Ford
Sierra
Owners
Workshop
Manual

A K Legg T Eng MIMI

Models covered
All Ford Sierra models with 2294 cc & 2792 cc V6 engines
2.3 Saloon & Estate, XR4i, XR4x4 & Ghia 4x4 Estate

Does not cover Diesel engine models

ABCDE
FGHIJ
KLMNO
PQR:

Haynes Publishing Group
Sparkford Nr Yeovil
Somerset BA22 7JJ England

Haynes Publications, Inc
861 Lawrence Drive
Newbury Park
California 91320 USA

Acknowledgements

Thanks are due to the Champion Sparking Plug Company Limited who supplied the illustrations showing the spark plug conditions, and Duckhams Oils who supplied lubrication data. Certain other illustrations are the copyright of Ford Motor Company Limited and are used with their permission. Thanks are also due to Sykes-Pickavant who supplied some of the workshop tools, and all those people at Sparkford who assisted in the production of this Manual.

© **Haynes Publishing Group 1988**

A book in the **Haynes Owners Workshop Manual Series**

Printed by J. H. Haynes & Co. Ltd, Sparkford, Nr Yeovil, Somerset BA22 7JJ, England

ISBN 0 85696 904 4

British Library Cataloguing in Publication Data
Legg, A. K.
    Ford Sierra 2.3 & 2.8 owners workshop manual.
    – (Owners Workshop Manuals).
    1. Automobiles – Maintenance and repair –
Amateurs' manuals
    I. Title   II. Series
    629.28'722   TL152
    ISBN 0-85696-904-4

Contents

Ford Sierra 2.3 Ghia

Ford Sierra XR4i

About this manual

Its aim

The aim of this manual is to help you get the best value from your vehicle. It can do so in several ways. It can help you decide what work must be done (even should you choose to get it done by a garage), provide information on routine maintenance and servicing, and give a logical course of action and diagnosis when random faults occur. However, it is hoped that you will use the manual by tackling the work yourself. On simpler jobs it may even be quicker than booking the car into a garage and going there twice, to leave and collect it. Perhaps most important, a lot of money can be saved by avoiding the costs a garage must charge to cover its labour and overheads.

The manual has drawings and descriptions to show the function of the various components so that their layout can be understood. Then the tasks are described and photographed in a step-by-step sequence so that even a novice can do the work.

Its arrangement

The manual is divided into twelve Chapters, each covering a logical sub-division of the vehicle. The Chapters are each divided into Sections, numbered with single figures, eg 5; and the Sections into paragraphs (or sub-sections), with decimal numbers following on from the Section they are in, eg 5.1, 5.2, 5.3 etc.

It is freely illustrated, especially in those parts where there is a detailed sequence of operations to be carried out. There are two forms of illustration: figures and photographs. The figures are numbered in sequence with decimal numbers, according to their position in the Chapter – eg Fig. 6.4 is the fourth drawing/illustration in Chapter 6. Photographs carry the same number (either individually or in related groups) as the Section or sub-section to which they relate.

There is an alphabetical index at the back of the manual as well as a contents list at the front. Each Chapter is also preceded by its own individual contents list.

References to the 'left' or 'right' of the vehicle are in the sense of a person in the driver's seat facing forwards.

Unless otherwise stated, nuts and bolts are removed by turning anti-clockwise, and tightened by turning clockwise.

Vehicle manufacturers continually make changes to specifications and recommendations, and these, when notified, are incorporated into our manuals at the earliest opportunity.

Whilst every care is taken to ensure that the information in this manual is correct, no liability can be accepted by the authors or publishers for loss, damage or injury caused by any errors in, or omissions from, the information given.

Project vehicles

The vehicles used in the preparation of this manual, and appearing in many of the photographic sequences, included a 1983 model XR4i, a 1986 model XR4x4 Saloon, and a 1987 model XR4x4 Saloon.

Introduction to the Ford Sierra V6

The Ford Sierra was first introduced in late 1982 with the option of seven different engines and four different trim levels. The range has since been considerably expanded and the latest models are equipped with improved instrumentation and trim. This manual covers models fitted with the 2.3 or 2.8 V6 engine and includes the automatic and 4x4 transmission in addition to the standard 4- and 5-speed gearboxes.

For the home mechanic, the Sierra is an ideal car to maintain and repair since design features have been incorporated to reduce the actual cost of ownership to a minimum, with the result that components requiring relatively frequent attention (eg the exhaust system) are easily removed.

Ford Sierra XR4x4 (1985 model)

Ford Sierra Ghia 4x4 Estate

Ford Sierra XR4x4 (1987 model)

General dimensions, weights and capacities

Dimensions – mm (in)	Pre-February 1987	February 1987-on
Overall length (nominal):		
Saloon	4407 (173.5)	4425 (174.2)
Estate	4505 (177.4)	4511 (177.7)
Overall width:		
Saloon	1920 (75.6)	1694 (66.7)
Estate	1920 (75.6)	1694 (66.7)
Overall height (unladen):		
Saloon (except XR4i and XR4x4)	1420 (55.9)	–
Saloon (XR4i and XR4x4)	1392 (54.8)	1352 (53.3)
Estate	1506 (59.3)	1386 (54.6)
Wheelbase:		
Except 4x4 models	2608 (102.7)	2608 (102.7)
4x4 models	2611 (102.8)	2611 (102.8)
Track:		
Front	1453 (57.2)	1453 (57.2)
Rear – Saloon	1468 (57.8)	1468 (57.8)
Rear – Estate	1458 (57.4)	1458 (57.4)

Weight – kg (lb)	
Kerb weight:	
2.3 Saloon	1165 (2568)
2.3 Estate	1200 (2646)
2.8 Saloon	1270 (2800)
2.8 Estate	1315 (2900)
Maximum roof rack load	75 (165)
Trailer nose weight	25 (55) to 50 (110)

Capacities – litres (pints)	
Engine oil (drain and refill, including filter):	
Except 4x4 models	4.25 (7.5)
4x4 models	4.65 (8.2)
Cooling system (including heater)	8.5 (15.0)
Fuel tank – litres (gallons)	60 (13.2)
Manual gearbox:	
Type B	1.46 (2.6)
Type N (except 4x4)	1.9 (3.3)
Type N (4x4)	1.25 (2.2)
Transfer box (4x4)	0.5 (0.9)
Automatic transmission	6.3 (11.1)
Final drive:	
Rear (except 4x4)	0.9 (1.6)
Rear (4x4)	1.0 (1.8)
Front (4x4)	0.96 (1.7)
Power steering	0.75 (1.3)

Jacking, towing and wheel changing

Jacking

Use the jack supplied with the vehicle only for wheel changing during roadside emergencies (photos). Chock the wheel diagonally opposite the one being removed.

When raising the vehicle for repair or maintenance, preferably use a trolley or hydraulic jack with a wooden block as an insulator to prevent damage to the underbody. Place the jack under a structural member at the points indicated, never raise the vehicle by jacking up under the engine sump or transmission casing.

It is to be preferred and is certainly recommended that the vehicle is positioned over an inspection pit or raised on a lift. When such equipment is not available, use ramps or jack up the vehicle as previously described, but always supplement the lifting device with axle stands.

Towing

Towing eyes are provided at both front and rear of the vehicle (photos). The rear towing eye should be used only for emergency towing of another vehicle.

Vehicles with automatic transmission must not be towed further than 30 miles (50 km) or faster than 30 mph (50 km/h). If these conditions cannot be met, or if transmission damage has already occurred, the propeller shaft must be removed or the vehicle towed with its rear wheels off the ground.

When being towed, disconnect the ignition coil LT leads or the wiring connector at the distributor, and turn the ignition key to position II. This will unlock the steering and allow the lights and direction indicators to be used. On models with ABS, it will also ensure that the rear brakes operate and the hydraulic system is pressurised. On models with a vacuum servo, additional effort will be required at the footbrake pedal.

Special precautions are necessary when towing 4x4 models *without* all four wheels on the road. If either the front or rear wheels are suspended, they must be allowed to rotate freely otherwise the transfer box differential gears and viscous couplings will be damaged. If all four wheels are on the road the car may be towed normally.

Wheel changing

Park on a firm flat surface if possible. Apply the handbrake and engage first or reverse gear or 'P'. Chock the wheel diagonally opposite the one being removed.

Remove the wheel trim, when applicable, for access to the wheel nuts. Prise the trim off if necessary using the plastic-tipped end of the wheelbrace. Use the other end of the wheelbrace to slacken each wheel nut by half a turn.

Jack up the vehicle until the wheel is clear of the ground. Remove the wheel nuts and lift the wheel off the studs. Transfer the wheel centre cap on alloy wheels, then fit the new wheel onto the studs and secure it with the nuts. Tighten the nuts in diagonal sequence until they are snug, but do not tighten them fully yet.

Lower the vehicle and remove the jack. Carry out the final tightening of the wheel nuts also in diagonal sequence. The use of a torque wrench is strongly recommended, especially when light alloy wheels are fitted. See Chapter 10 Specifications for the recommended tightening torque.

Refit the wheel trim, when applicable, and stow the tools.

Remove the cover in the luggage compartment ...

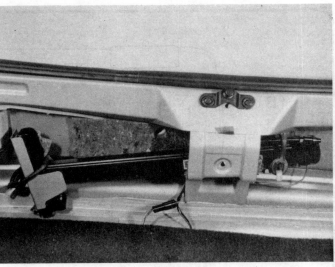

... for access to the jack

Spare wheel located in the luggage compartment

Using the wheel brace to remove the wheel cap

The cut-out in the wheel cap location over the tyre valve

Rear jacking point

Jack location by front wheel

Using an axle stand

Front towing eye

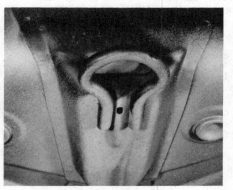

Rear towing eye

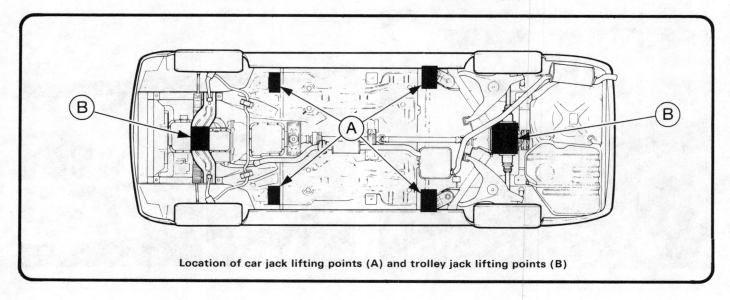

Location of car jack lifting points (A) and trolley jack lifting points (B)

Buying spare parts and vehicle identification numbers

Buying spare parts

Spare parts are available from many sources, for example: Ford garages, other garages and accessory shops, and motor factors. Our advice regarding spare parts sources is as follows:

Officially appointed Ford garages – This is the best source of parts which are peculiar to your car and are not generally available (eg complete cylinder heads, internal gearbox components, badges, interior trim etc). It is also the only place at which you should buy parts if your vehicle is still under warranty – non-Ford components may invalidate the warranty. To be sure of obtaining the correct parts it will always be necessary to give the storeman your car's vehicle identification number, and if possible, to take the 'old' part along for positive identification. Remember that some parts are available on a factory exchange scheme – any parts returned should always be clean! It obviously makes good sense to go straight to the specialists on your car for this type of part for they are best equipped to supply you.

Other garages and accessory shops – These are often very good places to buy materials and components needed for the maintenance of your car (eg oil filters, spark plugs, bulbs, drivebelts, oils and greases, touch-up paint, filler paste, etc). They also sell general accessories, usually have convenient opening hours, charge lower prices and can often be found not far from home.

Motor factors – Good factors will stock all of the more important components which wear out relatively quickly (eg clutch components, pistons, valves, exhaust systems, brake cylinders/pipes/hoses/seals and pads etc). Motor factors will often provide new or reconditioned components on a part exchange basis – this can save a considerable amount of money!

Vehicle identification numbers

When ordering spare parts, always give as much information as possible. Quote the car model, year of manufacture, body and engine numbers as appropriate.

The vehicle identification number (VIN) plate is mounted on the right-hand side of the body front panel, and may be seen once the bonnet is open (photo). Besides the VIN it also carries information on the vehicle equipment and permissible loads.

The engine number is located on the left-hand side of the cylinder block above the fuel pump or blanking plate.

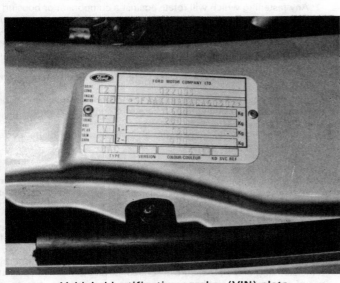

Vehicle identification number (VIN) plate

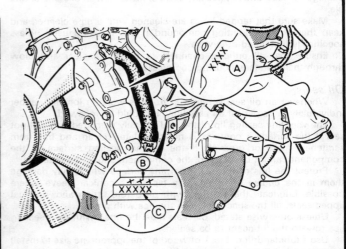

Engine identification

A   *Date code*   C   *Engine number*
B   *Engine code*

General repair procedures

Whenever servicing, repair or overhaul work is carried out on the car or its components, it is necessary to observe the following procedures and instructions. This will assist in carrying out the operation efficiently and to a professional standard of workmanship.

Joint mating faces and gaskets

Where a gasket is used between the mating faces of two components, ensure that it is renewed on reassembly, and fit it dry unless otherwise stated in the repair procedure. Make sure that the mating faces are clean and dry with all traces of old gasket removed. When cleaning a joint face, use a tool which is not likely to score or damage the face, and remove any burrs or nicks with an oilstone or fine file.

Make sure that tapped holes are cleaned with a pipe cleaner, and keep them free of jointing compound if this is being used unless specifically instructed otherwise.

Ensure that all orifices, channels or pipes are clear and blow through them, preferably using compressed air.

Oil seals

Whenever an oil seal is removed from its working location, either individually or as part of an assembly, it should be renewed.

The very fine sealing lip of the seal is easily damaged and will not seal if the surface it contacts is not completely clean and free from scratches, nicks or grooves. If the original sealing surface of the component cannot be restored, the component should be renewed.

Protect the lips of the seal from any surface which may damage them in the course of fitting. Use tape or a conical sleeve where possible. Lubricate the seal lips with oil before fitting and, on dual lipped seals, fill the space between the lips with grease.

Unless otherwise stated, oil seals must be fitted with their sealing lips toward the lubricant to be sealed.

Use a tubular drift or block of wood of the appropriate size to install the seal and, if the seal housing is shouldered, drive the seal down to the shoulder. If the seal housing is unshouldered, the seal should be fitted with its face flush with the housing top face.

Screw threads and fastenings

Always ensure that a blind tapped hole is completely free from oil, grease, water or other fluid before installing the bolt or stud. Failure to do this could cause the housing to crack due to the hydraulic action of the bolt or stud as it is screwed in.

When tightening a castellated nut to accept a split pin, tighten the nut to the specified torque, where applicable, and then tighten further to the next split pin hole. Never slacken the nut to align a split pin hole unless stated in the repair procedure.

When checking or retightening a nut or bolt to a specified torque setting, slacken the nut or bolt by a quarter of a turn, and then retighten to the specified setting.

Locknuts, locktabs and washers

Any fastening which will rotate against a component or housing in the course of tightening should always have a washer between it and the relevant component or housing.

Spring or split washers should always be renewed when they are used to lock a critical component such as a big-end bearing retaining nut or bolt.

Locktabs which are folded over to retain a nut or bolt should always be renewed.

Self-locking nuts can be reused in non-critical areas, providing resistance can be felt when the locking portion passes over the bolt or stud thread.

Split pins must always be replaced with new ones of the correct size for the hole.

Special tools

Some repair procedures in this manual entail the use of special tools such as a press, two or three-legged pullers, spring compressors etc. Wherever possible, suitable readily available alternatives to the manufacturer's special tools are described, and are shown in use. In some instances, where no alternative is possible, it has been necessary to resort to the use of a manufacturer's tool and this has been done for reasons of safety as well as the efficient completion of the repair operation. Unless you are highly skilled and have a thorough understanding of the procedure described, never attempt to bypass the use of any special tool when the procedure described specifies its use. Not only is there a very great risk of personal injury, but expensive damage could be caused to the components involved.

Tools and working facilities

Introduction

A selection of good tools is a fundamental requirement for anyone contemplating the maintenance and repair of a motor vehicle. For the owner who does not possess any, their purchase will prove a considerable expense, offsetting some of the savings made by doing-it-yourself. However, provided that the tools purchased are of good quality, they will last for many years and prove an extremely worthwhile investment.

To help the average owner to decide which tools are needed to carry out the various tasks detailed in this manual, we have compiled three lists of tools under the following headings: *Maintenance and minor repair*, *Repair and overhaul*, and *Special*. The newcomer to practical mechanics should start off with the *Maintenance and minor repair* tool kit and confine himself to the simpler jobs around the vehicle. Then, as his confidence and experience grow, he can undertake more difficult tasks, buying extra tools as, and when, they are needed. In this way, a *Maintenance and minor repair* tool kit can be built-up into a *Repair and overhaul* tool kit over a considerable period of time without any major cash outlays. The experienced do-it-yourselfer will have a tool kit good enough for most repair and overhaul procedures and will add tools from the *Special* category when he feels the expense is justified by the amount of use to which these tools will be put.

It is obviously not possible to cover the subject of tools fully here. For those who wish to learn more about tools and their use there is a book entitled *How to Choose and Use Car Tools* available from the publishers of this manual.

Maintenance and minor repair tool kit

The tools given in this list should be considered as a minimum requirement if routine maintenance, servicing and minor repair operations are to be undertaken. We recommend the purchase of combination spanners (ring one end, open-ended the other); although more expensive than open-ended ones, they do give the advantages of both types of spanner.

Combination spanners - 10, 11, 12, 13, 14 & 17 mm
Adjustable spanner - 9 inch
Engine sump/gearbox/rear axle drain plug key
Spark plug spanner (with rubber insert)
Spark plug gap adjustment tool
Set of feeler gauges
Brake adjuster spanner
Brake bleed nipple spanner
Screwdriver - 4 in long x 1/4 in dia (flat blade)
Screwdriver - 4 in long x 1/4 in dia (cross blade)
Combination pliers - 6 inch
Hacksaw (junior)
Tyre pump
Tyre pressure gauge
Grease gun
Oil can
Fine emery cloth (1 sheet)
Wire brush (small)
Funnel (medium size)

Repair and overhaul tool kit

These tools are virtually essential for anyone undertaking any major repairs to a motor vehicle, and are additional to those given in the *Maintenance and minor repair* list. Included in this list is a comprehensive set of sockets. Although these are expensive they will be found invaluable as they are so versatile - particularly if various drives are included in the set. We recommend the ½ in square-drive type, as this can be used with most proprietary torque wrenches. If you cannot afford a socket set, even bought piecemeal, then inexpensive tubular box spanners are a useful alternative.

The tools in this list will occasionally need to be supplemented by tools from the *Special* list.

Sockets (or box spanners) to cover range in previous list
Reversible ratchet drive (for use with sockets)
Extension piece, 10 inch (for use with sockets)
Universal joint (for use with sockets)
Torque wrench (for use with sockets)
'Mole' wrench - 8 inch
Ball pein hammer
Soft-faced hammer, plastic or rubber
Screwdriver - 6 in long x 5/16 in dia (flat blade)
Screwdriver - 2 in long x 5/16 in square (flat blade)
Screwdriver - 1 1/2 in long x 1/4 in dia (cross blade)
Screwdriver - 3 in long x 1/8 in dia (electricians)
Pliers - electricians side cutters
Pliers - needle nosed
Pliers - circlip (internal and external)
Cold chisel - 1/2 inch
Scriber
Scraper
Centre punch
Pin punch
Hacksaw
Valve grinding tool
Steel rule/straight-edge
Allen keys (inc. splined/Torx type if necessary)
Selection of files
Wire brush (large)
Axle-stands
Jack (strong trolley or hydraulic type)

Special tools

The tools in this list are those which are not used regularly, are expensive to buy, or which need to be used in accordance with their manufacturers' instructions. Unless relatively difficult mechanical jobs are undertaken frequently, it will not be economic to buy many of these tools. Where this is the case, you could consider clubbing together with friends (or joining a motorists' club) to make a joint purchase, or borrowing the tools against a deposit from a local garage or tool hire specialist.

The following list contains only those tools and instruments freely available to the public, and not those special tools produced by the vehicle manufacturer specifically for its dealer network. You will find occasional references to these manufacturers' special tools in the text of this manual. Generally, an alternative method of doing the job without the vehicle manufacturers' special tool is given. However, sometimes, there is no alternative to using them. Where this is the case and the relevant tool cannot be bought or borrowed, you will have to entrust the work to a franchised garage.

> Valve spring compressor (where applicable)
> Piston ring compressor
> Balljoint separator
> Universal hub/bearing puller
> Impact screwdriver
> Micrometer and/or vernier gauge
> Dial gauge
> Stroboscopic timing light
> Dwell angle meter/tachometer
> Universal electrical multi-meter
> Cylinder compression gauge
> Lifting tackle
> Trolley jack
> Light with extension lead

Buying tools

For practically all tools, a tool factor is the best source since he will have a very comprehensive range compared with the average garage or accessory shop. Having said that, accessory shops often offer excellent quality tools at discount prices, so it pays to shop around.

Remember, you don't have to buy the most expensive items on the shelf, but it is always advisable to steer clear of the very cheap tools. There are plenty of good tools around at reasonable prices, so ask the proprietor or manager of the shop for advice before making a purchase.

Care and maintenance of tools

Having purchased a reasonable tool kit, it is necessary to keep the tools in a clean serviceable condition. After use, always wipe off any dirt, grease and metal particles using a clean, dry cloth, before putting the tools away. Never leave them lying around after they have been used. A simple tool rack on the garage or workshop wall, for items such as screwdrivers and pliers is a good idea. Store all normal wrenches and sockets in a metal box. Any measuring instruments, gauges, meters, etc, must be carefully stored where they cannot be damaged or become rusty.

Take a little care when tools are used. Hammer heads inevitably become marked and screwdrivers lose the keen edge on their blades from time to time. A little timely attention with emery cloth or a file will soon restore items like this to a good serviceable finish.

Working facilities

Not to be forgotten when discussing tools, is the workshop itself. If anything more than routine maintenance is to be carried out, some form of suitable working area becomes essential.

It is appreciated that many an owner mechanic is forced by circumstances to remove an engine or similar item, without the benefit of a garage or workshop. Having done this, any repairs should always be done under the cover of a roof.

Wherever possible, any dismantling should be done on a clean, flat workbench or table at a suitable working height.

Any workbench needs a vice: one with a jaw opening of 4 in (100 mm) is suitable for most jobs. As mentioned previously, some clean dry storage space is also required for tools, as well as for lubricants, cleaning fluids, touch-up paints and so on, which become necessary.

Another item which may be required, and which has a much more general usage, is an electric drill with a chuck capacity of at least 5/16 in (8 mm). This, together with a good range of twist drills, is virtually essential for fitting accessories such as mirrors and reversing lights.

Last, but not least, always keep a supply of old newspapers and clean, lint-free rags available, and try to keep any working area as clean as possible.

Spanner jaw gap comparison table

Jaw gap (in)	Spanner size
0.250	1/4 in AF
0.276	7 mm
0.313	5/16 in AF
0.315	8 mm
0.344	11/32 in AF; 1/8 in Whitworth
0.354	9 mm
0.375	3/8 in AF
0.394	10 mm
0.433	11 mm
0.438	7/16 in AF
0.445	3/16 in Whitworth; 1/4 in BSF
0.472	12 mm
0.500	1/2 in AF
0.512	13 mm
0.525	1/4 in Whitworth; 5/16 in BSF
0.551	14 mm
0.563	9/16 in AF
0.591	15 mm
0.600	5/16 in Whitworth; 3/8 in BSF
0.625	5/8 in AF
0.630	16 mm
0.669	17 mm
0.686	11/16 in AF
0.709	18 mm
0.710	3/8 in Whitworth; 7/16 in BSF
0.748	19 mm
0.750	3/4 in AF
0.813	13/16 in AF
0.820	7/16 in Whitworth; 1/2 in BSF
0.866	22 mm
0.875	7/8 in AF
0.920	1/2 in Whitworth; 9/16 in BSF
0.938	15/16 in AF
0.945	24 mm
1.000	1 in AF
1.010	9/16 in Whitworth; 5/8 in BSF
1.024	26 mm
1.063	11/16 in AF; 27 mm
1.100	5/8 in Whitworth; 11/16 in BSF
1.125	11/8 in AF
1.181	30 mm
1.200	11/16 in Whitworth; 3/4 in BSF
1.250	11/4 in AF
1.260	32 mm
1.300	3/4 in Whitworth; 7/8 in BSF
1.313	15/16 in AF
1.390	13/16 in Whitworth; 15/16 in BSF
1.417	36 mm
1.438	17/16 in AF
1.480	7/8 in Whitworth; 1 in BSF
1.500	11/2 in AF
1.575	40 mm; 15/16 in Whitworth
1.614	41 mm
1.625	15/8 in AF
1.670	1 in Whitworth; 11/8 in BSF
1.688	111/16 in AF
1.811	46 mm
1.813	113/16 in AF
1.860	11/8 in Whitworth; 11/4 in BSF
1.875	17/8 in AF
1.969	50 mm
2.000	2 in AF
2.050	11/4 in Whitworth; 13/8 in BSF
2.165	55 mm
2.362	60 mm

Conversion factors

Length (distance)

Inches (in)	X	25.4	=	Millimetres (mm)	X	0.0394	= Inches (in)
Feet (ft)	X	0.305	=	Metres (m)	X	3.281	= Feet (ft)
Miles	X	1.609	=	Kilometres (km)	X	0.621	= Miles

Volume (capacity)

Cubic inches (cu in; in³)	X	16.387	=	Cubic centimetres (cc; cm³)	X	0.061	= Cubic inches (cu in; in³)
Imperial pints (Imp pt)	X	0.568	=	Litres (l)	X	1.76	= Imperial pints (Imp pt)
Imperial quarts (Imp qt)	X	1.137	=	Litres (l)	X	0.88	= Imperial quarts (Imp qt)
Imperial quarts (Imp qt)	X	1.201	=	US quarts (US qt)	X	0.833	= Imperial quarts (Imp qt)
US quarts (US qt)	X	0.946	=	Litres (l)	X	1.057	= US quarts (US qt)
Imperial gallons (Imp gal)	X	4.546	=	Litres (l)	X	0.22	= Imperial gallons (Imp gal)
Imperial gallons (Imp gal)	X	1.201	=	US gallons (US gal)	X	0.833	= Imperial gallons (Imp gal)
US gallons (US gal)	X	3.785	=	Litres (l)	X	0.264	= US gallons (US gal)

Mass (weight)

Ounces (oz)	X	28.35	=	Grams (g)	X	0.035	= Ounces (oz)
Pounds (lb)	X	0.454	=	Kilograms (kg)	X	2.205	= Pounds (lb)

Force

Ounces-force (ozf; oz)	X	0.278	=	Newtons (N)	X	3.6	= Ounces-force (ozf; oz)
Pounds-force (lbf; lb)	X	4.448	=	Newtons (N)	X	0.225	= Pounds-force (lbf; lb)
Newtons (N)	X	0.1	=	Kilograms-force (kgf; kg)	X	9.81	= Newtons (N)

Pressure

Pounds-force per square inch (psi; lbf/in²; lb/in²)	X	0.070	=	Kilograms-force per square centimetre (kgf/cm²; kg/cm²)	X	14.223	= Pounds-force per square inch (psi; lbf/in²; lb/in²)
Pounds-force per square inch (psi; lbf/in²; lb/in²)	X	0.068	=	Atmospheres (atm)	X	14.696	= Pounds-force per square inch (psi; lbf/in²; lb/in²)
Pounds-force per square inch (psi; lbf/in²; lb/in²)	X	0.069	=	Bars	X	14.5	= Pounds-force per square inch (psi; lbf/in²; lb/in²)
Pounds-force per square inch (psi; lbf/in²; lb/in²)	X	6.895	=	Kilopascals (kPa)	X	0.145	= Pounds-force per square inch (psi; lbf/in²; lb/in²)
Kilopascals (kPa)	X	0.01	=	Kilograms-force per square centimetre (kgf/cm²; kg/cm²)	X	98.1	= Kilopascals (kPa)
Millibar (mbar)	X	100	=	Pascals (Pa)	X	0.01	= Millibar (mbar)
Millibar (mbar)	X	0.0145	=	Pounds-force per square inch (psi; lbf/in², lb/in²)	X	68.947	= Millibar (mbar)
Millibar (mbar)	X	0.75	=	Millimetres of mercury (mmHg)	X	1.333	= Millibar (mbar)
Millibar (mbar)	X	1.40	=	Inches of water (inH₂O)	X	0.714	= Millibar (mbar)
Millimetres of mercury (mmHg)	X	1.868	=	Inches of water (inH₂O)	X	0.535	= Millimetres of mercury (mmHg)
Inches of water (inH₂O)	X	27.68	=	Pounds-force per square inch (psi, lbf/in², lb/in²)	X	0.036	= Inches of water (inH₂O)

Torque (moment of force)

Pounds-force inches (lbf in; lb in)	X	1.152	=	Kilograms-force centimetre (kgf cm; kg cm)	X	0.868	= Pounds-force inches (lbf in; lb in)
Pounds-force inches (lbf in; lb in)	X	0.113	=	Newton metres (Nm)	X	8.85	= Pounds-force inches (lbf in; lb in)
Pounds-force inches (lbf in; lb in)	X	0.083	=	Pounds-force feet (lbf ft; lb ft)	X	12	= Pounds-force inches (lbf in; lb in)
Pounds-force feet (lbf ft; lb ft)	X	0.138	=	Kilograms-force metres (kgf m; kg m)	X	7.233	= Pounds-force feet (lbf ft; lb ft)
Pounds-force feet (lbf ft; lb ft)	X	1.356	=	Newton metres (Nm)	X	0.738	= Pounds-force feet (lbf ft; lb ft)
Newton metres (Nm)	X	0.102	=	Kilograms-force metres (kgf m; kg m)	X	9.804	= Newton metres (Nm)

Power

Horsepower (hp)	X	745.7	=	Watts (W)	X	0.0013	= Horsepower (hp)

Velocity (speed)

Miles per hour (miles/hr; mph)	X	1.609	=	Kilometres per hour (km/hr; kph)	X	0.621	= Miles per hour (miles/hr; mph)

Fuel consumption*

Miles per gallon, Imperial (mpg)	X	0.354	=	Kilometres per litre (km/l)	X	2.825	= Miles per gallon, Imperial (mpg)
Miles per gallon, US (mpg)	X	0.425	=	Kilometres per litre (km/l)	X	2.352	= Miles per gallon, US (mpg)

Temperature

Degrees Fahrenheit = (°C x 1.8) + 32

Degrees Celsius (Degrees Centigrade; °C) = (°F - 32) x 0.56

*It is common practice to convert from miles per gallon (mpg) to litres/100 kilometres (l/100km), where mpg (Imperial) x l/100 km = 282 and mpg (US) x l/100 km = 235

Safety first!

Professional motor mechanics are trained in safe working procedures. However enthusiastic you may be about getting on with the job in hand, do take the time to ensure that your safety is not put at risk. A moment's lack of attention can result in an accident, as can failure to observe certain elementary precautions.

There will always be new ways of having accidents, and the following points do not pretend to be a comprehensive list of all dangers; they are intended rather to make you aware of the risks and to encourage a safety-conscious approach to all work you carry out on your vehicle.

Essential DOs and DON'Ts

DON'T rely on a single jack when working underneath the vehicle. Always use reliable additional means of support, such as axle stands, securely placed under a part of the vehicle that you know will not give way.

DON'T attempt to loosen or tighten high-torque nuts (e.g. wheel hub nuts) while the vehicle is on a jack; it may be pulled off.

DON'T start the engine without first ascertaining that the transmission is in neutral (or 'Park' where applicable) and the parking brake applied.

DON'T suddenly remove the filler cap from a hot cooling system – cover it with a cloth and release the pressure gradually first, or you may get scalded by escaping coolant.

DON'T attempt to drain oil until you are sure it has cooled sufficiently to avoid scalding you.

DON'T grasp any part of the engine, exhaust or catalytic converter without first ascertaining that it is sufficiently cool to avoid burning you.

DON'T allow brake fluid or antifreeze to contact vehicle paintwork.

DON'T syphon toxic liquids such as fuel, brake fluid or antifreeze by mouth, or allow them to remain on your skin.

DON'T inhale dust – it may be injurious to health (see *Asbestos* below).

DON'T allow any spilt oil or grease to remain on the floor – wipe it up straight away, before someone slips on it.

DON'T use ill-fitting spanners or other tools which may slip and cause injury.

DON'T attempt to lift a heavy component which may be beyond your capability – get assistance.

DON'T rush to finish a job, or take unverified short cuts.

DON'T allow children or animals in or around an unattended vehicle.

DO wear eye protection when using power tools such as drill, sander, bench grinder etc, and when working under the vehicle.

DO use a barrier cream on your hands prior to undertaking dirty jobs – it will protect your skin from infection as well as making the dirt easier to remove afterwards; but make sure your hands aren't left slippery. Note that long-term contact with used engine oil can be a health hazard.

DO keep loose clothing (cuffs, tie etc) and long hair well out of the way of moving mechanical parts.

DO remove rings, wristwatch etc, before working on the vehicle – especially the electrical system.

DO ensure that any lifting tackle used has a safe working load rating adequate for the job.

DO keep your work area tidy – it is only too easy to fall over articles left lying around.

DO get someone to check periodically that all is well, when working alone on the vehicle.

DO carry out work in a logical sequence and check that everything is correctly assembled and tightened afterwards.

DO remember that your vehicle's safety affects that of yourself and others. If in doubt on any point, get specialist advice.

IF, in spite of following these precautions, you are unfortunate enough to injure yourself, seek medical attention as soon as possible.

Asbestos

Certain friction, insulating, sealing, and other products – such as brake linings, brake bands, clutch linings, torque converters, gaskets, etc – contain asbestos. *Extreme care must be taken to avoid inhalation of dust from such products since it is hazardous to health.* If in doubt, assume that they *do* contain asbestos.

Fire

Remember at all times that petrol (gasoline) is highly flammable. Never smoke, or have any kind of naked flame around, when working on the vehicle. But the risk does not end there – a spark caused by an electrical short-circuit, by two metal surfaces contacting each other, by careless use of tools, or even by static electricity built up in your body under certain conditions, can ignite petrol vapour, which in a confined space is highly explosive.

Always disconnect the battery earth (ground) terminal before working on any part of the fuel or electrical system, and never risk spilling fuel on to a hot engine or exhaust.

It is recommended that a fire extinguisher of a type suitable for fuel and electrical fires is kept handy in the garage or workplace at all times. Never try to extinguish a fuel or electrical fire with water.

Note: *Any reference to a 'torch' appearing in this manual should always be taken to mean a hand-held battery-operated electric lamp or flashlight. It does NOT mean a welding/gas torch or blowlamp.*

Fumes

Certain fumes are highly toxic and can quickly cause unconsciousness and even death if inhaled to any extent. Petrol (gasoline) vapour comes into this category, as do the vapours from certain solvents such as trichloroethylene. Any draining or pouring of such volatile fluids should be done in a well ventilated area.

When using cleaning fluids and solvents, read the instructions carefully. Never use materials from unmarked containers – they may give off poisonous vapours.

Never run the engine of a motor vehicle in an enclosed space such as a garage. Exhaust fumes contain carbon monoxide which is extremely poisonous; if you need to run the engine, always do so in the open air or at least have the rear of the vehicle outside the workplace.

If you are fortunate enough to have the use of an inspection pit, never drain or pour petrol, and never run the engine, while the vehicle is standing over it; the fumes, being heavier than air, will concentrate in the pit with possibly lethal results.

The battery

Never cause a spark, or allow a naked light, near the vehicle's battery. It will normally be giving off a certain amount of hydrogen gas, which is highly explosive.

Always disconnect the battery earth (ground) terminal before working on the fuel or electrical systems.

If possible, loosen the filler plugs or cover when charging the battery from an external source. Do not charge at an excessive rate or the battery may burst.

Take care when topping up and when carrying the battery. The acid electrolyte, even when diluted, is very corrosive and should not be allowed to contact the eyes or skin.

If you ever need to prepare electrolyte yourself, always add the acid slowly to the water, and never the other way round. Protect against splashes by wearing rubber gloves and goggles.

When jump starting a car using a booster battery, for negative earth (ground) vehicles, connect the jump leads in the following sequence: First connect one jump lead between the positive (+) terminals of the two batteries. Then connect the other jump lead first to the negative (–) terminal of the booster battery, and then to a good earthing (ground) point on the vehicle to be started, at least 18 in (45 cm) from the battery if possible. Ensure that hands and jump leads are clear of any moving parts, and that the two vehicles do not touch. Disconnect the leads in the reverse order.

Mains electricity

When using an electric power tool, inspection light etc, which works from the mains, always ensure that the appliance is correctly connected to its plug and that, where necessary, it is properly earthed (grounded). Do not use such appliances in damp conditions and, again, beware of creating a spark or applying excessive heat in the vicinity of fuel or fuel vapour.

Ignition HT voltage

A severe electric shock can result from touching certain parts of the ignition system, such as the HT leads, when the engine is running or being cranked, particularly if components are damp or the insulation is defective. Where an electronic ignition system is fitted, the HT voltage is much higher and could prove fatal.

Routine maintenance

The maintenance schedules below are basically those recommended by the manufacturer. Servicing intervals are determined by mileage or time elapsed – this is because fluids and systems deteriorate with age as well as with use. Follow the time intervals if the appropriate mileage is not covered within the specified period.

Vehicles operating under adverse conditions may need more frequent maintenance. Adverse conditions' include climatic extremes, full-time towing or taxi work, driving on unmade roads, and a high proportion of short journeys.

Every 250 miles (400 km), weekly or before a long journey

Engine
Check the oil level and top up if necessary (Chapter 1).
Check the coolant level and top up if necessary (Chapter 2).

Tyres
Check the tyre pressures and adjust if necessary (Chapter 10)

Every 6000 miles (10 000 km) or 6 months, whichever comes first

Engine
Change engine oil, renew oil filter and clean oil filler cap (Chapter 1)
Check cooling system for leaks (Chapter 2)
Check condition of fuel system hoses (Chapter 3)
Check and adjust the idling speed and mixture (Chapter 3)

Brakes
Check and if necessary top up the brake fluid level (Chapter 9)
Check the disc pads/rear brake shoes for wear (Chapter 9)
Check the hydraulic brake lines and hoses for damage (Chapter 9)

Steering and tyres
Check steering components for damage (Chapter 10)
Check tyres for wear and damage (Chapter 10)

Bodywork
Check the seat belts (Chapter 11)

Electrical
Check operation of exterior lights (Chapter 12)
Top up washer reservoirs (Chapter 12)

Every 12 000 miles (20 000 km) or 12 months, whichever comes first

Engine
Check and adjust valve clearances (Chapter 1)

Tighten inlet manifold bolts (Chapter 3)
Renew spark plugs (Chapter 4)

Manual gearbox and automatic transmission
Check manual gearbox oil level (Chapter 6)
Check 4x4 transfer box oil level (Chapter 6)
Check manual gearbox/automatic transmission for leaks (Chapter 6)
Lubricate the automatic transmission linkage (Chapter 6)
Check automatic transmission fluid level (Chapter 6)

Final drive and driveshafts
Check and if necessary top up final drive oil level (Chapter 8)
Check driveshaft rubber gaiters for damage (Chapter 8)

Bodywork and fittings
Lubricate hinges and catches (Chapter 11)
Check air conditioning system (Chapter 11)
Check underbody protection (Chapter 11)

Electrical
Check operation of all electrical equipment (Chapter 12)
Check battery electrolyte level (Chapter 12)

Every 24 000 miles (40 000 km) or 2 years, whichever comes first

Engine
Renew the crankcase emission valve (Chapter 1)
Check the drivebelts (Chapter 2)
Renew the coolant – at 2 year intervals only (Chapter 2)
Renew the air filter element (Chapter 3)
Renew the fuel filter on fuel injection models (Chapter 3)
Check operation of air cleaner temperature control (carburettor models) (Chapter 3)
Clean and check the distributor cap, HT leads and coil (Chapter 4)

Automatic transmission
Adjust front brake band (Chapter 6)

Suspension and steering
Check power steering pump drivebelt(s) (Chapter 10)
Check steering and suspension components for wear and damage (Chapter 10)

Every 36 000 miles (60 000 km) or 3 years, whichever comes first

Brakes
Renew the hydraulic brake fluid (Chapter 9)

Under-bonnet view of an XR4x4

1 Fusebox
2 Windscreen wiper motor
3 Windscreen washer jet
4 Plastic cover over heater motor
5 Distributor
6 Windscreen wiper arm
7 Speedometer cable
8 Engine oil level dipstick
9 Battery
10 Engine oil filler cap
11 Ignition coil
12 Front suspension top mounting
13 Air chamber
14 Accelerator cable
15 Fuel distributor
16 Air cleaner
17 Fuel injector pipes
18 Bottom hose
19 Thermostat housing
20 Warm-up regulator
21 Water pump
22 Auxiliary air device
23 Water pump/power steering pump drivebelts
24 Heater feed hose
25 Top hose
26 Power steering pump
27 Headlamp rear cover
28 Power steering fluid reservoir
29 Washer fluid reservoir
30 Expansion tank to radiator hose
31 Degas hose
32 Expansion tank filler cap
33 Exhaust manifold
34 Clutch cable
35 Fuel start valve
36 Bonnet release cable
37 ABS hydraulic fluid reservoir

Front underside view of an XR4x4

1 Front propeller shaft
2 Main gearbox casing
3 Steering column intermediate shaft
4 Front final drive unit
5 Front brake caliper
6 Lower suspension arm
7 Track rod end
8 Track rod
9 Alternator
10 Power steering pressure hose
11 Heater return hose
12 Radiator
13 Alternator drivebelt
14 Engine sump (incorporating FWD intermediate shaft)
15 Connecting plate (no longer fitted, although bolt holes remain on some early models)
16 Engine oil drain plug
17 Thermo-viscous cooling fan
18 Power steering cooling tube
19 Front suspension crossmember
20 Bottom hose
21 Front driveshaft
22 Flexible hydraulic brake hose
23 Starter motor
24 Anti-roll bar
25 Hydraulic brake line
26 Fuel feed and return lines
27 Exhaust pipes
28 Transmission mounting crossmember
29 Rear propeller shaft
30 4x4 transfer box

Rear underside view of an XR4x4

1 Fuel tank
2 Rear driveshaft
3 Rear suspension lower arm
4 Rear suspension crossmember
5 Rear suspension front mounting
6 Exhaust mounting (right)
7 Exhaust system
8 Rear propeller shaft
9 Handbrake cables
10 Exhaust mounting (left)
11 Anti-roll bar
12 Fuel pump
13 Fuel accumulator
14 Fuel supply hose
15 Final drive rear mounting
16 Rear final drive unit
17 Fuel return line

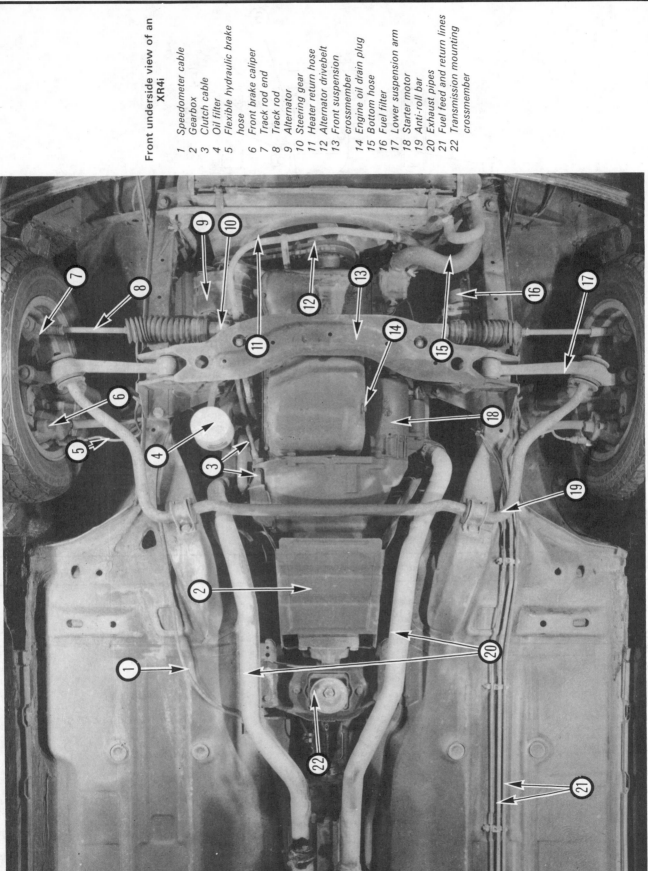

Front underside view of an XR4i

1 Speedometer cable
2 Gearbox
3 Clutch cable
4 Oil filter
5 Flexible hydraulic brake hose
6 Front brake caliper
7 Track rod end
8 Track rod
9 Alternator
10 Steering gear
11 Heater return hose
12 Alternator drivebelt
13 Front suspension crossmember
14 Engine oil drain plug
15 Bottom hose
16 Fuel filter
17 Lower suspension arm
18 Starter motor
19 Anti-roll bar
20 Exhaust pipes
21 Fuel feed and return lines
22 Transmission mounting crossmember

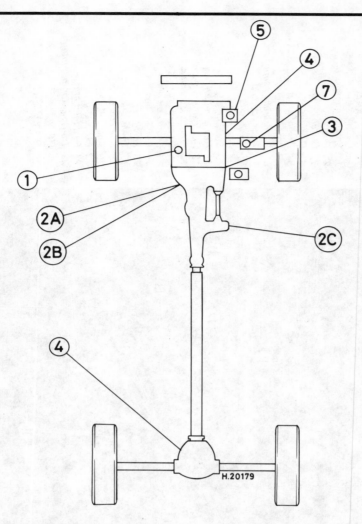

H.20179

Recommended lubricants and fluids

Component or system	Lubricant type/specification	Duckhams recommendation
1 Engine	Multigrade engine oil, viscosity range SAE 10W/30 to 10W/50, to API SF/CC or SF/CD	Duckhams QXR, Hypergrade, or 10W/40 Motor Oil
2A Manual gearbox (4-speed and 4x4)	Gear oil, viscosity SAE 80EP to Ford spec SQM 2C 9008-A	Duckhams Hypoid 80
2B Manual gearbox (5-speed non 4x4)		
Early models	Gear oil, viscosity SAE 80EP to Ford spec SQM 2C 9008-A	Duckhams Hypoid 80
Later models	Semi-synthetic gear oil to Ford spec ESD-M2C-175-A	Duckhams Hypoid 75W/90S
2C Transfer box (4x4)	ATF to Ford spec SQM-2C9010-A	Duckhams D-Matic
3 Automatic transmission	ATF to Ford spec SQM-2C9010-A	Duckhams D-Matic
4 Final drive	Hypoid gear oil, viscosity SAE 90 to API GL5	Duckhams Hypoid 90S
5 Power-assisted steering	ATF to Ford spec SQM-2C 9010-A	Duckhams D-Matic
6 Brake hydraulic system	Hydraulic fluid to Ford spec SAM-6C9103-A	Duckhams Universal Brake and Clutch Fluid
7 Cooling system	Antifreeze to Ford spec SSM-97B9103-A	Duckhams Universal Antifreeze and Summer Coolant

Fault diagnosis

Introduction

The vehicle owner who does his or her own maintenance according to the recommended schedules should not have to use this section of the manual very often. Modern component reliability is such that, provided those items subject to wear or deterioration are inspected or renewed at the specified intervals, sudden failure is comparatively rare. Faults do not usually just happen as a result of sudden failure, but develop over a period of time. Major mechanical failures in particular are usually preceded by characteristic symptoms over hundreds or even thousands of miles. Those components which do occasionally fail without warning are often small and easily carried in the vehicle.

With any fault finding, the first step is to decide where to begin investigations. Sometimes this is obvious, but on other occasions a little detective work will be necessary. The owner who makes half a dozen haphazard adjustments or replacements may be successful in curing a fault (or its symptoms), but he will be none the wiser if the fault recurs and he may well have spent more time and money than was necessary. A calm and logical approach will be found to be more satisfactory in the long run. Always take into account any warning signs or abnormalities that may have been noticed in the period preceding the fault – power loss, high or low gauge readings, unusual noises or smells, etc – and remember that failure of components such as fuses or spark plugs may only be pointers to some underlying fault.

The pages which follow here are intended to help in cases of failure to start or breakdown on the road. There is also a Fault Diagnosis Section at the end of each Chapter which should be consulted if the preliminary checks prove unfruitful. Whatever the fault, certain basic principles apply. These are as follows:

Verify the fault. This is simply a matter of being sure that you know what the symptoms are before starting work. This is particularly important if you are investigating a fault for someone else who may not have described it very accurately.

Don't overlook the obvious. For example, if the vehicle won't start, is there petrol in the tank? (Don't take anyone else's word on this particular point, and don't trust the fuel gauge either!) If an electrical fault is indicated, look for loose or broken wires before digging out the test gear.

Cure the disease, not the symptom. Substituting a flat battery with a fully charged one will get you off the hard shoulder, but if the underlying cause is not attended to, the new battery will go the same way. Similarly, changing oil-fouled spark plugs for a new set will get you moving again, but remember that the reason for the fouling (if it wasn't simply an incorrect grade of plug) will have to be established and corrected.

Don't take anything for granted. Particularly, don't forget that a 'new' component may itself be defective (especially if it's been rattling round in the boot for months), and don't leave components out of a fault diagnosis sequence just because they are new or recently fitted. When you do finally diagnose a difficult fault, you'll probably realise that all the evidence was there from the start.

Electrical faults

Electrical faults can be more puzzling than straightforward mechanical failures, but they are no less susceptible to logical analysis if the basic principles of operation are understood. Vehicle electrical wiring exists in extremely unfavourable conditions – heat, vibration and chemical attack – and the first things to look for are loose or corroded connections and broken or chafed wires, especially where the wires pass through holes in the bodywork or are subject to vibration.

All metal-bodied vehicles in current production have one pole of the battery 'earthed', ie connected to the vehicle bodywork, and in nearly all modern vehicles it is the negative (–) terminal. The various electrical components – motors, bulb holders etc – are also connected to earth, either by means of a lead or directly by their mountings. Electric current flows through the component and then back to the battery via the bodywork. If the component mounting is loose or corroded, or if a good path back to the battery is not available, the circuit will be incomplete and malfunction will result. The engine and/or gearbox are also earthed by means of flexible metal straps to the body or subframe; if these straps are loose or missing, starter motor, generator and ignition trouble may result.

Assuming the earth return to be satisfactory, electrical faults will be due either to component malfunction or to defects in the current supply. Individual components are dealt with in Chapter 12. If supply wires are broken or cracked internally this results in an open-circuit, and the easiest way to check for this is to bypass the suspect wire temporarily with a length of wire having a crocodile clip or suitable connector at each end. Alternatively, a 12V test lamp can be used to verify the presence of supply voltage at various points along the wire and the break can be thus isolated.

If a bare portion of a live wire touches the bodywork or other earthed metal part, the electricity will take the low-resistance path thus formed back to the battery: this is known as a short-circuit. Hopefully a short-circuit will blow a fuse, but otherwise it may cause burning of the insulation (and possibly further short-circuits) or even a fire. This is why it is inadvisable to bypass persistently blowing fuses with silver foil or wire.

Spares and tool kit

Most vehicles are supplied only with sufficient tools for wheel changing; the *Maintenance and minor repair* tool kit detailed in *Tools and working facilities*, with the addition of a hammer, is probably sufficient for those repairs that most motorists would consider attempting at the roadside. In addition a few items which can be fitted without too much trouble in the event of a breakdown should be carried. Experience and available space will modify the list below, but the following may save having to call on professional assistance:

Spark plugs, clean and correctly gapped
HT lead and plug cap – long enough to reach the plug furthest from the distributor
Distributor rotor
Drivebelt(s) – emergency type may suffice
Spare fuses
Set of principal light bulbs
Tin of radiator sealer and hose bandage
Exhaust bandage
Roll of insulating tape
Length of soft iron wire
Length of electrical flex
Torch or inspection lamp (can double as test lamp)
Battery jump leads
Tow-rope
Ignition waterproofing aerosol
Litre of engine oil
Sealed can of hydraulic fluid
Emergency windscreen
'Jubilee' clips
Tube of filler paste

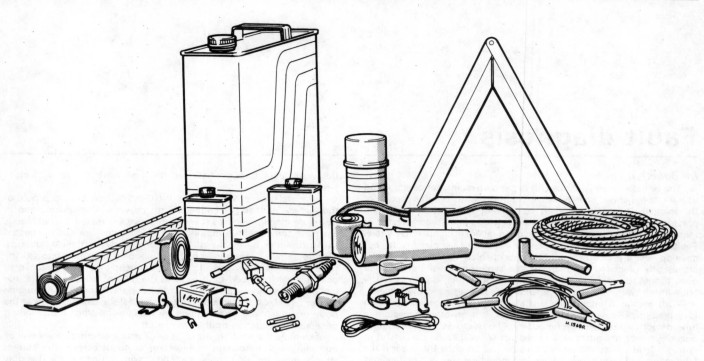

Carrying a few spares can save a long walk!

If spare fuel is carried, a can designed for the purpose should be used to minimise risks of leakage and collision damage. A first aid kit and a warning triangle, whilst not at present compulsory in the UK, are obviously sensible items to carry in addition to the above.

When touring abroad it may be advisable to carry additional spares which, even if you cannot fit them yourself, could save having to wait while parts are obtained. The items below may be worth considering:

Clutch and throttle cables
Cylinder head gasket
Alternator brushes
Tyre valve core

One of the motoring organisations will be able to advise on availability of fuel etc in foreign countries.

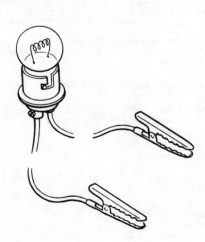

A simple test lamp is useful for tracing electrical faults

Engine will not start

Engine fails to turn when starter operated
   Flat battery (recharge, use jump leads, or push start)
   Battery terminals loose or corroded
   Battery earth to body defective
   Engine earth strap loose or broken
   Starter motor (or solenoid) wiring loose or broken
   Automatic transmission selector in wrong position, or inhibitor switch faulty

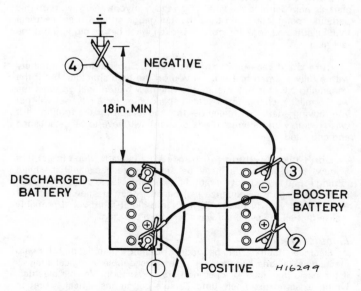

Jump start lead connections for negative earth vehicles – connect leads in order shown

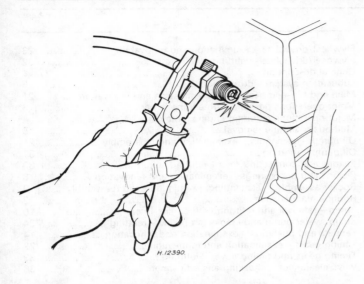

Crank engine and check for spark. Note use of insulated tool

Ignition/starter switch faulty
Major mechanical failure (seizure)
Starter or solenoid internal fault (see Chapter 12)

Starter motor turns engine slowly
Partially discharged battery (recharge, use jump leads, or push start)
Battery terminals loose or corroded
Battery earth to body defective
Engine earth strap loose
Starter motor (or solenoid) wiring loose
Starter motor internal fault (see Chapter 12)

Starter motor spins without turning engine
Flywheel gear teeth stripped
Starter motor mounting bolts loose

Engine turns normally but fails to start
Damp or dirty HT leads and distributor cap (crank engine and check for spark)
No fuel in tank (check for delivery at carburettor)
Fouled or incorrectly gapped spark plugs (remove, clean and regap)
Other ignition system fault (see Chapter 4)
Other fuel system fault (see Chapter 3)
Poor compression (see Chapter 1)
Major mechanical failure (eg camshaft gear teeth stripped)

Engine fires but will not run
Insufficient choke (cold engine)
Air leaks at carburettor or inlet manifold
Fuel starvation (see Chapter 3)
Ignition fault (see Chapter 4)

Engine cuts out and will not restart

Engine cuts out suddenly – ignition fault
Loose or disconnected LT wires
Wet HT leads or distributor cap (after traversing water splash)
Coil failure (check for spark)
Other ignition fault (see Chapter 4)

Engine misfires before cutting out – fuel fault
Fuel tank empty
Fuel pump defective or filter blocked (check for delivery)
Fuel tank filler vent blocked (suction will be evident on releasing cap)

Carburettor needle valve sticking
Carburettor jets blocked (fuel contaminated)
Other fuel system fault (see Chapter 3)

Engine cuts out – other causes
Serious overheating
Major mechanical failure (eg camshaft gear teeth stripped)

Engine overheats

Ignition (no-charge) warning light illuminated
Slack or broken drivebelt – retension or renew (Chapter 2)

Ignition warning light not illuminated
Coolant loss due to internal or external leakage (see Chapter 2)
Thermostat defective
Low oil level
Brakes binding
Radiator clogged externally or internally
Engine waterways clogged
Ignition timing incorrect or automatic advance malfunctioning
Mixture too weak

Note: *Do not add cold water to an overheated engine or damage may result*

Low engine oil pressure

Gauge reads low or warning light illuminated with engine running
Oil level low or incorrect grade
Defective gauge or sender unit
Wire to sender unit earthed
Engine overheating
Oil filter clogged or bypass valve defective
Oil pressure relief valve defective
Oil pick-up strainer clogged
Oil pump worn or mountings loose
Worn main or big-end bearings

Note: *Low oil pressure in a high-mileage engine at tickover is not necessarily a cause for concern. Sudden pressure loss at speed is far more significant. In any event, check the gauge or warning light sender before condemning the engine.*

Engine noises

Pre-ignition (pinking) on acceleration
Incorrect grade of fuel
Ignition timing incorrect
Distributor faulty or worn
Worn or maladjusted carburettor
Excessive carbon build-up in engine

Whistling or wheezing noises
Leaking vacuum hose
Leaking carburettor or manifold gasket
Blowing head gasket

Tapping or rattling
Incorrect valve clearances
Worn valve gear
Broken piston ring (ticking noise)

Knocking or thumping
Unintentional mechanical contact (eg fan blades)
Worn drivebelt
Peripheral component fault (alternator, water pump etc)
Worn big-end bearings (regular heavy knocking, perhaps less under load)
Worn main bearings (rumbling and knocking, perhaps worsening under load)
Piston slap (most noticeable when cold)

Chapter 1 Engine

Contents

Specifications

Type	6-cylinder ohv in 60°V formation

Firing order	1-4-2-5-3-6

General

	2.3	2.8
Engine code	YYT	PRT
Bore	90.02 mm (3.544 in)	93.03 mm (3.663 in)
Stroke	60.10 mm (2.366 in)	68.50 mm (2.697 in)
Cubic capacity	2294 cc (139.9 cu in)	2792 cc (170.3 cu in)
Compression ratio	9.0 : 1	9.2 : 1
Compression pressure at cranking speed	10.0 to 12.0 bar (145 to 174 lbf/in²)	11.5 to 12.5 bar (167 to 181 lbf/in²)

Lubrication system

Oil type/specification .... Multigrade engine oil, viscosity range SAE 10W/30 to 10W/50, to API SF/CC or SF/CD (Duckhams QXR, Hypergrade, or 10W/40 Motor Oil)

Capacity (with filter):
- Non-4x4 models .... 4.25 litres (7.5 pints)
- 4x4 models .... 4.65 litres (8.2 pints)

Oil pressure (minimum):
- At 750 rpm .... 1.0 bar (15.lbf/in²)
- At 2000 rpm .... 2.5 bar (36 lbf/in²)

Oil pressure relief valve opening pressure .... 4.0 to 4.7 bar (58 to 68 lbf/in²)
Oil pressure warning light switch setting .... 0.3 to 0.5 bar (4 to 7 lbf/in²)

Oil pump

Type .... Bi-rotor
Drive .... From camshaft

Operating clearances:
- Outer rotor-to-housing .... 0.15 to 0.30 mm (0.006 to 0.012 in)
- Inner-to-outer rotor .... 0.05 to 0.20 mm (0.002 to 0.008 in)
- Rotor endfloat .... 0.03 to 0.10 mm (0.001 to 0.004 in)

Cylinder block

	2.3	2.8
Cast identification mark	A	E
Bore diameter:		
Standard grade 1	90.000 to 90.010 mm (3.5433 to 3.5437 in)	93.010 to 93.020 mm (3.6618 to 3.6622 in)
Standard grade 2	90.010 to 90.020 mm (3.5437 to 3.5441 in)	93.020 to 93.030 mm (3.6622 to 3.6626 in)
Standard grade 3	90.020 to 90.030 mm (3.5441 to 3.5445 in)	93.030 to 93.040 mm (3.6626 to 3.6630 in)
Standard grade 4	90.030 to 90.040 mm (3.5445 to 3.5449 in)	93.040 to 93.050 mm (3.6630 to 3.6634 in)
Oversize grade A	90.510 to 90.520 mm (3.5634 to 3.5638 in)	93.520 to 93.530 mm (3.6819 to 3.6823 in)
Oversize grade B	90.520 to 90.530 mm (3.5638 to 3.5642 in)	93.530 to 93.540 mm (3.6823 to 3.6827 in)

Cylinder block (continued)

	2.3	2.8
Oversize grade C	90.530 to 90.540 mm (3.5642 to 3.5646 in)	93.540 to 93.550 mm (3.6827 to 3.6831 in)
Standard service grade	90.030 to 90.040 mm (3.5445 to 3.5449 in)	93.040 to 93.050 mm (3.6630 to 3.6634 in)
Oversize 0.5	90.530 to 90.540 mm (3.5642 to 3.5646 in)	93.540 to 93.550 mm (3.6827 to 3.6831 in)
Oversize 1.0	91.030 to 91.040 mm (3.5839 to 3.5843 in)	94.040 to 94.050 mm (3.7024 to 3.7028 in)

Crankshaft

Number of main bearings 4
Main bearing journal diameter (standard) .... 56.980 to 57.000 mm (2.2433 to 2.2441 in)
Main bearing running clearance .... 0.008 to 0.062 mm (0.0003 to 0.0024 in)
No. 3 (thrust) bearing shoulder width (standard) .... 26.390 to 26.440 mm (1.0390 to 1.0409 in)
No. 3 (thrust) flanged bearing shell width (standard) .... 26.240 to 26.290 mm (1.0331 to 1.0350 in)
Crankshaft endfloat:
    2.3 .... 0.08 to 0.28 mm (0.003 to 0.011 in)
    2.8 .... 0.08 to 0.20 mm (0.0032 to 0.0079 in)
Big-end bearing journal diameter (standard) .... 53.980 to 54.000 mm (2.1252 to 2.1260 in)
Big-end bearing running clearance .... 0.006 to 0.064 mm (0.0002 to 0.0025 in)

Pistons

Diameter:

	2.3	2.8
Standard grade 1	89.962 to 89.972 mm (3.5418 to 3.5422 in)	92.972 to 92.982 mm (3.6603 to 3.6607 in)
Standard grade 2	89.972 to 89.982 mm (3.5422 to 3.5426 in)	92.982 to 92.992 mm (3.6607 to 3.6611 in)
Standard grade 3	89.982 to 89.992 mm (3.5426 to 3.5430 in)	92.992 to 93.002 mm (3.6611 to 3.6615 in)
Standard grade 4	89.992 to 90.002 mm (3.5430 to 3.5434 in)	93.002 to 93.012 mm (3.6615 to 3.6619 in)
Standard service grade	89.978 to 90.002 mm (3.5424 to 3.5434 in)	93.000 to 93.020 mm (3.6614 to 3.6622 in)
Oversize 0.5	90.478 to 90.502 mm (3.5621 to 3.5631 in)	93.500 to 93.520 mm (3.6811 to 3.6819 in)
Oversize 1.0	90.978 to 91.002 mm (3.5818 to 3.5828 in)	94.000 to 94.020 mm (3.7008 to 3.7016 in)
Clearance in bore	0.028 to 0.062 mm (0.0011 to 0.0024 in)	0.020 to 0.050 mm (0.0008 to 0.0020 in)

Piston ring end gap

	2.3	2.8
Top and centre	0.38 to 0.58 mm (0.15 to 0.023 in)	0.38 to 0.58 mm (0.015 to 0.023 in)
Bottom	0.38 to 1.40 mm (0.015 to 0.055 in)	0.38 to 1.40 mm (0.015 to 0.055 in)

Gudgeon pins

Diameter:
    Red .... 23.994 to 23.997 mm (0.9446 to 0.9448 in)
    Blue .... 23.997 to 24.000 mm (0.9448 to 0.9449 in)
Clearance in piston:
    2.3 .... 0.005 to 0.011 mm (0.0002 to 0.0004 in)
    2.8 .... 0.008 to 0.014 mm (0.0003 to 0.0006 in)
Interference in connecting rod .... 0.018 to 0.042 mm (0.0007 to 0.0017 in)

Cylinder heads

Cast identification mark:
    2.3 .... A9
    2.8 .... EN
Valve seat angle .... 44° 30' to 45° 00'
Valve seat width .... 1.61 to 2.33 mm (0.0634 to 0.0917 in)
Valve guide bore:
    Standard .... 8.063 to 8.088 mm (0.3174 to 0.3184 in)
    Oversizes .... +0.2, 0.4, 0.6 and 0.8 mm (0.008, 0.016, 0.024 and 0.032 in)

Camshaft

Drive .... Gear
Gear backlash .... 0.17 to 0.27 mm (0.007 to 0.011 in)
Valve timing:

	2.3	2.8
Inlet opens	25° BTDC	24° BTDC
Inlet closes	51° ABDC	72° ABDC
Exhaust opens	67° BBDC	63° BBDC
Exhaust closes	9° ATDC	25° ATDC

Thrust plate thickness:
    Red .... 3.960 to 3.985 mm (0.1559 to 0.1569 in)
    Blue .... 3.986 to 4.011 mm (0.1569 to 0.1579 in)

Spacer thickness:	
Red	4.075 to 4.100 mm (0.1604 to 0.1614 in)
Blue	4.101 to 4.125 mm (0.1615 to 0.1624 in)
Camshaft endfloat	0.02 to 0.10 mm (0.0008 to 0.0039 in)
Bearing journal diameter:	
Front	43.903 to 43.923 mm (1.7285 to 1.7292 in)
Front centre	43.522 to 43.542 mm (1.7135 to 1.7142 in)
Rear centre	43.141 to 43.161 mm (1.6985 to 1.6992 in)
Rear	42.760 to 42.780 mm (1.6835 to 1.6843 in)
Bearing bush internal diameter:	
Front	43.948 to 43.968 mm (1.7302 to 1.7310 in)
Front centre	43.567 to 43.587 mm (1.7152 to 1.7160 in)
Rear centre	43.186 to 43.206 mm (1.7002 to 1.7010 in)
Rear	42.805 to 42.825 mm (1.6852 to 1.6860 in)

Valve clearances (cold)

Inlet	0.35 mm (0.014 in)
Exhaust	0.40 mm (0.016 in)

Inlet valves

Valve spring free length	52.5 mm (2.0669 in)
Stem diameter:	
Standard	8.025 to 8.043 mm (0.3159 to 0.3167 in)
Oversizes	+0.2, 0.4, 0.6 and 0.8 mm (0.008, 0.016, 0.024 and 0.032 in)
Stem-to-guide clearance	0.020 to 0.063 mm (0.0008 to 0.0025 in)

Exhaust valves

Valve spring free length	52.5 mm (2.0669 in)
Stem diameter:	
Standard	7.999 to 8.017 mm (0.3149 to 0.3156 in)
Oversizes	+0.2, 0.4, 0.6 and 0.8 mm (0.008, 0.016, 0.024 and 0.032 in)
Stem-to-guide clerance	0.046 to 0.089 mm (0.0018 to 0.0035 in)
Valve stem oil seal:	
Type	Nulon, selective sizes
Identification:	
Standard size	White
+0.2	Red
+0.4	Blue
+0.6	Green
+0.8	Black

Torque wrench settings

	Nm	lbf ft
Main bearing cap bolts	90 to 104	66 to 77
Big-end cap nuts	26 to 33	19 to 24
Crankshaft pulley/damper central bolt	115 to 130	85 to 96
Camshaft gear bolt	42 to 50	31 to 37
Camshaft thrust plate bolts	17 to 21	13 to 16
Timing cover to cylinder block	17 to 21	13 to 16
Timing cover to intermediate plate	13 to 17	10 to 13
Intermediate plate to cylinder block	17 to 21	13 to 16
Oil pump to cylinder block	14 to 17	10 to 13
Oil pump cover bolts	9 to 13	7 to 10
Rocker shaft securing bolts	59 to 67	44 to 50
Sump bolts:		
Non-4x4 models:		
Stage 1	4 to 7	3 to 5
Stage 2	7 to 10	5 to 7
4x4 models	5 to 11	4 to 8
Sump drain plug:		
Non-4x4 models	21 to 28	16 to 21
4x4 models	25 to 35	19 to 26
Oil pressure switch	12 to 15	9 to 11
Oil cooler threaded sleeve	20 to 40	15 to 30
Cylinder head – hexagon bolts:		
Stage 1	39 to 54	29 to 40
Stage 2	54 to 69	40 to 51
Stage 3 (after 10 to 20 minutes)	95 to 115	70 to 85
Stage 4 (after warm-up)	95 to 115	70 to 85
Cylinder head – Torx bolts:		
Stage 1	35 to 40	26 to 30
Stage 2	70 to 75	52 to 55
Stage 3 (after 5 minutes)	Tighten 90° further	Tighten 90° further
Rocker cover bolts	5 to 8	4 to 6
Fuel pump blanking plate	16 to 18	12 to 13
Flywheel bolts	64 to 70	47 to 52

1 General description

The engine is of 'German' V6 overhead valve type. The camshaft is located centrally in the cylinder block and is driven by helical gears from the crankshaft. The valves are operated by tappets, pushrods and rocker arms.

The cylinder heads are of the crossflow design with the inlet manifold located on top of the cylinder block between the two cylinder heads and the exhaust manifolds on the outside of the heads. The combined crankcase and cylinder block is made of cast iron; attached to the bottom of the crankcase is a pressed steel or aluminium sump which acts as a reservoir for the engine oil.

Aluminium alloy pistons are connected to the crankshaft by H-section forged steel connecting rods and gudgeon pins. Two compression rings and one oil control ring, all located above the gudgeon pin, are fitted.

The forged crankshaft runs in four main bearings, and endfloat is controlled by thrust washers on No 3 main bearing. The drive gear for the distributor and oil pump is located in front of the rear camshaft bearing.

Lubrication is by means of a bi-rotor oil pump.

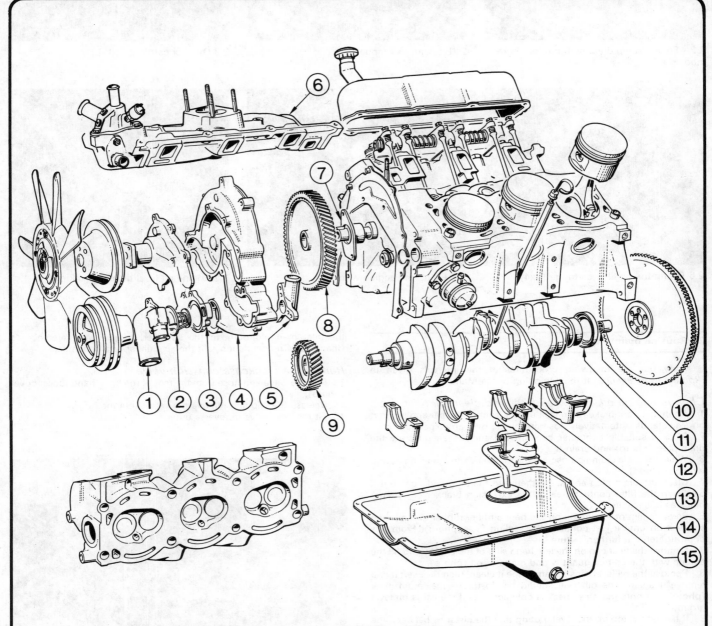

Fig. 1.1 Exploded view of the engine – 2.3 litre carburettor version shown (Sec 1)

1 Thermostat housing	5 By-pass hose flange	9 Crankshaft gear	13 Oil pump driveshaft
2 Thermostat	6 Inlet manifold	10 Flywheel	14 Main bearing cap
3 Water pump	7 Camshaft thrust plate	11 Crankshaft spigot bearing	15 Oil pump
4 Timing cover	8 Camshaft gear	12 Oil seal	

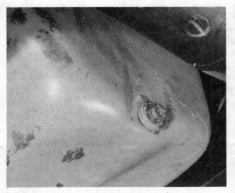

2.2A Engine sump drain plug on non-4x4 models ...

2.2B ... and 4x4 models

2.3 Oil filter cartridge (XR4i)

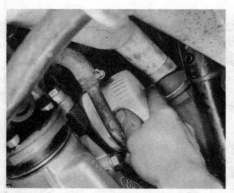

2.6 Fitting the oil filter cartridge (4x4)

2.7 Filling the engine with oil

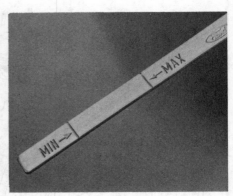

2.8 Engine oil level dipstick markings

2   Routine maintenance

Carry out the following procedures at the intervals given in 'Routine Maintenance' at the beginning of the Manual.

Change engine oil, renew oil filter and clean oil filler cap

1   Apply the handbrake, then jack up the front of the car and support on axle stands. Alternatively position the car over an inspection pit.
2   Place a suitable container beneath the sump then unscrew the drain plug (photo) and drain the oil.
3   While the oil is draining unscrew the oil filter cartridge using a strap wrench (photo).
4   Clean the drain plug and sump then refit the plug and tighten it.
5   Clean the filter contact area of the extension bracket or cylinder block as applicable.
6   Smear a film of engine oil on the new oil filter rubber gasket, then screw it on until it just contacts the sealing face (photo). From this point tighten it a further 3/4 turn.
7   Remove the filler cap on the left-hand side of the engine and fill the engine with the correct quantity and grade of oil (photo).
8   Remove the oil level dipstick and wipe it clean, then re-insert it and remove it again. The oil level should be up to the maximum mark (photo), but note that this check is only accurate if the car is on level ground.
9   If necessary, top up the level, noting that the distance between the minimum and maximum level marks represents approximately 1.0 litre (1.76 pint).
10   Clean the oil filler cap then refit it.

Check and adjust valve clearances

11   Refer to Section 36.

Tighten inlet manifold bolts

12   Remove the air cleaner, or air chamber, as applicable then tighten the inlet manifold bolts to the specified torque with reference to Chapter 3. On completion refit the air cleaner or air chamber.

Renew the crankcase emission valve

13   Pull the valve and hose from the rear of the right-hand rocker cover (photo).
14   Release the clip and remove the valve from the hose.
15   Fit the new valve in reverse order.

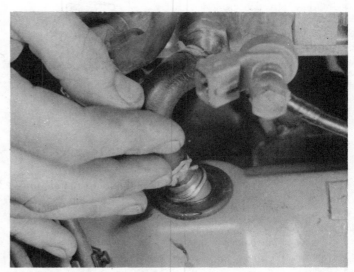

2.13 Removing the crankcase emission valve

3 Major operations possible with engine in car

The following major operations can be carried out without removing the engine from the car.

(a) *Removal and refitting of the cylinder heads*
(b) *Removal and refitting of rocker shaft and pushrods*
(c) *Removal and refitting of front engine mountings*
(d) *Removal and refitting of the flywheel (gearbox removed)*
(e) *Removal and refitting of the sump and oil pump*
(f) *Removal and refitting of the timing gears*
(g) *Removal and refitting of the big-end bearings*
(h) *Removal and refitting of the pistons and connecting rods*
(i) *Renewal of the crankshaft front oil seal in timing cover*
(j) *Removal and refitting of the camshaft*

4 Major operations requiring engine removal

The following major operations may be carried out after removal of the engine:

(a) *Removal and refitting of the crankshaft and main bearings*
(b) *Renewal of the crankshaft rear oil seal*

5 Methods of engine removal

1   Although it is possible to remove the engine together with the manual gearbox or automatic transmission, it is recommended that the home mechanic remove the engine separately. Even so, it is essential to have a good hoist, as the engine alone is of above-average weight.
2   If the work being undertaken requires the removal of the gearbox as well as the engine it is recommended that the gearbox is removed first (refer to Chapter 6).
3   On non-4x4 models the engine is removed upwards from the engine compartment, whereas on 4x4 models, it is removed downwards.
4   If access to a large hoist or four post lifting ramp is possible, then the engine may be removed together with the manual gearbox or automatic transmission. On non-4x4 models the assembly must be lifted out at a very steep angle, and for this a considerable lifting height is required. On 4x4 models the car should be lowered on the ramp until the engine/transmission is resting on a suitable bench, then afer disconnecting the assembly, the car can be raised.
5   The procedure described in paragraph 4 may be completed by referring to the relevant paragraphs of Sections 6 and 38, together with the relevant paragraphs of Chapter 6, Section 3 or 19.

6 Engine – removal

1   Remove the bonnet as described in Chapter 11.
2   Disconnect the battery negative lead.

3   Remove the air cleaner, or inlet air hose, as applicable with reference to Chapter 3.
4   Remove the radiator as described in Chapter 2.
5   Where applicable remove the carburettor cooling air hose.
6   Disconnect the heater hoses at the bulkhead.
7   Disconnect the coolant hoses from the thermostat housing, inlet manifold outlet, and where applicable the oil cooler.
8   Remove the thermo-viscous cooling fan as described in Chapter 2.
9   On non-4x4 models unbolt the heater water tube from the engine.
10   Disconnect the wiring from the alternator, temperature gauge sender unit and where applicable, the carburettor cooling thermo-switch and oil dipstick.
11   Disconnect the HT lead from the ignition coil and the wiring multi-plug from the distributor.
12   On the 2.8 litre engine disconnect the wiring from the cold start valve, thermotime switch, warm-up regulator, auxiliary air valve and overrun fuel cut-off.
13   Remove the distributor cap and rotor arm as described in Chapter 4 as a precaution against any damage when the engine is being removed.
14   Disconnect the accelerator cable and linkage, and remove the bracket with reference to Chapter 3.
15   On automatic transmission models disconnect the downshift cable at the carburettor.
16   As applicable disconnect the wiring from the carburettor or throttle housing (photo).
17   Disconnect the brake servo vacuum hose from the carburettor intermediate flange (2.3 engine) or air chamber (2.8 engine), except on models with ABS braking.
18   Disconnect the fuel lines from the fuel pump and carburettor (2.3 engine).
19   Disconnect the fuel lines from the fuel distributor with reference to Chapter 3 (2.8 engine).
20   Disconnect the wire from the oil pressure switch or gauge connector (photos).
21   Remove the power steering pump as described in Chapter 10. If preferred, the hoses may be left on the pump and the unit tied to one side of the engine compartment.
22   Disconnect the engine earth cable(s) (photo).
23   Apply the handbrake then jack up the front of the car and support on axle stands. On 4x4 models allow a minimum clearance of 700 mm (27.5 in) between the front panel and ground for the engine to be withdrawn.
24   Remove the starter motor as described in Chapter 12, then unbolt the cable bracket from the cylinder block (photo).
25   On non-4x4 models disconnect the exhaust downpipes from the exhaust manifolds; on 4x4 models remove the exhaust system complete (Chapter 3).
26   Remove the clutch cable where applicable from the gearbox with reference to Chapter 5.

Non-4x4 models

27   Unscrew the bolts securing the manual gearbox or automatic transmission to the engine, noting the location of the earth cable.
28   On automatic transmission models unscrew the unions and

6.16 Earthing wire connected to the throttle housing (2.8)

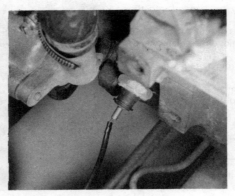

6.20A Oil pressure switch and wiring

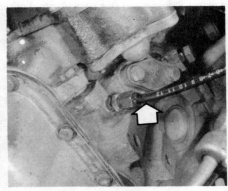

6.20B Oil pressure gauge line (arrowed) and connector

6.22 Engine earth cable on the bulkhead

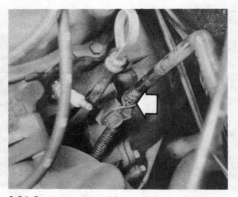

6.24 Starter motor wiring cable and bracket (arrowed)

6.42 Front suspension crossmember removed together with the steering gear

disconnect the oil cooler pipes from the transmission. Plug the pipe ends and apertures.

29 On automatic transmission models, working through the starter motor aperture, unscrew the driveplate nuts. There are four nuts, and it is necessary to turn the engine to locate each one in turn in the aperture.

30 Lower the car to the ground.

31 Support the gearbox/automatic transmission with a trolley jack.

32 Attach a hoist to the engine and just take its weight. To maintain balance, a suitable place to connect the hoist chains is around the front of the exhaust manifolds.

33 Unscrew the nuts from the two engine mountings. On the 2.8 litre engine unbolt the right-hand mounting bracket from the engine.

34 Raise the engine until the bellhousing touches the bulkhead, then also raise the trolley jack to support the gearbox/automatic transmission.

35 Pull the engine forwards to disengage it from the gearbox/automatic transmission and location dowels. On automatic transmission models make sure that the torque converter is held firmly in contact with the transmission oil pump, otherwise it could fall out, and fluid would be spilled.

36 When clear of the gearbox/automatic transmission lift the engine from the engine compartment while guiding it past the surrounding components.

4x4 models

37 Attach a hoist to the engine and just take its weight. To maintain balance, a suitable place to connect the hoist chains is around the front of the exhaust manifolds.

38 Disconnect the speedometer cable from the intermediate shaft bearing cover (Chapter 12).

39 Remove the front propeller shaft as described in Chapter 7.

40 Unscrew the bolts securing the gearbox to the engine, noting the location of the earth cable and heater hose bracket.

41 Support the front of the gearbox on a trolley jack. Alternatively a suitable 686 mm (27.0 in) long metal bar may be inserted into the holes in the underbody side members.

42 Remove the front suspension crossmember as described in Chapter 10, Section 3, however it is not necessary to remove the steering gear from the crossmember (photo).

43 Pull the engine forwards to disengage it from the gearbox and location dowels.

44 When clear of the gearbox lower the engine from the engine compartment while guiding it past the surrounding components (photo).

7 Engine dismantling – general

1 When the engine is removed from the car, it, and particularly its accessories, are vulnerable to damage. If possible mount the engine on a stand, or failing this, make sure it is supported in such a manner that it will not be damaged whilst undoing tight nuts and bolts.

2 Cleanliness is important when dismantling the engine to prevent exposed parts from contamination. Before starting the dismantling operations, clean the outside of the engine with paraffin, or a good grease solvent if it is very dirty. Carry out this cleaning away from the area in which the dismantling is to take place.

3 If an engine stand is not available carry out the work on a bench or wooden platform. Avoid working with the engine directly on a concrete floor, as grit presents a real source of trouble.

4 As parts are removed, clean them in a paraffin bath. Never immerse parts with internal oilways in paraffin but wipe down carefully with a petrol-dampened rag. Clean oilways with wire.

5 It is advisable to have suitable containers to hold small items in their groups as this will help when reassembling the engine and also prevent possible loss.

6 Always obtain complete sets of gaskets when the engine is being dismantled. It is a good policy to always fit new gaskets in view of the relatively small cost involved. Retain the old gaskets when dismantling the engine with a view to using them as a pattern to make a replacement gasket if a new one is not available.

7 When possible refit nuts, bolts and washers in their locations as this helps to protect the threads from damage and will also be helpful when the engine is being reassembled, as it establishes their location.

8 Retain unserviceable items until the new parts are obtained, so that the new part can be checked against the old part to ensure that the correct item has been supplied.

6.44 Lowering the engine from the engine compartment (4x4)

8 Engine ancillaries – removal

Although the items listed may be removed separately with the engine installed (as described in the relevant Chapters) it is more appropriate to take them off after the engine has been removed from the car when extensive dismantling is being carried out. The items are:

Carburettor or fuel injection components (Chapter 3)
Distributor (Chapter 4)
Water pump (Chapter 2)
Inlet and exhaust manifolds (Chapter 3)
Clutch (Chapter 5)
Spark plugs (Chapter 4)
Alternator (Chapter 12)
Engine mounting brackets (Section 11)
Temperature gauge sender unit (Chapter 2)
Front final drive unit and intermediate shaft on 4x4 models (Chapter 8)
Oil filter cartridge (Section 2)
Fuel pump on 2.3 engine (Chapter 3)

9 Engine – dismantling

1 If not done previously, unscrew the sump drain plug and drain the oil into a suitable container.
2 Where applicable, use a 27 mm spanner to unscrew the special nut securing the extension bracket to the oil cooler. Remove the bracket, together with the washers and O-ring. Unscrew the centre sleeve and remove the oil cooler and gasket (photo).
3 Unbolt and remove the power steering pump/alternator bracket (photo).
4 Disconnect the bypass hose from the timing cover rear elbow (photo).

5 Remove the rocker cover securing bolts and lift off the covers (photo). Disconnect the breather hose where applicable.
6 Undo the rocker shaft securing bolts and remove the rocker shafts and oil splash shields (photos). Note which way the splash shields are fitted. Mark the rocker shafts so that they can be refitted in their original positions.
7 Lift out the pushrods and keep them in their respective positions in relation to the rocker shafts to ensure that they are refitted in their original locations (photo).
8 Unscrew the cylinder head bolts progressively and in the reverse order to the tightening sequence shown in Fig. 1.8 (photo).
9 Each head can now be lifted from the block (photo). If the head sticks to the cylinder block try to break the seal by rocking it. If this does not free it a soft-faced hammer can be used to strike it sharply and break the cylinder head joint seal. Never use a metal hammer directly on the head as this may fracture the casting. Also never try to prise the head free by forcing a screwdriver or chisel between the cylinder head and cylinder block as this will damage the mating surfaces.
10 Remove the cylinder head gaskets.
11 Unscrew the oil pressure switch, or oil pressure connector.
12 Using a piece of bent wire, prise the valve tappets from the block (photos). Place the tappets with their respective pushrods to ensure correct refitting.
13 Invert the engine and unbolt the sump (photo). Remove the gaskets as applicable. Unbolt the heater tube if applicable.
14 Unbolt the pick-up pipe from the oil pump, and remove the gasket (photos).
15 Unbolt the oil pump and withdraw the driveshaft, noting which way round it is fitted (photos).
16 Remove the crankshaft pulley securing bolt and take the pulley off the crankshaft (photos). Restrain the crankshaft from turning by chocking the flywheel.
17 Index mark the position of the flywheel or driveplate in relation to the crankshaft so that it can be refitted in the same position.
18 Chock the flywheel or driveplate to restrain it from turning, then

9.2 Oil cooler showing centre sleeve

9.3 Power steering/pump alternator bracket

9.4 Disconnecting the bypass hose from the timing cover rear elbow

9.5 Unbolting the rocker covers

9.6A Unscrew the bolts ...

9.6B ... and remove the rocker shafts ...

9.6C ... and oil splash shields

9.7 Removing the pushrods

9.8 Removing the cylinder head bolts

9.9 Removing the right-hand cylinder head

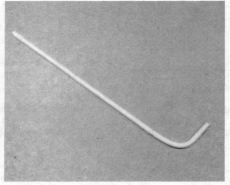

9.12A Using a piece of bent wire ...

9.12B ... prise up the tappets ...

9.12C ... and remove them from the block

9.13 Unbolting the sump (non-4x4 models)

9.14A Unbolt the oil pump pick-up pipe ...

9.14B ... and remove the gasket

9.15A Oil pump mounting bolts (arrowed)

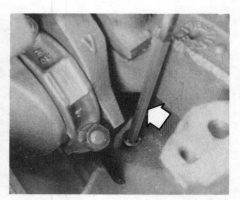

9.15B Removing the oil pump driveshaft (arrowed)

9.16A Unscrew the crankshaft pulley bolt ...

9.16B ... remove the bolt ...

9.16C ... and slide off the pulley

remove the six bolts securing the flywheel or driveplate to the crankshaft and lift off the flywheel (photo).

19 Remove the engine adaptor plate (photo).

20 Unbolt the thermostat rear water elbow. Remove the gasket.

21 Unbolt the timing cover and remove the gasket (photos).

22 Unscrew the bolt securing the camshaft gear to the camshaft and pull off the gear (photos).

23 Unscrew the front intermediate plate attaching bolts and remove the intermediate plate. Remove the gasket and guide sleeves (photos).

24 If the crankshaft gear needs to be removed use a standard puller to draw it off the crankshaft (photo).

25 Unscrew the camshaft thrust plate securing bolts, remove the thrust plate and withdraw the camshaft (photos).

26 Check that the big-end bearing caps and connecting rods have identification marks. This is to ensure that the correct caps are fitted to the correct connecting rods and at reassembly are fitted in their correct cylinder bores. Note that the pistons have an arrow (or notch) marked on the crown to indicate the forward facing side (photos).

27 Remove the No 1 cylinder big-end nuts, then tap off the big-end cap. Keep the shell bearings with the cap and connecting rod from which they are removed. To remove the shell bearings, press the bearing on the side opposite the groove in both the connecting rod and the cap, and the bearing will slide out (photos).

28 Withdraw the piston and connecting rod upwards out of the cylinder bore by tapping with the handle of a hammer from underneath.

29 Repeat the procedure given in paragraphs 27 and 28 to remove the remaining pistons and connecting rods.

9.18 Removing the flywheel bolts

9.19 Removing the engine adaptor plate

9.21A Unbolt the timing cover ...

9.21B ... and remove the gasket

9.22A Remove the securing bolt ...

9.22B ... and slide off the camshaft gear

9.23A Unscrew the bolts ...

9.23B ... and remove the intermediate plate ...

9.23C ... and gasket

9.24 Pulling off the crankshaft gear

9.25A Unscrew the bolts ...

9.25B ... and remove the camshaft thrust plate

9.25C Withdrawing the camshaft

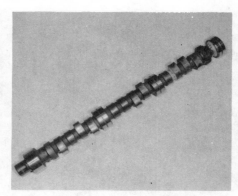

9.25D Camshaft removed from the engine

9.26A Check that the big-end bearing caps and connecting rods are marked for position (arrows)

9.26B The arrow on the piston crown faces the front of the engine

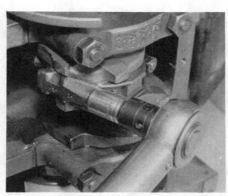

9.27A Removing the big-end nuts

9.27B Removing a shell bearing from the connecting rod

9.30A Main bearing cap number (A) and directional arrow (B)

9.30B The domed (top) and standard (bottom) main bearing bolts

9.31 Main bearing bolt removal

9.32 Removing the crankshaft

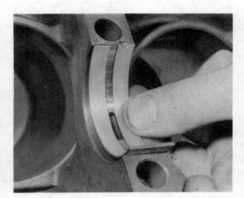

9.33A Removing an upper main bearing shell

9.33B Removing the upper half of No 3 main bearing shell (2.8)

30 Make sure that the identification marks are visible on the main bearing caps so that they can be refitted in their original positions at reassembly. The caps are numbered and an arrow indicates the front of the engine (photo). Note that on the 2.8 engine Nos 2 and 3 caps are retained with longer bolts incorporating a domed head (photo). Keep these identified for position.

31 Undo the securing bolts and lift off the main bearing caps and the bottom half of each bearing shell, taking care to keep the bearing shell in the right caps (photo). When removing the rear main bearing cap note that this also retains the crankshaft rear oil seal. When removing the No 3 main bearing cap, note the position of the two half thrust washers and mark them so that they can be refitted in the same position. On later models the thrust washers are integral with the main shell. It may be necessary to tap the main bearing caps with a soft-faced hammer to release them.

32 Lift the crankshaft out of the crankcase and remove the rear oil seal (photo).

33 Remove the upper halves of the main bearing shells and the upper half of the No 3 bearing thrust washers (where applicable) from the crankcase and place them with the respective main bearing caps (photos).

10 Sump – removal and refitting with engine in car

1 Disconnect the battery negative lead.
2 Apply the handbrake then jack up the front of the car and support on axle stands.
3 Unscrew the sump drain plug and drain the oil into a suitable container. When completed refit the plug and tighten.

Non-4x4 models
4 Remove the starter motor as described in Chapter 12.
5 Unscrew the nuts from both engine mountings.

6 Remove the adaptor plate bolt from the gearbox/automatic transmission.
7 Unscrew the bolt securing the steering intermediate shaft to the inner column, swivel the clamp plate to one side, and disconnect the intermediate shaft.
8 Unscrew the sump bolts and prise the sump from the crankcase.
9 Prise the engine as far as possible using a hoist, and support with stands beneath the gearbox/automatic transmission and the front of the engine.
10 Support the front suspension crossmember with a trolley jack, then unscrew the crossmember-to-underbody bolts sufficiently to lower the crossmember and withdraw the sump.
11 Scrape off the old gaskets and clean the mating faces.
12 Refitting is a reversal of removal, but fit the new gaskets with reference to Section 34. Finally fill the engine with oil.

4x4 models
13 Remove the front suspension crossmember as described in Chapter 10, Section 3, however it is not necessary to remove the steering gear from the crossmember.
14 Remove the front final drive unit and intermediate shaft as described in Chapter 8.
15 Loosen the heater tube front and side mounting bolt and nut, and move the tube forwards as far as possible (photos).
16 Unscrew the sump bolts, noting that there are three lengths and the two longer bolts go at the flywheel end (photo).
17 Remove the sump from the crankcase (photo). Do not prise the sump away as it is of aluminium and the sealing surfaces may be damaged. Careful tapping with a wooden or hide mallet should be sufficient to release the sump.
18 Remove the end gaskets from the rear main bearing cap and timing cover and clean all the mating faces (photo).
19 Refitting is a reversal of removal, but fit new end gaskets, and apply sealing compound to Ford specification SPM2G-9121-A to the sump sealing surfaces before fitting it to the crankcase (photos).

10.15A Heater tube front mounting bolt removal (4x4)

10.15B Heater tube side mounting nut (4x4)

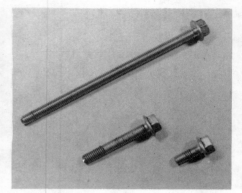

10.16 Sump bolts (4x4)

10.17 Sump removal from the crankcase (4x4)

10.18 Mating faces and inside view of sump (4x4)

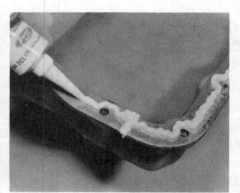

10.19A Apply the sealing compound to the sealing surfaces ...

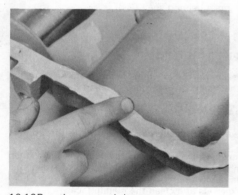

10.19B ... then smooth it to an even thickness

11.1A Left-hand engine mounting (4x4)

11.1B Right-hand engine mounting shown on front suspension crossmember

11 Engine mountings – renewal

1   Unscrew the nuts which secure the brackets to the mountings and recover the washers (photos).
2   Where applicable temporarily raise the front of the car, support on axle stands, and unscrew the lower mounting nuts.
3   Where the mountings are bolted to the top of the crossmember unscrew the bolts.
4   Raise the engine using a hoist or trolley jack and block of wood, and withdraw the mountings.
5   Fit the new mountings using a reversal of the removal procedure.

12 Engine components – examination for wear

When the engine has been stripped down and all the parts have been cleaned, they should be examined for wear. In cases where no definite wear limit is given, it must be a matter of judgement on whether or not a part is to be renewed or refitted, taking into consideration the further life expected from the engine, the degree of reliability required, the cost of the new part and the amount of dismantling which will be necessary to renew the part later.

13 Rocker assembly – dismantling, examination and reassembly

1   Tap out the roll pin from one end of the rocker shaft and remove the spring washer (photo).
2   Slide the rocker arms, rocker supports and springs off the rocker shaft. Keep them in the correct order so that they can be reassembled in the same position. If a rocker support sticks it can be removed by tapping it with a soft-faced hammer.

13.1 The rocker shaft has a retaining pin at each end (arrowed)

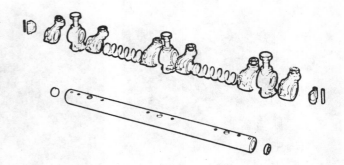

Fig. 1.2 Exploded view of rocker shaft assembly (Sec 13)

3   Examine the rocker shaft and rocker arms for wear. If the rocker arm surface that contacts the valve stem is considerably worn, renew the rocker arm. If it is worn slightly step-shaped it may be cleaned up with a fine oil stone.
4   Commencing January 1984, modified rocker shaft springs have been fitted. Where tappet nojse is evident on earlier models between engine speeds of 1500 and 2000 rpm, the later type of springs may be fitted.
5   Oil the parts and reassemble them on their shafts in the original order. With both rocker shafts fitted the oil holes must face downwards to the cylinder heads. This position is indicated by a notch on one end face of the rocker shaft.

14 Tappets and pushrods – examination and renovation

1   Examine the valve tappets for wear and damage, renew if suspect.
2   Check the pushrods for signs of bending or wear. Correct or renew as necessary.

15 Camshaft and camshaft bearings – examination and renovation

1   If there is excessive wear in the camshaft they will have to be renewed. As the fitting of new bearings requires special tools this should be left to your local Ford dealer.

2   The camshaft may show signs of wear on the bearing journals or cam lobes. The main decision to take is what degree of wear necessitates renewing the camshaft, which is expensive. Scoring or damage to the bearing journals cannot be removed by regrinding; renewal of the camshaft is the only solution.
3   The cam lobes may show signs of ridging or pitting on the high points. If ridging is slight then it may be possible to remove it with a fine oil stone or emery cloth. The cam lobes, however, are surface hardened and once the hard skin is penetrated wear will be very rapid.

16 Cylinder heads – dismantling, renovation and reassembly

1   Clean the dirt and oil off the cylinder heads. Remove the carbon deposits fom the combustion chambers and valve heads with a scraper or rotary wire brush.
2   Remove the valves by compressing the valve springs with a suitable valve spring compressor and lifting out the collets. Release the valve spring compressor and remove the valve spring retainer, spring and valve (photos). Mark each valve so that they can be fitted in the same location.
3   With the valves removed, clean out the carbon from the ports.
4   Examine the heads of the valves and the valve seats for pitting and burning. If the pitting on valve and seat is slight it can be removed by grinding the valves and seats together with coarse, and then fine, valve grinding paste. If the pitting is deep the valves will have to be reground on a valve grinding machine and the seats will have to be recut with a valve seat cutter. Both these operations are a job for your local Ford dealer or motor engineering specialist.
5   Check the valves guides for wear by inserting the valve in the guide, the valve stem should move easily in the guide without side play. Renewal of worn guides requires special tools and should be left to your local Ford dealer.
6   When grinding slightly pitted valves and valve seats with carborundum paste proceed as follows: Apply a little coarse grinding paste to the valve seat and using a suction type valve grinding tool,

16.2A Compress the spring with a valve spring compressor ...

16.2B ... then remove the collets (magnetic probe shown) ...

16.2C ... followed by the retainer ...

16.2D ... and valve spring

16.2E Removing an inlet valve

16.2F Inlet valve (top) and exhaust valve (bottom) components

grind the valve into its seat with a semi-rotary movement, lifting the valve from time to time. A light spring under the valve head will assist in this operation. When a dull matt even surface finish appears on both the valve and the valve seat, clean off the coarse paste and repeat the grinding operation with a fine grinding paste until a continuous ring of light grey matt finish appears on both valve and valve seat. Carefully clean off all traces of grinding paste. Blow through the gas passages with compressed air.

7   Check the valve springs for damage and also check the free length, refer to the Specifications at the beginning of this Chapter. Renew if defective.

8   Lubricate the valve stem with engine oil and insert it in the valve guide. Slide on a new oil seal. The light plastic seals go on the exhaust valves (photo).

16.8 Inlet valve seal (left) and exhaust valve seal (right)

9   Fit the valve spring and valve spring retainer.

10 Use a suitable valve spring compressor to compress the valve spring until the collets can be fitted in position in the slots in the valve stem. Release the valve spring compressor.

11 After fitting all the parts, tap the top of the valve springs lightly with a plastic hammer to ensure correct seating of the collets.

17 Cylinder bores – examination and renovation

1   A new cylinder is perfectly round and the walls parallel throughout its length. The action of the piston tends to wear the walls at right angles to the gudgeon pin due to side thrust. This wear takes place principally on that section of the cylinder swept by the piston rings.

2   It is possible to get an indication of bore wear by removing the cylinder heads with the engine still in the car. With the piston down in the bore first signs of wear can be seen and felt just below the top of the bore where the top piston ring reaches and there will be a noticeable lip (other than normal carbon build-up). If there is no lip it is fairly reasonable to expect that bore wear is not severe and any lack of compression or excessive oil consumption is due to worn or broken piston rings or pistons.

3   If it is possible to obtain a bore measuring micrometer, measure the bore in the thrust plane below the lip and again at the bottom of the cylinder in the same plane. If the difference is more than 0.076 mm (0.003 in) then a rebore is necessary. Similarly a difference of 0.076 mm (0.003 in) or more across the bore diameter is a sign of ovality calling for a rebore.

4   Any bore which is significantly scratched or scored will need reboring. This symptom usually indicates that the piston or rings are damaged. Even if only one cylinder is in need of reboring it will still be necessary for all cylinders to be bored and fitted with new oversize pistons and rings. Your Ford agent or local motor engineering specialist will be able to rebore and obtain the necessary matched pistons. If the crankshaft is undergoing regrinding also, it is a good idea to let the same firm renovate and reassemble the crankshaft and pistons to the block. A reputable firm normally gives a guarantee for such work. In cases where engines have been rebored already to their maximum, cylinder liners are available which may be fitted. In such cases the same reboring processes have to be followed and the services of a specialist engineering firm are required.

18 Pistons and piston rings – examination and renovation

1   Worn pistons and rings can usually be diagnosed when the symptoms of excessive oil consumption and low compression occur and are sometimes, though not always, associated with worn cylinder bores. Compression testers that fit onto the spark plug holes are available and these can indicate where low pressure is occurring. Wear usually accelerates the more it is left so when the symptoms occur early action can possibly save the expense of a rebore.

2   Another symptom of piston wear is piston slap – a knocking noise from the crankcase, not to be confused with big-end bearing failure. It can be heard clearly at low engine speed when there is no load (idling for example) and is much less audible when the engine speed increases. Piston wear usually occurs in the skirt or lower end of the piston on the thrust side. It can also be seen where the skirt thickness is different.

3   Piston ring wear can be checked by first removing the rings from the pistons as described later in this Section. Then place the rings in the cylinder bores from the top, pushing them down about 40 mm (1.5 in) with the head of the piston (from which the rings have been removed) so that they rest square in the cylinder. Then measure the gap at the ends of the ring with a feeler gauge (photo). If it exceeds the specified maximum then the ring needs renewal.

18.3 Checking the piston ring end gap with a feeler gauge

11 The easiest method to use when fitting rings is to wrap a feeler gauge round the top of the piston and place the rings on one at a time, starting with the bottom oil control ring, over the feeler gauge. The feeler gauge, complete with ring, can then be slid down the piston over the other piston ring grooves until the correct groove is reached. The piston ring is then slid off the feeler gauge into the groove.
12 An alternative method is to fit the rings by holding them slightly open with the thumbs and both of the index fingers. This method requires a steady hand and great care as it is easy to open the ring too much and break it.

19 Connecting rods and gudgeon pins – examination and renovation

1 Gudgeon pins are a shrink fit into the connecting rods. Neither of these would normally need renewal unless the pistons were being changed, in which case the new pistons would automatically be supplied with new gudgeon pins.
2 Connecting rods are not subject to wear but in extreme circumstances such as engine seizure they could be distorted. Such conditions may be visually apparent but where doubt exists they should be checked for alignment and if necessary renewed or straightened. The bearing caps should also be examined for indications of filing down which may have been attempted in the mistaken idea that bearing slackness could be remedied in this way. If there are such signs then the connecting rods and caps should be renewed by your Ford agent or local engineering specialist.

20 Crankshaft – examination and renovation

1 Examine the main bearing journals and crankpins for score marks or scratches. Also check them for ovality using a micrometer (photo). Ovality in excess of 0.025 mm (0.001 in) should be regarded as excessive.
2 Regrinding of the crankshaft on the 2.3 litre engine is permitted, but contrary to normal practise Ford stipulate that under no circumstances should the 2.8 litre crankshaft be reground. This means that if the 2.8 litre crankshaft is damaged or excessively worn, it must be renewed.
3 Before being refitted, the crankshaft must be thoroughly cleaned, including the internal oilways. This can be done by probing with wire or by blowing through with an air line. Then insert the nozzle of an oil gun into the respective oilways, each time blanking off the previous hole, and squirt oil through the shaft. It should emerge through the next hole. Any oilway blockage must obviously be cleaned out prior to refitting the crankshaft.
4 Check the spigot bearing in the rear of the crankshaft and if necessary renew it on manual gearbox models (photo).

4 The grooves in which the rings locate in the piston can also become enlarged in use. The clearance between ring and piston, in the groove, should not exceed 0.102 mm (0.004 in) for the top two compression rings and 0.076 mm (0.003 in) for the lower oil control ring.
5 However, it is rare that a piston is only worn in the ring grooves and the need to renew them for this fault alone is hardly ever encountered. Wherever pistons are renewed the weight of the four piston/connecting rod assemblies should be kept within the limit variation of 8 g (0.28 oz) to maintain engine balance.
6 To remove the piston rings, slide them carefully over the top of the piston, taking care not to scratch the aluminium alloy; never slide them off the bottom of the piston skirt. It is very easy to break the cast iron piston rings if they are pulled off roughly, so this operation should be done with extreme care. It is helpful to make use of old feeler gauges.
7 Lift one end of the piston ring to be removed out of its groove and insert under it the end of the feeler gauge.
8 Turn the feeler gauge slowly round the piston and, as the ring comes out of its groove, apply slight upward pressure so that it rests on the land above. It can then be eased off the piston, with the feeler gauge stopping it from slipping into an empty groove if it is any but the top piston ring that is being removed (photos).
9 The piston rings must always be removed from the top of the piston.
10 Check that the piston ring grooves and oilways are thoroughly clean and unblocked. Piston rings must always be fitted over the head of the piston and never from the bottom.

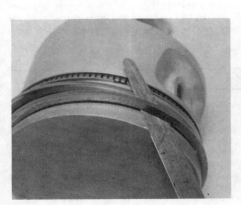

18.8A Removing the top compression ring

18.8B Removing the second compression ring

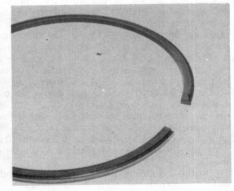

18.8C The second compression ring is stepped

20.1 Checking the crankpins for ovality

20.4 Spigot bearing in rear of crankshaft

21.6A Markings on the reverse of a big-end bearing shell

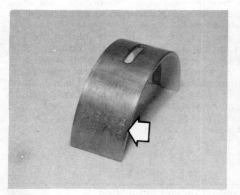

21.6B 'Standard' markings on the reverse of a main bearing shell (arrowed)

21.7A Plastigage used to check the running clearance of main and big-end bearings (arrowed)

21.7B Card gauge for checking width of Plastigage

21 Main and big-end bearings – examination and renovation

1   With careful servicing and regular oil and filter changes, bearings will last for a very long time, but they can still fail for unforeseen reasons. With big-end bearings the indication is a regular rhythymic loud knocking from the crankcase. The frequency depends on engine speed and is particularly noticeable when the engine is under load. This symptom is accompanied by a fall in oil pressure, although this is not normally noticeable unless an oil pressure gauge is fitted. Main bearing failure is usually indicated by serious vibration, particularly at higher engine revolutions, accompanied by a more significant drop in oil pressure and a 'rumbling' noise.

2   Bearing shells in good condition have bearing surfaces with a smooth, even matt silver/grey colour all over. Worn bearings will show patches of a different colour when the bearing metal has worn away and exposed the underlay. Damaged bearings will be pitted or scored. If the crankshaft is in good condition it is merely a question of obtaining another set of bearings the same size. A reground or new crankshaft will need new bearing shells as a matter of course.

3   The original bore in the cylinder block may have been standard or the first grade oversize and in the latter instance this will be indicated by the bearing caps which will be marked with white paint.

4   On the 2.3 engine, the original size of the crankshaft main bearing journals may have been standard or 0.25 mm (0.010 in) undersize. If the journals were undersize originally, this will be indicated by a green stripe on the first balance weight. The original size of the big-end journal was either standard or 0.25 mm (0.010 in) undersize. If undersize, the corresponding journal web will be marked with a green spot.

5   On the 2.8 litre engine, both the main and big-end journals are standard size only.

6   If the bearing shells are to be renewed, take the old ones along to your supplier and this will act as a check that you are getting the

correct size bearings. Undersize bearings are marked as such on the reverse face (photos).

7   The running clearance of the bearings may be checked using Plastigage. The plastic thread is positioned on the journal then the bearing shell and cap assembled, and the bolts/nuts tightened to the specified torque. When the cap is removed, the width of the thread is measured with a card gauge which indicates the running clearance (photos).

22 Timing gears – examination and renovation

1   Inspect the gear teeth for damage, or signs of excessive wear which will cause noisy operation.

2   The backlash between the camshaft gear and the crankshaft gear must not exceed 0.27 mm (0.011 in) and the backlash should be checked at four different points around the periphery of the gear (photo).

23 Flywheel/driveplate – examination and renovation

1   Inspect the flywheel/driveplate for damage and check the ring gear for wear and damage.

2   If the ring gear is badly worn or has missing teeth it should be renewed. The old ring can be removed by cutting a notch between two teeth with a hacksaw and then splitting it with a cold chisel.

3   To fit a new ring gear requires heating the ring to 204°C (400°F). This can be done by polishing four equal spaced sections of the gear laying it on a suitable heat resistant surface (such as fire bricks) and heating it evenly with a blow lamp or torch until the polished areas turn a light yellow tint. Do not overheat or the hard wearing properties will be lost. The gear has a chamfered inner edge which should go against

22.2 Checking the timing gear backlash

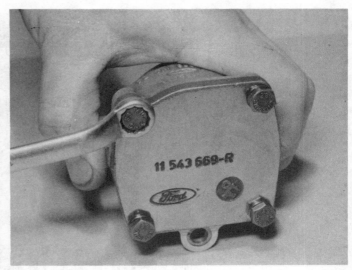

24.3 Unbolting the oil pump cover

the shoulder when put on the flywheel/driveplate. When hot enough place the gear in position quickly, tapping it home if necessary, and let it cool naturally without quenching in any way.

24 Oil pump – dismantling, examination and reassembly

1   If oil pump wear is suspected it is possible to obtain a repair kit. Check for wear first as described later in this Section and if confirmed, obtain an overhaul kit or a new pump. The two rotors are a matched pair and form a single replacement unit. Where the rotor assembly is to be re-used and the outer rotor, prior to dismantling, must be marked on its front face in order to ensure correct reassembly.
2   Remove the intake pipe and oil strainer if not already removed.
3   Note the relative position of the oil pump cover and body and then undo and remove the bolts and spring washers (photo). Lift away the cover.
4   Carefully remove the rotors from the housing.
5   Using a centre punch, tap a hole in the centre of the pressure relief valve sealing plug, (make a note to obtain a new one).
6   Screw in a self-tapping screw and, using an open-ended spanner, withdraw the sealing plug.
7   Thoroughly clean all parts in petrol or paraffin and wipe dry using a non-fluffy rag. The necessary clearances may now be checked using a machined straight-edge (a good steel rule) and a set of feeler gauges. The critical clearances are between the lobes of the centre rotor and convex faces of the outer rotor; between the rotor and the pump body; and between both rotors and the end cover plate.
8   The rotor lobe clearance may be checked using feeler gauges and

should be within the limits 0.05 to 0.20 mm (0.002 to 0.008 in) (photo).
9   The clearance between the outer rotor and pump body should be within the limits 0.15 to 0.30 mm (0.006 to 0.012 in) (photo).
10 The endfloat may be measured by placing a steel straight-edge across the end of the pump and measuring the gap between the rotors and the straight-edge (photo). The gap in either rotor should be within the limits 0.03 to 0.10 mm (0.0012 to 0.004 in).
11 If the only excessive clearances are endfloat it is possible to reduce them by removing the rotors and lapping the face of the body on a flat bed until the necessary clearances are obtained. It must be emphasised, however, that the face of the body must remain perfectly flat and square to the axis of the rotor spindle, otherwise the clearances will not be equal and the end cover will not be a pressure tight fit to the body. It is worth trying, of course, if the pump is in need of renewal anyway but unless done properly, it could seriously jeopardise the rest of the overhaul. Any variations in the other two clearances should be overcome with a new unit.
12 With all parts scrupulously clean, first refit the relief valve and spring and lightly lubricate with engine oil.
13 Using a suitable diameter drift, drive in a new sealing plug, flat side outwards until it is flush with the intake pipe mating face.
14 Lubricate both rotors with engine oil and fit them in the body. Fit the oil pump cover and secure with the bolts tightened in a diagonal and progressive manner to the torque wrench setting given in the Specifications.
15 Fit the driveshaft into the rotor driveshaft and ensure that the rotor turns freely.
16 Fit the intake pipe and oil strainer to the pump body together with a new gasket.

24.8 Checking the rotor lobe clearance

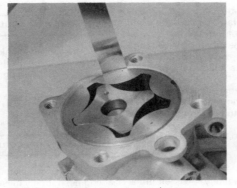

24.9 Checking the outer rotor clearance

24.10 Checking the endfloat

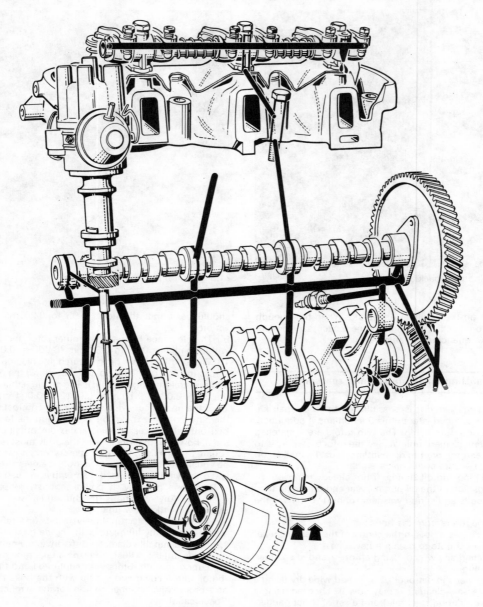

Fig. 1.3 Engine lubrication system (Sec 25)

25 Lubrication system – description

The oil sump is attached to the underside of the crankcase and acts as a reservoir for the engine oil. The oil pump draws oil from the sump via an oil strainer and intake pipe, then passes it into the full-flow oil filter. The filtered oil flows from the centre of the oil filter element and passes through a short drilling, on the right-hand side, to the oil pressure switch and to the main gallery (on the left-hand side of the crankcase) through a transverse drilling.

Four drillings connect the main gallery to the four main bearings and the camshaft bearings in their turn are connected to all the main bearings. The big-end bearings are supplied with oil through diagonal drillings from the nearest main bearing.

When the crankshaft is rotating, oil is thrown from the hole in each big-end bearing and ensures splash lubrication of the gudgeon pins and thrust side of the cylinders. The timing gears are also splash lubricated through an oil drilling.

The crankshaft third bearing journal intermittently feeds oil under pressure, to the rocker shafts through a drilling in the cylinder block

and cylinder head. The oil then passes back to the engine sump, via large drillings in the cylinder block and cylinder head.

26 Crankcase ventilation system – description

The closed crankcase ventilation system is used to control the emission of crankcase vapour. It is controlled by the amount of air drawn in by the engine when it is running and the throughput of the vent valve.

The system is known as the PCV system (positive crankcase ventilation).

27 Engine reassembly – general

1   To ensure maximum life with minimum trouble from an overhauled engine, not only must every part be correctly assembled but everything must be spotlessly clean, all oilways must be clean, locking washers

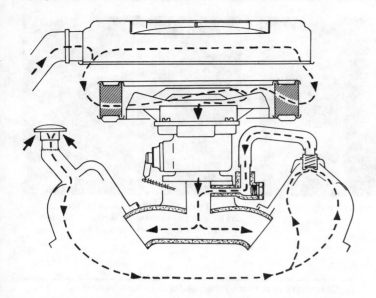

Fig. 1.4 Crankcase ventilation system (Sec 26)

2.3 litre carburettor engine shown

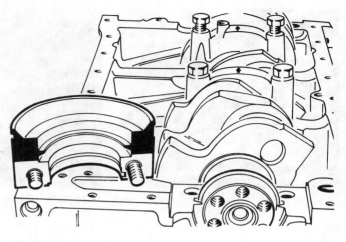

Fig. 1.5 Apply sealing compound to the shaded area of the rear main bearing cap (Sec 28)

and spring washers must always be fitted where needed and all bearings and other sliding surfaces must be thoroughly lubricated during assembly.

2   Before assembly, renew any bolts, studs and nuts whose threads are in any way damaged and whenever possible use new spring washers. Obtain a complete set of new gaskets and all new parts as necessary.

3   When refitting parts ensure that they are refitted in their original positions and directions. Oil seal lips should be smeared with grease before fitting. A liquid gasket sealant should be used where specified to prevent leakage.

4   Apart from your normal tools, a supply of clean rags, an oil can filled with clean engine oil and a torque wrench are essential.

28 Crankshaft – refitting

1   Wipe the bearing shell locations in the crankcase with a clean rag and fit the main bearing upper half shells in position.

2   Clean the main bearing shell locations and fit the half shells in the caps (photo). If the old bearings are being refitted (although this is a

false economy unless they are practically new) make sure they are fitted in their original positions.

3   Apply a little grease to each side of the No. 3 main bearing so as to retain the thrust washers (2.3 models only).

4   Fit the upper halves of the thrust washers into their grooves each side of the main bearing. The slots must face outwards with the tag located in the groove (2.3 models only).

5   Lubricate the crankshaft main bearing journals and the main bearing shells with engine oil (photo).

6   Place the rear main bearing oil seal in position on the end of the crankshaft. Alternatively fit it later.

7   Carefully lower the crankshaft into the crankcase.

8   Apply a thin coating of sealing compound to the mating faces of the crankcase and the rear main bearing cap (photo).

9   Apply a smear of grease to both sides of the No 3 main bearing cap so as to retain the thrust washers. Fit the thrust washers with the tag located in the groove and the slots facing outwards (2.3 models only).

10 Fit the main bearing caps with the arrows on the caps pointing to the front of the engine (photo).

11 Progressively tighten the main bearing securing bolts to the specified torque, except No 3 bearing bolts which should only be finger-tight. Now press the crankshaft fully to the rear then slowly press it fully forward, hold it in this position and tighten the No 3 main bearing cap securing bolts to the specified torque (photo). This ensures that the thrust washers are correctly located.

12 Press the rear main bearing oil seal firmly against the rear main bearing. If fully fitting it, protect the seal lips with adhesive tape (photo).

28.2 Fitting a shell bearing to the rear main bearing cap

28.5 Oiling No 3 main bearing upper shell

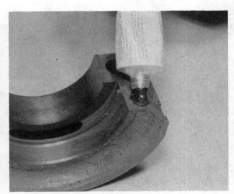

28.8 Applying sealing compound to the rear main bearing cap

28.10 Fitting the rear main bearing cap

28.11 Tightening the main bearing cap bolts

28.12 Temporarily stick adhesive tape on the rear of the crankshaft when fitting the rear oil seal to protect the seal lips

13 Using feeler gauges, check the crankshaft endfloat by inserting the feeler gauge between the crankshaft journal side and the thrust washers. The clearance must not exceed the figure given in the Specifications. The check can also be made using a dial gauge (photos).
14 Rotate the crankshaft to ensure that it is not binding or sticking. Should it be very stiff to turn or have high spots it must be removed and thoroughly checked.
15 Coat the rear main bearing cap dowel seals with sealing compound and fit in position. Use a blunt screwdriver or similar tool to press them fully in (photos). They should be fitted with the rounded face pointing towards the bearing cap.

29 Camshaft and front intermediate plate – refitting

1 Slide the spacer onto the camshaft with the chamfered side first and fit the key (photos).
2 Lubricate the camshaft bearings, the camshaft and the thrust plate.
3 Carefully insert the camshaft from the front and fit the thrust plate and self-locking securing bolts. Tighten the bolts to the specified torque.
4 Fit the timing cover guide sleeves and O-ring seals onto the crankcase. The chamfered end of the guide sleeves must face outward towards the timing cover.

28.13A Crankshaft endfloat can be checked with feeler gauges ...

28.13B ... or a dial gauge

28.15A Locate the dowel seals on the main bearing cap ...

28.15B ... and press fully in with a screwdriver

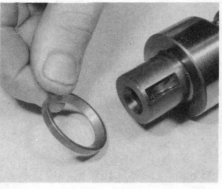

29.1A Fit the chamfered spacer ...

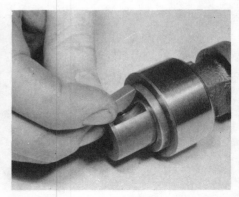

29.1B ... and key on the camshaft

5 Ensure the mating faces of the crankcase and the front intermediate plate are clean and then apply sealing compound to both faces. Position the gasket on the crankcase and then fit the intermediate plate (photo).

6 Fit the two centre bolts finger-tight then fit another two bolts temporarily for locating purposes. Tighten the centre securing bolts then remove the temporary fitted locating bolts (photo).

30 Pistons and connecting rods – refitting

1 Wipe clean the connecting rod half of the big-end bearing and the underside of the shell bearing and fit the shell bearing in position with its locating tongue engaged with the corresponding cut-out in the rod.

2 If the old bearings are nearly new, and are being refitted, then ensure they are refitted in their correct locations on the correct rods.

3 The pistons, complete with connecting rods, are fitted to their bores from the top of the block.

4 Locate the piston ring gaps in the following manner:

Top: 150° from one side of the oil control ring helical expander gap

Centre: 150° from the opposite side of the oil control ring helical expander gap

Bottom: oil control ring Helical expander: opposite the marked piston front side

Oil control ring, intermediate rings: 25 mm (1.0 in) each side of the helical expander gap

5 Well lubricate the piston and rings with engine oil (photo).

6 Fit a universal ring compressor and prepare to insert the first piston into the bore. Make sure it is the correct piston-connecting rod assembly for that particular bore, that the connecting rod is the correct way round and that the front of the piston (marked with an arrow or a notch) is to the front of the engine.

7 Lubricate the cylinder bore (photo) and insert the connecting rod and piston assembly into the cylinder bore up to the bottom of the piston ring compressor.

8 Gently but firmly tap the piston through the piston ring compressor and into the cylinder bore, using the shaft of a hammer (photo).

9 Generously lubricate the crankpin journals with engine oil, and turn the crankshaft so that the crankpin is in the most advantageous position for the connecting rods to be drawn onto it.

10 Wipe clean the connecting rod bearing cap and back of the shell bearing, and fit the shell bearing in position, ensuring that the locating tongue at the back of the bearing engages with the locating groove in the connecting rod cap.

11 Generously lubricate the shell bearing and offer up the connecting rod bearing cap to the connecting rod.

12 Refitting the connecting rod nuts.

13 Tighten the nuts with a torque wrench to the specified setting.

14 When all the pistons and connecting rods have been fitted, rotate the crankshaft to check that everything is free, and that there are no high spots causing binding.

31 Oil pump – refitting

1 Ensure the mating faces of the oil pump and the crankcase are clean.

2 Insert the hexagonal oil pump driveshaft with the pointed end towards the distributor location. The stop washer (photo) must be positioned 127.5 mm (5.020 in) from the rounded end of the driveshaft.

3 Fit the oil pump to the crankcase and secure with two bolts tightened to the specified torque. **Note:** *When a new or overhauled oil pump is being fitted, it should be filled with engine oil and turned by hand for one complete revolution before being fitted, this will prime the pump.*

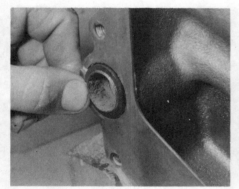
29.5 Fitting the intermediate plate

29.6 Temporary bolt for locating the intermediate plate

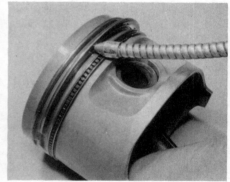
30.5 Oiling the piston rings

30.7 Oiling the cylinder bore

30.8 Using a piston ring compressor when inserting the piston into the bore

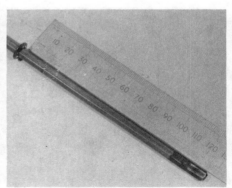
31.2 Checking the stop washer position on the oil pump driveshaft

32 Flywheel/driveplate – refitting

1   Fit the engine adaptor plate on the two locating dowels.
2   Ensure the mating faces of the flywheel/driveplate and crankshaft are clean and fit the flywheel/driveplate to the crankshaft, aligning the marks made at dismantling, unless new parts are being fitted.
3   Fit the six securing bolts (oiled) and lightly tighten (photo).
4   Chock the flywheel/driveplate to restrain it from turning, and tighten the securing bolts in a diagonal and progressive manner to the specified torque.
5   Refit the clutch disc and pressure plate assembly, making sure the disc is the correct way round (see Chapter 5).
6   Secure the pressure plate assembly with the retaining bolts, centralise the clutch disc using an old gearbox input shaft or suitable mandrel, and then tighten the retaining bolts to the specified torque in a diagonal and progessive manner.

33 Timing gears and timing cover – refitting

1   Check that the keyways in the end of the crankshaft are clean and the keys are free from burrs. Fit the keys into the keyways.
2   If the crankshaft gear was removed refit it to the crankshaft using a suitable diameter tube to drive it fully home. Alternatively temporarily use the pulley and bolt to press it on (photos).
3   Fit the camshaft gear on the camshaft with the punch mark in alignment with the mark on the crankshaft gear (photo). Note that if there are two punch marks on the crankshaft gear, ensure that the correct mark is aligned (Fig. 1.6).
4   Fit the camshaft gear retaining washer and bolt. Tighten the bolt to the specified torque.
5   If available use a dial gauge to check the camshaft endfloat (photo).

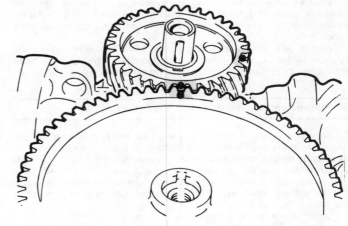

Fig. 1.6 Correct timing gear mark alignment where the crankshaft gear has two marks (Sec 33)

6   Determine the position of the oil seal in the timing cover, then drive out the old seal (photos).
7   Clean the front face of the intermediate plate and the face of the timing cover, then coat both mating faces with sealing compound.
8   Position a new gasket on the intermediate plate and fit the timing cover to the cylinder block. Insert the bolts finger-tight.
9   Centre the timing cover around the nose of the crankshaft using vernier calipers at four diametric points, then fully tighten the bolts (photo).
10 Fit the front oil seal to the timing cover and draw it into the position determined in paragraph 6 using a socket and bolt (photos).
11 Trim any protruding gasket from the sump mating face (photo).

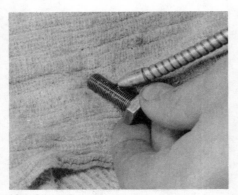

32.3 Oil the flywheel/driveplate bolts before fitting

33.2A Locate the crankshaft gear on the crankshaft ...

33.2B ... and use the pulley to press it on

33.3 Alignment dots on the timing gears

33.5 Checking the camshaft endfloat with a dial gauge

33.6A Checking the position of the old oil seal in the timing cover

33.6B Driving out the timing cover oil seal

33.9 Using vernier calipers to check that the timing cover is centred on the crankshaft nose

33.10A Fitting the crankshaft front oil seal using a socket and bolt

33.10B Fitted position of the crankshaft front oil seal in the timing cover

33.11 Trimming the gasket from the sump mating face

34.2A Fitting the rubber seal to the timing cover

34.2B Apply sealing compound beneath the rubber seal

34.3 Locating the side gasket tabs beneath the seals

34.8 Applying sealing compound to the crankshaft pulley washer

34 Sump, water pump and crankshaft pulley – refitting

Non-4x4 models

1 Clean the mating faces of the crankcase and sump. Ensure that the grooves in the seal carriers are clean.
2 Fit the rubber seals in the grooves of the seal carriers. Apply sealing compound beneath the ends of the rear seal (photos).
3 Locate the side gaskets with their tabs under the cut-outs in the rubber seals (photo). Retain the gaskets with a little sealing compound if necessary.
4 Locate the sump on the gaskets, making sure that the bolt holes are still aligned.
5 Fit the sump securing bolts and tighten them to the correct torque, as specified in Specifications at the beginning of this Chapter.

4x4 models

6 Refit the sump with reference to Section 10.

All models

7 Place a new gasket on the timing cover and fit the water pump. Fit the thermostat and thermostat housing, refer to Chapter 2. Fit the rear water elbow together with a new gasket.
8 Coat the crankshaft pulley washer with sealing compound. Fit the pulley, washer and securing bolt. Tighten the bolt to the specified torque (photo).
9 Refit and tighten the oil pressure switch or oil pressure connector.
10 Fit the bypass hose to the timing cover rear elbow.
11 Where applicable locate the oil cooler on the cylinder block, together with a new seal, then insert the sleeve and tighten it with the cooler pipes angled as shown in Fig. 1.7.

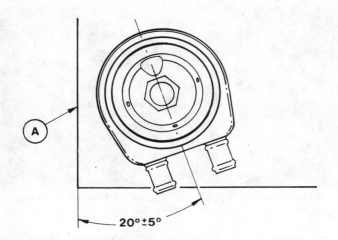

Fig. 1.7 Oil cooler fitting angle (Sec 34)

A   Rear face of cylinder block

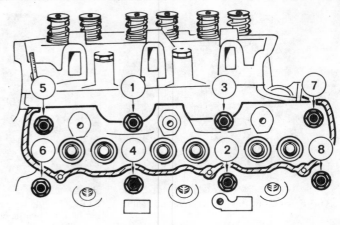

Fig. 1.8 Tightening sequence for cylinder head bolts (Sec 35)

35 Cylinder heads, rocker gear and inlet manifold – refitting

1   Lubricate the valve tappets with clean engine oil and insert them in the cylinder block. Ensure they are fitted in their original locations.
2   Ensure that the mating faces of the cylinder block and the cylinder heads are clean.
3   Position the new cylinder head gaskets over the guide bushes on the cylinder block. Check that they are correctly located. The right and left-hand gaskets are different. The gaskets are marked FRONT TOP (photos).

4   Carefully lower the cylinder heads onto the cylinder block and fit the holding down bolts which should be first lightly oiled.
5   Tighten the bolts, in the sequence shown in Fig. 1.8, in the stages given in the Specifications (photo).
6   Lubricate the pushrods with engine oil and insert them in the cylinder block.
7   Place the oil splash shields in position on the cylinder heads and fit the rocker shaft assemblies. Guide the rocker arm adjusting screws into the pushrod sockets (photo).
8   Tighten the rocker shaft securing bolts progressively to the specified torque (photo).
9   Refit the inlet manifold as described in Chapter 3.
10 Adjust the valve clearances as described in Section 36.
11 Refit the power steering pump/alternator bracket and tighten the bolts.

35.3A Cylinder head gaskets – the arrow indicates front

35.3B Cylinder head gasket position markings

35.3C Fitting the head gaskets on the cylinder block

35.5 Tightening the cylinder head bolts

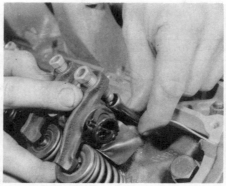

35.7 Guiding the rocker arm adjusting screws into the pushrods

35.8 Tightening the rocker shaft bolts

36 Valve clearances – checking and adjustment

1 Adjust the inlet and exhaust valve clearances when the engine is cold, between 20 and 40°C (68 and 104°F). Clearances are important. If the clearance is too great the valves will not open as fully as they should. They will also open late and close early, this will affect the engine performance. If the clearances are too small the valves may not close completely, which could result in lack of compression and very soon, burnt out valves and valve seats.

2 When turning the engine during valve clearance adjustments always turn the engine in the direction of normal rotation by means of a spanner on the pulley bolt.

3 Turn the engine and align the crankshaft pulley mark with the O-mark on the timing cover.

4 If the crankshaft pulley is rotated backwards and forwards slightly, the valves of No 1 or 5 cylinder will be seen to be rocking (the two rocker arms moving in opposite directions). If the valves of No 1 cylinder are rocking, rotate the crankshaft through 360° so that those on No 5 cylinder are rocking.

5 When the valves of No 5 cylinder are in this position, check the valve clearances of No 1 cylinder by inserting a feeler gauge of the specified thickness between the rocker arm and the valve stem. Adjust the clearance, if necessary, by turning the rocker arm adjusting screw until the specified clearance is obtained (photo). Inlet and exhaust valve clearances are different.

6 If the engine is now rotated $1/3$ of a turn the valves of No 3 cylinder will be rocking and the valves of No 4 cylinder can be checked and adjusted.

7 Proceed to adjust the clearances according to the firing order as follows. Fig. 1.9 shows the cylinder numbers and valves listed in their correct order, working from the front of the engine.

Valves rocking	Valves to adjust
No 5 cylinder	*No 1 cylinder (in, ex)*
No 3 cylinder	*No 4 cylinder (in, ex)*
No 6 cylinder	*No 2 cylinder (in, ex)*
No 1 cylinder	*No 5 cylinder (ex, in)*
No 4 cylinder	*No 3 cylinder (ex, in)*
No 2 cylinder	*No 6 cylinder (ex, in)*

8 Fit the rocker cover gaskets and rocker covers (photo). Tighten the securing bolts to the specified torque.

37 Engine ancillaries – refitting

Refer to Section 8 and refit the listed components with reference to the Chapters indicated.

38 Engine – refitting

Refitting the engine is a reversal of the removal procedure given in Section 6, but in addition note the following points:

(a) *Lightly grease the manual gearbox input shaft*
(b) *Check that the clutch release arm is correctly located on manual gearbox models*
(c) *Adjust the clutch cable on manual gearbox models as described in Chapter 5*
(d) *On automatic transmission models, check that the torque converter is fully engaged with the oil pump, with reference to Chapter 6, Section 19*
(e) *Adjust the tension of the power steering pump and water pump/alternator drivebelts as described in Chapters 10 and 2 respectively*
(f) *Fill the cooling system (Chapter 2) and power steering system (Chapter 10), then fill the engine with oil (Section 2)*

39 Engine – initial start-up after major overhaul or repair

1 Make sure that the battery is fully charged and that all lubricants, coolant and fuel are replenished.

36.5 Adjusting the valve clearances

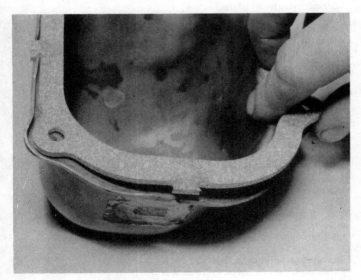

36.8 Fitting the gasket to a rocker cover

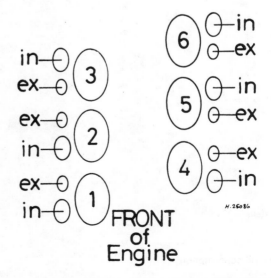

Fig. 1.9 Location of inlet and exhaust valves (Sec 36)

2   Double check all fittings and electrical connections. Ensure that the distributor is correctly fitted and that the ignition timing static setting is correct. If in doubt refer to Chapter 4.

3   Remove the spark plugs and the '–' connection from the ignition coil. Turn the engine over on the starter motor until the oil pressure warning light is extinguished or until oil pressure is recorded on the gauge. This will ensure that the engine is not starved of oil during the critical few minutes running after initial start-up. The fuel system will also be primed during this operation.

4   Reconnect the '–' connection on the ignition coil and refit the spark plugs and leads. Start the engine.

5   As soon as the engine fires and runs, keep it going at a fast tickover only (no faster) and bring it up to normal working temperature.

6   As the engine warms up there will be odd smells and some smoke from parts getting hot and burning off oil deposits. The signs to look for are leaks of water or oil, which will be obvious if serious. Check also the exhaust pipe and manifold connections as these do not always find their exact gas tight position until the warmth and vibration have acted on them, and it is almost certain that they will need tightening further. This should be done, of course, with the engine stopped.

7   When normal running temperature has been reached, adjust the engine idle speed as described in Chapter 3.

8   Stop the engine and wait a few minutes to see if any lubricant or coolant is dripping out when the engine is stationary.

9   After the engine has run for 20 minutes remove the engine rocker covers and rocker shafts and recheck the tightness of the cylinder head bolts (photo). Also check the tightness of the sump bolts. In both cases use a torque wrench.

10   Road test the car to check that the timing is correct and that the engine is giving the necessary smoothness and power. Do not race the engine – if new bearings and/or pistons have been fitted it should be treated as a new engine and run in at a reduced speed for the first 1000 miles (1600 km).

39.9 Rechecking the tightness of the cylinder head bolts

40 Fault diagnosis – engine

Symptom	Reason(s)
Engine fails to start	Discharged battery
	Loose battery connection
	Loose or broken ignition leads
	Moisture on spark plugs, distributor cap or HT leads
	Incorrect spark plug gap
	Cracked distributor cap or rotor
	Dirt or water in fuel
	Empty fuel tank
	Faulty fuel pump
	Faulty starter motor
	Low cylinder compression
	Faulty electronic ignition system
Engine idles erratically	Inlet manifold air leak
	Leaking cylinder head gasket
	Worn camshaft lobes
	Incorrect valve clearances
	Loose crankcase ventilation hoses
	Incorrect idle adjustment
	Uneven cylinder compressions
	Incorrect ignition timing
Engine misfires	Incorrect spark plug gap
	Faulty coil or electronic ignition
	Dirt or water in fuel
	Idle adjustment incorrect
	Leaking cylinder head gasket
	Distributor cap cracked
	Incorrect valve clearances
	Uneven cylinder compressions
	Moisture on spark plugs, distributor cap or HT leads
Engine stalls	Idle adjustment incorrect
	Inlet manifold air leak
	Ignition timing incorrect
Excessive oil consumption	Worn pistons and cylinder bores
	Valve guides and valve stem seals worn
	Oil leaking from gasket or oil seal

Chapter 2 Cooling system

Contents

Specifications

System type ....

Pressurised, with belt-driven pump, crossflow radiator, thermo-viscous cooling fan, thermostat, and expansion (degas) tank

Expansion tank cap
Release pressure:
    Pre-February 1987 models ....

0.85 to 1.10 bar (12.3 to 16.0 lbf/in²)

    February 1987-on models ....

1.2 to 1.5 bar (17.4 to 21.8 lbf/in²)

Thermostat
Norminal temperature rating ....

82°C (180°F)

Opening temperature ....

79° to 83°C (174° to 181°F)

Drivebelt tension
Deflection midway between pulleys (longest run) ....

10.0 mm (0.4 in) approx

Coolant
Coolant type/specification ....

Antifreeze to Ford spec SSM-97B9103-A (Duckhams Universal Antifreeze and Summer Coolant)

Capacity (including heater) ....

8.5 litres (15.0 pints)

Specific gravity (at 45 to 50% antifreeze concentration) ....

1.069 to 1.077

Torque wrench settings

	Nm	lbf ft
Radiator upper mountings	20.5 to 25.5	15.1 to 18.8
Radiator lower mountings	8.0 to 12.0	5.9 to 8.9
Thermostat housing	16.6 to 20.4	12.2 to 15.1
Water pump	9.0 to 13.0	6.6 to 9.6
Outlet to inlet manifold	16.6 to 20.4	12.2 to 15.1
Cooling fan shroud	8.0 to 11.0	5.9 to 8.1
Water pump pulley	21.0 to 28.0	15.5 to 20.7
Fan blade to viscous clutch	8.0 to 10.0	5.9 to 7.4

1 General description

.The cooling system is of pressurised type and includes a front mounted crossflow radiator, belt-driven water pump, temperature conscious thermo-viscous fan, wax type thermostat, and an expansion and degas tank.

The radiator matrix is of copper and brass construction and the end tanks are of plastic. On automatic transmission models the right-hand side end tank incorporates the transmission oil cooler.

The thermostat is located on the front of the water pump. Its purpose is to ensure rapid engine warm-up by restricting the flow of coolant in the engine when cold, and also to assist in regulating the normal operating temperature of the engine.

The expansion tank incorporates a pressure cap, which effectively pressurises the cooling system as the coolant temperature rises, thereby increasing the boiling point temperature of the coolant. The tank also has a further degas function. Any accumulation of air bubbles in the coolant is returned to the tank and released in the air space, thus maintaining the efficiency of the coolant.

On models fitted with the auxiliary warning system, the expansion tank contains a level sensor which operates a warning light if the coolant level falls significantly.

When the engine is started from cold, the water pump circulates coolant around the cylinder block, cylinder heads and inlet manifold. The warm coolant passes through the automatic choke housing (when applicable) and through the heater matrix before returning to the engine. As the coolant expands, the level in the expansion tank rises. Circulation of coolant through the radiator is prevented while the thermostat is shut.

When the coolant reaches the predetermined temperature the thermostat opens and hot water circulates down through the radiator. It is cooled by the passage of air past the radiator when the car is in forward motion, supplemented by the action of the thermo-viscous fan when necessary. Having reached the bottom of the radiator, the water is now cool and the cycle is repeated. Circulation of water continues through the expansion tank, inlet manifold and heater at all times, the heater temperature control being by an air flap.

The thermo-viscous fan is controlled by the temperature of air behind the radiator. When the air temperature reaches a predetermined level, a bi-metallic coil commences to open a valve within the unit and silicon fluid is fed through a system of vanes. Half of the vanes are driven directly by the water pump, and the remaining half are connected to the fan blades. The vanes are arranged so that drive is transmitted to the fan blades in relation to the drag or viscosity of the fluid, and this in turn depends on ambient temperature and engine speed. The fan is therefore only operated when required, and compared with direct drive type fans, represents a considerable improvement in fuel economy, drivebelt wear and fan noise.

2 Routine maintenance

Carry out the following procedures at the intervals given in 'Routine Maintenance' at the beginning of the Manual.

Check coolant level

1 With the engine cold, check that the coolant level in the expansion tank is up to the 'MAX' mark. Note that it is quite normal for the level to rise above the 'MAX' mark when the engine is hot.
2 If topping-up is necessary remove the pressure (with the engine cold) and add more coolant. If possible the antifreeze specific gravity should be checked before adding the additional coolant, so that adjustment may be made to the antifreeze concentration.
3 **Do not** add cold water to an overheated engine whilst it is still hot, since this may result in a cracked cylinder head or block.
4 Refit the pressure cap on completion.

Check cooling system for leaks

5 If frequent topping-up is required, check all the hoses for condition and security. Check the thermostat and water pump gasket joints for signs of leakage, and similarly check the radiator matrix and end tanks.

Check drivebelts

6 Examine the full length of the drivebelts for damage, fraying or glazing.
7 Check that the drivebelt tension is as given in the Specifications, and if necessary adjust it as described in Section 12.

Renew coolant

8 Drain and flush the cooling system as described in Sections 3 and 4.
9 Fill the system with new antifreeze mixture as described in Section 5.

3 Cooling system – draining

1 Remove the expansion tank filler cap. If the engine is hot place a thick cloth over the cap before removing it slowly, otherwise there is a danger of scalding.
2 Check if a drain plug is fitted to the right-hand side of the radiator (photo) – some early models may not be fitted with one.
3 Place a suitable container beneath the radiator.
4 Either unscrew the drain plug, without removing it, or disconnect the bottom hose from the left-hand side of the radiator. Drain the coolant into the container.
5 Place another container beneath the cylinder block drain plug, which is located just in front of the oil filter. Remove the drain plug and drain the coolant.
6 Dispose of the old coolant, or keep it in a covered container if it is to be re-used.

3.2 Radiator drain plug

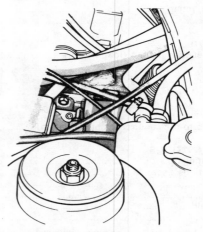

Fig. 2.1 Cylinder block drain plug location (Sec 3)

4 Cooling system – flushing

1 Flushing should not be necessary unless periodic renewal of the coolant has been neglected, or unless plain water has been used as a coolant. In either case the coolant will appear rusty and dark in colour. Flushing is then required and should be carried out as follows.
2 Drain the system as described in the previous Section, and if not already done, disconnect the bottom hose.
3 Disconnect the top hose from the radiator. Insert a garden hose into the top of the radiator and run the water until it flows clear from the bottom outlet.
4 Similarly flush the expansion tank. The heater matrix may be flushed by disconnecting the hoses on the bulkhead.
5 Reverse-flush the engine by inserting the garden hose in the top hose and running the water until it flows clear from the cylinder block drain plug.
6 In severe cases of contamination the radiator should be removed, inverted and flushed in the reverse direction to normal flow, *ie* with the water going in at the bottom and out at the top. Shake the radiator gently while doing this to dislodge any deposits.
7 The use of chemical cleaners should only be necessary as a last resort. Make sure that such cleaners are suitable for use in 'mixed metal' (aluminium and iron) engines.

5 Cooling system – filling

1 Reconnect the hoses and tighten the drain plug(s). Make sure that the hose clips are in good condition.
2 Pour coolant into the expansion tank (photo) until it reaches the maximum ('MAX') level mark. Squeeze the radiator hoses to help disperse air-locks.
3 Refit and tighten the expansion tank filler cap.
4 Run the engine at a fast idle speed for approximately ten seconds, then stop the engine and top up the coolant again to the 'MAX' mark.
5 With the filler cap refitted, run the engine to operating temperature while checking for leaks. Stop the engine and allow it to cool completely, then recheck the coolant level.

6 Antifreeze mixture – general

Warning: *Antifreeze mixture is poisonous. Keep it out of reach of children and pets. Wash splashes off skin and clothing with plenty of water. Wash splashes off vehicle paintwork, too, to avoid discoloration.*

1 The antifreeze/water mixture must be renewed every two years to preserve its anti-corrosive properties. In climates where antifreeze protection is unnecessary, a corrosion inhibitor may be used instead – consult a Ford dealer. Never run the engine for long periods with plain water as coolant.
2 Only use the specified antifreeze (see *'Recommended lubricants and fluids'*). Inferior brands may not contain the necessary corrosion inhibitors, or may break down at high temperatures. Antifreeze containing methanol is particularly to be avoided, as the methanol evaporates.
3 The specified mixture is 45 to 50% antifreeze and 55 to 50% clean soft water (by volume). Mix the required quantity in a clean container and then fill the system as described in Section 5. Save any surplus mixture for topping-up.

7 Radiator – removal and refitting

1 Disconnect the battery negative lead.
2 Drain the radiator as described in Section 3 – there is no need to drain the cylinder block.
3 Apply the handbrake, then jack up the front of the car and support on axle stands.
4 Disconnect the top hose, and where applicable the bottom hose (photo) and expansion tank hose from the radiator. Where the expansion tank hose incorporates an intermediate tube, disconnect the hose on the right-hand side and unbolt the tube from the bottom of the radiator. Where the expansion tank hose connects directly with the bottom hose, leave it connected but unclip it from the radiator.
5 On automatic transmission models place a suitable container beneath the oil cooler pipe connections to the radiator. Unscrew the union and plug the upper pipe, then unscrew the union and plug the lower pipe.
6 On 2.8 models disconnect the accelerator cable from the fan shroud.
7 Disconnect the fan upper and lower shrouds by pressing out the plastic dowels and prising out the clips (photo).
8 Unbolt and remove the fan upper shroud (photo).
9 On models with air conditioning disconnect the condenser, fan and motor with reference to Chapter 11.
10 Unscrew the top mounting nuts, then support the radiator and unscrew the lower bracket mounting bolts. Release the radiator from the top mountings then lower it from the car, tilting it as necessary to clear the fan blades (photos).
11 Unbolt the fan lower shroud from the radiator.
12 If a new radiator is being fitted, transfer the lower shroud to the new unit. Examine the hoses, clips and mountings and renew them if necessary (photo).

5.2 Filling the cooling system

7.4 Bottom hose connection to radiator

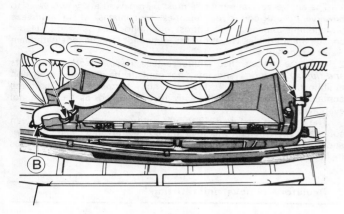

Fig. 2.2 Radiator lower connections (Sec 7)

A *Expansion tank hose to intermediate tube clip*
B *Intermediate tube to U-hose clip*
C *U-hose to radiator clip*
D *Bottom hose to radiator clip*

13 Refitting is a reversal of removal. Refill the cooling system as described in Section 5. On automatic transmission models, tighten the oil cooler unions to the torque setting given in Chapter 6, and also top up the transmission fluid level.

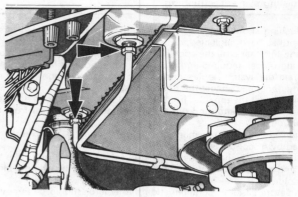

Fig. 2.3 Automatic transmission oil cooler pipe connections to the radiator (Sec 7)

2 Clean dirt and debris from the radiator fins, using an air jet or water and a soft brush. Be careful not to damage the fins, or cut your fingers.
3 A radiator specialist can perform a 'flow test' on the radiator to establish whether an internal blockage exists.
4 A leaking radiator must be referred to a specialist for permanent repair. Do not attempt to weld or solder a leaking radiator, as damage to the plastic parts may result.
5 Temporary 'cold' repairs may be made using proprietary compounds sold for this purpose.

8 Radiator – inspection and repair

1 If the radiator has been removed because of suspected blockage, reverse-flush it as described in Section 4.

9 Thermostat – removal and refitting

1 Disconnect the battery negative lead.
2 Drain the radiator and cylinder block as described in Section 3.

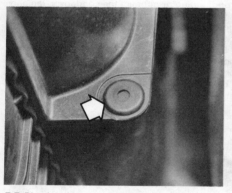

7.7 Plastic clip connecting the upper and lower fan shrouds (arrowed)

7.8 Unbolting the fan upper shroud

7.10A Radiator lower bracket and mounting bolt

7.10B Lowering the radiator from the car

7.12 Radiator top mounting

9.4 Removing the thermostat housing ...

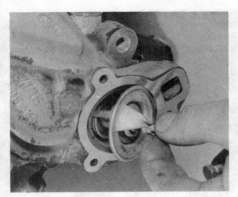

9.5 ... and thermostat

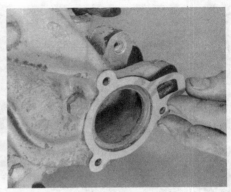

9.6 Thermostat housing gasket removal

3 Disconnect the bottom hose and heater return hose from the thermostat housing on the left-hand side of the engine.
4 Unscrew the bolts and remove the housing (photo).
5 Remove the thermostat together with the sealing ring (photo).
6 Peel the gasket from the water pump housing (photo).
7 Clean the gasket faces of the thermostat housing and water pump housing.
8 Refit by reversing the removal procedure, but fit a new housing gasket and thermostat sealing ring. Refill the cooling system as described in Section 5.

10 Thermostat – testing

1 A rough test of the thermostat may be made by suspending it with a piece of string in a saucepan full of water. Bring the water to the boil: the thermostat must open by the time the water boils. If not, renew it.
2 If a thermometer is available, the precise opening temperature of the thermostat may be determined and compared with that given in the Specifications.
3 A thermostat which fails to close as the water cools must also be renewed.

11 Water pump – removal and refitting

1 Remove the thermostat as described in Section 9.
2 Remove the thermo-viscous cooling fan as described in Section 13.
3 Where fitted, remove the air conditioning compressor and place it to one side, with reference to Chapter 11.
4 Remove the drivebelt(s) from the power steering pump (Chapter 10).

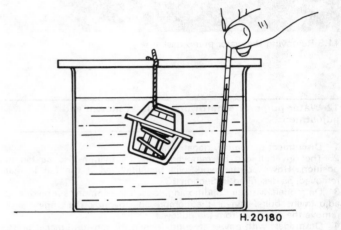

H.20180

Fig. 2.4 Checking the thermostat opening temperature (Sec 10)

5 Remove the water pump/alternator drivebelt with reference to Section 12.
6 Unbolt the pulley from the water pump hub (photo).
7 Unscrew the twelve securing bolts and remove the water pump from the timing cover (photos).
8 Remove the gasket (photo) and clean both mating faces.
9 If the water pump is faulty, renew it, as it is not possible to obtain individual components.
10 Refitting is a reversal of removal, but use a new gasket and tighten the securing bolts to the specified torque. Tension the drivebelts with reference to Section 12, and refit the thermo viscous cooling fan with reference to Section 13. Refit the thermostat with reference to Section 9.

11.6 Unbolting the water pump pulley

11.7A Unbolting the water pump from the timing cover

11.7B Water pump removed from the engine

11.8 Removing the water pump gasket

12.7 Adjusting the power steering pump drivebelt

12 Water pump/alternator drivebelt – renewal and adjustment

1   Disconnect the battery negative lead.
2   The drivebelt can be removed with the thermo-viscous fan in position. However, the work will be simplified if the fan is first removed, as described in Section 13.
3   On models with air conditioning, loosen the compressor pivot and adjustment bolts, swivel the compressor towards the engine and remove the drivebelt from the pulleys.
4   On models with power steering, loosen the tension bracket bolts, on the pump pivot and adjustment bolts as applicable. Slide the bracket or swivel the pump towards the engine and remove the drivebelt(s) from the pulleys.
5   Loosen the alternator pivot and adjustment bolts, swivel the alternator towards the engine and remove the drivebelt from the pulleys.
6   Fit the drivebelts loosely over their respective pulleys.
7   Where a single drivebelt drives the water pump, power steering pump and alternator, lever the alternator away from the cylinder block until the specified tension is achieved, then tighten the adjustment bolt. Where two drivebelts are fitted, depending on the arrangement, it may be necessary to adjust the power steering pump drivebelt before adjusting the water pump/alternator drivebelt or *vice versa* (photo). On some models an adjustable bracket is provided to tension the power steering pump drivebelt (Fig. 2.5).
8   The air conditioning compressor drivebelt should be tensioned last.
9   Tighten all the bolts, then refit the thermo-viscous fan, if removed, with reference to Section 13.
10   Reconnect the battery negative lead.
11   The drivebelt tension should be rechecked, and if necessary adjusted, after the engine has run for approximately ten minutes.

13 Thermo-viscous cooling fan – removal and refitting

1   Disconnect the battery negative lead.
2   Disconnect the fan upper and lower shrouds by pressing out the plastic dowels and prising out the clips.
3   Unbolt and remove the fan upper shroud.
4   Using a 32 mm (non-4x4 models) or 36 mm (4x4 models) spanner unscrew the fan hub nut from the water pump drive flange, noting that the nut has a **left-hand thread**. A thin, slightly cranked spanner is ideal, however if two of the pulley bolts are removed a normal spanner, or even an adjustable spanner can be used. Alternatively, careful use of

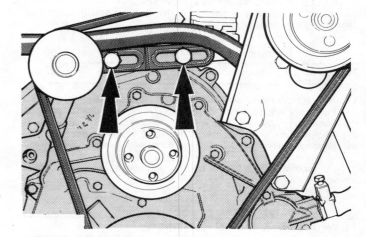

Fig. 2.5 Tension bracket bolts (arrowed) for adjusting the power steering pump drivebelt on some models (Sec 12)

a soft metal drift has been found to work extremely well, without any damage to the nut.
5   If required, the fan blades may now be unbolted from the thermo-viscous clutch hub (photo).
6   Refitting is a reversal of removal, but do not overtighten the fan blade bolts otherwise thread damage may occur.

14 Expansion tank and coolant level sensor – removal and refitting

1   Partially drain the cooling system until the level is below the expansion tank, with reference to Section 3.
2   Loosen the clips and disconnect the hoses from the tank.
3   Where applicable disconnect the coolant level sensor wiring.
4   Unscrew the mounting screws and remove the expansion tank from the engine compartment.
5   Where applicable unscrew the collar from the coolant level sensor and withdraw the spacer, sensor and seal. Note that the sensor can only be fitted in one position.
6   Refitting is a reversal of removal. Refill the cooling system with reference to Section 5.

13.5 Fan blade to clutch hub bolts

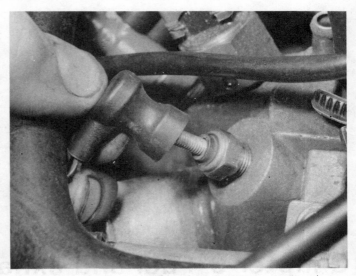

15.4 Disconnecting the wiring from the temperature gauge sender unit

15 Temperature gauge sender unit – removal and refitting

1   The temperature gauge sender unit is located on the outlet housing at the front of the inlet manifold.
2   If the engine is hot, allow it to cool before attempting to remove the unit.
3   Remove the expansion tank filler cap to release any remaining pressure, then refit the cap to help reduce the loss of coolant.
4   Pull the wiring connector from the terminal on the sender unit (photo).
5   Unscrew and remove the sender unit, and temporarily plug the aperture with a suitable rubber or cork bung.
6   Smear a little sealing compound on the sender unit threads and refit it using a reversal of the removal procedure. Top up the cooling system if necessary.

16 Fault Diagnosis – cooling system

Symptom	Reason(s)
Overheating	Low coolant level
	Drivebelt slipping
	Radiator blocked
	Thermostat sticking shut
	Faulty thermo-viscous fan unit
	Retarded ignition timing
	Weak mixture
	Faulty expansion tank pressure cap
Overcooling	Thermostat sticking open
Coolant loss	Damaged or perished hose
	Damaged radiator
	Blown cylinder head gasket
	Faulty expansion tank pressure cap
	Pressure cap sealing face distorted in expansion tank filler neck (early) models with metal neck)
	Cylinder head or block cracked

Chapter 3 Fuel and exhaust systems

Contents

Specifications

General
System type:
    2.3 litre engine .... Solex twin venturi carburettor
    2.8 litre engine .... Bosch K-Jetronic fuel injection system
Fuel tank capacity .... 60 litres (13.2 gallons)

Fuel pump
Delivery pressure (2.3) .... 0.24 to 0.38 bar (3.5 to 5.5 lbf/in²)
Delivery rate (2.8) .... 0.75 litre (1.32 pints) in 30 seconds

Carburettor
Idle speed .... 800 ± 20 rpm
Idle CO% .... 1.5 ± 1.5
Accelerator pump jet (A) .... 2.0 to 5.0 mm (0.08 to 0.20 in)
Float level setting .... 11.0 ± 0.5 mm (0.43 ± 0.02 in)
Fast idle speed .... 3000 ± 100 rpm
Choke plate pull-down .... 3.2 ± 0.2 mm (0.13 ± 0.01 in)
Choke phasing .... 0.3 to 0.6 mm (0.012 to 0.024 in)
Modulator spring gap .... 1.8 ± 0.1 mm (0.071 ± 0.004 in)
Barrel diameter .... 35.0 mm (1.378 in)
Venturi diameter .... 26.0 mm (1.024 in)
Main jet 137.5
Idle jet 47.5

Fuel injection system
Idle speed .... 900 ± 25 rpm
Idle CO% .... 1.0 to 1.5
Thermotime switch operating temperature .... 35°C (95°F)

Torque wrench settings

Inlet manifold:	Nm	lbf ft
Stage 1	4 to 8	3 to 6
Stage 2	8 to 15	6 to 11
Stage 3	15 to 21	11 to 16
Stage 4	21 to 25	16 to 19
Stage 5 (engine at normal operating temperature)	21 to 25	16 to 19
Fuel pump (2.3)	16 to 18	12 to 13
Exhaust manifold	25 to 30	19 to 22
Air chamber (2.8)	7 to 10	5 to 7
Fuel distributor (2.8)	32 to 38	24 to 28
Air sensor plate (2.8)	9 to 11	7 to 8
Warm-up regulator (2.8)	7 to 10	5 to 7
Fuel start valve (2.8)	7 to 10	5 to 7
Auxiliary air device (2.8)	7 to 10	5 to 7
Banjo bolts (2.8):		
Fuel distributor	18 to 20	13 to 15
Warm-up regulator inlet (M10)	11 to 15	8 to 11
Warm-up regulator outlet (M8)	5 to 8	4 to 6
Injection pipes	5 to 8	4 to 6
Fuel pump, filter and accumulator	18 to 20	13 to 15

1 General description

The fuel system consists of a rear-mounted fuel tank, a mechanical fuel pump and twin venturi Solex carburettor on 2.3 models, or an electrical fuel pump and Bosch K-Jetronic fuel injection system on 2.8 models.

The exhaust system fitted in production is made of aluminised steel, with stainless steel used in the endplates and baffles of the rear silencer. Individual sections of the system are easily renewed in service.

2 Routine maintenance

Carry out the following procedures at the intervals given in 'Routine Maintenance' at the beginning of the Manual.

Check and adjust the idling speed and mixture
1   Refer to Section 16 or 24.

Check condition of fuel system hoses
2   Examine all the fuel hoses for damage, deterioration and security. Also check all air and vacuum hoses associated with the fuel system.

Tighten the inlet manifold bolts and nuts
3   Refer to Section 25 and tighten the inlet manifold bolts and nuts in the sequence given.

Renew the air filter element
4   Refer to Section 5.

Renew the fuel filter (fuel injection models)
5   Refer to Section 9.

Check operation of air cleaner temperature control (carburettor models)
6   Refer to Section 6.

3 Tamperproof adjustment screws – description

1   Certain adjustment points in the fuel system (and elsewhere) are protected by 'tamperproof' caps, plugs or seals. The purpose of such tamperproofing is to discourage, and to detect, adjustment by unqualified operators.
2   In some EEC countries (though not yet in the UK) it is an offence to drive a vehicle with missing or broken tamperproof seals.
3   Before disturbing a tamperproof seal, satisfy yourself that you will not be breaking local or national anti-pollution regulations by doing so. Fit a new seal when adjustment is complete when this is required by law.

4   Do not break tamperproof seals on a vehicle which is still under warranty.

4 Unleaded fuel – general

1   Unleaded fuel will theoretically be available in all EEC countries as time progresses, and may eventually replace leaded fuel completely.
2   It is generally believed that continuous use of unleaded fuel can cause rapid wear of conventional valve seats. Valve seat inserts which can tolerate unleaded fuel are fitted to some engines. These engines are identified by a letter stamped on the cylinder head exhaust flange as follows:

2.3 litre – 'B' or 'F'
2.8 litre – 'D' or 'E'

3   Engines which are marked as above can be run entirely on unleaded fuel.
4   Engines which are not fitted with the special valve seat inserts can still be run on unleaded fuel, but one tankful of leaded fuel should be used for every three tankfuls of unleaded. This will protect the valve seats.
5   When using unleaded fuel, the ignition timing must be retarded as described in Chapter 4, for all engines.

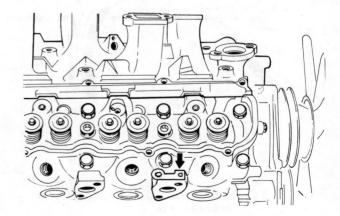

Fig. 3.1 Identification letter on cylinder head modified for use of unleaded fuel (Sec 4)

5.8 Air cleaner cover spring clip

5.9 Removing the air filter element

5.14 Fuel shut-off valve location in the air cleaner body (arrowed)

5 Air cleaner and element – removal and refitting

Carburettor models

1 Release the air duct from the air cleaner inlet tube.
2 Remove the two screws securing the air cleaner to the carburettor.
3 Lift the air cleaner from the carburettor, at the same time disconnecting the hot air hose and the vacuum supply hose.
4 Release the spring clips and lift off the cover. The element may now be removed from the air cleaner body.
5 Wipe clean the inside of the body and cover.
6 Refit by reversing the removal operations.

Fuel injection models

7 Unscrew the clip and disconnect the air inlet duct from the air cleaner cover.
8 Release the spring clips and lift off the cover (photo).
9 Remove the element from the groove in the lower body (photo).
10 Wipe clean the inside of the body and cover.
11 To remove the lower body, unscrew the clip and lift the ducting from the mixture control assembly. Place the ducting to one side.

12 Remove the screws securing the fuel distributor/mixture control assembly to the air cleaner body. Do not remove the assembly at this stage.
13 Loosen the clip and slide the fuel filter from the bracket below the air cleaner.
14 Pull the fuel shut-off valve from the rubber grommet in the front of the air cleaner body (photo).
15 Turn the steering wheel to full left lock.
16 Working under the left-hand side wheel arch unscrew the air cleaner securing bolts.
17 Lift the fuel distributor/mixture control assembly and withdraw the air cleaner body. Remove the gasket.
18 Refit by reversing the removal operations, but renew the fuel distributor/mixture control assembly gasket.

6 Air cleaner temperature control – description and testing

1 On carburettor models only, the air cleaner can take in both hot and cold air. Hot air is obtained from a shroud bolted to the exhaust manifold.
2 A flap valve in the air cleaner spout determines the mix of hot and cold air. The valve is operated by a vacuum diaphragm. Vacuum is obtained from the inlet manifold and is applied via a heat sensing valve, which cuts off the vacuum as the temperature of the incoming air rises.
3 If the system fails and the flap remains in one position, the engine may run roughly and/or not develop full power. If only cold air is admitted problems will be noticeable in the warm-up stage, but if only hot air is admitted normal running will suffer.
4 To check the system, carry out the following tests. With the engine stopped, disconnect the cold air inlet trunking from the spout. Look into the spout and check that the flap valve is covering the hot air intake.
5 Start the engine and allow it to idle. Check that the flap moves to

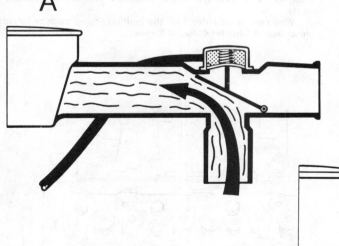

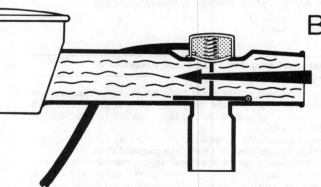

Fig. 3.2 Air cleaner temperature control operation (Sec 6)

A Flap open, admitting hot air
B Flap closed, admitting cold (or ambient) air

cover the cold air intake. If the flap does not move, check the diaphragm and heat sensor as follows.

6   Stop the engine. Disconnect the diaphragm vacuum pipe from the heat sensor. Apply vacuum to the diaphragm, using a vacuum hand pump or by connecting the pipe directly to manifold vacuum. If the flap now moves, the heat sensor or vacuum line was faulty. If the flap still does not move, the diaphragm is faulty or the flap is jammed.

7   On completion reconnect the vacuum pipe and the cold air trunking.

7   Fuel pump (mechanical) – testing, removal and refitting

1   Carburettor models are fitted with a mechanical fuel pump, located on the left-hand side of the engine block.

2   To test the pump, disconnect the ignition coil LT lead. Disconnect the outlet hose from the pump and place a wad of rag next to the pump outlet. Take appropriate fire precautions.

3   Have an assistant crank the engine on the starter. Well-defined spurts of fuel must be ejected from the pump outlet – if not, the pump is probably faulty (or the tank is empty). Dispose of the fuel-soaked rag safely.

4   To remove the fuel pump, first disconnect the battery negative lead.

5   Disconnect and plug the pump inlet and outlet hoses. Be prepared for fuel spillage.

6   Unscrew the two bolts and withdraw the pump from the cylinder block. Remove the gasket. If necessary extract the pushrod.

7   Clean the exterior of the pump in paraffin and wipe dry. Clean all traces of gasket from the cylinder block and pump flange.

8   If the fuel pump has a removable cover, remove the screw and withdraw the cover and nylon mesh filter with seal. Clean the filter, cover and pump in fuel. Locate the filter in the cover and fit the cover to the pump so that the pip and indentation are aligned. Tighten the screw.

9   Refitting is a reversal of removal, but fit a new gasket and tighten the bolts to the specified torque. If necessary discard the crimped type hose clips and fit screw type clips.

8   Fuel pump (electrical) – testing, removal and refitting

1   Fuel injection models are fitted with an electric fuel pump, located next to the fuel tank beneath the rear of the car.

2   If the fuel pump appears to have failed completely, check the appropriate fuse and relay.

3   A rough check of the fuel pump may be made by disconnecting the inlet pipe to the fuel filter, then having an assistant temporarily switch on the ignition. Catch the flow of fuel in a wad of rag or suitable container.

4   To check the fuel pump accurately, measure the delivery (see Specifications) with a calibrated container.

5   To remove the pump first disconnect the battery negative lead.

6   Loosen the warm-up regulator fuel inlet union to relieve any pressure in the system, using a wad of rag to soak up the fuel.

7   Raise and support the rear of the car. Clean the fuel pump and surrounding area.

8   Clamp the tank-to-pump hose, or make arrangements to collect the contents of the fuel tank which will otherwise be released.

9   Place a drain pan beneath the pump. Disconnect the inlet and outlet pipes; be prepared for fuel spillage (photo).

10 Disconnect the wiring from the two terminals.

11 Unscrew the two nuts securing the mounting bracket to the underbody. Recover the washers.

12 Unscrew the clamp bolt in the centre of the mounting bracket and withdraw the fuel pump.

13 Refitting is a reversal of removal, but make sure that the rubber sleeve is correctly located around the pump.

9   Fuel filter (fuel injection models) – renewal

1   Disconnect the battery negative lead.

2   Loosen the warm-up regulator fuel inlet union to relieve any pressure in the system, using a wad of rag to soak up the fuel.

3   The fuel filter is located on the left-hand side of the engine compartment (photo). Place a suitable container beneath it to catch any spilled fuel.

4   Wipe clean the fuel filter, then unscrew the inlet and outlet unions.

5   Loosen the clamp screw and slide out the fuel filter.

6   Fit the new filter using a reversal of the removal procedure, but renew the copper washers on the inlet and outlet unions.

10   Fuel tank – removal and refitting

Note: *For safety the fuel tank must always be removed in a well ventilated area, never over a pit.*

1   Disconnect the battery negative lead.

2   Remove the tank filler cap, then syphon or pump out all the fuel (there is no drain plug).

3   From inside the filler cap recess remove the filler neck retaining screws.

4   Chock the front wheels, then jack up the rear of the car and support on axle stands.

5   Where applicable, disconnect the outlet and return hoses from the bottom of the fuel tank (photo). Be prepared for some loss of fuel.

6   Unscrew the two mounting bolts from the left-hand side tank flange (photo).

8.9 Fuel pump outlet pipe (arrowed)

9.3 Fuel filter

10.5 Fuel tank outlet (large) and return hoses

10.6 Fuel tank mounting bolt

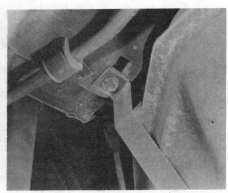

10.7 Fuel tank retaining strap and mounting bolt

7   Support the tank then remove the bolt from the retaining strap (photo). Unhook the strap from the underbody.
8   Lower the tank sufficiently to disconnect the wiring plugs from the sender unit.
9   As applicable identify then disconnect and plug the fuel lines and breather pipe from the sender unit.
10 Withdraw the fuel tank from under the car.
11 Remove the sender unit with reference to Section 11.
12 Loosen the clips where necessary and remove the filler and ventilation pipes. Remove the seal.
13 If the tank is contaminated with sediment or water, swill it out with clean fuel. If the tank leaks or is damaged, it should be repaired by specialists or alternatively renewed. *Do not under any circumstances solder or weld a fuel tank.*
14 Refitting is a reversal of removal, but locate the ventilation pipe in the groove provided in the top of the tank. If necessary discard the crimped type hose clips and fit screw type clips. Refit the sender unit with reference to Section 11.

11 Fuel gauge sender unit – removal and refitting

1   Remove the fuel tank as described in the previous Section.
2   Unscrew the sender unit from the tank. There is a Ford tool (No.

23-014) which engages with the lugs on the unit, but with patience a pair of crossed screwdrivers or similar items can be used instead.
3   Remove the sender unit, taking care not to damage the float or bend the float arm. Recover the seal.
4   A defective sender unit must be renewed; spares are not available. Renew the seal in any case, as it distorts when removed.
5   Refit by reversing the removal operations.

12 Accelerator cable – removal, refitting and adjustment

1   Disconnect the battery negative lead.
2   Remove the panel from beneath the facia, inside the car on the right-hand side.
3   Prise off the clip retaining the cable to the accelerator pedal, and unhook the cable.
4   Working in the engine compartment release the cable from the bulkhead and pull it through.
5   Remove the air cleaner on carburettor models as described in Section 5.
6   Disconnect the inner cable from the throttle lever on the carburettor or throttle housing Where necessary prise off the spring clip to detach the cable end socket from the lever ball (photo).

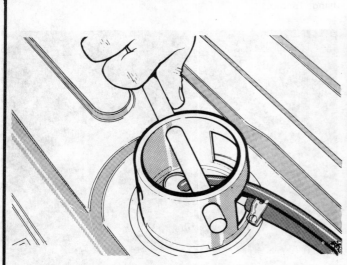

Fig. 3.3 Using the special Ford tool to remove the fuel gauge sender unit (Sec 11)

12.6 Disconnecting the accelerator cable from the throttle lever

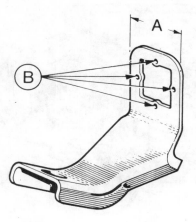

Fig. 3.4 Tool for removing the accelerator cable (Sec 12)

A = 25.4 mm (1.0 in)   *B Centre punch holes*

7 Prise the spring clip from the cable bracket using a screwdriver.
8 Depress the four plastic legs and withdraw the cable from the bracket. If difficulty is experienced, make up a tool as shown in Fig. 3.4 and push it onto the plastic fitting to depress the legs.
9 Where applicable disconnect the outer cable from the clip on the radiator upper shroud (photo).
10 Refitting is a reversal of removal, but adjust the cable as follows. Using a broom or length of wood fully depress the accelerator pedal and retain it in this position. On automatic transmission models make sure that the downshift cable does not restrict the accelerator pedal movement. Unscrew the cable ferrule at the bracket on the engine until the throttle lever is fully open. Release the accelerator pedal, and then check that the full throttle position is achieved again with the pedal fully depressed.

13 Accelerator pedal – removal and refitting

1 Disconnect the battery negative lead.
2 Remove the lower facia panel on the right-hand side.
3 Prise off the clip retaining the cable to the accelerator pedal, and unhook the cable.
4 Unscrew the retaining ntus, one inside the car and one inside the engine compartment, and withdraw the accelerator pedal.
5 Refitting is a reversal of removal, but adjust the accelerator cable as described in Section 12.

14 Fuel pressure regulator (carburettor models) – removal and refitting

1 The fuel pressure regulator is located on the left-hand side of the engine compartment. Identify the two or three hoses then disconnect them from the regulator.
2 Remove the cross-head screws and withdraw the regulator from the engine compartment.
3 Refitting is a reversal of removal, but if necessary discard the crimped type hose clips and fit screw type clips.

15 Solex carburettor – general description

The Solex dual venturi carburettor is of the synchronous type, where both throttle valves operate in unison and are linked by toothed segments. The choke is electrically operated and controlled by a thermo-switch located in the cooling system. A pull-down unit opens the choke valves under full throttle operation.

An accelerator pump delivers additional fuel when the throttle is opened suddenly, and a power valve provides mixture enrichment under sustained full throttle operation. A throttle damper is fitted to prevent an excessively weak mixture when the throttle is shut

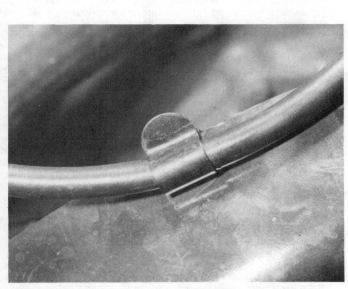

12.9 Accelerator cable clip on the radiator upper shroud

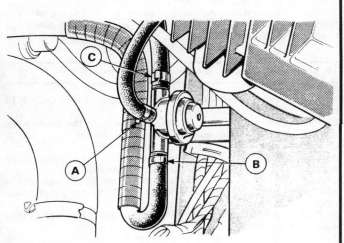

Fig. 3.5 Fuel pressure regulator hose positions (Sec 14)

A   Return to tank   *C   Outlet to carburettor*
B   Inlet

suddenly. An anti-stall device is fitted in order to temporarily enrich the mixture if the engine threatens to stall during idling.

16 Solex carburettor – idle speed and mixture adjustment

1   An accurate tachometer (rev. counter) will be needed to adjust the idle speed, and an exhaust gas analyser (CO meter) or other proprietary device will be needed to adjust the mixture.
2   The engine must be at operating temperature, the air cleaner element must be clean and the vacuum hoses fitted, and the engine valve clearances must be correct. The ignition system must also be in good condition.
3   Connect the meters to the engine as instructed by the manufacturers.
4   Run the engine at 3000 rpm for 30 seconds, then allow it to idle.
5   If the idle speed is not as given in the Specifications, turn the idle speed adjustment screw (Fig. 3.6) as necessary.
6   Read the CO level, and compare with the information given in Specifications.
7   If mixture adjustment is required, stop the engine, then fully screw in both idle mixture screws until lightly contacting their seatings. Unscrew each screw 5 turns exactly. This is the initial setting.
8   Start the engine and repeat the procedure in paragraphs 4 to 6.
9   Turn both idle mixture screws by equal amounts (also in the same direction) until the CO level is correct. Turning the screws clockwise weakens the mixture, and turning them anti-clockwise richens the mixture.
10 Finally repeat paragraphs 4 to 6 to check that the idle speed and mixture are correct.
11 Stop the engine and remove the meters.

17 Solex carburettor – removal and refitting

1   Disconnect the battery negative lead.
2   Remove the air cleaner as described in Section 5.
3   Disconnect the wiring from the automatic choke.
4   Disconnect the accelerator cable and throttle rod.
5   Loosen the clip and disconnect the fuel supply pipe.
6   Pull off the distributor vacuum advance pipe.
7   Unscrew and remove the four mounting nuts and washers, then lift the carburettor from the inlet manifold studs. Remove the gasket.
8   Clean the mating surfaces of the inlet manifold and carburettor, taking care not to drop debris inside the inlet manifold.
9   Refit by reversing the removal operations, but fit a new gasket and tighten the mounting nuts evenly. Finally adjust the idle speed and mixture as described in Section 16.

18 Solex carburettor – dismantling and reassembly

1   Remove the carburettor from the engine as described in Section 17 and thoroughly clean the exterior.
2   Remove the screws securing the upper body to the lower body, then extract the U-clip, disconnect the lower choke link and lift off the carburettor upper body.
3   Lever out the nylon float locking tab with a small screwdriver, lift out the float retaining pin, then the float and needle valve.
4   Unscrew the four jets shown in Fig. 3.9, noting the positions in which they are fitted, and then lever out the accelerator pump supply tubes.
5   Remove the four securing screws and detach the accelerator pump diaphragm assembly, taking care not to lose the spring.
6   Undo the three securing screws and remove the power valve diaphragm assembly.
7   Break off the tamperproof caps and remove the mixture adjusting screws.
8   Remove the single screw and detach the throttle damper and bracket.
9   Remove the four securing screws and remove the anti-stall diaphragm and spring.
10 Clean out the float chamber and the upper body. Clean all the jets and passageways using clean, dry compressed air. Check the float

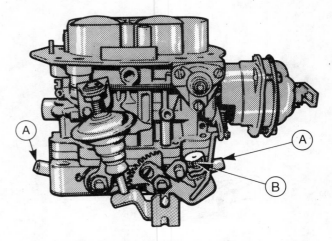

Fig. 3.6 Adjustment screws on the Solex carburettor (Sec 16)

A   Idle mixture screws   *B   Idle speed screws*

assembly for signs of damage or leaking. Inspect the power valve and pump diaphragms for splits or deterioration. Examine the mixture screws, needle valve, throttle damper and throttle spindle for signs of wear and damage. Renew defective parts as necessary.
11 Refit the two mixture adjusting screws, and set to the initial setting (see Section 16).
12 Fit the accelerator and power valve assemblies and tighten the screws.
13 Fit the anti-stall diaphragm assembly, taking care that the diaphragm does not get kinked or twisted.
14 Refit the four jets in the correct locations.
15 Check the O-ring, then refit the accelerator pump supply tubes.
16 Refit the throttle damper and bracket and tighten the screw. If the damper has been renewed, adjust it well clear of the throttle linkage and carry out the final adjustment later.
17 Fit the needle valve, making sure the spring clip is on the valve, and then fit the retaining pin to the float. Position the assembly with the float tag behind the needle valve spring and fit the nylon locking tag.
18 To check the float level setting, lift the float with a wire or elastic band until the adjusting tag just contacts the spring-tensioned ball in the needle valve. Measure the distance between the gasket face and float using a depth gauge, and compare the reading with the dimension given in the Specifications. If adjustment is necessary bend the adjusting tag as required.
19 To check the pump stroke fuel direction partly fill the float chamber with petrol. Operate the accelerator pump and check the fuel direction in relation to the throttle plates, see Fig. 3.10. Adjust the position of the pump discharge tubes to obtain the specified dimension at A.
20 Reconnect the choke link, position a new gasket on the lower body then fit the upper body and the securing screws.
21 On early models, to synchronise the throttle plates, unscrew the basic idle speed adjusting screw until it is clear of the throttle mechanism. Loosen the synchronisation adjusting screw. Hold the choke plates open and flick the throttle to close both throttle plates. Press down both plates to ensure that they are fully closed and tighten the synchronising screw. Note that the synchronisation screw has a left-hand thread.
22 On later models, the basic idle adjusting screw is preset during manufacture and its end sheared off. Adjustment by this means is therefore no longer possible.
23 Refit the carburettor and adjust the idle settings as described in Section 16.
24 With the locknut loosened, adjust the throttle damper upwards or downwards until a clearance of 0.05 mm (0.002 in) exists between the plunger and the throttle lever. Make a reference mark on the damper casing, then screw the damper downwards (towards the throttle lever) exactly 3 turns. Tighten the locknut without altering the damper setting. Operate the throttle several times and check that the damper does not bind or stick, and that the idle speed adjusting screw contacts its stop correctly.

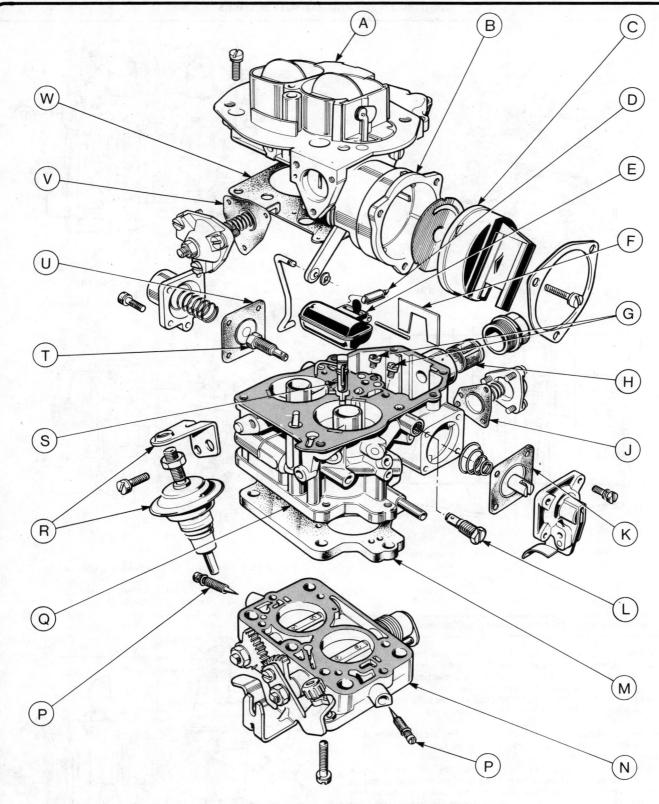

Fig. 3.7 Exploded view of the Solex carburettor (Sec 18)

A	Upper body	G	Main jets	M	Insulator	S	Accelerator pump jets
B	Automatic choke body	H	Fuel filter	N	Throttle body	T	Idle jet
C	Automatic choke housing	J	Power valve diaphragm	P	Mixture screws	U	Anti-stall diaphragm
D	Needle valve	K	Accelerator pump diaphragm	Q	Lower body	V	Pull-down diaphragm
E	Float	L	Idle jet	R	Throttle damper and bracket	W	Gasket
F	Locking tab						

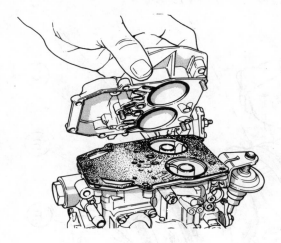

Fig. 3.8 Upper body removal (Sec 18)

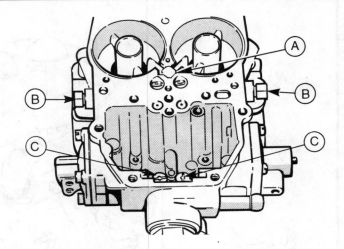

Fig. 3.9 Jet locations (Sec 18)

A   Accelerator pump jets   C   Main jets
B   Idle jets

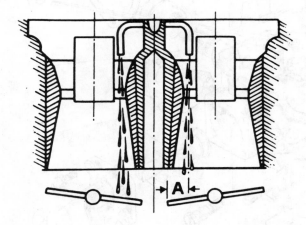

Fig. 3.10 Checking the pump stroke fuel direction (Sec 18)

A = 2.0 to 5.0 mm (0.08 to 0.20 in)

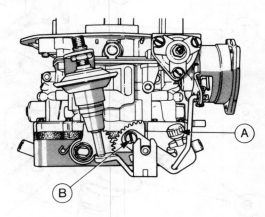

Fig. 3.11 Synchronizing the throttle plates (Sec 18)

A   Idle speed adjusting screw
B   Throttle synchronising
    adjusting screw

19 Solex carburettor fast idle speed – adjustment

1   Run the engine to normal operating temperature, then stop it and connect a tachometer as instructed by the manufacturer.
2   Remove the air cleaner and without disconnecting the vacuum supply pipe, position it clear of the carburettor.
3   Open the throttle partially, hold the choke plates fully closed, then release the throttle so that the choke mechanism is held in the fast idle position.
4   Release the choke plates and check that they return to the fully open position. (If not, the assembly is faulty or the engine is not at operating temperature.)
5   Without touching the accelerator pedal, start the engine and check the fast idle speed. Adjust by screwing the fast idle screw in or out as necessary. To gain access to the screw, stop the engine and fully open the throttle. A $1/2$ turn of the screw alters the engine speed by approximately 400 rpm.
6   Refit the air cleaner.

20 Solex carburettor automatic choke – adjustment

1   Check and if necessary adjust the idle speed and mixture as described in Section 16.

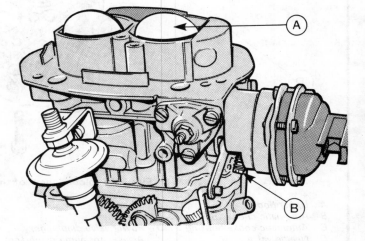

Fig. 3.12 Fast idle speed adjustment (Sec 19)

A   Choke plates fully open   B   Fast idle adjusting screw

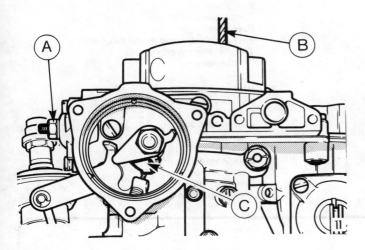

Fig. 3.13 Vacuum pull-down adjustment (Sec 20)

A Adjusting screw   C Choke mechanism on high
B Twist drill   cam

2   Remove the air cleaner and without disconnecting the vacuum
supply pipe, position it clear of the carburettor.
3   Disconnect the wiring, remove the securing screws and pull the
choke housing and bi-metal spring assembly clear of the carburettor.
4   Detach the internal heat shield.

Vacuum pull-down

5   With the engine at normal operating temperature, partially open the
throttle then hold the choke plates fully closed and release the throttle.
The choke mechanism will now be held in the high cam position (fast
idle).
6   Release the choke plates and start the engine without touching the
accelerator pedal. Carefully close the choke plates until resistance is
felt and then hold in this position.
7   Measure the clearance using an unmarked twist drill shank
between the edge of the choke plate and the air horn wall, and
compare it with the specified figure. Adjust, if necessary, by screwing
the diaphragm adjusting screw in or out as required.

Choke phasing

8   With the engine at the normal operating temperature and the choke
mechanism at the fast idle position, start the engine without touching
the accelerator pedal, then close the choke plates to the pull-down
position. Hold the choke plates, partly open the throttle and allow the
fast idle cam to return to its normal position.
9   Release the throttle and stop the engine. With the choke plates held
in the pull-down position the fast idle screw should locate on the cam
next to the high cam stop, leaving a small operating clearance. If
necessary, adjust by bending the phasing adjusting tag.

Modulator spring gap

10 Remove the carburettor upper body as described in Section 18
paragraph 2. Measure the clearance between the modulator spring and
the choke lever with a twist drill shank. If the clearance is not as
specified, adjust by bending the spring to obtain the correct clearance
(Fig. 3.15).

Reassembly

11 Refit the internal heat shield making sure it is the correct way round
to complete the earth circuit.
12 Connect the bi-metal spring to the choke lever, fit the choke
housing and ring, and loosely fit the three retaining screws. Rotate the
cover until the marks are aligned, then tighten the three screws.
Reconnect the wiring.
13 Adjust the fast idle as described in Section 19.
14 Refit the air cleaner assembly.

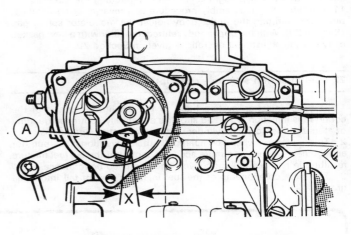

Fig. 3.14 Choke phasing adjustment (Sec 20)

X   Operating clearance   B Adjusting tag
A   Fast idle cam

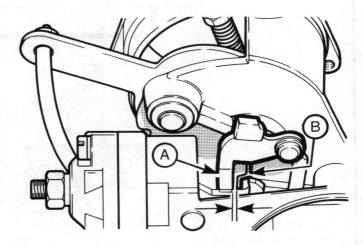

Fig. 3.15 Modulator spring adjustment (Sec 20)

A Automatic choke lever   B Modulator spring

21 Solex carburettor automatic choke – dismantling and reassembly

1   Remove the air cleaner as described in Section 5.
2   Disconnect the wiring from the automatic choke.
3   Remove the screws and withdraw the automatic choke housing
and ring.
4   Detach the internal heat shield.
5   Remove the screws securing the upper body to the lower body,
then extract the U-clip, disconnect the lower choke link and lift off the
carburettor upper body.
6   Unclip the dust cover, then extract the spring clip and disconnect
the upper choke link from the choke plate spindle.
7   Remove the two screws and detach the automatic choke from the
upper body.
8   Remove the three screws and withdraw the vacuum pull-down
housing, spring and diaphragm.
9   Clean all the parts, inspect them for wear and damage and wipe
them dry with a clean cloth. Do not use any lubricants during
reassembly.

10 Refit the vacuum pull-down diaphragm, spring and housing, ensuring that the diaphragm is flat before tightening the screws.

11 The remaining reassembly procedure is a reversal of dismantling, but before refitting the upper body adjust the modulator spring gap (Section 20). With the upper body refitted, together with a new gasket, carry out the adjustment operations given in Section 20.

22 Fuel injection system – description

1 The fuel injection system fitted to the 2.8 litre engine is of the continuous injection type, and supplies a precisely controlled quantity of atomized fuel to each cylinder under all operating conditions.

2 This system, when compared with conventional carburettor arrangements, achieves a more accurate control of the air/fuel mixture resulting in reduced emission levels and improved performance.

3 The main components of the fuel injection system fall into three groups.

A   Fuel tank
     Fuel pump
     Fuel accumulator
     Fuel filter
     Fuel distributor and mixture control
     Throttle and injector valves
     Air chamber

B   Warm-up regulator
     Auxiliary air device
     Starter valve
     Thermotime switch

C   Wiring
     Safety module and fuse
     Speed sensor module
     Fuel shut-off valve
     Impulse module

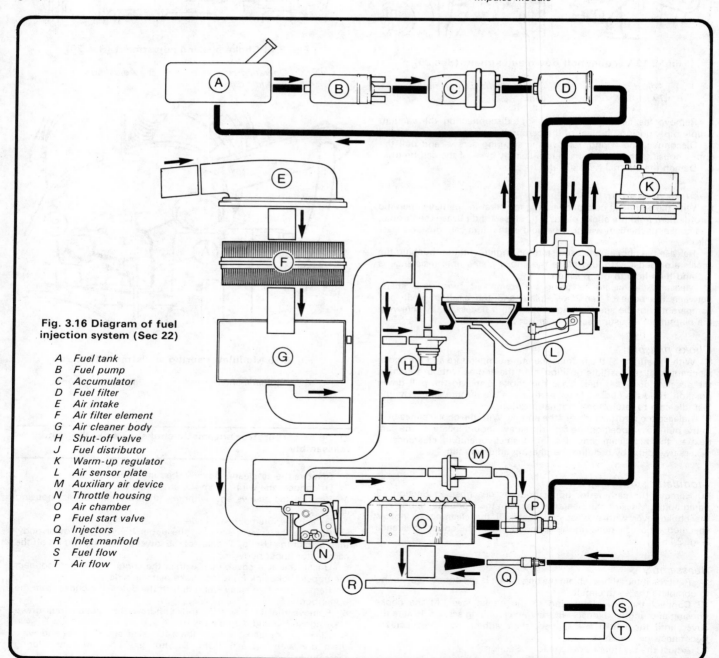

Fig. 3.16 Diagram of fuel injection system (Sec 22)

    A   Fuel tank
    B   Fuel pump
    C   Accumulator
    D   Fuel filter
    E   Air intake
    F   Air filter element
    G   Air cleaner body
    H   Shut-off valve
    J   Fuel distributor
    K   Warm-up regulator
    L   Air sensor plate
    M   Auxiliary air device
    N   Throttle housing
    O   Air chamber
    P   Fuel start valve
    Q   Injectors
    R   Inlet manifold
    S   Fuel flow
    T   Air flow

4 **The fuel pump** is of electrically operated, roller cell type. A pressure relief valve is incorporated in the pump to prevent excessive pressure build up in the event of a restriction in the pipelines.

5 **The fuel accumulator** has two functions, (i) to dampen the pulsation of the fuel flow, generated by the pump and (ii) to maintain fuel pressure after the engine has been switched off. This prevents a vapour lock developing with consequent hot starting problems.

6 **The fuel filter** incorporates two paper filter elements to ensure that the fuel reaching the injection system components is completely free from dirt.

7 **The fuel distributor/mixture control assembly.** The fuel distributor controls the quantity of fuel being delivered to the engine, ensuring that each cylinder receives the same amount The mixture control assembly incorporates an air sensor plate and control plunger. The air sensor plate is located in the main air stream between the air cleaner and the throttle butterfly. During idling, the airflow lifts the sensor plate which in turn raises a control plunger which allows fuel to flow past the plunger and out of the injector valves. Increases in engine speed cause increased air flow which raises the control plunger and so admits more fuel.

8 **The throttle valve** assembly is mounted in the main air intake between the mixture control assembly and the air chamber. The throttle valve plate is controlled by a cable connected to the accelerator cable.

9 **The injector valves** are located in the inlet manifold and are designed to open at a fuel pressure of 3.3 kgf/cm² (46.9 lbf/in²).

10 **The air chamber** is mounted on the top of the engine, and functions as an auxiliary inlet manifold directing air from the sensor plate to each individual cylinder.

11 **The warm-up regulator** is located on the front of the engine and incorporates a bi-metal strip, vacuum diaphragm and control valve. The function of the regulator is to enrich the fuel/air mixture during the warm up period and also at full throttle operation (photo).

12 **The auxiliary air device** is located on the front face of the air chamber. it consists of a pivoted plate, bi-metal strip and heater coil. The purpose of this device is to supply an increased volume of fuel/air mixture during cold idling rather similar to the fast idle system on carburettor layouts.

13 **The fuel start valve** is located on the main air chamber and is an electrically operated injector. Its purpose is to spray fuel into the air chamber at cold starting. This fuel comes from the fuel distributor and is atomized in the air chamber with air from the auxiliary air device.

14 **The thermotime switch** is screwed into the coolant outlet adjacent to the warm up regulator. The switch incorporates a contact set, bi-metal strip and two heated elements. The switch controls the start valve by limiting the period of fuel injection from the valve and also preventing the valve from injecting any fuel at all when starting a hot engine.

15 **The impulse module** is located behind the glovebox, and its purpose is to pulse the fuel start valve when the starter motor is operating. This improves starting with a warm engine.

16 **The fuel-shut off valve** is located on the front of the air cleaner main body, and improves fuel economy by cutting the fuel supply on the overrun. The valve is controlled by manifold vacuum and electrically via an earthing switch on the throttle housing. When

activated, the valve opens a link either side of the air sensor plate which causes the plate to drop and cut off the fuel supply. The valve is only operational with the engine temperature above 35°C (95°F), and when the engine is decelerating from 1700 rpm or more.

17 **The speed sensor module** is located on the left-hand side of the engine compartment (photo). It senses the engine speed from the ignition coil LT circuit, and it de-activates the fuel shut-off valve when the engine speed reaches 1400 rpm.

18 **The safety module and fuse** are located behind the glovebox. The module is coloured purple and it supplies power to the fuel pump, provided that it is receiving pulses from the ignition coil, these pulses being evidence that the engine is running. When the engine stops for whatever reason, the safety control module cuts off power to the fuel pump.

23 Fuel injection system components – removal and refitting

Fuel accumulator

1 The fuel accumulator is located next to the fuel pump beneath the rear of the car (photo).

2 Check the front wheels, raise the rear of the car, and support on axle stands.

3 Disconnect the battery negative lead.

4 Loosen the warm-up regulator fuel inlet union to relieve any pressure in the system, using a wad of rag to soak up the fuel. Tighten the union.

5 Disconnect the fuel pipes from the fuel accumulator and catch the small quantity of fuel which will be released.

6 Unscrew the clamp bolt and slide the accumulator from the mounting bracket. If necessary lower the bracket from the underbody to facilitate removal of the unit.

7 Refitting is a reversal of removal.

Fuel distributor

8 The fuel distributor is located on the mixture control assembly next to the air cleaner (photo).

9 Disconnect the battery negative lead.

10 Loosen the warm-up regulator fuel inlet union to relieve any pressure in the system, using a wad of rag to soak up the fuel. Tighten the union.

11 Note the location of the fuel pipes, then disconnect them by unscrewing the union bolts. There are six injector pipes, the warm-up regulator return pipe, and the fuel inlet and return pipes.

12 Remove the screws and lift the fuel distributor from the mixture control assembly. Note that early models have three cross-head screws, whereas later models have two slot-head and two Torx head screws.

13 Remove the O-ring.

14 Refitting is a reversal of removal, but clean the mating surfaces and renew the O-ring. Adjust the idle speed and mixture as described in Section 24. Have the system pressure checked by your dealer at the earliest opportunity.

22.11 Warm-up regulator (A), auxiliary air device (B), and thermotime switch (C)

22.17 Speed sensor module

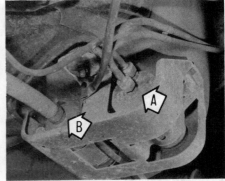

23.1 Fuel accumulator (A) and fuel pump (B)

23.8 Fuel distributor

23.18 Disconnecting the wiring plug from the warm-up regulator

23.26 Disconnecting the wiring plug from the fuel start valve

Warm-up regulator

15 The warm-up regulator is located on the front of the engine next to the cooling system outlet elbow.
16 Disconnect the battery negative lead.
17 Loosen the fuel inlet union to relieve any pressure in the system, using a wad of rag to soak up the fuel.
18 Disconnect the vacuum hose and wiring plug (photo). Use a small screwdriver to prise out the spring clip when removing the wiring plug.
19 Unscrew the union bolts and disconnect the fuel lines. Recover the copper washers.
20 Unscrew the two socket-headed bolts and withdraw the warm-up regulator.
21 Refitting is a reversal of removal, but fit new copper washers to the unions, taking care not to overtighten the union bolts.

Fuel start valve

22 The fuel start valve is located on the right-hand side of the air chamber.
23 Disconnect the battery negative lead.
24 Loosen the warm-up regulator fuel inlet union to relieve any pressure in the system, using a wad of rag to soak up the fuel. Tighten the union.
25 Disconnect the battery negative lead.
26 Disconnect the wiring plug (photo).
27 Unscrew the union bolt and disconnect the fuel line.
28 Unscrew the two socket-headed bolts and withdraw the fuel start valve.
29 Refitting is a reversal of removal, but use a new mounting flange gasket. Renew the union copper washers.

Auxiliary air device

30 The auxiliary air device is located on the front of the engine near the warm-up regulator.
31 Disconnect the battery negative lead.
32 Disconnect the wiring plug and the two air hoses (photo).

33 Unbolt the auxiliary air device from the coolant outlet housing.
34 Refitting is a reversal of removal.

Fuel injectors

35 Disconnect the battery negative lead.
36 Loosen the fuel supply union bolt on the fuel start valve to relieve any pressure in the system, using a wad of rag to soak up the fuel. Unscrew the union bolt and disconnect the fuel line.
37 Disconnect the start valve wiring plug, also the auxiliary air supply hose to the valve.
38 Disconnect the brake servo vacuum hose from the air chamber (except on models with ABS braking), also the vacuum hose(s) next to the start valve.
39 Disconnect the crankcase ventilation hose.
40 Disconnect the accelerator cable and unbolt the bracket (photo).
41 Disconnect the main air supply hose, the auxiliary air device hose, and the vacuum hose from the throttle housing.
42 Unbolt the air chamber (eight bolts) and lift it from the inlet manifold. Remove the gasket (photo).
43 Using two spanners, loosen the union nuts and disconnect the fuel lines from the injectors.
44 Unscrew the mounting bolts and pull the injectors from the inlet manifold.
45 Refitting is a reversal of removal, but make sure that the injectors are clean, and fit new O-ring seals (photo). Also renew the air chamber gasket.

24 Fuel injection system – idle speed and mixture adjustment

Note: The mixture setting is preset during production of the car and should not normally require adjustment. If new components of the system have been fitted, however, the mixture can be adjusted as

23.32 Disconnecting the wiring plug from the auxiliary air device

23.40 Unbolting the accelerator cable bracket from the air chamber

23.42 Removing the air chamber gasket from the inlet manifold

23.45 Injector O-ring seal (arrowed)

24.4 Idle speed adjustment screw (arrowed)

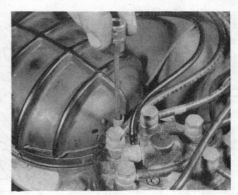

24.7 Adjusting the mixture screw

25.7 Removing the inlet manifold bolts

25.8 Inlet manifold removal

25.9 Inlet manifold gasket

follows using an exhaust gas analyser and tachometer. Adjustment is not possible without an exhaust gas analyser.

1   Run the engine until it is at the normal operating temperature.
2   Connect an exhaust gas analyser and a tachometer (if not fitted as standard equipment) in accordance with the manufacturer's instructions.
3   Increase the engine speed to 3000 rpm and hold it there for 30 seconds to stabilise the exhaust gases and then allow the engine to return to idling.
4   Check the readings on the test instruments with those specified. If adjustment is required first turn the idle speed screw to give the correct idle speed (photo).
5   Break off the tamperproof cap from the mixture control screw on top of the fuel distributor.
6   Stabilise the exhaust gases as described in paragraph 3.
7   Insert a 3 mm Allen key into the head of the mixture screw and turn the screw until the correct CO reading is obtained (photo). Readjust the idle speed screw.
8   If the mixture adjustment cannot be finalised within 30 seconds from the moment of stabilising the exhaust gases, repeat the operations described in paragraph 3 before continuing the adjustment procedure.
9   Stop the engine and disconnect the meters.

25 Inlet manifold – removal and refitting

1   Remove the carburettor (Section 17) or fuel injectors (Section 23).
2   Drain the cooling system (Chapter 2), then disconnect the radiator top hose and the hose connections at the front of the manifold.
3   On 2.8 models remove the warm-up regulator and auxiliary air device (Section 23).
4   Unbolt the outlet housing from the front of the inlet manifold and remove the gasket.
5   On 2.3 models disconnect the crankcase ventilation hose.
6   Where applicable unscrew the single nuts at each end of the manifold.

7   Progressively unscrew the bolts in the reverse order to that shown in Fig. 3.18 (photo).
8   Lift the inlet manifold from the cylinder heads (photo).
9   Remove the gasket and clean the mating faces (photo).
10 Clean the areas where the corners of the cylinder heads meet the cylinder block (Fig. 3.17) and apply sealing compound (photo).
11 Apply a thin film of sealing compound on both sides of the new gasket around the inlet ports and coolant passages.
12 The refitting procedure is now a reversal of removal, but tighten the bolts to the specified torque using the sequence shown in Fig. 3.18. Refill the cooling system with reference to Chapter 2.

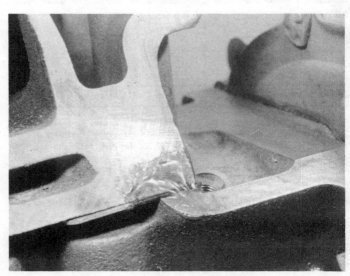

25.10 Sealing compound location before fitting the inlet manifold gasket

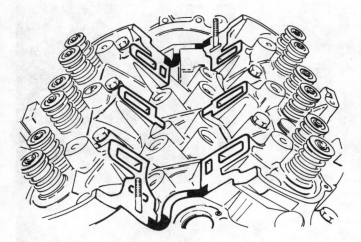

Fig. 3.17 Apply sealing compound to the shaded areas
(Sec 25)

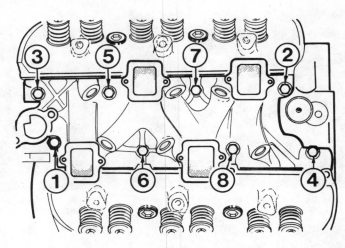

Fig. 3.18 Inlet manifold bolt tightening sequence (Sec 25)

26.2 Exhaust manifold flange (right-hand side)

26.3 Exhaust manifold removal

26 Exhaust manifold – removal and refitting

1   On 2.3 models remove the air cleaner as described in Section 5.
2   Unscrew the nuts securing the downpipe collar to the exhaust manifold flange (photo). If necessary soak the nuts with penetrating oil before unscrewing them.
3   Unbolt the exhaust manifold from the cylinder head and remove the gaskets (photo).
4   Refitting is a reversal of removal but clean the mating surfaces, fit new gaskets, and tighten the nuts and bolts to the specified torque.

27 Exhaust system – removal and refitting

1   The original production exhaust system is in two or three sections. However, the system is divided into six sections for service replacements, as shown in Fig. 3.19. The service sections are provided with sockets which locate over the original system after cutting to the dimensions shown.
2   To remove the complete system, jack up the front and rear of the car and support on axle stands, or position the car over an inspection pit.
3   Unscrew the nuts securing both downpipe collars to the exhaust manifold flanges (photo).
4   With the help of an assistant, unhook the rubber mountings. If necessary the left-hand mounting bracket may be unbolted from the underbody (photos).
5   Move the exhaust system rearwards to clear the front anti-roll bar, then lower the system and remove from under the car.
6   Clean the downpipe and manifold flange mating faces. Examine the rubber mountings for damage and deterioration and renew them if necessary.
7   Refitting is a reversal of removal, but do not fully tighten the downpipe flange nuts until the rubber mountings have been reconnected. To ensure gastight joints, smear the mating faces with suitable exhaust sealing compound.

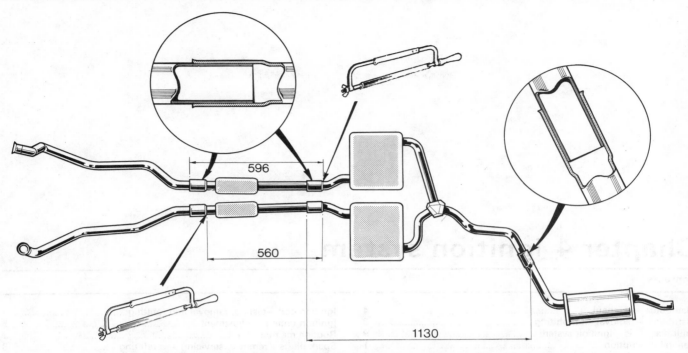

Fig. 3.19 Exhaust cutting dimensions when fitting service sections to the original system (Sec 27)

596 mm = 23.5 in   560 mm = 22.0 in   1130 mm = 44.5 in

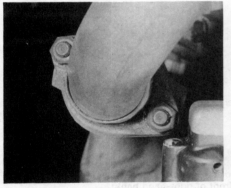

27.3 Exhaust manifold flange (left-hand side)

27.4A Right-hand exhaust mounting

27.4B Left-hand exhaust mounting

28 Fault diagnosis – fuel and exhaust systems

Symptom	Reason(s)
Excessive fuel consumption	Air cleaner element choked
	Fuel leakage
	Carburettor float level incorrect, or needle valve sticking
	Mixture adjustment incorrect
	Carburettor excessively worn
Insufficient fuel supply or weak mixture	Faulty fuel pump
	Mixture adjustment incorrect
	Air leak on induction component
	Fuel filter blocked
	Fuel leakage
Difficult starting	Faulty automatic choke or cold start system

Chapter 4 Ignition system

Contents

Specifications

System type .... Electronic, breakerless distributor with remote module and coil

Ignition coil
Make .... Bosch, Femsa or Polmot
Primary resistance .... 0.72 to 0.86 ohm
Secondary resistance .... 4.5 to 7.0 k ohms
Output voltage (open-circuit) .... 25 kV minimum

HT leads
Resistance .... 30 k ohms maximum per lead

Distributor
Make .... Bosch
Rotation .... Clockwise (viewed from above)
Dwell angle .... Controlled by module
Automatic advance .... Centrifugal weights on distributor shaft, and vacuum unit
Firing order .... 1–4–2–5–3–6 (No 1 at front of right-hand bank)

Spark plugs
Make and type .... Champion RN7YC, Motorcraft Super AGR22C, or equivalent
Electrode gap:
    Champion .... 0.60 mm (0.024 in)
    Motorcraft .... 0.75 mm (0.030 in)

Ignition timing (vacuum hose disconnected)
Using leaded (97 octane) fuel:
    2.3 engine .... 9° BTDC at 800 ± 20 rpm
    2.8 engine .... 12° BTDC at 900 ± 25 rpm
Using unleaded (95 octane) fuel – all engines, refer also
to Chapter 3 .... 6° BTDC

Torque wrench setting

	Nm	lbf ft
Spark plugs	30 to 40	22 to 30

1 General description

To achieve optimum performance from an engine and to meet stringent exhaust emission requirements, it is essential that the fuel/air mixture in the combustion chamber is ignited at exactly the right time relative to engine speed and load. The ignition system provides the spark necessary to start the mixture burning and the instant at which ignition occurs is varied automatically as engine operating conditions change.

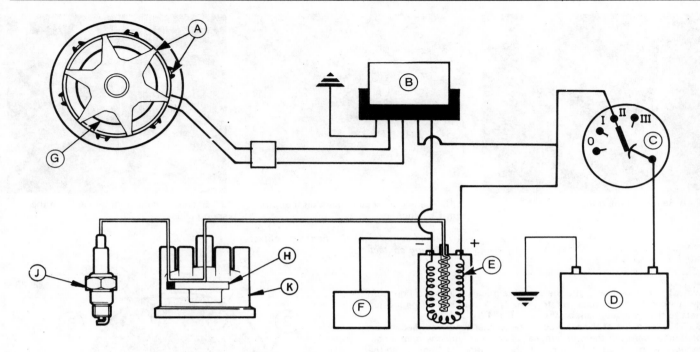

Fig. 4.1 Diagram of the breakerless ignition system (Sec 1)

A Trigger and stator arms D Battery   G Trigger coil   J Spark plug
B Amplifier module   E Coil   H Rotor arm   K Distributor cap
C Ignition switch   F Tachometer

The ignition system consists of a primary LT (low tension) circuit and a secondary HT (high tension) circuit. When the ignition is switched on, current is fed to the coil primary windings and a magnetic field is established. At the required point of ignition, the primary circuit is interrupted electronically by the trigger arm within the distributor passing the stator arm. The magnetic field collapses and a secondary high voltage is induced in the secondary windings. This HT voltage is fed via the distributor rotor arm to the relevant spark plug. After delivering the spark the primary circuit is re-energised and the cycle is repeated.

The ignition timing is controlled centrifugally and by a vacuum unit to compensate for engine speed and load.

When working on the electronic ignition system, remember that the high tension voltage can be considerably higher than on a conventional system, and in certain circumstances could prove fatal. Depending on the position of the distributor trigger components it is also possible for a single high tension spark to be generated simply by knocking the distributor with the ignition switched on. It is therefore important to keep the ignition system clean and dry at all times, and to make sure that the ignition switch is off when working on the engine.

2 Routine maintenance

Carry out the following procedures at the intervals given in *Routine Maintenance* at the beginning of the Manual.

Renew the spark plugs
1 Refer to Section 8.

Clean and check the distributor cap, HT leads and coil
2 Release the two clips securing the distributor cap to the distributor body and lift away the cap. Clean the cap inside and out with a dry cloth. Closely inspect the inside of the cap and the six segments. If there are any signs of cracking, or if the segments are burned or scored excessively the cap will have to be renewed.

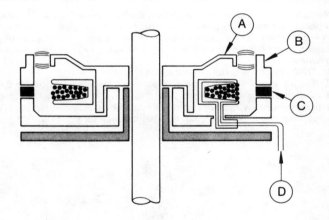

Fig. 4.2 Cross-sectional diagram of the distributor reluctance trigger system (Sec 1)

A Trigger arm   C Permanent magnet
B Stator arm   D Wires

3 Also check that the carbon brush in the centre of the cap is not broken or excessively worn.

4 Pull the rotor arm from the distributor shaft and check it for cracking and burning of the metal segment. On the 2.8 engine check the spring-tensioned engine speed limiter incorporated in the rotor arm for free movement (photos).

5 With the rotor arm removed, lubricate the felt pad in the centre of the distributor shaft with two drops of engine oil.

6 Refit the rotor arm and distributor cap (photo).

7 Wipe clean the HT leads and check them for condition. Pull the leads from the distributor cap one at a time, and make sure that no

2.4A Removing the rotor arm

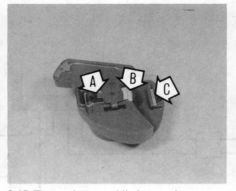

2.4B The engine speed limiter on the rotor arm (2.8 engine)

A   Spring contact   C   Earthing contact
B   Moving contact

2.6 Securing the distributor cap with the spring clips

water has found its way into the socket terminals. Clean any corrosion away, then refit the leads (photo). The No 1 lead should be located next to the moulded mark on the cap (Fig. 4.3).
8   The resistance of the HT leads may be checked by connecting an ohmmeter between the end terminal of the lead and the appropriate terminal within the distributor cap. If the resistance is greater than the maximum given in the Specifications, check that the lead connection in the cap is good before renewing the lead.
9   Clean the ignition coil tower and check that it is free of any 'tracking' lines.

3   Distributor – removal and refitting

Note: *During manufacture the ignition timing is set using a microwave process, and sealant applied to the distributor clamp bolt. Removal of the distributor will therefore only be necessary where excessive bearing wear has occurred due to high mileage, or during an engine overhaul.*
1   Disconnect the battery negative lead.
2   On 2.3 engines remove the air cleaner as described in Chapter 3.
3   Remove the distributor cap only (Section 2). If required the cap may be completely removed from the engine by disconnecting the HT leads, however make sure each lead is identified for position.

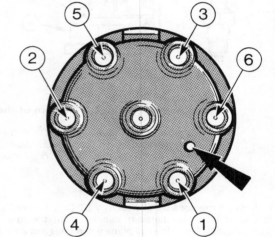

Fig. 4.3 HT lead positions on the distributor cap (Sec 2)

Arrow indicates moulded mark adjacent to No 1 HT lead

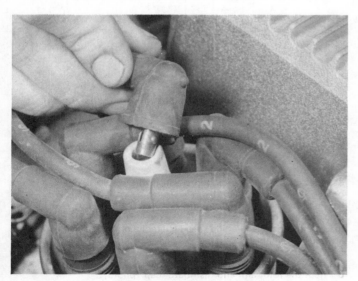

2.7 Refitting the HT lead terminals on the distributor

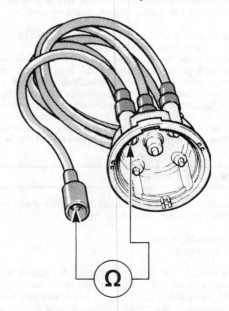

Fig. 4.4 Method of testing an HT lead with an ohmmeter (Sec 2)

3.4 Disconnecting the vacuum advance pipe

3.5 Disconnecting the earth lead

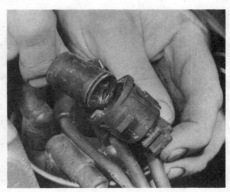

3.6 Disconnecting the multi-plug

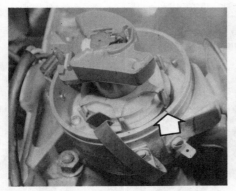

3.7 Rotor arm alignment mark (arrowed) before removal from engine

3.8 Crankshaft pulley notch (arrowed) and timing cover gradation

3.10A Unscrew the clamp bolt ...

3.10B ... and remove the distributor

3.10C Rotor arm alignment after removal from engine

4   Disconnect the vacuum advance pipe (photo).
5   Where applicable, disconnect the earth lead from the terminal on the distributor body (photo).
6   Disconnect the distributor multi-plug connector. To disconnect the plug, the wires must be held and pulled, not the plug itself (photo).
7   Turn the engine until the rotor arm is pointing to the No 1 cylinder segment in the distributor cap. On later models, this is also indicated by a slot on the distributor body rim (photo).
8   Check also that the notch in the crankshaft pulley is in line with the correct mark on the timing cover (photo). The marks are in 3° intervals (see Specifications for the correct setting).
9   Mark the position of the distributor body in relation to the cylinder block.
10 Remove the single bolt and clamp from the base of the distributor, and slowly lift out the distributor without turning its body. As the

distributor is removed, the skew gear will turn the rotor arm clockwise. Mark the new position of the rotor arm on the rim if there is not already a mark there (photos).
11 To refit the distributor ensure that the timing marks are still aligned as detailed in paragraph 8 of this Section. Hold the distributor over the cylinder head so that the body-to-cylinder block marks are in alignment.
12 Position the rotor arm towards the mark on the distributor body and slide the assembly into position on the engine. As the gears mesh, the rotor will turn and align with No 1 segment in the distributor cap.
13 Refit the securing bolt and clamp to the base of the distributor, but do not fully tighten at this stage.
14 Check that the previously made marks on the distributor body and cylinder block are aligned. The correct position of the distributor is when a line through the centre of the vacuum capsule (ie from the

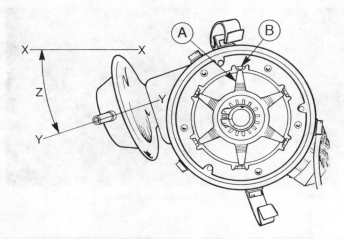

Fig. 4.5 Distributor fitting position (Sec 3)

XX Rear face of cylinder block   *Z = 0° to 14°*
YY Vacuum unit axis   *A Trigger arm*
                                         B Stator arm

distributor through the capsule) is parallel to, or a maximum of 14° anti-clockwise from, the rear face of the cylinder block.

15 Reconnect the multi-plug connector.

16 Reconnect the earth lead (if applicable) and the vacuum advance pipe.

17 Refer to Section 5 and set the ignition timing.

18 If removed, refit the air cleaner on 2.3 engines.

4 Distributor – overhaul

1 There are only two overhaul tasks possible, these being the fitting of a trigger coil kit, and the renewal of the vacuum advance unit. Excessive wear or damage to the distributor body or driveshaft will mean the renewal of the complete distributor.

2 Refer to Fig. 4.3 for the order of removal of the components, and lightly oil the shaft and vacuum unit arm during reassembly (photos).

5 Ignition timing – adjustment

1 With the distributor fitted as described in Section 3, check that the correct timing marks are aligned.

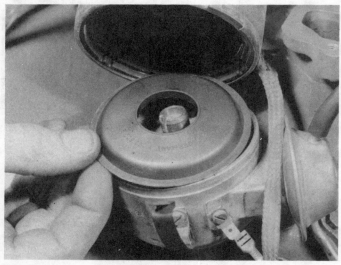

4.2A Removing the plastic dust cover

4.2B Upper view of the trigger arm and coil

4.2C Wiring connector and securing screw (arrowed)

4.2D Vacuum unit securing screw with earth lead terminal (arrowed)

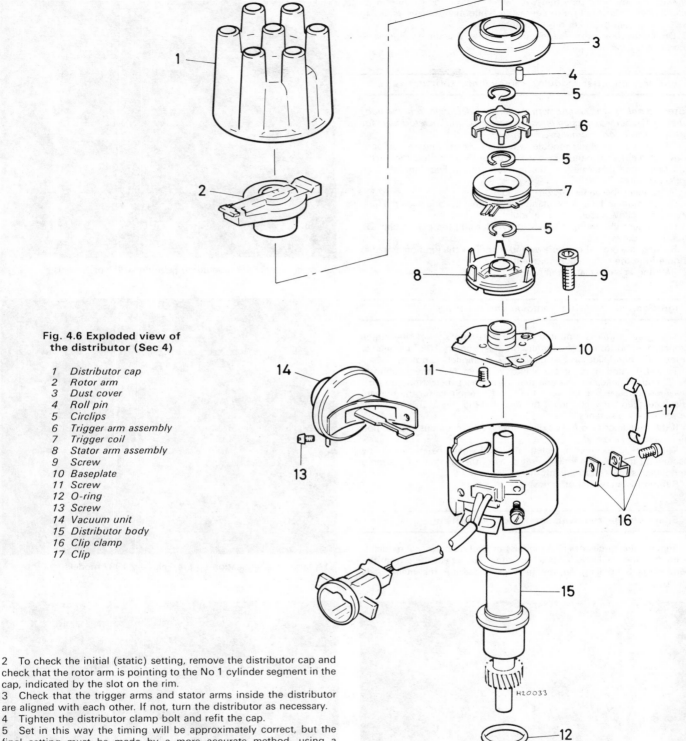

Fig. 4.6 Exploded view of the distributor (Sec 4)

1 Distributor cap
2 Rotor arm
3 Dust cover
4 Roll pin
5 Circlips
6 Trigger arm assembly
7 Trigger coil
8 Stator arm assembly
9 Screw
10 Baseplate
11 Screw
12 O-ring
13 Screw
14 Vacuum unit
15 Distributor body
16 Clip clamp
17 Clip

2   To check the initial (static) setting, remove the distributor cap and check that the rotor arm is pointing to the No 1 cylinder segment in the cap, indicated by the slot on the rim.

3   Check that the trigger arms and stator arms inside the distributor are aligned with each other. If not, turn the distributor as necessary.

4   Tighten the distributor clamp bolt and refit the cap.

5   Set in this way the timing will be approximately correct, but the final setting must be made by a more accurate method, using a stroboscopic timing light.

6   Highlight the specified timing marks on the timing cover and crankshaft pulley with white paint or chalk.

7   Connect a timing light to the No 1 spark plug lead.

8   Disconnect the vacuum advance pipe at the carburettor or air chamber (fuel injection) and plug the pipe. Run the engine until normal operating temperature is reached.

9   With the engine idling point the timing light at the crankshaft pulley. The white painted marks will appear stationary, and if the timing is correct they will be in alignment.

10 To adjust the timing, stop the engine, slacken the clamp bolt and

turn the distributor slightly in the required direction. To retard the ignition (move the mark nearer TDC) turn the distributor body clockwise, and *vice versa* to advance the ignition. Tighten the clamp bolt, start the engine and recheck the timing. Repeat this procedure until the marks are in line.

11 To check the mechanical advance, increase the engine speed and note whether the white mark on the pulley moves away from the mark on the pointer. If it does the mechanical advance is functioning.

12 With the engine idling the vacuum advance can be checked by

sucking the advanced pipe that was removed from the carburettor or air chamber. This should also cause the white mark on the pulley to move away from the mark on the pointer.
13 On completion stop the engine, remove the timing light and reconnect the vacuum pipe.

6 Ignition amplifier module – removal and refitting

Note: *Do not run the engine with the module detached from the body panel, as the body acts as an effective heat sink, and therefore damage may occur through internal overheating.*
1   The ignition amplifier module is located on the engine compartment left-hand side panel on pre-February 1987 models, or on the right-hand side panel next to the ignition coil on February 1987-on models (photo).
2   Disconnect the battery negative lead.
3   On 2.8 models, loosen the clamp on the fuel filter and slide the filter forwards to allow access to the module.
4   Disconnect the wiring multi-plug by releasing the plastic clip. Do not pull on the wiring.
5   Remove the cross-head screws and withdraw the ignition amplifier module from the engine compartment.
6   Refitting is a reversal of removal.

6.1 Ignition amplifier module on February 1987-on models

7 Ignition coil – testing, removal and refitting

1   The ignition coil is mounted on the left-hand side of the engine compartment, in front of the battery on pre-February 1987 models, or on the right-hand side on February 1987-on models (photos).
2   To test the coil an ohmmeter will be required. Note the location of the LT and HT leads on the coil then disconnect them (ignition off). Measure the resistance between the two LT terminals for the primary resistance, then between the HT terminal and the +/15 LT terminal for the secondary resistance.
3   If the resistances are not as given in the Specifications the ignition coil should be renewed.
4   With all leads disconnected the coil may be removed by unscrewing the two mounting screws. Note the location of the radio interference suppressor beneath one of the screws.
5   Refitting is a reversal of removal.

7.1A Ignition coil location on pre-February 1987 models

8 Spark plugs – removal, servicing and refitting

1   Remove the air cleaner (2.3 models) or inlet ducting (2.8 models).
2   Identify the HT leads for position, then disconnect them from the spark plugs by pulling on the terminal ends, not the main leads (photo).

7.1B Ignition coil location on February 1987-on models

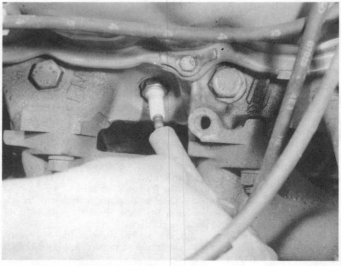
8.2 Disconnect the HT lead ...

Measuring plug gap. A feeler gauge of the correct size (see ignition system specifications) should have a slight 'drag' when slid between the electrodes. Adjust gap if necessary

Adjusting plug gap. The plug gap is adjusted by bending the earth electrode inwards, or outwards, as necessary until the correct clearance is obtained. Note the use of the correct tool

Normal. Grey-brown deposits, lightly coated core nose. Gap increasing by around 0.001 in (0.025 mm) per 1000 miles (1600 km). Plugs ideally suited to engine, and engine in good condition

Carbon fouling. Dry, black, sooty deposits. Will cause weak spark and eventually misfire. Fault: over-rich fuel mixture. Check: carburettor mixture settings, float level and jet sizes; choke operation and cleanliness of air filter. Plugs can be re-used after cleaning

Oil fouling. Wet, oily deposits. Will cause weak spark and eventually misfire. Fault: worn bores/piston rings or valve guides; sometimes occurs (temporarily) during running-in period. Plugs can be re-used after thorough cleaning

Overheating. Electrodes have glazed appearance, core nose very white — few deposits. Fault: plug overheating. Check: plug value, ignition timing, fuel octane rating (too low) and fuel mixture (too weak). Discard plugs and cure fault immediately

Electrode damage. Electrodes burned away; core nose has burned, glazed appearance. Fault: pre-ignition. Check: as for 'Overheating' but may be more severe. Discard plugs and remedy fault before piston or valve damage occurs

Split core nose (may appear initially as a crack). Damage is self-evident, but cracks will only show after cleaning. Fault: pre-ignition or wrong gap-setting technique. Check: ignition timing, cooling system, fuel octane rating (too low) and fuel mixture (too weak). Discard plugs, rectify fault immediately

8.3A ... unscrew the spark plug ...

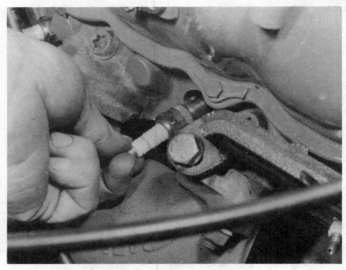

8.3B ... and remove it

3   Using a spark plug spanner, unscrew the plugs from the cylinder heads (photos).
4   If the insulator nose of the spark plug is clean and white, with no deposits, this is indicative of a weak mixture, or too hot a plug (a hot plug transfers heat away from the electrode slowly – a cold plug transfers it away quickly).
5   The plugs fitted as standard are as listed in the Specifications at the beginning of this Chapter. If the tip and insulator nose are covered with hard black-looking deposits, then this is indicative that the mixture is too rich. Should the plug be black and oily, then it is likely that the engine is fairly worn, as well as the mixture being too rich.
6   If the insulator nose is covered with light tan to greyish brown deposits, then the mixture is correct and it is likely that the engine is in good condition.
7   If there are any traces of long brown tapering stains on the outside of the white portion of the plug, then the plug will have to be renewed, as this shows that there is a faulty joint between the plug and body and the insulator, and compression is being allowed to leak away.
8   Plugs should be cleaned by a sand blasting machine, which will free them from carbon more thoroughly than cleaning by hand. The machine will also test the condition of the plugs under compression. Any plug that fails to spark at the recommended pressure should be renewed.
9   The spark plug gap is of considerable importance, as, if it is too large or too small, the size of the spark and its efficiency will be seriously impaired. The spark plug should be set to the figure given in the Specifications at the beginning of this Chapter.
10 To set it, measure the gap with a feeler gauge, and then bend open, or close, the outer plug electrode until the correct gap is achieved. The centre electrode should never be bent as this may crack the insulation and cause plug failure, if nothing worse.
11 Refit the plugs, and refit the leads from the distributor in the correct firing order (Fig. 4.7) which is given in the Specifications. Screw the plugs in by hand initially, then tighten them to the specified torque using the plug spanner.

9   Fault diagnosis – ignition system

The electrode ignition fitted is far less likely to cause trouble than the contact breaker type fitted to many cars, largely because the low tension circuit is electronically controlled. However the high tension circuit remains identical and therefore the associated faults are the same. There are two main symptoms indicating ignition faults. Either the engine will not start or fire, or the engine is difficult to start and misfires. If it is a regular misfire, the fault is almost sure to be in the secondary or high tension circuit.

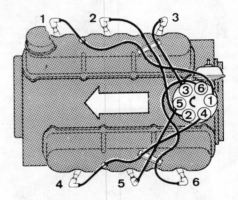

Fig. 4.7 Correct HT lead positions (Sec 8)

Arrow indicates front of engine

Engine fails to start

1   If the starter motor fails to turn the engine check the battery and starter motor with reference to Chapter 12.
2   Disconnect an HT lead from any park plug and hold the end of the cable approximately 5 mm (0.2 in) away from the cylinder head using *well insulated pliers*. While an assistant spins the engine on the starter motor, check that a regular blue spark occurs. If so, remove, clean, and re-gap the spark plugs as described in Section 8.
3   If no spark occurs, disconnect the main feed HT lead from the distributor cap and check for a spark as in paragraph 2. If sparks now occur, check the distributor cap, rotor arm, and HT leads as described in Section 2 and renew them as necessary.
4   If no sparks occur check the resistance of the main feed HT lead as described in Section 2 and renew as necessary. Should the lead be serviceable check that all wiring and multi-plugs are secure on the electronic module and distributor.
5   Check the coil as described in Section 7.
6   If the above checks reveal no faults but there is still no spark, the distributor or the control module must be suspect. Consult a Ford dealer for further testing, or tests by substitution.

Engine misfires

7   If the engine misfires regularly, run it at a fast idling speed. Pull off each of the plug HT leads in turn and listen to the note of the engine.

Hold the plug leads with a well insulated pair of pliers as protection against a shock from the HT supply.

8   No difference in engine running will be noticed when the lead from the defective circuit is removed. Removing the lead from one of the good cylinders will accentuate the misfire.

9   Remove the plug lead from the end of the defective plug and hold it about 5 mm (0.2 in) away from the cylinder head. Restart the engine. If the sparking is fairly strong and regular, the fault must lie in the spark plug.

10 The plug may be loose, the insulation may be cracked, or the points may have burnt away, giving too wide a gap for the spark to jump. Worse still, one of the points may have broken off. Either renew the plug, or clean it, reset the gap, and then test it.

11 If there is no spark at the end of the plug lead, or if it is weak and intermittent, check the HT lead from the distributor to the plug. If the insulation is cracked or perished or if its resistance is incorrect, renew the lead. Check the connections at the distributor cap.

12 If there is still no spark, examine the distributor cap carefully for tracking. This can be recognised by a very thin black line running between two or more electrodes, or between an electrode and some other part of the distributor. These lines are paths which now conduct electricity across the cap, thus letting it run to earth. The only answer in this case is a new distributor cap. Tracking will also occur if the inside or outside of the distributor cap is damp. If this is evident use a proprietary water repellent spray or alternatively thoroughly dry out the cap.

Chapter 5 Clutch

Contents

Specifications

General

Clutch type	Single dry plate, diaphragm spring, cable-operated (self-adjusting)
Clutch pedal free play	10 to 15 mm (0.39 to 0.59 in)

Friction disc

Diameter:

2.3 engine	232 mm (9.1 in)
2.8 engine	242 mm (9.5 in)
Lining thickness (new)	3.81 ± 0.13 mm (0.15 ± 0.005 in)

Torque wrench setting

	Nm	lbf ft
Clutch pressure plate	20 to 25	15 to 18

1 General description

The clutch is of single dry plate type with a diaphragm spring pressure plate. The unit is dowelled and bolted to the rear face of the flywheel.

The clutch friction disc is free to slide along the splined gearbox input shaft and is held in position between the flywheel and the pressure plate by the pressure of the diaphragm spring. Friction lining material is riveted to the friction disc, and it has a spring cushioned hub to absorb transmission shocks and to help ensure a smooth take off.

The circular diaphragm spring is mounted on shoulder pins and held in place in the cover by two fulcrum rings. The spring is also held to the pressure plate by three spring steel clips which are riveted in position.

The clutch is actuated by a cable controlled by the clutch pedal. Wear of the friction linings is compensated for by an automatic pawl and quadrant adjuster on the top of the clutch pedal. The clutch release mechanism consists of a self-centring ball bearing which slides on a guide sleeve at the front of the gearbox, and a release arm which pivots inside the clutch bellhousing.

Depressing the clutch pedal actuates the clutch release arm by means of the cable. The release arm pushes the release bearing forwards to bear against the release fingers, so moving the centre of the diaphragm spring inwards. The spring is sandwiched between two annular rings which act as fulcrum points. As the centre of the spring is

pushed in, the outside of the spring is pushed out, so moving the pressure plate backwards and disengaging the pressure plate from the friction disc.

When the clutch pedal is released, the diaphragm spring forces the pressure plate into contact with the friction linings on the friction disc and at the same time pushes the friction disc a fraction of an inch forwards on its splines, so engaging the friction disc with the flywheel. The friction disc is now firmly sandwiched between the pressure plate and the flywheel so the drive is taken up.

2 Clutch pedal – removal, overhaul and refitting

1   Disconnect the clutch cable from the release arm and clutch pedal as described in Section 4, but do not remove the cable.
2   Prise the spring clip from the end of the pedal shaft and remove the spacer washer.
3   Withdraw the pedal complete with automatic adjuster from the shaft.
4   Prise the bushes from each side of the pedal and extract the toothed segment. Unhook the spring.
5   Prise one of the clips from the pawl shaft, withdraw the shaft and remove the pawl and spring.
6   Clean all the components and examine them for wear and damage. Renew them as necessary.

Fig. 5.1 Clutch pedal, washer and retaining spring clip (Sec 2)

7 Lubricate the bores of the pawl and segment with graphite grease.
8 Assemble the pawl, spring and shaft to the pedal with reference to Fig. 5.2, then refit the clip.
9 Attach the spring to the toothed segment, then insert the segment into the pedal and press in the two pivot bushes.
10 Lift the pawl and turn the segment so that the pawl rests on the smooth curved surface at the end of the teeth.
11 Attach the segment spring to the pedal.
12 Lubricate the pedal shaft with a molybdenum disulphide based grease, then fit the pedal assembly.
13 Fit the spacer washer and spring clip.
14 Reconnect the clutch cable to the clutch pedal and release arm as described in Section 4.

3 Clutch pedal self-adjusting mechanism – seizure

1 It is possible for the pawl on the self-adjusting mechanism to become permanently locked to the toothed segment, particularly if the components are worn. Where this has happened, the cable free play will eventually be lost resulting in clutch slip and rapid wear of the clutch plate lining.
2 To check if the mechanism has seized, open the bonnet and pull the clutch outer cable sharply out from the bulkhead. This will have the effect of pulling the inner cable and turning the toothed segment. If the mechanism is working normally, a clicking sound will be heard as the pawl moves over the segment teeth, and as the outer cable is released, the mechanism will regain its original adjustment. However, if the pawl is locked, it will not be possible to pull the outer cable from the bulkhead.
3 Where the pawl is locked, the clutch cable will be difficult to remove. Levering the release arm to disconnect the inner cable is possible, or alternatively the inner cable should be cut. If the latter course of action is decided upon, remember that the release arm will fly back smartly, so keep fingers well away from the aperture in the clutch housing and wear safety glasses to prevent possible injury from the inner cable end fitting.
4 Pulling the clutch outer cable from the bulkhead will sometimes release a seized mechanism, however it is recommended that new components are fitted to prevent a possible recurrence.

4 Clutch cable – removal and refitting

1 Apply the handbrake, then jack up the front of the car and support it on axle stands.
2 Working beneath the car squeeze the sides of the rubber boot and release it from the gearbox (photos).

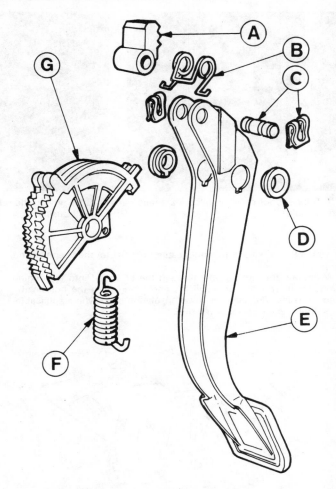

Fig. 5.2 Clutch pedal and self-adjusting mechanism (Sec 2)

A Pawl
B Spring
C Pawl pin and clip
D Bush
E Clutch pedal
F Toothed segment tension spring
G Toothed segment

Fig. 5.3 Clutch pedal toothed segment at initial setting (Sec 2)

3 Pull down on the inner cable to release the self-adjusting mechanism on the pedal, then hold the cable with a pair of pliers and unhook it from the release arm. Remove the insulator pad if fitted (photo).
4 Remove the rubber boot over the inner cable.
5 Remove the lower facia panel inside the car.

4.2A Rubber boot covering release arm and end of cable

4.2B Removing the rubber boot from the clutch housing

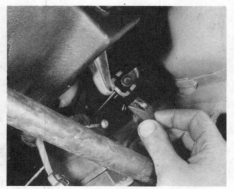

4.3 Removing the insulator pad from the inner cable

6   Unhook and remove the inner cable from the toothed segment on the pedal.
7   Withdraw the clutch cable through the bulkhead into the engine compartment (photo), and pull the end fitting from the hole in the clutch housing. Remove the rubber insulation bush where applicable.
8   Refitting is a reversal of removal.

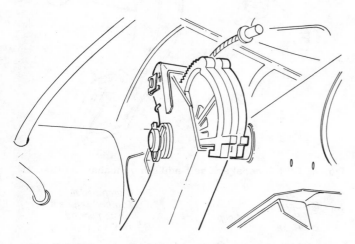

Fig. 5.4 Disconnecting the clutch inner cable from the toothed segment (Sec 4)

5   Clutch – removal

1   The clutch may be removed by two alternative methods. Either remove the engine (Chapter 1) or remove the gearbox (Chapter 6). Unless the engine requires a major overhaul or the crankshaft rear oil seal requires renewal, it is easier and quicker to remove the gearbox.
2   With a file or scriber mark the relative positions of the pressure plate and flywheel, which will ensure identical positioning on refitting. This is not necessary if a new clutch is to be fitted.
3   Unscrew, in a diagonal progressive manner, the six bolts and spring washers that secure the pressure plate to the flywheel. This will prevent distortion of the plate, and also prevent it from suddenly flying off due to binding on the dowels.
4   With all the bolts removed lift the clutch assembly from the locating dowels. Note which way round the friction disc is fitted and lift it from the pressure plate (photo).

6   Clutch – inspection

1   Examine the surfaces of the pressure plate and flywheel for scoring. If this is only light, the parts may be re-used. But, if scoring is excessive the pressure plate must be renewed and the flywheel friction face reground, provided the amount of metal being removed is minimal. If any doubt exists renew the flywheel.
2   Renew the friction disc if the linings are worn down to or near the rivets. If the linings appear oil stained, the cause of the oil leak must be found and rectified. This is most likely to be a failed gearbox input shaft

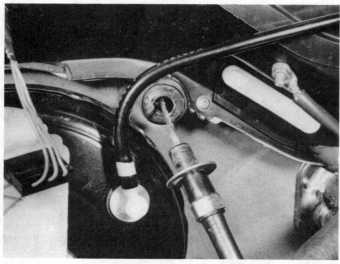

4.7 Removing the clutch cable from the bulkhead

5.4 Pressure plate and friction disc removal

oil seal or crankshaft rear oil seal. Check the friction disc hub and centre splines for wear.

3   Examine the pressure plate and diaphragm spring for wear which will be indicated by loose components. If the diaphragm spring has any blue discoloured areas, the clutch has probably been overheated at some time and the pressure plate should be renewed.

4   Spin the release bearing in the clutch housing and check it for roughness. Hold the outer race and attempt to move it laterally against the inner race. If any excessive movement or roughness is evident, renew the release bearing as described in Section 7.

7   Clutch release bearing and arm – removal and refitting

1   With the gearbox and engine separated to provide access to the clutch, attention can be given to the release bearing located in the clutch housing, over the input shaft.

2   If the gearbox is still in the car, remove the rubber boot and disconnect the clutch cable from the release arm with reference to Section 4.

3   Free the release bearing from the release arm and withdraw it from the guide sleeve (photo).

4   Pull the release arm from the fulcrum pin, then withdraw the arm over to the input shaft (photo).

5   Check the release bearing as described in Section 6. If there are any signs of grease leakage, renew the bearing (photo).

6   Refitting is a reversal of removal.

8   Clutch – refitting

1   It is important that no oil or grease gets on the clutch friction disc linings, or the pressure plate and flywheel faces. It is advisable to refit the clutch with clean hands, and to wipe down the pressure plate and flywheel faces with a clean rag before assembly begins.

2   Place the friction disc against the flywheel, ensuring that it is the correct way round. The flatter side of the disc (marked 'FLYWHEEL SIDE') must go towards the flywheel (photo).

3   Fit the pressure plate loosely on the flywheel dowels, aligning the previously made marks if the original plate is being refitted. Insert the six bolts and spring washers. Tighten the bolts finger tight, so that the driven plate is just gripped but can still be moved.

4   The friction disc must now be centralised so that when the engine and gearbox are mated, the gearbox input shaft splines will pass through the splines in the centre of the disc. Ideally a universal clutch centralising tool should be used (photo) or if available an old gearbox

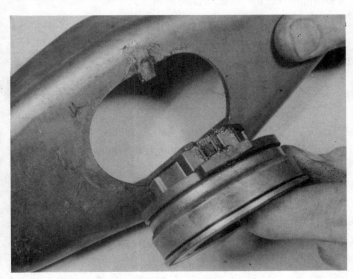

7.3 Showing how the release bearing is connected to the release arm

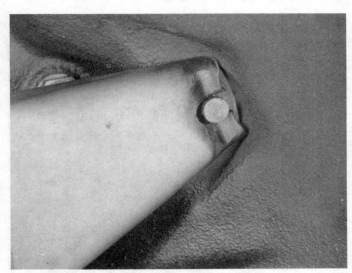

7.4 Release arm and fulcrum pin

7.5 Clutch release bearing

8.2 'FLYWHEEL SIDE' mark on the friction disc

8.4 Centralising the clutch friction disc

8.5A Tightening the pressure plate bolts

8.5B Clutch fitted to flywheel, ready for fitting of gearbox

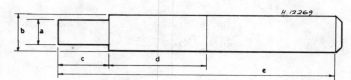

Fig. 5.5 Clutch centralising mandrel dimensions (Sec 8)

a = *Spigot bearing inner diameter = 16.3 mm (0.64 in)*
b = *Friction disc inner diameter = 25.45 mm (1.00 in)*
c = *31.75 mm (1.25 in)*
d = *44.45 mm (1.75 in) minimum*
e = *152.4 mm (6.0 in) approximately*

input shaft. Alternatively, a wooden mandrel can be made to the dimensions shown in Fig. 5.5.
5   Make sure that the centralising tool is located correctly in the friction disc and in the crankshaft spigot bearing then tighten the pressure plate bolts progressively in a diagonal sequence to the specified torque. Remove the tool (photos).
6   Make sure that the release bearing and arm have been refitted, then refit the gearbox (Chapter 6) or engine (Chapter 1) as applicable.

9   Fault diagnosis – clutch

Symptom	Reason(s)
Judder when taking up drive	Worn friction disc linings or contamination with oil Worn splines on friction disc or gearbox input shaft Engine/gearbox mountings loose or deteriorated
Clutch drag (failure to disengage)	Friction disc sticking on input shaft splines Crankshaft spigot bearing seizing Faulty cable self-adjusting mechanism
Clutch slip (engine speed increases without increasing road speed)	Friction disc linings worn or contaminated with oil Pressure plate defective
Noise when depressing clutch pedal (engine stopped)	Worn diaphragm spring Pedal shaft dry
Noise when depressing clutch pedal (engine running)	Dry or worn release bearing

Chapter 6 Manual gearbox and automatic transmission

Contents

Specifications

Manual gearbox

Type .... Four or five forward speeds and reverse, synchromesh on all forward speeds, constant four-wheel-drive on 4x4 models

Application
2.3 engine .... Four-speed (type B) or optional five-speed (type N1)
2.8 engine .... Five-speed (type N3)

Ratios

	B	N1	N3
1st	3.65:1	3.65:1	3.36:1
2nd	1.97:1	1.97:1	1.81:1
3rd	1.37:1	1.37:1	1.26:1
4th	1.00:1	1.00:1	1.00:1
5th	–	0.82:1	0.83:1
Reverse	3.66:1	3.66:1	3.36:1

Lubrication
Lubricant type/specification:
    4-speed and 4x4 gearbox .... Gear oil, viscosity SAE 80EP to Ford spec SQM 2C 9008-A (Duckhams Hypoid 80)

    5-speed non 4x4 gearbox:
        Early models .... Gear oil, viscosity SAE 80EP to Ford spec SQM 2C 9008-A (Duckhams Hypoid 80)

        Later models .... Semi-Synthetic gear oil to Ford spec ESD-M2C-175-A (Duckhams Hypoid 75W/90S)
    Transfer box (4x4) .... ATF to Ford spec SQM-2C 9010-A (Duckhams D-Matic)
Lubricant capacity:
    Type B .... 1.46 litres (2.6 pints)
    Type N (except 4x4) .... 1.9 litres (3.3 pints)
    Type N (4x4) .... 1.25 litres (2.2 pints)
    Transfer box (4x4) .... 0.5 litre (0.9 pint)

Torque wrench settings

	Nm	lbf ft
Clutch housing to gearbox casing	70 to 90	52 to 66
Clutch housing to engine	40 to 51	30 to 38
Clutch guide sleeve	9 to 11	7 to 8
Extension housing	45 to 49	33 to 36
Gearbox cover	9 to 11	6 to 8
Crossmember	20 to 25	14 to 18
Insulator to crossmember (except 4x4)	16 to 20	12 to 15
Insulator to gearbox (except 4x4)	50 to 57	37 to 42
Reversing light switch	1 to 2	0.7 to 1.5
Selector interlock	17 to 19	13 to 14
Filler plug (except 4x4)	33 to 41	24 to 30
5th gear collar nut	120 to 150	89 to 111
5th gear lockplate	21 to 26	15 to 19
Gear lever to extension housing	21 to 26	15 to 19
Countershaft cluster spigot	14 to 19	10 to 14
Insulator to crossmember (4x4)	20 to 26	15 to 19
Insulator to transfer box (4x4)	40 to 50	30 to 37
Filler plug (4x4)	40 to 60	30 to 44
Transfer box to transmission	45 to 49	33 to 36

Transfer box housing outer bolts	21 to 28	16 to 21
Transfer box housing central bolt	50 to 70	37 to 52

Automatic transmission
Type
Ford (Bordeaux) C3 three forward speeds and one reverse, epicyclic geartrain with hydraulic control and torque converter

Ratios
1st	2.47:1
2nd	1.47:1
3rd	1.0:1
Reverse	2.11:1
Torque converter	2.15:1

Lubrication
Fluid type/specification	ATF to Ford spec SQM-2C 9010-A (Duckhams D-Matic)
Fluid capacity	6.3 litres (11.1 pints)

Torque wrench settings
	Nm	lbf ft
Driveplate to converter	30 to 40	22 to 30
Sump	13 to 21	10 to 16
Downshift cable bracket	16 to 24	12 to 18
Starter inhibitor switch	10 to 14	7 to 10
Brake band adjusting screw locknut	47 to 61	35 to 45
Oil cooler pipe to connector	22 to 24	16 to 18
Oil pipe connector to transmission	24 to 31	18 to 23
Transmission to engine	30 to 37	22 to 27
Drain plug	27 to 40	20 to 30

1 Manual gearbox – general description

The manual gearbox fitted is either a four-speed (type B) or five-speed (type N). 4x4 models are fitted with a modified five-speed (type N) gearbox with a transfer box instead of the rear extension housing.

The gearbox construction is conventional. Drive from the clutch is transmitted to the input shaft which runs in line with the mainshaft. The input shaft and mainshaft forward gears are in constant mesh with the countershaft gear cluster, and selection of gears is by sliding the synchromesh sleeves, which lack the appropriate mainshaft gear to the mainshaft. Drive in 4th gear in direct (ie the input shaft is locked to the mainshaft). Reverse gear is obtained by sliding an idler gear into mesh with two spur-cut gears on the mainshaft and countershaft. All forward gear teeth are helically cut to reduce noise and improve wear characteristics.

The transfer box on 4x4 models incorporates a centre differential. Drive from the gearbox mainshaft is transmitted to the differential gear pivot shafts, and is then split to the rear wheels via an outer ring, and to the front wheels via an inner sun gear shaft. Due to the take-off diameters from the differential gears, 66% torque is transmitted to the rear wheels and 34% torque to the front wheels. Drive from the inner sun gear shaft to the front wheels is via a silent chain and specially cut chain wheels, front propeller shaft, final drive unit, and driveshafts. A viscous coupling is fitted between the front and rear drive outputs to improve traction, by limiting any speed difference between the front and rear wheels.

When overhauling the gearbox, due consideration should be given to the costs involved, since it is often more economical to obtain a service exchange or good secondhand gearbox rather than fit new parts to the existing gearbox.

2 Routine maintenance – manual gearbox and automatic transmission

Carry out the following procedures at the intervals given in 'Routine Maintenance' at the beginning of the Manual.

Check manual gearbox oil level
1 Either position the car over an inspection pit or jack up the front and rear of the car. The car must be level.
2 If the transmission is hot after a run, allow it to cool for a few minutes. This is necessary because the oil can foam when hot and give a false level reading.
3 Wipe clean around the filler/level plug, which is located on the left-hand side of the gearbox (photo). Unscrew the plug with a square drive key and remove it.

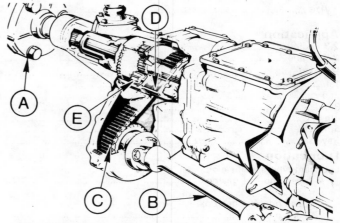

Fig. 6.1 Cutaway view of the transfer box fitted to 4x4 models (Sec 1)

A	*Rear propeller shaft*	D *Viscous coupling*
B	*Front propeller shaft*	E *Epicyclic centre differential*
C	*Drive chain*	

4 Using a piece of bent wire, chock that the oil level is in accordance with the following table.

Gearbox type	Oil level
All four-speed gearboxes	0 to 5 mm (0.197 in) below lower edge of filler hole
All five-speed gearboxes up to April 1984 (build code EG)	Level with bottom edge of oil filler hole
All five-speed gearboxes built from May 1984 (build code EC) to end of April 1985 (build code FP) and all vehicles built prior to April 1984 and subsequently fitted with a modified transmission extension housing	20 to 25 mm (0.788 to 0.985 in) below lower edge of filler hole
All five-speed gearboxes built from May 1985 onwards (build code FB)	1 to 5 mm (0.197 in) below lower edge of filler hole

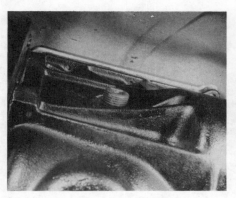

2.3 Manual gearbox (type B) filler/level plug

2.5 Topping-up the manual gearbox (type N)

2.12 Topping-up the 4x4 transfer box

5   Top up if necessary but do not overfill, as this can cause overheating leading to leakage and difficult gear changing (photo).

6   On the early five-speed (type N) gearbox, if persistent difficulty is experienced in engaging 1st or 2nd gear, the use of a semi-synthetic oil (see *'Recommended lubricants and fluids'*) may improve matters. Since no drain plug is fitted, it will be necessary to syphon the old oil out via the filler/level plug. Measure the volume of oil removed to be certain that it has all been recovered.

7   Refit and tighten the filler/level plug.

8   The frequent need for topping-up indicates a leakage, possibly through an oil seal. The cause should be investigated and rectified.

Check transfer box oil level (4x4)

9   Raise the car as described in paragraph 1.

10 Wipe clean the area around the filler/level plug. Unscrew and remove the plug.

11 Check that the oil is level with the lower edge of the filler hole.

12 Top up if necessary with the correct fluid (see *'Recommended lubricants and fluids'*), then refit and tighten the plug (photo).

Check manual gearbox/automatic transmission for leaks

13 Raise the car as described in paragraph 1.

14 Examine the manual gearbox/automatic transmission for leakage of oil or fluid. In particular check the rear oil seal and, on 4x4 models, the front propeller shaft oil seal in the transfer box.

Lubricate the automatic transmission linkage

15 Raise the car as described in paragraph 1.

16 Oil the selector rod end bushes, also the downshift cable end. Oil the downshift cable end at the carburettor as well.

Check automatic transmission fluid level

17 Refer to Section 18.

Adjust automatic transmission front brake band

18 Refer to Section 20.

3   Manual gearbox – removal and refitting

Note: *The gearbox can be removed together with the engine as described in Chapter 1, then separated from the engine on the bench. However if work is only necessary on the gearbox or clutch, it is better to remove the gearbox from under the car. The latter method is described in this Section.*

1   Position the car over an inspection pit, or alternatively on car ramps and/or axle stands so that there is sufficient working room beneath the car.

2   Disconnect the battery negative lead.

3   Working inside the car unscrew the gear lever knob.

4   Remove the centre console tray with reference to Chapter 11 if necessary.

5   Pull the outer rubber gaiter from the plastic frame and slide it from the gear lever (photo).

6   Remove the screws, or release the plastic clips, and withdraw the inner rubber gaiter and plastic frame from the gear lever (photo).

7   Using a Torx key remove the screws securing the gear lever to the gearbox and withdraw the gear lever (photo). Note how the gear lever locates over the selector shaft.

8   Remove the exhaust system as described in Chapter 3.

9   Remove the distributor cap and rotor arm as a precaution against possible damage when the engine is lowered.

10 Disconnect and plug the short heater hose at the bulkhead.

11 Unbolt the rear mounting clamps of the front anti-roll bar from the underbody (see Chapter 10).

12 Where fitted unbolt and remove the transmission heat shield.

3.5 Removing the gear lever outer rubber gaiter

3.6 Removing the plastic frame and gear lever inner rubber gaiter

3.7A Remove the Torx screws ...

3.7B ... and withdraw the gear lever

3.15 Reversing light switch and wiring

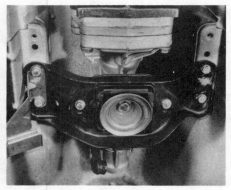
3.17A Gearbox (type B) mounting crossmember

3.17B Gearbox (type B) mounting cup removal

3.17C Gearbox (4x4) mounting crossmember

13 Remove the rear propeller shaft, and also the front propeller shaft on 4x4 models, as described in Chapter 7.

14 Except on 4x4 models, extract the circlip and withdraw the speedometer cable from the extension housing.

15 Disconnect the wiring from the reversing light switch (photo).

16 Support the gearbox with a suitable jack.

17 Unbolt the mounting crossmember from the underbody. If required, the crossmember may also be unbolted from the gearbox at this stage (photos).

18 Remove the starter motor as described in Chapter 12.

19 Disconnect the clutch cable from the release arm with reference to Chapter 5.

20 On 4x4 models support the front suspension crossmember with a suitable jack, then unscrew the four bolts securing the crossmember to the underbody until they are flush with the tops of the nuts. Lower the engine as far as possible.

21 Unscrew the bolts securing the gearbox bellhousing to the engine, and detach the heat shield where applicable. Note the location of the engine earth cable on the left-hand, second-from-top bolt, and the heater hose bracket on the right-hand, second-from-top bolt.

22 Lower the gearbox on the jack, then with the help of an assistant lift the gearbox direct from the engine and withdraw it from under the car (photos). Do not allow the weight of the gearbox to hang on the input shaft, and make sure that the car is adequately supported, since a little rocking may be necessary to free the gearbox from the dowels.

23 Refitting is a reversal of removal. Check that the clutch release arm and bearing are correctly fitted, and lightly grease the input shaft splines. Reconnect the clutch cable with reference to Chapter 5, refit the starter motor with reference to Chapter 12 and refit the propeller shaft(s) with reference to Chapter 7. Note that the clutch friction disc must be centralised in order for the gearbox input shaft to enter the crankshaft spigot bearing. Also check that the rear engine plate is correctly located on the dowels. Check and if necessary top up the gearbox oil level with reference to Section 2. On 4x4 models do not tighten the rear crossmember mounting nuts until the front suspension crossmember bolts are fully tightened (photos).

3.22A Lowering the gearbox (4x4)

3.22B Rear of engine with gearbox (4x4) removed

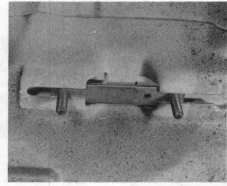
3.23A Right-hand gearbox mounting plate (4x4)

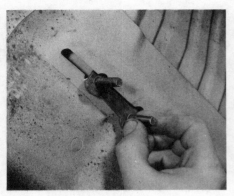

3.23B Left-hand gearbox mounting plate (4x4)

4.4 Extension housing rear cover removal

4.7 Selector locking pin and spring

4 Manual gearbox (type B) – dismantling into major assemblies

1 Clean the exterior of the gearbox with paraffin and wipe dry.
2 Remove the clutch release bearing and arm with reference to Chapter 5.
3 Where applicable unbolt the clutch bellhousing from the front of the gearbox.

4 Working through the gear lever aperture, use a screwdriver or small drift to tap out the extension housing rear cover (photo).
5 Unscrew the bolts and remove the top cover and gasket.
6 Invert the gearbox and allow the oil to drain, then turn it upright again.
7 Using a screwdriver, unscrew the selector locking mechanism plug then extract the spring and locking pin if necessary using a pen magnet (photo).
8 Extract the blanking plug from the rear of the gearbox casing and

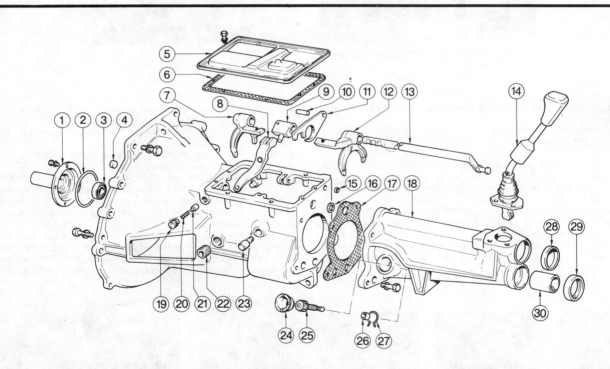

Fig. 6.2 Exploded view of type B gearbox housings and selector mechanism (Sec 4)

1 Guide sleeve	9 Selector boss	16 Oil seal	24 Cap
2 O-ring	10 Roll pin	17 Gasket	25 Speedometer drive pinion
3 Oil seal	11 Selector locking plate	18 Extension housing	26 Gasket
4 Plug	12 1st/2nd gear selector fork	19 Threaded plug	27 Retainer
5 Cover	13 Selector shaft	20 Spring	28 Cover
6 Gasket	14 Gear lever assembly	21 Locking pin	29 Oil seal
7 3rd/4th gear selector fork	15 Plug	22 Oil filler plug	30 Bush
8 Rev. gear relay lever		23 Plug	

4.8 Blanking plug removal

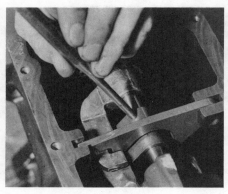

4.9A Removing the selector boss roll pin

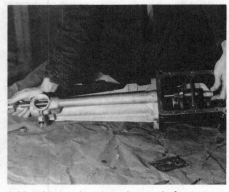

4.9B Withdrawing the selector shaft

4.10A Removing the selector locking plate and selector boss ...

4.10B ... and the selector forks

using a suitable drift through the hole, drive out the selector locking plate roll pin (photo).

9   Drive the roll pin from the selector boss, then withdraw the selector shaft through the selector forks and out of the rear extension housing (photos).

10 Note the location of the components then withdraw the selector forks, selector locking plate and selector boss (photos).

11 Unscrew the bolts securing the extension housing to the main gearbox casing.

12 Release the extension housing complete with mainshaft from the main casing, then turn the extension housing so that the cut-away reveals the countershaft.

13 Invert the gearbox and use a soft metal drift to tap the countershaft rearwards until it can be removed from the rear of the main casing (photo).

14 Turn the gearbox upright and allow the countershaft gear cluster to move to the bottom of the main casing.

15 Withdraw the extension housing complete with mainshaft from the main casing (photo).

16 Remove the input shaft needle roller bearing from the end of the mainshaft or from the centre of the input shaft.

17 Unscrew the bolts and withdraw the clutch release bearing guide sleeve from the front of the main casing. Note that the cut-out on the sleeve faces to the bottom of the casing. Remove the O-ring (photos).

18 Using a soft metal drift from inside the main casing, drive out the input shaft and bearing.

19 Remove the countershaft gear cluster together with the thrust washers, keeping them identified for location (photo). Take care not to lose the needle roller bearings and spacers from inside the gear cluster.

20 Insert an suitable bolt into the reverse gear idler shaft, and using a

4.13 Removing the countershaft

4.15 Withdrawing the extension housing and mainshaft

4.17A Unscrew the bolts ...

4.17B ... and remove the clutch release bearing guide sleeve ...

4.17C ... and O-ring

4.19 Removing the countershaft gear cluster

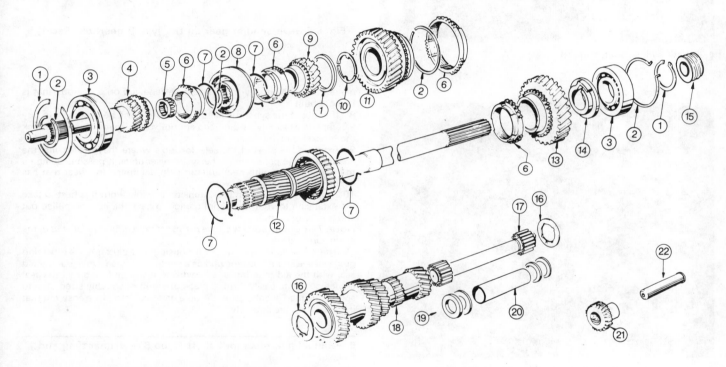

Fig. 6.3 Exploded view of type B gearbox gear assemblies (Sec 4)

1	Circlip	12	Mainshaft with synchroniser
2	Circlip	13	1st gear
3	Grooved ball bearing	14	Oil scoop ring
4	Input shaft	15	Speedometer drivegear
5	Needle roller bearing	16	Thrust washer
6	Synchroniser ring	17	Needle rollers
7	Retaining spring	18	Countershaft gear cluster
8	Synchroniser hub	19	Spacer
9	3rd gear	20	Spacer tube
10	Thrust half washers	21	Reverse gear idler
11	2nd gear	22	Idler shaft

nut, washer and socket pull out the idler shaft (photo). Note the fitted position of the reverse idler gear, then remove it.

21 Extract the circlip and withdraw the reverse relay lever from the pivot pin. Also disengage the return spring.

22 Prise out the speedometer drivegear cover from the extension housing and withdraw the drive pinion.

23 Squeeze the ends of the mainshaft bearing circlip together and extract it from the extension housing. Then using a soft-faced mallet drive the mainshaft from the extension housing (photo).

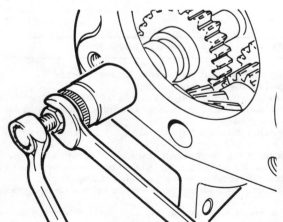

Fig. 6.4 Method of removing the reverse gear idler shaft on the type B gearbox (Sec 4)

4.20 Reverse idler shaft removal

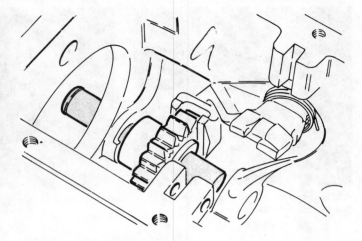

Fig. 6.5 Reverse idler gear on the type B gearbox (Sec 4)

4.23 Separating the mainshaft from the extension housing

5 Manual gearbox (type B) – inspection

1   Thoroughly clean the interior of the gearbox, and check for dropped needle rollers and roll pins.
2   Carefully clean and then examine all the component parts for general wear, distortion, slackness of fit, and damage to machined faces and threads.
3   Examine the gears for excessive wear and chipping of the teeth. Renew them as necessary.
4   Examine the countershaft for signs of wear, where the needle rollers bear. If a small ridge can be felt at either end of the shaft it will be necessary to renew it. Renew the thrust washers at each end.
5   The four synchroniser rings should be renewed as a matter of course.
6   The needle roller bearing and cage, located between the nose of the mainshaft and the annulus in the rear of the input shaft, is also liable to wear, and should be renewed as a matter of course.
7   Examine the condition of the two ball bearing assemblies, one on the input shaft and one on the mainshaft. Check them for noisy operation, looseness between the inner and outer races, and for

general wear. Normally they should be renewed on a gearbox that is being rebuilt.
8   If either of the synchroniser units is worn it will be necessary to buy a complete assembly as the parts are not sold individually. Also check the blocker bars for wear.
9   Examine the ends of the selector forks where they rub against the channels in the periphery of the sychroniser units. If possible compare the selector forks with new units to help determine the wear that has occurred. Renew them if worn.
10 If the bearing bush in the extension is badly worn it is best to take the extension to your local Ford garage to have the bearing pulled out and a new one fitted.
Note: *This can be done with the mainshaft assembly still located in the extension housing.*
11 The oil seals in the extension housing and clutch release bearing guide sleeve should be renewed as a matter of course. Drive out the old seal with the aid of a drift or screwdriver. It will be found that the seal comes out quite easily. With a piece of wood or suitably sized tube to spread the load evenly, carefully tap a new seal into place ensuring that it enters the bore squarely.

6 Manual gearbox input shaft (type B) – dismantling and reassembly

1   Extract the small circlip from the input shaft (photo).
2   Locate the bearing outer track on top of an open vice, then using a soft-faced mallet, drive the input shaft down through the bearing.
3   Remove the bearing from the input shaft noting that the groove in the outer track is towards the front splined end of the shaft.
4   Place the input shaft on a block of wood and lightly grease the bearing location shoulder.
5   Locate the new bearing on the input shaft with the circlip groove facing the correct way. Then using a metal tube on the inner track drive the bearing fully home.
6   Refit the small circlip.

7 Manual gearbox mainshaft (type B) – dismantling and reassembly

1   Remove the 4th gear synchroniser ring from the 3rd/4th synchroniser unit.
2   Extract the circlip and slide the 3rd/4th synchroniser unit together with the 3rd gear from the front of the mainshaft, using a two-legged puller where necessary. Remove the 3rd gear synchroniser ring (photos).
3   Remove the outer ring from the 2nd gear then extract the thrust washer halves.

6.1 Removing the input shaft bearing retaining circlip

7.2A Remove the circlip ...

7.2B ... and withdraw the 3rd/4th synchroniser unit, 3rd synchroniser ring, and 3rd gear

7.4 2nd gear and synchroniser ring removal

7.6 Removing the mainshaft bearing retaining circlip

7.10 Assembling the 1st/2nd synchroniser unit

4   Slide the 2nd gear from the front of the mainshaft and remove the 2nd gear synchroniser ring and thrust ring where applicable (photo).

5   Mark the 1st/2nd synchroniser unit hub and sleeve in relation to each other and note the location of the selector fork groove. Then slide the sleeve forward from the hub and remove the blocker bars and springs.

6   Extract the circlip retaining the mainshaft bearing. Then using a suitable puller remove 1st gear complete with the oil scoop ring, mainshaft bearing and speedometer drivegear (photo). Alternatively, support the 1st gear and press the mainshaft downwards.

7   Remove the 1st gear sychroniser ring.

8   If necessary the 3rd/4th synchroniser unit may be dismantled, but first mark the hub and sleeve in relation to each other. Slide the sleeve from the hub and remove the blocker bars and springs. Note that the 1st/2nd synchroniser hub cannot be removed from the mainshaft.

9   Clean all the components in paraffin, wipe dry and examine them for wear and damage. Obtain new components as necessary. During reassembly lubricate the components with gearbox oil and where new parts are being fitted lightly grease contact surfaces.

10 Commence reassembly by assembling the synchroniser units. Slide the sleeves on the hubs in their previously noted positions then insert the blocker bars and fit the springs as shown in Fig. 6.7 (photo).

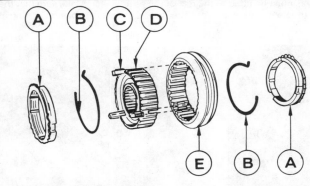

Fig. 6.6 Exploded view of a synchroniser unit (Sec 7)

A   Synchroniser ring
B   Springs
C   Blocker bars

D   Hub
E   Sleeve

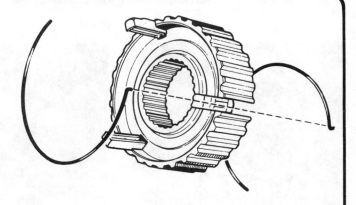

Fig. 6.7 Correct assembly of the synchroniser springs (Sec 7)

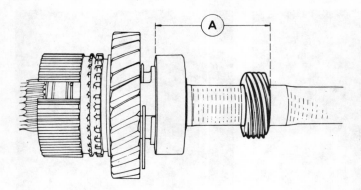

Fig. 6.8 Speedometer drivegear fitting dimension on the type B gearbox (Sec 7)

A = 49.25 mm (1.939 in)

8.1 Fitting the mainshaft to the extension housing

11 Fit the 1st gear synchroniser ring to the 1st/2nd synchroniser unit with the blocker bars located in the slots.

12 Slide the 1st gear and oil scoop ring (with the oil groove towards 1st gear) into the mainshaft.

13 If a new mainshaft bearing or extension housing is being fitted, the thickness of the retaining circlip in the extension housing must be determined at this stage. Using vernier calipers measure the width of the bearing outer track (B) then measure the total width of the bearing location in the extension housing (A) – the difference (ie A minus B) represents the thickness of the retaining circlip.

14 Fit the small circlip if applicable, then loosely locate the bearing retaining circlip as determined from paragraph 13 on the mainshaft.

15 Smear a little grease on the mainshaft, then fit the bearing and drive it fully home using a metal tube on the inner track. Fit the circlip.

16 Locate the speedometer drivegear on the mainshaft and use a metal tube to tap it into the position shown in Fig. 6.8.

17 Fit the 2nd gear synchroniser ring to the 1st/2nd synchroniser unit with the blocker bars located in the slots. Fit the thrust ring where applicable.

18 Slide the 2nd gear onto the front of the mainshaft and retain with the thrust washer halves and outer ring.

19 Slide the 3rd gear onto the front of the mainshaft then locate the synchroniser ring on the gear cone.

20 Locate the 3rd/4th synchroniser unit on the mainshaft splines with the long side of the hub facing the front. Tap the unit fully home using a metal tube then fit the circlip. Make sure that the slots in the 3rd gear synchroniser ring are aligned with the blocker bars as the synchroniser unit is being fitted.

21 Fit the 4th gear synchroniser ring to the 3rd/4th synchroniser unit with the blocker bars located in the slots.

8 Manual gearbox (type B) – reassembly

1 Immerse the extension housing in hot water for several minutes. Then remove it and quickly insert the mainshaft and push the bearing fully home. If necessary place the extension housing on the edge of the bench and use a soft-faced mallet to drive the mainshaft home (photo).

2 Using long nose pliers and a screwdriver refit the bearing circlip (photo).

3 Apply a little grease to the extension housing mating face and fit a new gasket (photo).

4 Insert the speedometer drive pinion in the extension housing, smear a little sealer on the cover then tap the cover into the housing.

5 Fit the reverse relay lever and return spring onto the pivot pin in the main casing, and fit the circlip.

6 Position the reverse idler gear in the main casing with the long shoulder facing the rear and engaged with the relay lever. Slide in the idler shaft and tap fully home with a soft-faced mallet.

7 Smear grease inside the ends of the countershaft gear cluster, then fit the spacers and needle roller bearings (photo). Make sure that the central spacer tube is fitted with thin spacers either side followed by 19 needle rollers and thick spacers on each side. Note that the long needle rollers must be fitted to the rear of the gear cluster. Make sure that there is sufficient grease to hold the needle rollers in position during the

8.2 Fitting the mainshaft bearing circlip to the extension housing

8.3 Locating a new gasket on the extension housing

8.7 Fitting the outer spacer to the countershaft gear cluster needle rollers

subsequent operation, and if available fit a dummy shaft of a length slightly less than the gear cluster.

8   Stick the thrust washers on the inner faces of the main casing with the location tabs correctly positioned.

9   Lower the gear cluster to the bottom of the main casing keeping the thrust washers in position.

10 Insert the input shaft fully into the main casing using a soft metal drift if necessary.

11 Fit the clutch release bearing guide sleeve together with a new O-ring. Check that the cut-out on the sleeve faces the bottom of the casing then apply sealer to the bolt threads. Insert them, and tighten to the specified torque in diagonal sequence.

12 Oil the needle roller bearing and locate it in the centre of the input shaft.

13 Insert the mainshaft together with the extension housing into the main casing so that the front of the mainshaft enters the needle roller bearing in the centre of the input shaft. Turn the extension housing so that the cut-away reveals the countershaft bore.

14 While keeping the thrust washers in place, invert the gearbox so that the countershaft gear cluster meshes with the mainshaft and input shaft.

15 Line up the thrust washers and insert the countershaft from the rear of the main casing. Using a soft metal drift drive the countershaft into the main casing until flush. The flat on the rear end of the countershaft must be horizontal (Fig. 6.9).

16 Fully insert the extension housing and make sure that the 4th gear synchroniser ring is correctly aligned with the synchroniser unit.

17 Apply sealer to the bolt threads then insert them and tighten to the specified torque in diagonal sequence.

18 Locate the selector locking plate in the main casing and retain with the roll pin.

19 Coat the new blanking plug with sealer and tap it into the rear of the casing.

20 Fit the selector forks and selector boss, then insert the selector shaft from the rear and guide it through the selector components.

21 Align the holes then drive the roll pin into the selector boss and selector shaft.

22 Insert the selector locking pin and spring, apply sealer to the plug threads, then insert and tighten the plug.

23 Fit the gearbox top cover together with a new gasket and tighten the bolts to the specified torque in diagonal sequence.

24 Fit the extension housing rear cover using a little sealer, and stake it in several places to secure.

25 Where applicable fit the clutch bellhousing to the front of the gearbox, apply sealer to the bolt threads, then insert the bolts and tighten them to the specified torque in diagonal sequence.

26 Fit the clutch release bearing and arm with reference to Chapter 5.

9 Manual gearbox (type N) – dismantling into major assemblies

Note: *On 4x4 models, disregard paragraphs 8 to 13 inclusive and instead remove the transfer box assembly as described in Section 14.*

1   Clean the exterior of the gearbox with paraffin and wipe dry.

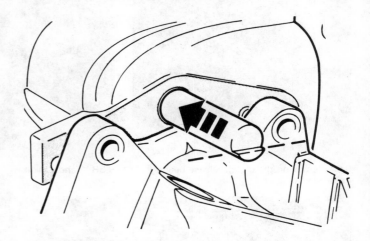

Fig. 6.9 Countershaft flat alignment on the type B gearbox (Sec 8)

2   Remove the clutch release bearing and arm with reference to Chapter 5.

3   Unscrew and remove the reversing light switch (photo).

4   Unbolt the clutch bellhousing from the front of the gearbox. Remove the gasket (photos).

5   Unscrew the bolts and withdraw the clutch release bearing guide sleeve and gasket from the front of the gearbox (photos).

6   Unscrew the bolts and remove the top cover and gasket (photos).

7   Invert the gearbox and allow the oil to drain, then turn it upright again.

8   Unscrew the bolts and lift the 5th gear locking plate from the extension housing.

9   Extract the 5th gear locking spring and pin from the extension housing (photos). Use a screw to remove the pin.

10 Working through the gear lever aperture, use a screwdriver or small drift to tap out the extension housing rear cover (photo).

11 Select reverse gear and pull the selector shaft fully to the rear. Support the shaft with a piece of wood then drive out the roll pin and withdraw the connector from the rear of the selector rod (photos).

12 Unbolt and remove the extension housing from the rear of the gearbox. If necessary tap the housing with a soft-faced mallet to release it from the dowels. Remove the gasket (photos).

13 Prise the cover from the extension housing and withdraw the speedometer drivegear (photo).

14 Select neutral then using an Allen key, unscrew the selector locking mechanism plug from the side of the main casing then extract the spring and locking pin if necessary using a pen magnet (photos).

15 Drive the roll pin from the selector boss and selector shaft.

16 If necessary the selector shaft centralising spring and 5th gear locking control may be removed. Using a small screwdriver push out

9.3 Reversing light switch removal

9.4A Clutch bellhousing bolts (arrowed)

9.4B Clutch bellhousing removal

9.5A Removing the clutch release bearing guide sleeve ...

9.5B ... and gasket

9.6A Remove the bolts ...

9.6B ... top cover ...

9.6C ... and gasket

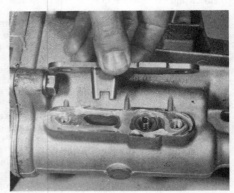

9.8 Removing the 5th gear locking plate

9.9A Extracting the 5th gear locking spring ...

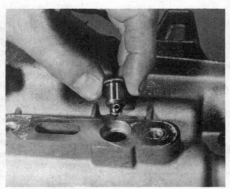

9.9B ... and pin

9.10 Extension housing rear cover removal

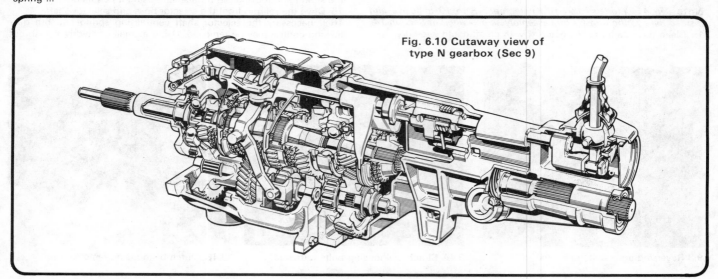

Fig. 6.10 Cutaway view of type N gearbox (Sec 9)

9.11A Drive out the roll pin ...

9.11B ... and remove the selector rod connector

9.11C Selector rod connector

9.12A Removing the extension housing ...

9.12B ... and gasket

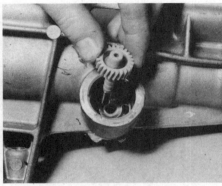
9.13 Speedometer drivegear removal

9.14A Unscrew the plug ...

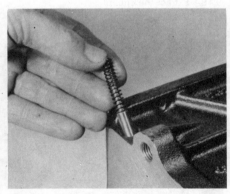
9.14B ... and remove the selector locking spring and pin

9.16A Insert a small screwdriver ...

9.16B ... and push out the plug ...

9.16C ... and pin from the selector shaft centralising spring and 5th gear locking control

9.17A Removing the selector boss and locking plate ...

9.17B ... 1st/2nd selector fork ...

9.17C ... 3rd/4th selector fork ...

9.17D ... 5th gear interlock sleeve ...

9.17E ... and 5th gear selector fork

9.18A Extract the circlip ...

9.18B ... and remove the 5th gear synchroniser dog hub ...

9.18C ... and 5th gear synchroniser unit

9.19 Removing the 5th driven gear

9.21 5th driving gear retaining nut removal

the pin and plug and slide the control from the selector shaft (photos).

17 Note the location of the selector components then withdraw the selector shaft from the rear of the gearbox and remove the selector boss and locking plate. 1st/2nd and 3rd/4th selector forks, and 5th gear selector fork and sleeve. Note that the roll pin hole in the selector boss is towards the front (photos).

18 Extract the circlip and pull the 5th gear synchroniser unit from the main casing leaving it loose on the mainshaft (photos).

19 Slide the 5th driven gear from the synchroniser unit hub (photo).

20 Select 3rd gear and either 1st or 2nd gear by pushing the respective synchroniser sleeves – this will lock the mainshaft and countershaft gear cluster.

21 Unscrew and remove the 5th driving gear retaining nut while an assistant holds the gearbox stationary (photo). The nut is tightened to a high torque setting and an additional extension bar may be required.

22 Remove the washer and pull the 5th driving gear from the countershaft gear cluster using a two-legged puller and socket in contact with the cluster. Remove the spacer ring (photos). Select neutral.

23 Extract the circlip retaining the countershaft gear cluster bearing in the intermediate housing (photo).

24 Using a soft-faced mallet tap the intermediate housing free of the main casing and pull the intermediate housing rearwards as far as possible. Using a screwdriver inserted between the intermediate housing and main casing, prise the bearing from the shoulder on the countershaft gear cluster and remove it from the intermediate housing (photo).

25 On June 1986-on models (build code GU), unbolt the spigot from

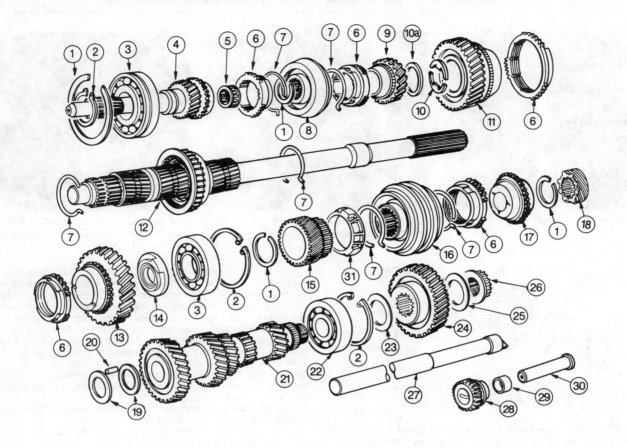

Fig. 6.11 Exploded view of type N gearbox gear assemblies (Sec 9)

1	Circlip	10	Thrust half washers	17	5th gear synchroniser hub	24	5th gear (countershaft gear cluster)
2	Circlip	10a	Thrust washer circlip	18	Speedometer drivegear	25	Washer
3	Ball bearing	11	2nd gear	19	Spacer	26	Twelve-sided nut
4	Input shaft	12	Mainshaft with synchroniser	20	Needle rollers	27	Countershaft
5	Needle roller bearing	13	1st gear	21	Countershaft gear cluster	28	Reverse idler gear
6	Synchroniser ring	14	Oil scoop ring	22	Roller bearing	29	Bush
7	Retaining spring	15	5th gear	23	Washer	30	Idler shaft
8	3rd/4th gear synchroniser	16	5th gear synchroniser			31	Blocker bar retainer
9	3rd gear						

9.22A Removing the washer from the 5th driving gear

9.22B Pull the 5th driving gear from the splines with a puller ...

9.22C ... and remove the gear from the countershaft gear cluster

9.22D Spacer ring removal

9.23 Removing the countershaft gear cluster bearing retaining circlip

9.24 Using a screwdriver to remove the countershaft gear cluster bearing from the intermediate housing

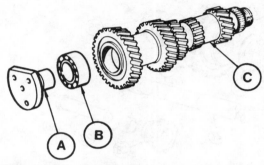

Fig. 6.12 Spigot (A) and roller bearing (B) fitted to the gear cluster (C) on the type N gearbox from June 1986 (Sec 9)

the front of the casing then drive it out from the roller bearing by inserting a soft metal drift through the countershaft gear cluster. Remove the drift and lower the gear cluster to the bottom of the casing.

26 On pre-June 1986 models, using a soft metal drift from the front of the main casing, drive the countershaft rearwards sufficiently to allow the gear cluster to be lowered to the bottom of the casing.

27 Ease the input shaft from the front of the casing, if necessary using a small drift inside the gearbox to move the bearing slightly forwards, then using levers beneath the bearing circlip (photo).

28 Remove the 4th gear synchroniser ring. Remove the input shaft needle roller bearing from the end of the mainshaft or from the centre of the input shaft (photo).

29 Remove the mainshaft and intermediate housing from the main casing. Remove the gasket (photos).

30 Withdraw the countershaft where applicable and gear cluster from the main casing (photos).

9.27 Input shaft removal

9.28A Removing the 4th gear synchroniser ring

9.28B Removing the input shaft needle roller bearing

9.29A Removing the mainshaft and intermediate housing ...

9.29B ... and gasket

9.30A Countershaft and gear cluster removal

9.30B Countershaft gear cluster

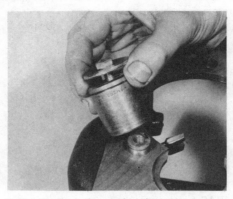

9.31A Method of removing the reverse gear idler shaft

9.31B Reverse idler gear removal

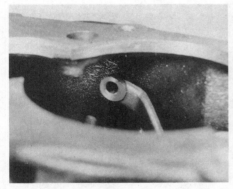

9.32A Location for reverse idler gear guide in the relay lever

9.32B Reverse relay lever and spring

31 Insert a suitable bolt into the reverse gear idler shaft, and using a nut, washer and socket pull out the idler shaft. Note the fitted position of the reverse idler gear then remove it (photos).
32 Remove the guide from the reverse relay lever then extract the circlip and remove the relay lever and spring from the pivot (photos).
33 Remove the magnetic disc from the bottom of the main casing. Also remove any needle rollers which may have been displaced from the countershaft gear cluster, if applicable (photo).

two ball-bearings and either one or two roller bearings (photos).
2 On June 1986-on models (build code GU) if the roller bearing is difficult to remove from the end of the countershaft gear cluster, break the bearing cage and remove the rollers, then use Ford tool 16-025 or a similar tool to extract the outer track. Drive the new bearing into position until flush with the cluster end face, making sure that the lettering faces outwards and using a suitable metal tube on the outer track only.

10 Manual gearbox (type N) – inspection

1 The procedure is basically as given in Section 5, however there are five synchroniser rings, no countershaft gear cluster thrust washers,

11 Manual gearbox input shaft (type N) – dismantling and reassembly

1 The procedure is identical to that described in Section 6 (photos).

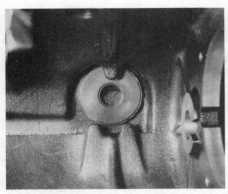

9.33 Magnetic disc location in the bottom of the main casing

10.1A Oil seal removal from the clutch release bearing guide sleeve

10.1B Fitting a new oil seal to the clutch release bearing guide sleeve

10.1C Location of the speedometer drivegear oil seal in the extension housing (except 4x4)

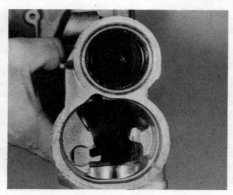

10.1D Rear view of the extension housing, showing the mainshaft oil seal and bush (except 4x4)

11.1A Extract the circlip from the input shaft ...

11.1B ... and remove the bearing

11.1C Using a metal tube to fit the input shaft bearing

12 Manual gearbox mainshaft (type N) – dismantling and reassembly

1   Extract the circlip and slide the 3rd/4th synchroniser unit together with the 3rd gear from the front of the mainshaft, using a two-legged puller where necessary. Separate the gear and unit, then remove the 3rd gear synchroniser ring (photos).

2   Remove the outer ring from the 2nd gear then extract the thrust washer halves (photos).

3   Slide the 2nd gear from the front of the mainshaft and remove the 2nd gear synchroniser ring (photos).

4   Mark the 1st/2nd synchroniser unit hub and sleeve in relation to each other and note the location of the selector fork groove, then slide the sleeve forward from the hub and remove the blocker bars and springs. Note that the synchroniser hub cannot be removed from the mainshaft (photos).

5   Using a suitable puller, pull the speedometer drivegear off the rear of the mainshaft (photo).

6   Remove the 5th gear synchroniser unit and 5th driven gear from the mainshaft.

7   Extract the circlip retaining the mainshaft bearing, then support the intermediate housing on blocks of wood and drive the mainshaft through the bearing with a soft-faced mallet (photos).

8   Remove the oil scoop ring, 1st gear, and 1st gear synchroniser ring (photos).

12.1A Extract the circlip ...

12.1B ... and remove the 3rd/4th synchroniser and ring ...

12.1C ... and 3rd gear

12.2A 2nd gear thrust washers and retaining ring location

12.2B Removing the outer retaining ring ...

12.2C ... and thrust washer halves

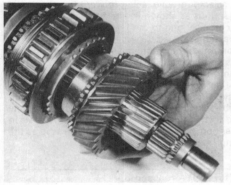

12.3A Removing the 2nd gear ...

12.3B ... and synchroniser ring

12.4A Removing the 1st/2nd synchroniser sleeve ...

12.4B ... and blocker bars

12.5 Speedometer drivegear removal

12.7A Mainshaft bearing circlip removal

12.7B Method of driving the mainshaft through the intermediate housing and bearing

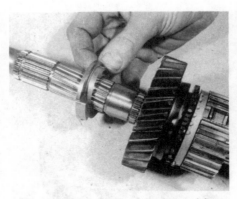

12.8A Removing the oil scoop ring and 1st gear

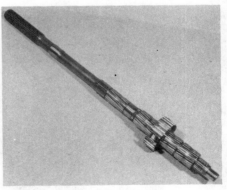

12.8B The dismantled mainshaft

12.9 Extracting the bearing retaining circlip from the intermediate housing

9   If necessary extract the circlip and drive the ball bearing from the intermediate housing using a metal tube (photo). Also the sychroniser units may be dismantled, but first mark the hub and sleeve in relation to each other. Slide the sleeve from the hub and remove the blocker bars and springs.

10 Clean all the components in paraffin, wipe dry and examine them for wear and damage. Obtain new components as necessary. During reassembly lubricate the components with gearbox oil and where new parts are being fitted lightly grease contact surfaces.

11 Commence reassembly by assembling the synchroniser units. Slide the sleeves on the hubs in their previously noted positions, then insert the blocker bars and fit the springs as shown in Fig. 6.7.

12 Support the intermediate housing then, using a metal tube on the outer track, drive in the new bearing and fit the circlip (photo).

13 Fit the blocker bar spring to the rear of the 1st/2nd synchroniser hub, followed by the 1st gear synchroniser ring (photo).

14 Slide the 1st gear and oil scoop ring (with the oil groove towards 1st gear) onto the mainshaft.

15 Using a metal tube on the mainshaft bearing inner track, drive the intermediate housing onto the mainshaft and fit the circlip (photo). Make sure the large circlip is towards the rear of the mainshaft.

16 Locate the 5th driven gear and 5th gear synchroniser with circlip, loose on the mainshaft. Tap the speedometer drivegear lightly onto its shoulder – its final position will be determined later (photo).

17 Fit the 1st/2nd synchroniser sleeve to the hub in its previously noted position with the selector groove facing forward then insert the blocker bars and fit the springs as shown in Fig. 6.7.

18 Fit the 2nd gear synchroniser ring to the 1st/2nd synchroniser unit with the blocker bars located in the slots.

19 Slide the 2nd gear onto the front of the mainshaft and retain with the thrust washer halves and outer ring (photo).

20 Slide the 3rd gear onto the front of the mainshaft, then locate the synchroniser ring on the gear cone.

21 Locate the 3rd/4th synchroniser unit on the mainshaft splines with the long side of the hub facing the front (photo). Tap the unit fully home using a metal tube then fit the circlip. Make sure that the slots in the 3rd gear synchroniser ring are aligned with the blocker bars as the synchroniser unit is being fitted.

13 Manual gearbox (type N) – reassembly

Note: *On 4x4 models, disregard paragraphs 24 to 31 inclusive, and instead refit the transfer box assembly as described in Section 14.*

12.12 Intermediate housing and mainshaft bearing

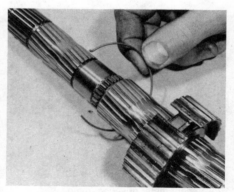

12.13 Fitting the blocker bar spring to the rear of the 1st/2nd sychroniser hub

12.15 Assembling the intermediate housing and bearing to the mainshaft

12.16 Fitting the speedometer drivegear

12.19 Location hole for 2nd gear thrust washer halves (arrowed)

12.21 Fitting the 3rd/4th synchroniser unit

1 Locate the magnetic disc in the bottom of the main casing.
2 Fit the reverse relay lever and spring onto the pivot and retain with the circlip. Fit the guide to the lever.
3 Position the reverse idler gear in the main casing with the long shoulder facing the rear and engaged with the relay lever. Slide in the idler shaft and tap fully home with a soft-faced mallet.
4 Where applicable, smear grease inside the end of the countershaft gear cluster then fit the spacers and needle roller bearings – there are 21 needle rollers. Make sure that there is sufficient grease to hold the needle rollers in position during the subsequent operation (photos). Note that on early models the countershaft bearing bore was 33 mm (1.3 in) long; on later models it is 25.75 mm (1.01 in) long, and the needle rollers are correspondingly shorter. When rebuilding an old pattern gearbox, use the new shorter rollers and insert two extra spacers behind them (Fig. 6.13).
5 Where applicable, insert the countershaft in the gear cluster until the front end is flush with the front gear on the cluster (photo).
6 Locate the gear cluster in the bottom of the main casing.
7 Position a new gasket on the main casing then fit the mainshaft and intermediate housing, and temporarily secure with two bolts.
8 Fit the input shaft needle roller bearing to the end of the mainshaft, or in the centre of the input shaft (photo).
9 Fit the 4th gear synchroniser ring to the 3rd/4th synchroniser unit with the cut-outs over the blocker bars, then fit the input shaft assembly and tap the bearing fully into the casing up to the retaining circlip (photo).
10 Invert the gearbox so that the countershaft gear cluster meshes with the input shaft and mainshaft gears.
11 On pre-June 1986 models, using a soft metal drift, drive the countershaft into the main casing until flush at the front face – the flat on the rear end of the countershaft must be horizontal (photo).
12 On June 1986-on models, apply sealing compound to the mating face of the spigot, insert it into the countershaft gear cluster front roller bearing, then insert and tighten the bolts. Tap the cluster onto the spigot as it is being fitted.

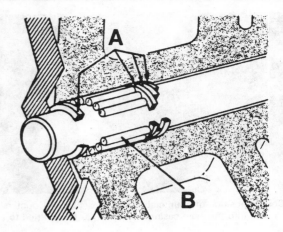

Fig. 6.13 Shorter countershaft rollers require extra spacers when fitted to early type N gearbox (Sec 13)

A Spacers   *B Rollers*

13 Using a metal tube tap the countershaft gear cluster bearing into the intermediate housing and secure with the circlip (photo).
14 Fit the spacer ring then, using a metal tube, tap the 5th driving gear onto the splines of the countershaft gear cluster.
15 Fit the thrust washer and retaining nut. Select 3rd gear and either 1st or 2nd gear by pushing the respective synchroniser sleeves. While an assistant holds the gearbox stationary, tighten the nut to the specified torque, then lock it by peening the collar on the nut into the slot in the gear cluster (photos).

13.4A Inserting the spacers in the countershaft gear cluster ...

13.4B ... followed by the needle rollers ...

13.4C ... and outer spacers

13.5 Countershaft inserted in the gear cluster

13.8 Fitting the input shaft needle roller bearing on the mainshaft

13.9 Fitting the input shaft

13.11 Correct position of countershaft before driving into the main casing

13.13 Countershaft gear cluster bearing being fitted to the intermediate housing

13.15A Tightening the 5th driving gear nut

13.15B Using a chisel to peen the nut collar

13.15C 5th driving gear nut locked to the countershaft gear cluster

13.17A Fitting the spacer to the 5th gear synchroniser unit

13.17B Fitting the 5th gear synchroniser unit to 5th driven gear

13.17C Fitting the 5th gear synchroniser ring and dog hub to the mainshaft

13.17D Fitting the circlip to the dog hub

16 Select neutral, then slide the 5th driven gear into mesh with the driving gear.
17 Slide the 5th gear synchroniser unit complete with spacer onto the 5th driven gear. Then using a metal tube, drive the dog hub and 5th synchroniser ring onto the mainshaft splines, while guiding the synchroniser ring onto the blocker bars. Fit the circlip (photos).
18 Tap the speedometer drivegear into its correct position on the mainshaft – the distance between the gear and the 5th gear dog hub circlip should be 123.0 to 124.0 mm (4.84 to 4.88 in) (photo).
19 Locate the 5th gear selector fork in its synchroniser sleeve and locate the interlock sleeve in the groove (short shoulder to front), then insert the selector shaft through the sleeve and selector fork into the main casing (photo).
20 Locate the 1st/2nd and 3rd/4th selector forks in their respective synchroniser sleeves, position the selector boss and locking plate, and

insert the selector shaft through the components into the front of the main casing. The roll pin hole in the selector boss must be towards the front.
21 If removed refit the selector shaft centralising spring and 5th gear locking control by inserting the pin and plug.
22 Align the holes then drive the roll pin into the selector boss and selector shaft (photo).
23 Insert the selector locking pin and spring, apply sealer to the plug threads, then insert and tighten the plug using an Allen-key.
24 Fit the speedometer drivegear to the rear extension housing. Apply a little sealer to the cover, then press it into the housing (photo).
25 Remove the temporarily fitted bolts from the intermediate housing, then select 4th gear.
26 Stick a new gasket to the extension housing with grease, and fit the housing to the intermediate housing. Take care not to damage the rear

13.18 Checking the distance between the circlip and speedometer drivegear

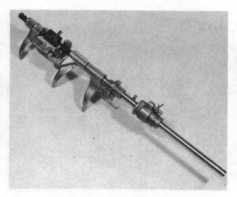

13.19 Selector shaft and components assembled on the bench to show relative positions

13.22 Driving the roll pin into the selector boss

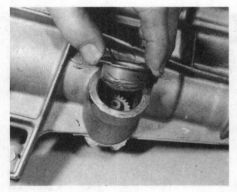

13.24 Fitting the speedometer drivegear cover (except 4x4)

13.26 Location of the selector shaft centralising spring pin (except 4x4)

13.27 Tightening the extension housing bolts (except 4x4)

oil seal, and make sure that the selector shaft centralising spring locates on the pin (photo).

27 Insert the bolts and tighten them to the specified torque in diagonal sequence (photo). Before inserting the three bolts which go right through the main casing, apply sealer to their threads.

28 Select reverse gear and locate the connector on the rear of the selector rod. Support the rod with a piece of wood then drive in the roll pin. Select neutral.

13.31 Applying sealer to the 5th gear locking plate location

29 Press the rear cover into the extension housing.

30 Check that the 5th gear interlock sleeve is correctly aligned, then insert the 5th gear locking pin and spring.

31 Apply some sealer to the 5th gear locking plate, locate it on the extension housing, and insert and tighten the bolts to the specified torque (photo).

32 Fit the gearbox top cover together with a new gasket, and tighten the bolts to the specified torque in diagonal sequence.

33 Fit the clutch release bearing guide sleeve (oil slot downwards) together with a new gasket, and tighten the bolts to the specified torque in diagonal sequence. Where necessary apply sealer to the bolt threads.

34 Fit the clutch bellhousing to the front of the gearbox together with a new gasket. Apply sealer to the bolt threads, then insert the bolts and tighten them to the specified torque in diagonal sequence.

35 Insert and tighten the reversing light switch in the extension housing.

36 Fit the clutch release bearing and arm with reference to Chapter 5.

14 Transfer box assembly (4x4) – removal and refitting

Note: *The transfer box assembly may be removed from the rear of the gearbox with the gearbox remaining in position. However, considering the relative inaccessibility of some of the components it is recommended that the gearbox is first removed from the car.*

1 Unscrew the transfer box oil filler plug, then tilt the gearbox and drain the oil into a suitable container.

2 Working through the gear lever aperture, use a screwdriver or small drift to tap out the transfer box housing rear cover (photo).

3 Select 3rd gear then support the selector shaft with a piece of wood, drive out the roll pin, and withdraw the gear lever connector through the rear aperture (photos).

4 Unscrew the bolts and lift the 5th gear locking plate from the transfer box housing (photos).

14.2 Transfer box housing rear cover

14.3A Drive out the roll pin (arrowed) ...

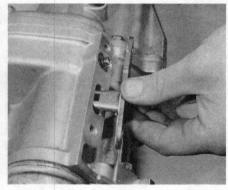

14.3B ... and withdraw the gear lever connector

14.4A Unscrew the bolts ...

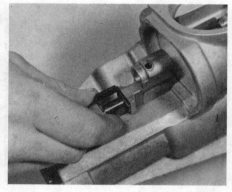

14.4B ... and remove the 5th gear locking plate

14.5 5th gear locking spring and pin removal

14.10A Wrap adhesive over the mainshaft splines before sliding on the oil seal

14.10B Checking the oil seal position on the mainshaft

14.11 Shift sleeve guide pin in the selector shaft (arrowed)

5   Extract the 5th gear locking spring and pin from the transfer box housing (photo). Use a screw to remove the pin.
6   Unbolt the transfer box assembly from the gearbox intermediate housing. Lightly top the transfer box housing to separate it from the intermediate housing, then withdraw the assembly over the mainshaft.
7   Remove the gasket.
8   Slide the mainshaft-to-sun gear shaft oil seal from the mainshaft.
9   Clean all traces of the old gasket from the housing faces.
10 Wrap adhesive tape over the mainshaft splines, then slide on the new oil seal until the outer edge of the oil seal is 23 mm (0.9 in) from the 5th synchroniser hub (photos).
11 Centralise the shift sleeve guide pin within the selector shaft (photo).
12 Position a new gasket on the gearbox intermediate housing (photo).

13 With the clutch bellhousing on the bench, lower the transfer box assembly onto the intermediate housing.
14 Apply sealant to the bolt threads, then insert them and tighten progressively to the specified torque (photo).
15 Refit the gear lever connector and drive the roll pin into the selector shaft.
16 Press the rear cover into the transfer box housing and secure by staking around the perimeter.
17 Insert the 5th gear locking spring and pin, and refit the locking plate. Before tightening the bolts, temporarily refit the gear lever and push it fully to the right in neutral. Tighten the bolts and remove the gear lever.
18 After refitting the gearbox, fill the transfer box with oil with reference to Section 2.

14.12 Intermediate housing with gasket fitted

14.14 Inserting the transfer box to main casing bolts

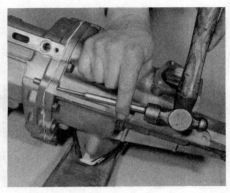

15.2 Driving out the dowel pins

15 Transfer box assembly (4x4) – dismantling and reassembly

1   Clean the exterior of the assembly and wipe dry.
2   Using a drift, drive out the dowel pins from the front and rear housings (photo).
3   Unscrew the housing bolts, including the central one by the oil filler hole (photo).
4   Place the assembly upright on the bench with the rear housing uppermost.
5   Withdraw the rear housing upwards, while tapping the driving chain wheel with a soft metal drift through the oil filler hole, to keep it in its normal position (photo).
6   Remove the endfloat shim from the output shaft or from the epicyclic centre stub (photo).
7   Remove the magnetic disc from the front housing (photo).
8   Mark the driver disc in relation to the ring gear, then slide them from the epicyclic centre differential and viscous coupling (photo).
9   Slide the epicyclic centre differential off the front-wheel-drive sun gear shaft (photo).
10 Mark the outer edge of the driving chain so that it can be refitted the same way round.
11 Simultaneously remove the viscous coupling, driven chain wheel

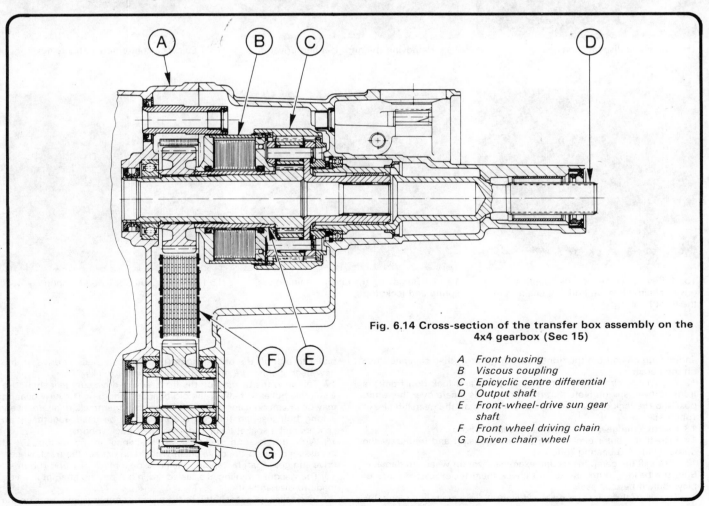

Fig. 6.14 Cross-section of the transfer box assembly on the 4x4 gearbox (Sec 15)

A   Front housing
B   Viscous coupling
C   Epicyclic centre differential
D   Output shaft
E   Front-wheel-drive sun gear shaft
F   Front wheel driving chain
G   Driven chain wheel

15.3 Removing the housing bolts

15.5 Separating the rear housing from the front housing

15.6 Endfloat shim (arrowed) located on the input shaft

15.7 Magnetic disc location

15.8 Removing the ring gear and driver disc

15.9 Epicyclic centre differential removal

15.11 Removing the viscous coupling, driven chain wheel and driving chain from the front housing

15.12A Removing the circlip retaining the spring and lock dog

15.12B Spring and lock dog location

and driving chain from the front housing (photo), then separate them on the bench.

12 Extract the circlip and remove the spring and lock dog from the front housing spigot. Note that the spring ends locate over the return post and the lock dog slot locates over the pin on the gearshift sleeve (photos).

13 Remove the gearshift sleeve and spacer (photo).

14 Extract the outer circlip from the rear housing and withdraw the output shaft and bearing (photos).

15 Clean all the components and examine them for wear and damage. Spin the bearing outer tracks and check them for excessive noise or play. Obtain new oil seals.

16 To renew the bearings on the driven chain wheel, use a suitable

puller to pull off the old bearings (photo), then press or drive on the new bearings using a metal tube on the inner tracks.

17 To renew the bearing on the front-wheel-drive sun gear shaft, use a suitable puller to pull off the old bearing (photos). The new bearing may be driven on using a metal tube on the inner track, or alternatively a long bolt inserted through the shaft may be used, together with spacers and a socket located on the inner track (photo).

18 With the bearing removed as described in paragraph 17, if necessary slide off the drive chain wheel and extract the front-wheel-drive sun gear shaft by tapping the latter on a block of wood (photos).

19 The viscous coupling is a sealed assembly, and no attempt must be made to dismantle it.

20 Insert the sun gear shaft into the viscous coupling, and press on the

15.13A Removing the gearshift sleeve ...

15.13B ... and spacer

15.14A Extract the outer circlip (arrowed) ...

15.14B ... and withdraw the output shaft

15.16 Using a puller to remove a bearing from the driven chain wheel

15.17A Removing the bearing from the sun gear shaft

15.17B Locate the new bearing on the sun gear shaft ...

15.17C ... and press into position with a long bolt and socket

15.18A Removing the drive chain wheel

15.18B Removing the sun gear shaft from the viscous coupling

15.20 Fitting the drive chain wheel

15.21A Extract the circlip ...

15.21B ... and remove the output shaft bearing with a puller

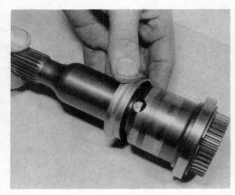

15.22 Removing the oil guide ring

15.24A Sun gear shaft front oil seal in the front housing

15.24B Sun gear shaft rear oil seal removal from the front housing

15.25 Fitting a new front propeller shaft oil seal to the front housing

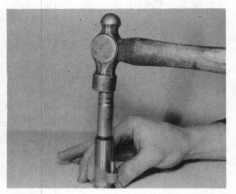

15.26 Fitting a new oil seal to the gearshift sleeve

drive chain wheel with the protruding collar facing away from the coupling (photo).

21 To renew the output shaft bearing, extract the circlip and use a suitable puller to pull off the old bearing (photos). Drive on the new bearing using a metal tube on the inner track.

22 Check that the oil guide ring is correctly located on the output shaft. Carefully tap it off and renew it if it is damaged (photo).

23 Refit the circlip to the output shaft.

24 Prise out one of the sun gear shaft oil seals from the front housing, then drive out the remaining oil seal using a drift. Press the new oil seals into position, noting that the rear seal has a metal insert which must face rearwards (see Fig. 6.15) (photos).

25 Prise the front propeller shaft oil seal from the front housing and drive in the new one using a metal tube or suitable socket (photo).

26 Prise the oil seal from the gearshift sleeve and drive in the new seal, using a 20 mm diameter metal tube or socket (photo).

27 Prise the gearshift sleeve oil seal from the front housing, and drive in the new seal using a metal tube or socket (photo).

28 Prise the selector shaft oil seal from the rear housing and drive in the new seal (photo).

29 Prise the oil seal from the rear of the rear housing. Check the rear bush, and if necessary renew it (photos). Ford tool 16-011 may be used to remove the bush, and a metal tube used to drive in the new bush. Similarly drive in the new oil seal.

30 Commence reassembly by inserting the output shaft and bearing into the rear housing. Fit the outer circlip in its groove.

31 Locate the gearshift sleeve and spacer in the front housing oil seal, with the housing on the bench.

32 Fit the lock dog and spring on the front housing spigot and secure with the circlip.

33 Engage the viscous coupling and driven chain wheel with the driving chain, then lower them into the front housing (photo). Make sure that the plain bore end of the driven chain wheel faces the oil seal, and that the previously made mark on the driving chain is uppermost.

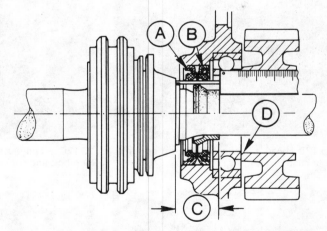

Fig. 6.15 Cross-section of oil seals between transfer box and main gearbox on 4x4 models (Sec 15)

A   Sun gear shaft front oil seal
B   Sun gear shaft rear oil seal
C   Mainshaft-to-sun gear shaft oil seal fitting dimension – 23 mm (0.91 in)
D   Drive chain wheel protruding collar

34 Slide the epicyclic centre differential into the splines of the front-wheel-drive sun gear shaft.

35 Fit the ring gear over the differential gears and engage it with the viscous coupling splines.

36 Fit the driver disc in the end of the ring gear.

15.27 Fitting a new gearshift sleeve oil seal to the front housing

37 Fit the magnetic disc in its location inside the front housing.
38 Before refitting the rear housing, check the correct thickness of the endfloat shim as follows. Measure the distance (A) between the output shaft bearing inner circlip and the rear housing mating surface (photo). Then measure the distance (B) between the ground surface of the driver disc and the front housing mating surface (photo). The difference between the two measurements (A – B), less a further 0.4 to 0.6 mm (0.016 to 0.024 in) for the end clearance, is the thickness of the endfloat shim.
39 Apply some grease to the endfloat shim and stick it against the output shaft bearing inner circlip.
40 Apply sealant to the mating surfaces of the front and rear housings.
41 Lower the rear housing onto the front housing, then tap in the dowel pins until centralised.
42 Insert the bolts and tighten them progressively to the specified torque. Note that the central bolt must be tightened more than the outer bolts.

16 Transfer box viscous coupling (4x4) – checking

1   Apply the handbrake and select neutral.
2   Jack up one of the front wheels and support the car on an axle stand. The remaining three wheels must be on the ground.
3   Remove the wheel cap and fit a socket on the driveshaft nut.
4   Using a torque wrench, turn the wheel clockwise approximately half a turn, taking approximately one second to complete the movement. The turning torque must be 70 ± 30 Nm (52 ± 22 lbf ft).
5   A low reading indicates a possible leak of fluid from the viscous coupling, or a deterioration of the fluid. A high reading indicates a partial seizure.
6   Renew the viscous coupling if the correct turning torque cannot be obtained.

17 Automatic transmission – general description

The automatic transmission which is fitted to 2.3 models in the Ford Bordeaux C3 type.
The unit has a large aluminium content, which helps to reduce its overall weight and it is of compact dimensions. A transmission oil cooler is fitted as standard and ensures cooler operation of the

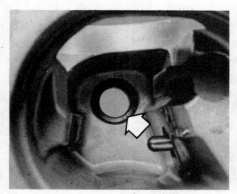

15.28 Selector shaft oil seal (arrowed) in the rear housing

15.29A Rear oil seal removal from the rear housing

15.29B Rear bush (arrowed) in the rear housing

15.33 Viscous coupling, driven chain wheel and driving chain fitted to the front housing

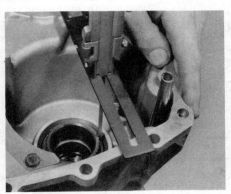

15.38A Measuring distance 'A' in the rear housing

15.38B Measuring distance 'B' in the front housing

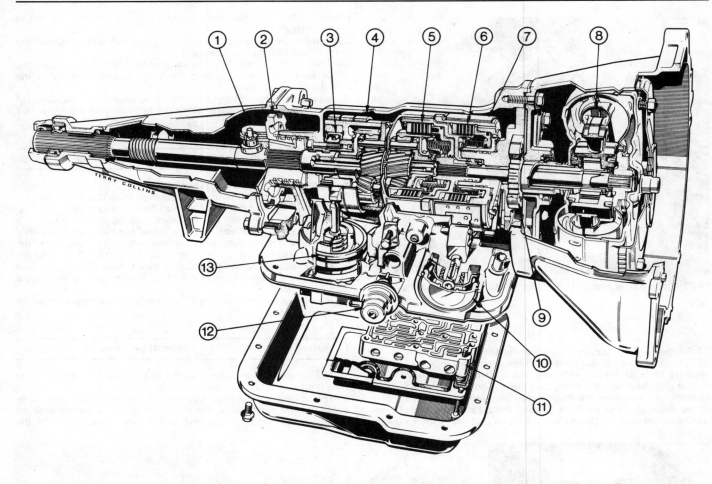

Fig. 6.16 Cutaway view of the C3 automatic transmission (Sec 17)

1	Centrifugal governor	5	Forward clutch	8	Torque converter	11	Valve body
2	Parking gear	6	Reverse and top gear clutch	9	Hydraulic pump	12	Vacuum diaphragm
3	One way clutch	7	Front brake band	10	Front servo	13	Rear servo
4	Rear brake band						

transmission under trailer towing conditions. A vacuum connection to the inlet manifold provides smoother and more consistent downshifts under load than is the case with units not incorporating this facility.

The system consists of two main components:

(a) A three element hydrokinetic torque converter coupling, capable of torque multiplication.

(b) A torque/speed responsive and hydraulically operated epicyclic gearbox, comprising planetary gearsets providing three forward ratios and one reverse ratio. Due to the complexity of the automatic transmission unit, if performance is not up to standard, or overhaul is necessary, it is imperative that this be left to the local main agents who will have the special equipment for fault diagnosis and rectification.

The content of the following sections is therefore confined to supplying general information and any service information and instruction that can be used by the owner.

18 Automatic transmission – fluid level checking

1 Locate the car on level ground and apply the handbrake.
2 Start the engine and let it idle, then apply the footbrake pedal and move the selector lever through all positions three times, ending at position P.
3 Wait for approximately one minute, then with the engine still idling

withdraw the transmission dipstick, wipe it clean with non fluffy rag, re-insert it and withdraw it again. The fluid level should be between the MIN and MAX marks. If necessary top up the level with the correct specified fluid through the dipstick tube.
4 Refit the dipstick and switch off the engine.

19 Automatic transmission – removal and refitting

Note: *Any suspected faults must be referred to the main agent or specialist before unit removal, as with this type of transmission the fault must be confirmed using specialist equipment before it has been removed from the car.*

1 Disconnect the battery negative lead.
2 Working in the engine compartment unscrew the four upper transmission-to-engine bolts, noting the location of the earth lead, vacuum line bracket, and dipstick tube bracket.
3 Jack up the car and support on axle stands. Make sure that there is sufficient working room beneath the car.
4 Remove the exhaust system as described in Chapter 3.
5 Remove the propeller shaft as described in Chapter 7.
6 Bend back the lock tabs, then unscrew and remove the bolts from the anti-roll bar rear mounting clamps, and lower the anti-roll bar as far as possible.
7 Remove the oil filler tube and plug the aperture.
8 Unscrew the unions and disconnect the oil cooler pipes from the

transmission. Plug the pipe ends and apertures. Remove the bracket from the engine mounting if necessary.

9 Remove the starter motor as described in Chapter 12.

10 Unclip and remove the selector rod.

11 Unscrew the locknut and disconnect the downshift cable from the transmission.

12 Disconnect the wiring plug from the starter inhibitor switch.

13 Unscrew the bolt and remove the speedometer cable from the extension housing.

14 Support the transmission with a trolley jack.

15 Unscrew the central mounting bolt from the crossmember and remove the cup.

16 Unscrew the bolts and remove the mounting crossmember from the underbody.

17 Lower the transmission three or four inches.

18 Disconnect and unclip the vacuum line.

19 Working through the starter motor aperture, unscrew the driveplate nuts. There are four nuts, and it is necessary to turn the engine to locate each one in turn in the aperture.

20 Unbolt the engine adaptor plate, then unscrew the remaining transmission-to-engine bolts.

21 With the help of an assistant lift the transmission from the engine, using the trolley jack to take most of the weight. Make sure that the torque converter is held firmly in contact with the transmission oil pump, otherwise it could fall out and fluid would be spilled. The car must be adequately supported since it will be necessary to rock the transmission a little to release it.

22 Refitting is a reversal of removal, but first make sure that the torque converter is fully engaged with the oil pump by checking the distance shown in Fig. 6.18. The torque converter drain plug must be aligned with the cut-out in the driveplate. Adjust the downshift cable as described in Section 22, and the selector rod as described in Section 23. Check, and if necessary top up, the transmission fluid level as described in Section 18.

20 Automatic transmission front brake band – adjustment

1 Apply the handbrake, then jack up the front of the car and support on axle stands.

2 Disconnect the downshift cable from the transmission.

3 Loosen the adjustment screw locknut and back off the screw several turns.

4 Using a suitable torque wrench tighten the screw to 14 Nm (10 lbf ft), then back off two complete turns and tighten the locknut.

5 Reconnect the downshift cable.

21 Automatic transmission starter inhibitor switch – removal and refitting

1 Apply the handbrake, then jack up the front of the car and support on axle stands.

2 Disconnect the wiring plug from the switch.

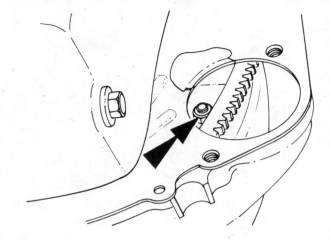

Fig. 6.17 Driveplate nut positioned in the starter motor aperture (Sec 19)

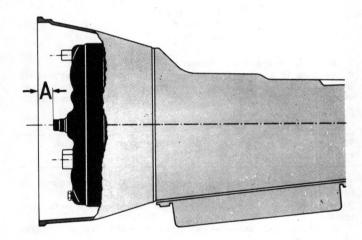

Fig. 6.18 With torque converter correctly fitted, dimension A should be 10.0 mm (0.4 in) minimum (Sec 19)

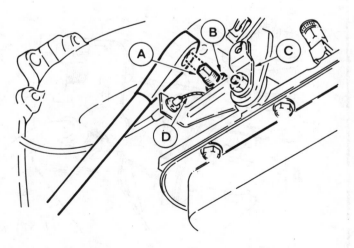

Fig. 6.20 Adjusting the front brake band (Sec 20)

A   Adjustment screw   C   Downshift lever
B   Locknut   D   Downshift cable

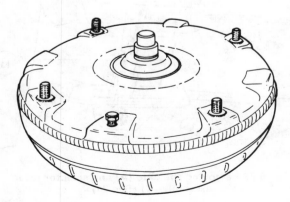

Fig. 6.19 Torque converter studs and drain plug (Sec 19)

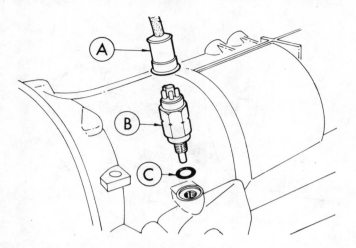

Fig. 6.21 Starter inhibitor switch components (Sec 21)

A   *Wiring plug*
B   *Switch*
C   *O-ring*

3   Unscrew the switch and remove the O-ring.
4   Refitting is a reversal of removal. Taking the necessary safety precautions, check that the engine will only start with the selector lever in positions P and N, and that the reversing light only glows in position R.

22 Automatic transmission downshift cable – removal, refitting and adjustment

1   Disconnect the downshift inner cable from the carburettor by removing the clip and pin.
2   Unscrew the locknut and release the cable from the carburettor bracket.
3   Apply the handbrake, then jack up the front of the car and support on axle stands.
4   Unscrew the locknut and disconnect the cable from the transmission bracket and lever.

5   Withdraw the downshift cable from the car.
6   Refitting is a reversal of removal, but adjust it as follows before lowering the car to the ground.
7   To adjust the cable, first check that the carburettor throttle fully opens when the accelerator pedal is depressed. While an assistant depresses the accelerator pedal, turn the lever on the transmission to the kickdown position and lock it in this position. Adjust the cable locknuts to give the dimension shown in Fig. 6.22, then tighten the locknuts.

23 Automatic transmission selector rod – removal, refitting and adjustment

1   Apply the handbrake, then jack up the front of the car and support on axle stands.
2   Unclip and remove the selector rod.
3   Move the selector lever to position 'D' and move the transmission lever two notches from the front stop. Fit the selector rod to the transmission lever, then adjust the rod so that it locates directly on the selector lever. Tighten the locknut.

24 Automatic transmission selector lever – removal, overhaul and refitting

1   Apply the handbrake, then jack up the front of the car and support on axle stands.
2   Pull off the clip and remove the selector rod from the selector lever.
3   Working inside the car unscrew the selector lever handle.
4   Remove the centre console tray with reference to Chapter 11.
5   Remove the gate cover and unclip the bulbholder.
6   Unscrew the four screws and withdraw the gate and selector lever assembly from the transmission tunnel.
7   Pull off the clip and push through the link pin to disconnect the upper and lower assemblies. Recover the two bushes and spring.
8   Pull off the clip and slide out the lower selector lever and shaft. Lift out the upper selector lever assembly and recover the washer and two guide bushes.
9   Remove the selector lever and spring from the guide.
10 Clean all the components and examine them for wear and damage. Renew them as necessary.
11 Reassembly is a reversal of dismantling, but lightly grease the bushes.
12 Refit using a reversal of the removal procedure, and finally adjust the selector rod with reference to Section 23.

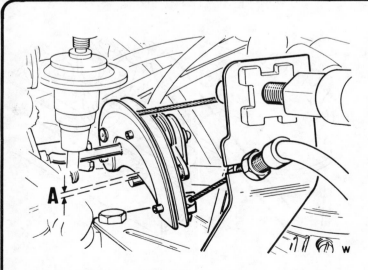

Fig. 6.22 Downshift cable adjustment dimension (Sec 22)

A = 0.8 to 1.0 mm (0.03 to 0.04 in)

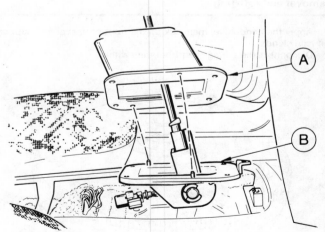

Fig. 6.23 Removing the gate (A) and selector lever assembly (B) (Sec 24)

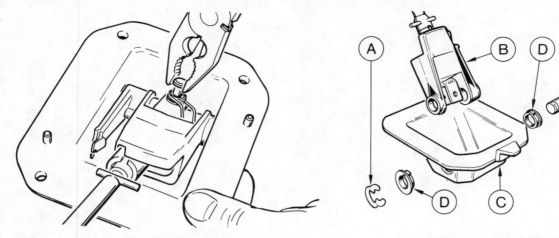

Fig. 6.24 Removing the link pin (Sec 24)

Fig. 6.25 Selector lever components (Sec 24)

A   Clip   D   Guide bushes
B   Upper lever assembly   E   Washer
C   Housing   F   Lower lever and shaft

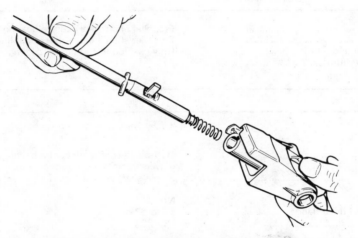

Fig. 6.26 Upper selector lever and spring removal (Sec 24)

25 Fault diagnosis – manual gearbox and automatic transmission

Symptom	Reason(s)
Manual gearbox	
Noisy operation	Oil level low, or incorrect grade Worn bearings or gears
Ineffective synchromesh	Worn synchro rings
Jumps out of gear	Worn synchro units Worn gears Worn selector forks Worn locking pins and springs
Difficulty in engaging gears	Clutch fault Worn selector components Seized input shaft spigot bearing

Automatic transmission

Faults in these units are nearly always the result of low fluid level, or incorrect adjustment of the selector linkage or downshift mechanism. Internal faults should be diagnosed by a main Ford dealer who has the necessary equipment to carry out the work.

Chapter 7 Propeller shaft

Contents

Specifications

General

Type:

Rear propeller shaft .... Two-piece shaft with centre bearing, standard centre and rear universal joints, front rubber coupling

Front propeller shaft (4x4) .... Single shaft with standard universal joints

Torque wrench settings

	Nm	lbf ft
Propeller shaft (front and rear) to final drive flange	57 to 67	42 to 49
Centre bearing to floor	18 to 23	13 to 17

1 General description

Drive is transmitted from the gearbox to the rear final drive unit by means of a two-piece propeller shaft, incorporating standard universal joints at the centre and rear, and a rubber coupling at the front. The centre of the propeller shaft is supported by a ball bearing in a soft rubber bush. Because the rear final drive unit is attached to the underbody, the working angles of the universal joints are minimal, and therefore wear in the joints is not likely to be excessive until very high mileages have been completed. The universal joints are of sealed type and cannot be serviced, however it is possible to renew the centre bearing and rubber coupling.

On four-wheel-drive models, a single propeller shaft transmits drive from the transfer box on the rear of the gearbox to the front final drive unit. The propeller shaft incorporates two standard universal joints, and the bearing end caps are retained with circlips (photo). Although it is possible to dismantle the joints, no spares are available at the present time.

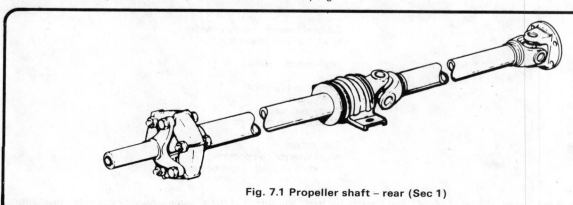

Fig. 7.1 Propeller shaft – rear (Sec 1)

1.1 Front propeller shaft universal joint (4x4 models)

2.4 Rear propeller shaft to final drive pinion flange bolts

2 Propeller shaft (rear) – removal and refitting

1   Jack up the rear of the car and support it on axle stands. Check both front wheels.
2   Unhook the exhaust rubber mountings and lower the exhaust system as far as possible without straining the manifold joints. The centre exhaust mounting bracket can be unbolted from the underbody if preferred. Support the exhaust system on axle stands, or by tying to the underbody.
3   Mark the rear universal joint and final drive flanges in relation to each other.
4   Unscrew and remove the bolts securing the propeller shaft to the final drive unit while holding the shaft stationary with a long screwdriver inserted between the joint spider (photo). If necessary apply the handbrake as an additional means of holding the shaft stationary.
5   Unscrew the two bolts securing the centre bearing to the underbody and lower the bearing noting the location and number of slotted shims on top of the mounting bracket (photos).
6   Detach the propeller shaft from the final drive unit then pull it from the rear of the gearbox (photo). To prevent any loss of oil/fluid from the gearbox a chamfered plastic cap can be inserted into the oil seal. Alternatively a plastic bag can be positioned on the gearbox and retained with an elastic band.
7   Withdraw the propeller shaft from under the car.
8   Select top gear. Remove the plastic cap or bag and wipe clean the gearbox rear oil seal and the propeller shaft splined spigot.

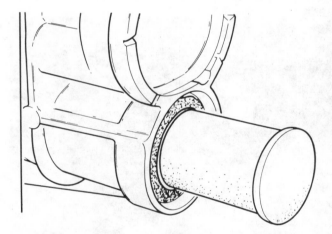

Fig. 7.2 Using a chamfered plastic cap to prevent loss of oil from the gearbox (Sec 2)

9   Insert the propeller shaft splined spigot into the gearbox rear extension, being careful to avoid damage to the oil seal.
10 Locate the rear of the propeller shaft on the final drive unit, then loosely attach the centre mounting bracket to the underbody with the two bolts.

2.5A Rear propeller shaft centre bearing

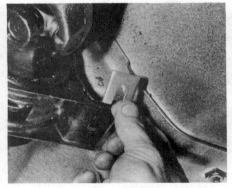

2.5B Removing a slotted shim from the centre bearing

2.6 Removing the rear propeller shaft from the gearbox

11 Insert the slotted shims over the top of the bracket.
12 Align the previously made marks if applicable. Then insert the rear flange bolts together with new spring washers and tighten them in diagonal sequence to the specified torque.
13 Tighten the centre mounting bracket bolts to the specified torque.
14 Using a length of board, check that the front and rear sections of the propeller shaft are accurately aligned, and if necessary adjust the shim thickness accordingly.
15 Lift the exhaust system and reconnect the rubber mountings, then lower the car to the ground.
16 With the car level, check and if necessary top up the level of oil/fluid in the gearbox. Refer to Chapter 6 for the correct procedure.

3 Propeller shaft (rear) centre bearing – renewal

1 Remove the propeller shaft as described in Section 2.
2 Mark the front and rear sections of the propeller shaft in relation to each other. Mark also the exact position of the U-shaped washer beneath the bolt located in the central universal joint.
3 Bend back the locking plate and loosen the bolt in the central universal joint so that the U-shaped washer can be removed (photo).
4 With the U-shaped washer removed, slide the rear section from the front section.
5 Pull the centre bearing bracket, together with the insulator rubber, from the centre bearing.

3.3 Rear propeller shaft centre bearing showing location of bolt (arrowed)

6 Remove the outer protective dust cap then, using a suitable puller, pull the centre bearing and inner dust cap from the front propeller shaft section.
7 Wipe clean the centre bearing components. Fit the inner protective dust cap to the new bearing and pack the cavity between the cap and bearing with grease.
8 Using a suitable metal tube on the inner race, push the centre bearing and inner cap onto the front propeller shaft section. Note that the red double seal end of the bearing must face the yoke.
9 Fit the outer dust cap and pack the cavity between the cap and bearing with grease.
10 Ease the centre bearing bracket together with the insulator rubber onto the centre bearing.
11 Screw the bolt and locking plate into the end of the front propeller shaft section, leaving a sufficient gap for the U-shaped washer to be inserted.
12 Slide the rear section onto the front section, making sure that the previously made marks are aligned (refer to Fig. 7.1 if necessary).
13 Refit the U-shaped washer in its previously noted position with the small peg towards the splines.
14 Tighten the bolt and bend over the locking plate to secure.

4 Propeller shaft (rear) rubber coupling – renewal

1 Remove the propeller shaft as described in Section 2.
2 Note which way round the bolts are fitted to the rubber coupling. The bolt heads are located on the flange arms and the nuts on the coupling (photo).
3 Unscrew the nuts, remove the washers, and pull out the bolts.

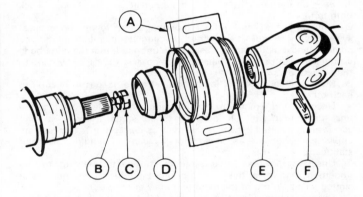

Fig. 7.3 Exploded view of the centre bearing (Sec 3)

A   Mounting bracket with   D   Ball bearing and dust caps
    rubber insulator   E   Splined universal joint yoke
B   Locking plate   F   U-shaped washer
C   Bolt

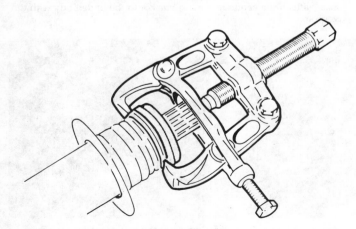

Fig. 7.4 Removing the centre bearing (Sec 3)

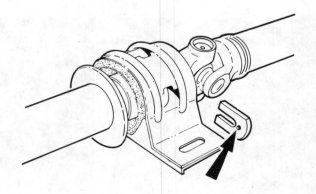

Fig. 7.5 Correct position of peg (arrowed) when refitting the U-shaped washer (Sec 3)

4   Fit the new coupling using a reversal of the removal procedure, but renew the bolts and self-locking nuts. To facilitate inserting the bolts it may be necessary to slightly compress the coupling, using a strap such as an oil filter removal tool strap.

5   Propeller shaft (front, 4x4) – removal and refitting

1   Apply the handbrake, then jack up the front of the car and support on axle stands.
2   Position a suitable container beneath the transfer box on the rear of the gearbox to catch any spilled fluid.
3   Mark the front universal joint and final drive flanges in relation to each other.
4   Unscrew and remove the bolts securing the propeller shaft to the final drive unit (photo), while holding the shaft stationary with a long screwdriver inserted between the joint spider. A Torx key will be required.
5   Detach the propeller shaft from the final drive unit, then pull it forwards from the splined chain wheel in the transfer box (photos).
6   Clean the flanged mating surfaces, the splined end of the propeller shaft, and the oil seal in the transfer box housing.
7   Insert the propeller shaft into the transfer box chain wheel.
8   Bring the two flanges together so that the previously made marks are aligned, then insert the bolts together with new spring washers and tighten them in diagonal sequence to the specified torque.
9   With the car level, check and if necessary top up the level of fluid in the transfer box (refer to Chapter 6 for the correct procedure).
10 Lower the car to the ground.

4.2 Rubber coupling fitted to the front of the rear propeller shaft

joint. Any movement within the universal joint is indicative of considerable wear, and if evident the complete propeller shaft must be renewed.
3   Wear in the centre bearing is characterised by a rumbling noise in the transmission.
4   The centre bearing is a little more difficult to test for wear. If bearing movement (as distinct from universal joint or rubber insulator movement) can be felt when lifting the propeller shaft front section next to the mounting bracket, the bearing should be removed as described in Section 3 and checked for roughness while spinning the outer race by hand. If excessive wear is evident, renew the bearing.

6   Universal joints and centre bearing – testing for wear

1   Wear in the universal joints is characterised by vibration in the transmission, or a knocking noise on taking up the drive.
2   To test a universal joint, jack up the car and support it on axle stands. Then attempt to turn the propeller shaft either side of the joint in alternate opposite directions. Also attempt to lift each side of the

5.4 Front propeller shaft to final drive pinion flange bolts

5.5A Withdrawing the front propeller shaft from the transfer box

5.5B Front propeller shaft (4x4 models)

7   Fault diagnosis – propeller shaft

Symptom	Reason(s)
Vibration	Worn universal joints or centre bearing
	Propeller shaft out of balance
	Deteriorated rubber insulator on centre bearing
Knock or 'clunk' when taking up drive	Worn universal joints
	Loose flange bolts
	Deteriorated rubber coupling
Excessive 'rumble' increasing with road speed	Worn centre bearing

Chapter 8 Final drive and driveshafts

Contents

Specifications

General

Final drive:
  Front (4x4) .... Bolted to right-hand side of engine sump, with intermediate shaft passing through sump
  Rear .... Unsprung, attached to rear underbody and crossmember
Driveshaft type .... Maintenance-free double Tripode type

Final drive ratio

Front (4x4) 3.62:1
Rear:
  2.3 models 3.38:1
  2.8 models 3.62:1

Final drive adjustment

Crownwheel and pinion backlash .... 0.10 to 0.17 mm (0.004 to 0.007 in)
Pinion turning torque:
  Front (4x4) .... 2.4 to 2.8 Nm (1.8 to 2.1 lbf ft)
  Rear .... 1.6 to 2.1 Nm (1.2 to 1.6 lbf ft)

Final drive oil

Type/specification .... Hypoid gear oil, viscosity SAE 90 to API GL5 (Duckhams Hypoid 90S)
Capacity:
  Front (4x4) .... 0.96 litre (1.69 pints)
  Rear (4x4) .... 1.00 litre (1.76 pints)
  Rear (except 4x4) .... 0.90 litre (1.58 pints)

Torque wrench settings

	Nm	lbf ft
Rear final drive unit cover	45 to 60	33 to 44
Oil filler plug	35 to 45	26 to 33
Rear final drive unit pinion flange nut	130 to 150	96 to 111
Rear driveshaft nut	250 to 290	185 to 214
Rear final drive unit to crossmember	70 to 90	52 to 66
Rear final drive unit rear mounting to body	30 to 35	22 to 26
Rear driveshaft bolts (Lobro)	38 to 43	28 to 32
Front final drive unit cover	9 to 11	7 to 8
Front final drive unit pinion flange nut	100 to 120	74 to 89
Front driveshaft nut (4x4)	205 to 235	151 to 173

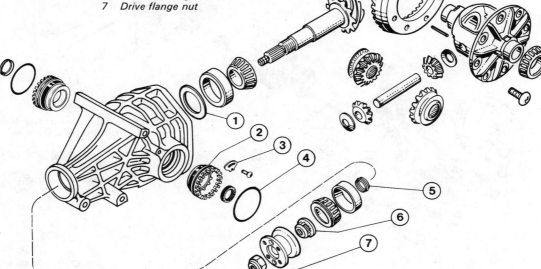

Fig. 8.1 Exploded view of the rear final drive unit with Tripode type driveshafts (Sec 1)

1   *Compensating washer*
2   *Bearing carrier*
3   *Locking plate*
4   *O-ring*
5   *Collapsible spacer*
6   *Pinion bearing nut*
7   *Drive flange nut*

Fig. 8.2 Cross-sectional diagram of the rear final drive unit without viscous limited-slip differential (Sec 1)

A   Collapsible spacer   *B   Drive pinion shim*   *C   Bearing carrier*

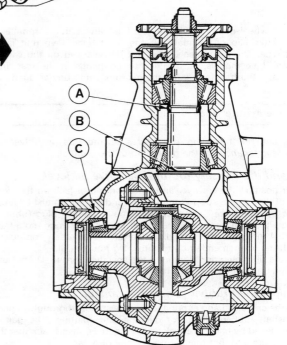

1   General description

The rear final drive unit is of unsprung type, and is attached to the rear underbody and crossmember. Two driveshafts transmit drive from the final drive unit to the rear wheels mounted on the fully independent rear suspension. The driveshafts may be of two types. The Tripode type includes stub axle shafts at each end, to engage with the final drive and rear hubs, whereas the Lobro type is bolted to flanges at each end. The final drive pinion runs in two taper roller bearings, which are preloaded by a collapsible spacer.

The front final drive unit on 4x4 models is bolted to the right-hand side of the aluminium engine sump. The right-hand driveshaft transmits drive directly from the final drive unit to the right-hand front wheel. Drive to the left-hand driveshaft is via an intermediate shaft enclosed in a tube, which passes directly through the sump. The front driveshafts are of the Tripode type, and the final drive pinion runs in two taper roller bearings.

Overhaul of the final drive unit is not covered in this Chapter, owing to the need for special tools and fixtures not normally available to the home mechanic.

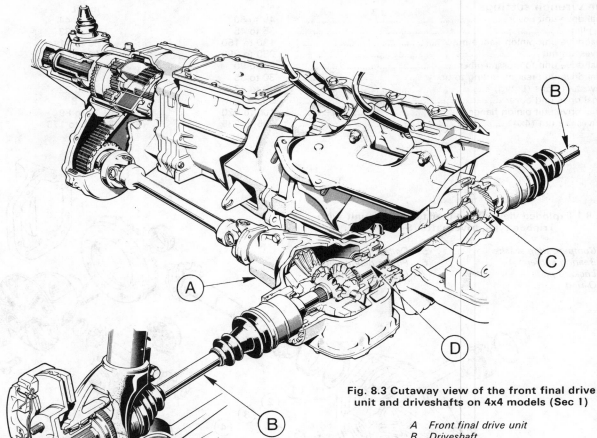

Fig. 8.3 Cutaway view of the front final drive unit and driveshafts on 4x4 models (Sec 1)

A   Front final drive unit
B   Driveshaft
C   Speedometer drivegear
D   Intermediate shaft

On four-wheel-drive models, the rear final drive unit incorporates a viscous limited-slip differential, but the front final drive unit is of standard type. The roadwheels must not be balanced on the car on four-wheel-drive models, as the viscous couplings in the rear final drive unit and the transfer box on the gearbox could be damaged.

2 Routine maintenance

Carry out the following procedures at the intervals given in *'Routine Maintenance'* at the beginning of the Manual.

Check and if necessary top up final drive oil level

1   Either position the car over an inspection pit, or jack up the front and rear of the car and support it on axle stands. The car must be level.
2   Using a hexagon key, unscrew and remove the filler plug (photo).
3   Using a piece of bent wire check that the oil level is no more than 10 mm (0.4 in) below the filler plug aperture. If necessary top up the level with the recommended oil (photo). Do not overfill.
4   Refit the filler plug and tighten to the specified torque. Do not use any sealing compound on the threads.

Check driveshaft rubber gaiters for damage

5   With the car raised and supported on axle stands, thoroughly check the driveshaft rubber gaiters for damage and splitting. The gaiters should be flexed by hand to check inside the folds. Also check that the clips are secure and that there is no leakage of grease.

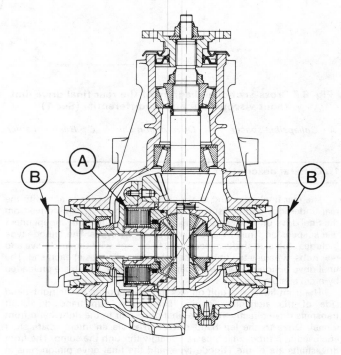

Fig. 8.4 Cross-sectional diagram of the rear final drive unit with viscous limited-slip differential (Sec 1)

A   Viscous coupling   B   Drive flange

2.2 Filler plug (arrowed) on the rear final drive unit (all models)

2.3 Topping-up the front final drive unit (4x4 models)

3.3A Removing a rear driveshaft outer joint plastic cover (non-4x4 models)

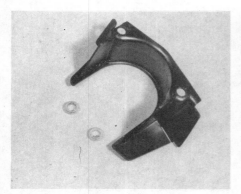

3.3B Rear driveshaft outer joint plastic cover and plastic retainers (non-4x4 models)

3.4 Removing rear hub retaining bolts (non-4x4 models)

3.6 Withdrawing the rear hub and brake assembly (non-4x4 models)

3 Final drive unit (rear) – removal and refitting

Non – 4x4 models

1 Loosen the rear roadwheel nuts, then jack up the rear of the car and support it on axle stands. Chock the front wheels and remove the rear wheels.

2 Remove the rear brake drums with reference to Chapter 9.

3 Unclip the driveshaft outer joint plastic covers from the upper brake backplate bolts (photos).

4 Using a socket through the holes in the hub flanges, unscrew the bolts securing the rear hubs to the lower suspension arms (photo).

5 Place a container beneath the final drive unit to catch any spilled oil.

6 Working on one side at a time pull the hub and brake assembly from the suspension arm sufficient to withdraw the driveshaft from the final drive unit (photo).

7 Refit the hub and brake assemblies and secure them with two bolts on each side. Tie the driveshafts to one side making sure that the deflection of each tripod joint does not exceed 13°.

8 Unhook the exhaust rubber mountings and lower the exhaust system as far as possible without straining the manifold joints. The centre exhaust mounting bracket can be unbolted from the underbody if preferred. Support the system on axle stands or by tying to the underbody.

9 Mark the propeller shaft rear universal joint and final drive flanges in relation to each other.

10 Unscrew and remove the bolts securing the propeller shaft to the final drive unit, while holding the shaft stationary with a long screwdriver inserted between the joint spider.

11 Unscrew the two bolts securing the centre bearing to the underbody and lower the bearing, noting the location and number of slotted shims on top of the mounting bracket.

12 Detach the propeller shaft from the final drive unit and tie it to one side.

13 Support the final drive unit with a trolley jack.

14 Unbolt the final drive rear mounting from the underbody, and remove the vent pipe from the hole in the underbody (photos).

15 Unscrew the two short bolts securing the front of the final drive unit to the rear suspension crossmember.

16 Lower the final drive unit slightly, then unscrew the nuts and remove the final drive unit mounting through-bolts (photo). Note the location of the U-shaped shims, if fitted.

17 Lower the final drive unit and withdraw it from under the car. Unbolt the mounting if required (photos).

18 Refitting is a reversal of removal, but do not tighten the mounting nuts and bolts until the final drive unit has been raised so that the rear mounting is touching the underbody. Check if any gaps exist between the tops of the side plates and the final drive unit, and if so use U-shaped shims to eliminate the gaps. Refer to Chapters 7 and 3 if necessary when refitting the propeller shaft and exhaust system. Top up the final drive unit oil level with reference to Section 2.

4x4 models

19 Chock the front wheels, then jack up the rear of the car and support on axle stands.

20 Mark the propeller shaft rear universal joint and final drive flanges in relation to each other.

21 Unscrew and remove the bolts securing the propeller shaft to the final drive unit, while holding the shaft stationary with a long screwdriver inserted between the joint spider.

22 Unscrew the two bolts securing the centre bearing to the underbody and lower the bearing, noting the location and number of slotted shims on top of the mounting bracket.

23 Detach the propeller shaft from the final drive unit and position it to one side on the exhaust system.

3.14A Removing the rear final drive unit mounting bolts ...

3.14B ... and vent pipe

3.16 Rear final drive mounting bolt locations (arrowed)

3.17A Remove the rear final drive unit ...

3.17B ... and unbolt the mounting bolts (arrowed)

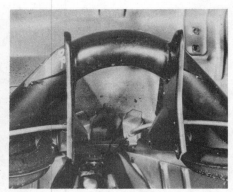

3.17C Rear final drive unit mounting bracket on rear suspension crossmember

24 Mark the rear driveshaft flanges and final drive output flanges in relation to each other.
25 Using a Torx key, unscrew the flange bolts, then tie the driveshafts to one side.
26 Support the final drive unit with a trolley jack.
27 Unbolt the final drive rear mounting from the underbody, and remove the vent pipe from the hole in the underbody.
28 Lower the final drive unit slightly, then unbolt the rear mounting from the rear cover.
29 Unscrew the two short bolts and the two through-bolts securing the final drive unit to the rear suspension crossmember, then lower the unit and withdraw it from under the car.
30 Refitting is a reversal of removal, but when locating the unit on the crossmember, insert the bottom through-bolt first and swivel the unit upwards before inserting the upper through-bolt. Refer to Chapter 7 when refitting the propeller shaft, and finally check and if necessary top up the final drive unit oil level, with reference to Section 2.

4 Final drive unit (rear) pinion oil seal – renewal

1 Remove the propeller shaft as described in Chapter 7.
2 Hold the final drive flange stationary by bolting a long bar to it, or by fitting two long bolts to it and inserting a long bar between them.
3 Unscrew the self-locking pinion flange nut (photo).
4 Using a suitable puller, pull the drive flange from the pinion (photos). As there may be some loss of oil, place a sutable container beneath the final drive unit.
5 Using a screwdriver, lever the oil seal from the final drive unit (photo).
6 Clean the oil seal seating within the housing, the drive flange, and the end of the pinion.
7 Fill the space between the lips of the new oil seal with grease. Then

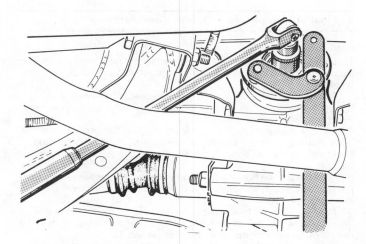

Fig. 8.5 Using a special tool to hold the final drive flange stationary while unscrewing the nut (Sec 4)

using a suitable metal tube or block of wood with a hole in it, drive the seal squarely into the final drive housing until flush.
8 Slide the drive flange onto the pinion splines, taking care not to damage the oil seal.
9 Fit the self-locking nut and tighten it to the specified torque while holding the drive flange stationary using the method described in paragraph 2 (photo). Ideally a new self-locking nut should be used,

4.3 Rear final drive unit pinion flange nut removal

4.4A Using a puller to remove the rear final drive unit pinion flange

4.4B Showing splines on the drive flange and pinion

4.5 Pinion oil seal location in the rear final drive unit

4.9 Tightening the final drive pinion flange nut

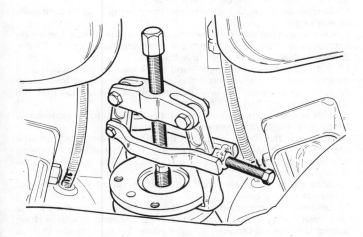

Fig. 8.6 Removing the final drive flange (Sec 4)

Fig. 8.7 Final drive unit pinion oil seal installation (Sec 4)

and it should not be unscrewed and tightened more than three times, otherwise it will lose its self-locking characteristic.
10 Refit the propeller shaft as described in Chapter 7.
11 Top up the final drive unit oil level with reference to Section 2.

5 Final drive unit (rear, except 4x4) differential bearing oil seals – renewal

1 Remove the driveshafts as described in Section 11.
2 Using vernier calipers, measure the fitted depth of the oil seals in the differential bearing housings. This should be approximately 11.23

mm (0.442 in) measured from the outer face of the retaining ring.
3 Using a screwdriver or hooked instrument, lever the oil seals from the differential bearing housings (photo). If available, Ford tool 15 048 may be used. This tool has internally expanding legs which grip the oil seal.
4 Clean the oil seal seatings in the housings.
5 Smear the lips of both oil seals with a little grease. Then using a suitable metal tube, press each seal squarely into its differential bearing housing to the previously noted depth. Alternatively use Ford tool 15 076, noting that the tool can be used in two different positions according to the size of crownwheel fitted. A 177.8 mm (7.0 in) diameter crownwheel is fitted on all models.
6 Refit the driveshafts as described in Section 11.

5.3 Differential bearing oil seal (arrowed) in the rear final drive unit

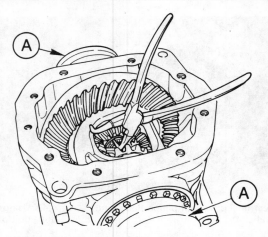

Fig. 8.8 Extracting the circlips in order to remove the final drive output shafts 'A' (Sec 6)

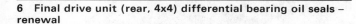

6 Final drive unit (rear, 4x4) differential bearing oil seals – renewal

1   Remove the final drive unit as described in Section 3.
2   Place the unit in a suitable container, then using a Torx key, unbolt and remove the rear cover and allow the oil to drain.
3   Using circlip pliers, extract the circlips securing the output shafts to the differential side gears, and withdraw the shafts. Note that the left-hand shaft is longer than the right-hand shaft, because the viscous coupling is on the left-hand side of the final drive unit.
4   Fit the new oil seals by following the procedure described in Section 5, paragraphs 2 to 5 inclusive.
5   Clean the output shafts and insert them into the differential side gears, then refit the circlips.
6   Clean the rear cover and the rear face of the final drive casing. Apply a bead of liquid sealant to the mating faces.
7   Refit the rear cover, insert the bolts and tighten them progressively in diagonal sequence to the specified torque.
8   Refit the final drive unit with reference to Section 3.

7 Final drive unit (rear, 4x4) viscous differential – checking

1   Chock the front wheels, then jack up the rear of the car and support on axle stands.
2   Remove one of the rear wheels, then fully release the handbrake.
3   Fit a socket on the driveshaft nut, then using a torque wrench, turn the hub clockwise approximately half a turn, taking approximately one second to complete the movement. The turning torque must be 70 ± 30 Nm (52 ± 22 lbf ft). Note that the propeller shaft must not turn during the check, if necessary it should be held stationary, or top gear engaged.
4   If the correct turning torque is not obtained, the viscous differential is faulty and will need to be renewed.

8 Final drive unit (front, 4x4) – removal and refitting

1   Disconnect the battery negative lead.
2   Working in the engine compartment, unscrew the bolt securing the steering intermediate shaft to the inner column, swivel the clamp plate to one side, and disconnect the intermediate shaft.
3   Unscrew the union bolt and disconnect the pressure line from the power steering pump. Position a suitable container beneath the pump to catch any spilled fluid.

4   Unscrew the upper nuts from the left and right engine mountings.
5   Apply the handbrake, then jack up the front of the car and support on axle stands. Remove the front roadwheels.
6   Position a suitable container beneath the engine, then unscrew the sump drain plug and drain the engine oil. Clean and refit the drain plug on completion.
7   Attach a suitable hoist to the engine and raise it slightly.
8   Disconnect the power steering return hose from the return pipe on the lower right-hand side of the engine compartment, and catch any spilled fluid in a suitable container.
9   Remove the steering intermediate shaft by unscrewing the clamp bolt and sliding the shaft from the splined steering gear pinion. A master spline ensures correct refitment, but it is helpful to also mark the shaft and pinion in relation to each other.
10 Disconnect the track rod ends from the steering arms on both sides by referring to Chapter 10.
11 Disconnect the lower suspension arms from the spindle carriers on both sides by unscrewing the nuts and removing the Torx bolts. Do not attempt to turn the Torx bolts, only the nuts.
12 Pull the bottom of the right-hand suspension strut outwards until the inner end of the driveshaft is clear of the final drive unit, then tie the driveshaft to one side. Similarly, pull the left-hand driveshaft from the intermediate shaft and tie it to one side.
13 Unscrew the bolts securing the front anti-roll bar to the underbody.
14 Support the front crossmember on a trolley jack.
15 Unscrew the bolts securing the front crossmember to the underbody, then lower the crossmember together with the steering gear, lower suspension arms, anti-roll bar and engine mountings to the floor.
16 Mark the front propeller shaft universal joint and final drive flanges in relation to each other.
17 Unscrew and remove the bolts securing the propeller shaft to the final drive unit, while holding the shaft stationary with a long screwdriver inserted between the joint spider. Tie the propeller shaft to one side.
18 Unscrew the three bolts securing the final drive unit to the engine sump, then support the unit and carefully lever it out (photos).
19 Remove the O-ring seals (photos).
20 Refitting is a reversal of removal, but fit new O-ring seals after dipping them in engine oil. Tighten all nuts and bolts to the specified torque. With the car level, fill the engine and final drive unit with oil. Fill and bleed the power steering system with reference to Chapter 10.

9 Final drive unit (front, 4x4) pinion oil seal – renewal

1   Remove the propeller shaft as described in Chapter 7.
2   Using a screwdriver, prise the special locking washer from the cut-outs in the pinion flange.
3   Hold the final drive flange stationary by bolting a long bar to it, or

8.18A Front final drive unit to engine sump mounting bolts (arrowed)

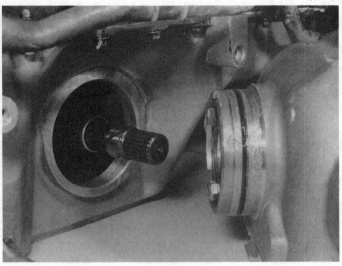

8.18B Removing the front final drive unit from the engine sump

8.19A Front final drive unit outer O-ring ...

8.19B ... and inner O-ring

by fitting two long bolts to it and inserting a long bar between them.

4   Unscrew the pinion flange nut after marking it in relation to the pinion.

5   Using a suitable puller, pull the drive flange from the pinion. As there may be some loss of oil, place a suitable container beneath the final drive unit.

6   Using a screwdriver, lever the oil seal from the final drive unit, noting its location depth.

7   Clean the oil seal seating within the housing, the drive flange, and the end of the pinion.

8   Check that the space between the lips of the new oil seal is filled with grease. Using a suitable metal tube or block of wood with a hole in it, drive the seal squarely into the final drive housing to the previously noted depth.

9   Slide the drive flange onto the pinion splines, taking care not to damage the oil seal.

10 Fit the nut and tighten it until the previously made marks are aligned. Hold the drive flange as described in paragraph 3 and after tightening the nut, check that the pinion turning torque is within the tolerance given in Specifications. Note that if the nut is over tightened it will be necessary to strip the final drive unit and review the

collapsible spacer on the pinion, and then to tighten the nut until the turning torque of the pinion is as specified.

11 Coat the nut with locking fluid, then fit a new locking washer and stake it into the cut-outs in the drive flange.

12 Refit the propeller shaft as described in Chapter 7.

13 Top up the final drive unit oil level with reference to Section 2.

10 Final drive unit (front, 4x4) differential bearing and intermediate shaft oil seals – renewal

Differential bearing oil seal

1   Disconnect the battery negative lead.

2   Apply the handbrake, then jack up the front of the car and support on axle stands. Remove the right-hand front roadwheel.

3   Disconnect the right-hand track rod end from the steering arm by referring to Chapter 10.

4   Disconnect the lower suspension arm from the right-hand spindle carrier by unscrewing the nut and removing the Torx bolt. Do not attempt to turn the Torx bolt, only the nut.

5 Pull the bottom of the suspension strut outwards until the inner end of the driveshaft is clear of the final drive unit, then tie the driveshaft to one side. Catch any spilled oil in a suitable container, and note that the driveshaft joints must not be inclined more than 20°.
6 Note the fitted depth of the oil seal, then use a screwdriver to prise it out of the bearing housing.
7 Clean the oil seal seating.
8 Smear the lip of the new oil seal with a little grease, then using a suitable metal tube press it squarely into the differential bearing housing to the previously noted depth.
9 Refit the driveshaft, lower suspension arm, and track rod end using a reversal of the removal procedure. Refit the roadwheel and reconnect the battery negative lead.
10 With the car level, top up the final drive unit with oil then lower the car to the ground.

Intermediate shaft oil seal

11 The procedure is basically as described in the previous paragraphs 1 to 10, working on the left-hand side of the car.

11 Driveshaft (rear) – removal and refitting

Tripode type

1 Remove the wheel cap as applicable and loosen the wheel nuts.
2 Loosen the driveshaft nut at the centre of the hub, noting that from September 1983 (build code DJ), the left-hand nut has a **left-hand thread.**
3 Jack up the rear of the car and support it on axle stands. Chock the front wheels and release the handbrake.
4 Remove the wheel and the driveshaft nut.
5 Remove the brake drum, with reference to Chapter 9 if necessary.
6 Using a suitable puller, pull the drive flange from the hub and off the driveshaft.
7 Unclip the driveshaft outer joint plastic cover from the upper brake backplate bolts.
8 Unscrew the four bolts securing the hub and brake backplate to the lower suspension arm.
9 Place a container beneath the final drive unit to catch any spilled oil.
10 Pull the hub and brake assembly from the suspension arm sufficient to withdraw the driveshaft from the final drive unit, then withdraw the driveshaft from the hub (photos). Note that the deflection of each tripod joint should not exceed 13°.
11 In order to prevent possible damage to the hydraulic brake pipe, attach the hub and brake assembly loosely to the suspension arm with two bolts.
12 Refitting is a reversal of removal. Tighten the driveshaft nut (new) to the specified torque after lowering the car to the ground. Then, except where the nut is self-locking, lock the nut by staking its outer ring into the groove in the driveshaft. Top up the final drive unit oil level with reference to Section 2.

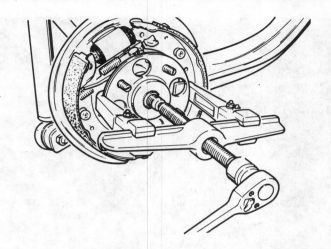

Fig. 8.9 Removing a rear wheel drive flange during Tripode type driveshaft removal (Sec 11)

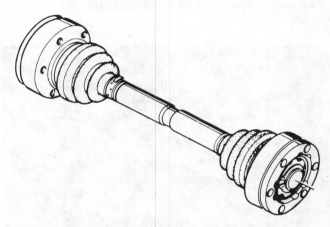

Fig. 8.10 Lobro type rear driveshaft (Sec 11)

Lobro type

13 Chock the front wheels, then jack up the rear of the car and support on axle stands.
14 Using a Torx key unscrew the six bolts (photo) and detach the inner end of the driveshaft from the final drive flange. Remove the spacers where fitted and temporarily support the driveshaft.

11.10A Tripode type driveshaft removal from rear final drive unit

11.10B Tripode type driveshaft inner joint

11.14 Lobro type driveshaft and flange bolts

15 Unscrew the six outer bolts and detach the driveshaft from the stub axle. Remove the spacers where fitted.

16 Clean the mating surfaces and if necessary check that the driveshaft joints are correctly filled with grease.

17 Refitting is a reversal of removal, but tighten the bolts progressively to the specified torque.

12 Driveshaft (front, 4x4) – removal and refitting

1 Remove the wheel cap and loosen the wheel nuts. Also loosen the driveshaft nut at the centre of the hub.

2 Apply the handbrake, then jack up the front of the car and support on axle stands. Remove the roadwheel and the driveshaft nut.

3 Remove the brake disc as described in Chapter 9.

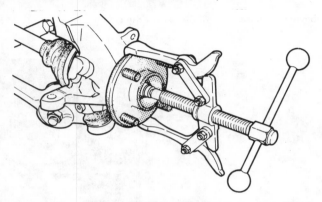

Fig. 8.11 Removing a front wheel drive flange during driveshaft removal (Sec 12)

4 Disconnect the track rod end from the steering arm with reference to Chapter 10.

5 Using a suitable puller, pull the drive flange from the hub and off the driveshaft.

6 Disconnect the lower suspension arm from the spindle carrier by unscrewing the nut and removing the Torx bolt. Do not attempt to turn the Torx bolt, only the nut.

7 Place a container beneath the final drive unit or intermediate shaft to catch any spilled oil.

8 Pull the bottom of the suspension strut outwards until the inner end of the driveshaft is clear of the final drive unit or intermediate shaft, then pull the outer end from the spindle carrier (photos).

9 Refitting is a reversal of removal. Tighten the driveshaft nut to the specified torque after lowering the car to the ground (photo), then lock the nut by staking its outer ring into the groove in the driveshaft. If necessary top up the final drive unit oil level with reference to Section 2.

13 Front intermediate shaft (4x4) – removal and refitting

1 Apply the handbrake, then jack up the front of the car and support on axle stands. Remove the left-hand roadwheel.

2 Disconnect the track rod end from the steering arm with reference to Chapter 10.

3 Disconnect the lower suspension arm from the spindle carrier by unscrewing the nut and removing the Torx bolt. Do not attempt to turn the Torx bolt, only the nut.

4 Pull the bottom of the suspension strut outwards until the inner end of the driveshaft is clear of the intermediate shaft, then tie the driveshaft to one side.

5 Disconnect the speedometer cable from the intermediate shaft bearing cover by unscrewing the nut.

6 Unbolt the intermediate shaft bearing cover from the sump (photos).

12.8A Removing the left-hand front driveshaft (4x4 models) from the intermediate shaft

12.8B Removing the right-hand front driveshaft from the spindle carrier

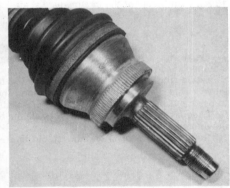

12.8C Outer stub end of a front driveshaft

12.9 Tightening a front driveshaft nut

13.6A Unscrew the bolts ...

13.6B ... and remove the intermediate shaft bearing cover

13.7A Speedometer drivegear retaining circlip (arrowed)

13.7B Removing the speedometer drivegear

13.8A Extract the circlip ...

13.8B ... and pull out the intermediate shaft

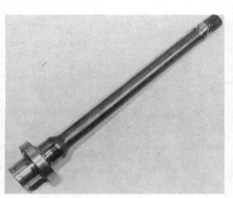

13.8C The intermediate shaft removed

13.9 Intermediate shaft bearing and circlip (arrowed)

7   Extract the circlip and slide the speedometer drivegear from the intermediate shaft (photos).
8   Extract the circlip from the mouth of the tube, then pull out the intermediate shaft together with the bearing (photos). There is no need to use a puller, as the bearing is not a press-fit in the tube.
9   If required, remove the circlip and slide the bearing from the end of the intermediate shaft (photo).
10   Refitting is a reversal of removal, but tighten all nuts and bolts to

the specified torque. Before refitting the driveshaft, the bearing cover oil seal should be renewed unless it is known to be in good condition (refer to Section 10) (photo).

14 Driveshaft – overhaul

Tripode type

1   Remove the clips from the rubber gaiter.
2   Using a hacksaw, cut the joint cover in line with the driveshaft, then use a pair of pliers to peel the cover from the joint until the swaged end is released.
3   Pull the driveshaft stub from the tripod joint together with the compression spring.
4   Mark the tripod joint in relation to the driveshaft centre section, then extract the retaining circlip.
5   Push the rubber gaiter and the remains of the joint cover along the driveshaft away from the joint.
6   Using a suitable three-legged puller pull the tripod joint off the splined driveshaft centre section.
7   Remove the plastic washer, joint cover and rubber gaiter from the driveshaft.
8   Remove the rubber O-ring from the groove in the driveshaft stub.
9   Wash all the components in paraffin and wipe dry, then examine them for wear and damage. In particular check the tripod joint bearings for rough operation and excessive wear. Renew the components as necessary and obtain a new joint cover and rubber O-ring.
10   Locate the rubber gaiter followed by the joint cover and plastic washer (convex side first) onto the driveshaft centre section.
11   Locate the tripod joint on the driveshaft with the previously made marks aligned, and drive it on the splines using a suitable metal tube. Note that the joints on each end of the driveshaft must be offset as shown in Fig. 8.15.
12   Fit the retaining circlip to the end of the driveshaft.

13.10 Renewing the intermediate shaft bearing cover oil seal before refitting the cover

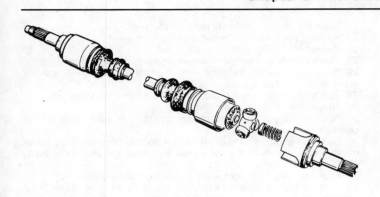

Fig. 8.12 Exploded view of the Tripode driveshaft (Sec 14)

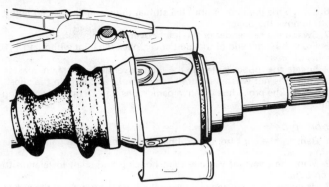

Fig. 8.13 Removing the joint cover on a Tripode driveshaft (Sec 14)

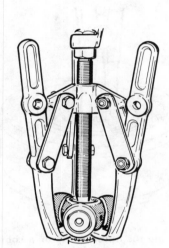

Fig. 8.14 Removing the tripod joint on a Tripode driveshaft (Sec 14)

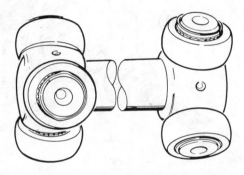

Fig. 8.15 Showing the correct tripod offset on a Tripode driveshaft (Sec 14)

13 Fit the rubber O-ring into the groove in the driveshaft stub, and also locate the spring and pressure pad in the hole inside the stub.

14 Mount the driveshaft centre section in a vice and fit the stub over the tripod joint. Pack the joint with approximately 15 grams of grease, and smear a little grease onto the rubber O-ring.

15 Push the stub onto the driveshaft so that the internal spring is compressed then, using a suitable puller, pull the joint cover over the stub making sure that the six notches engage with the cut-outs in the stub.

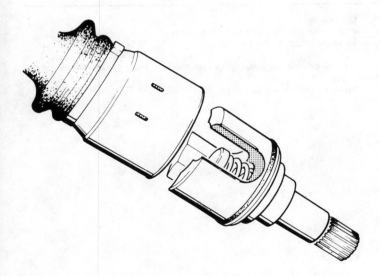

Fig. 8.16 The notches on the joint cover must engage the cut-outs in the Tripode driveshaft stub (Sec 14)

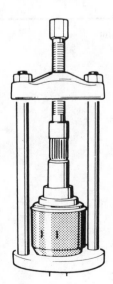

Fig. 8.17 Using a puller to fit the joint cover on a Tripode driveshaft (Sec 14)

16 Swage the joint cover onto the stub at three equally spaced points then remove the puller.

17 Swage the remainder of the joint cover onto the stub.

18 From the inner end of the joint cover, pack the joint with 90 to 110 grams of grease.

19 Locate the rubber gaiter on the joint cover and driveshaft, making sure that it is not twisted or stretched. Then fit and tighten the clips.

20 Repeat the procedure given in paragraphs 1 to 19 on the remaining joint.

Lobro type

21 Remove the clips from the rubber gaiter, and pull the gaiter off the joint cover.

22 Mark the constant velocity joint housing and shaft in relation to each other.

23 Using circlip pliers, remove the circlip from the groove in the end of the shaft.

24 Slide the constant velocity joint off the shaft.

25 Remove the remaining circlip and the joint cover.

26 Pull off the rubber gaiter.

27 Clean the components and obtain a new gaiter and clips.

28 Smear the inside of the gaiter with grease and locate it on the shaft, together with the new clips.

29 Locate the joint cover in the gaiter and tighten the large clip.

30 Fit the inner circlip on the shaft.

31 Apply sealing compound to the face of the joint cover which contacts the joint.

32 Slide the joint onto the shaft splines so that the previously made marks are aligned, with the outer groove towards the end of the shaft.

33 Fit the outer circlip.

34 Pack the joint from both sides with 85 grams of grease.

35 Align the joint cover holes with the joint housing holes, and position the gaiter on the shaft, so that it is not twisted or distorted.

36 Fit and tighten the small gaiter clip.

37 Repeat the procedure given in paragraphs 21 to 36 on the remaining joint.

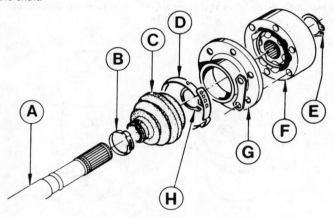

Fig. 8.18 Exploded view of the Lobro driveshaft (Sec 14)

A	Shaft	E	Outer circlip
B	Clip	F	Constant velocity joint
C	Rubber gaiter	G	Joint cover
D	Clip	H	Inner circlip

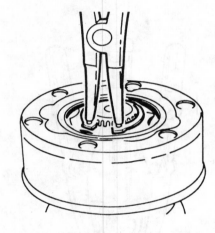

Fig. 8.19 Removing the outer circlip on a Lobro driveshaft (Sec 14)

15 Fault diagnosis – final drive and driveshafts

Symptom	Reason(s)
Noise from final drive unit	Lack of lubricant Worn bearings, crownwheel or pinion Loose final drive unit mountings
Oil leakage	Pinion, differential bearing, or intermediate shaft (4x4) oil seals worn
Noise from driveshafts	Worn driveshaft joints

Chapter 9 Braking system

Contents

Specifications

System type .... Front discs, rear discs or drums, hydraulic system split front/rear, vacuum servo unit and rear brake deceleration valve, or anti-lock braking system (ABS). Cable-operated handbrake on rear wheels

Brake fluid type/specification .... Hydraulic fluid to Ford spec SAM-6C 9103-A (Duckhams Universal Brake and Clutch Fluid)

Brake discs

	Front	Rear
Type	Ventilated	Solid
Diameter:		
All models except XR4i	240 mm (9.4 in)	253 mm (10.0 in)
XR4i	260 mm (10.2 in)	–
Thickness variation (max)	0.015 mm (0.0006 in)	0.015 mm (0.0006 in)
Minimum thickness	22.8 mm (0.90 in)	8.9 mm (0.35 in)
Run-out (max)	0.15 mm (0.006 in)	0.15 mm (0.006 in)
Minimum pad lining thickness	1.5 mm (0.06 in)	1.5 mm (0.06 in)

Brake drums

Internal diameter (max)	228.6 mm (9.0 in)
Minimum lining thickness	1.0 mm (0.04 in)

ABS hydraulic system

Operating pressure	130 to 190 bar (1885 to 2755 lbf/in²)
Pressure warning switch operates at	100 to 110 bar (1450 to 1595 lbf/in²)

Torque wrench settings

	Nm	lbf ft
Caliper carrier	51 to 61	38 to 45
Caliper guide bolts (front)	20 to 25	15 to 18
Caliper guide bolts (rear)	31 to 35	23 to 26
Servo unit	35 to 45	26 to 33
Master cylinder	20 to 25	15 to 18
Rear (drum) brake backplate	52 to 64	38 to 47
Hydraulic unions	7 to 9	5 to 7
ABS unit to bulkhead	41 to 51	30 to 38
ABS accumulator	34 to 46	25 to 34
ABS pump	7 to 9	5 to 7
ABS wheel sensor	8.5 to 11	6 to 8

1 General description

The braking system is of dual hydraulic circuit type, with discs at the front and either drum or disc brakes at the rear. The front and rear hydraulic circuits are operated independently, so that in the event of a failure in one circuit the remaining circuit still functions. The handbrake operates by cable on the rear wheels. Both the footbrake and handbrake are self-adjusting in use. The handbrake lever operates a switch which illuminates a warning light on the instrument panel; the same light is used as a warning for low fluid level in the reservoir. Models fitted with an auxiliary warning system have a disc pad wear warning light included on the facia panel.

Ford's anti-lock braking system (ABS) is fitted to some models. The system monitors the rotational speed of each roadwheel. When a wheel begins to lock under heavy braking, the ABS reduces the hydraulic pressure to that wheel, so preventing it from locking. When this happens a pulsating effect will be noticed at the brake pedal. On some road surfaces the tyres may squeal when braking hard even though the wheels are not locked.

The main components of the system are the hydraulic unit, the wheel sensors, and the control module. The hydraulic unit contains the elements of a traditional master cylinder, plus an electric motor and pump, a pressure accumulator and control valves. The pump is the source of pressure for the system and does away with the need for a

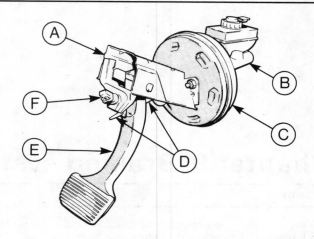

Fig. 9.1 Standard braking system components (Sec 1)

A Bracket
B Master cylinder
C Servo unit
D Pushrod
E Pedal
F Stoplamp switch

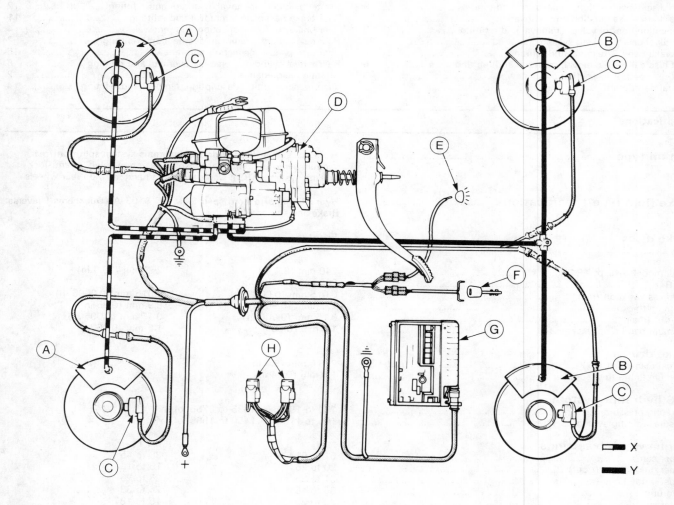

Fig. 9.2 Schematic diagram of the anti-lock braking system – ABS (Sec 1)

A Front calipers
B Rear calipers
C Wheel sensors
D Hydraulic unit
E Warning light
F Ignition switch
G ABS module
H Relays and diodes
X Front hydraulic circuit
Y Rear hydraulic circuit

vacuum servo. In the event that the hydraulic pump fails, unassisted braking effort is still available on the front calipers only.

Warning lights inform the driver of low brake fluid level, ABS failure and (on some models) disc pad wear. The low fluid level light doubles as a 'handbrake on' light; if it illuminates at the same time as the ABS warning light, it warns of low hydraulic pressure.

ABS cannot overturn the laws of physics; stopping distances will inevitably be greater on loose or slippery surfaces. However, the system should allow even inexperienced drivers to retain directional control under panic braking.

Overhaul of the ABS hydraulic unit is not included in this Chapter as it is considered to be outside the scope of the home mechanic. Furthermore, a pressure check is necessary, requiring the use of a specialised pressure gauge.

2   Routine maintenance

Carry out the following procedures at the intervals given in 'Routine Maintenance' at the beginning of the Manual.

Check and if necessary top up the brake fluid level
1   On models not fitted with ABS, check that the fluid level is at or near the maximum mark on the translucent reservoir. Note that the level will drop slightly as the front brake pads wear and topping up to correct this is not necessary. If the level is near the minimum mark the hydraulic circuit should be thoroughly checked for leaks.
2   A different procedure is necessary in order to check the brake fluid level on models fitted with ABS. First, with the ignition switched off, pump the brake pedal at least 20 times, or until the pedal feels hard.
3   With the bonnet open, switch on the ignition, then when the hydraulic unit pump stops, check the fluid level in the reservoir. If the fluid level is not on the maximum mark, top it up with fresh brake fluid.

Check the disc pads/rear brake shoes for wear
4   Wear of the front disc pad linings can be checked by supporting the front of the car on axle stands and using a mirror between the caliper and wheel. However, a more accurate check can be made by removing the wheels completely.
5   The rear brake shoe linings can be checked without removing the rear wheels by supporting the rear of the car on axle stands, then prising the rubber plugs from the brake backplates. Here again, a more accurate check can be made by removing the drums.
6   It is necessary to remove the rear wheels in order to check the rear disc pad linings. The spring clip can be prised from the caliper aperture to view the pads (photo) but, as it is quite difficult to refit it, a better method is to remove a guide bolt and swivel the caliper upwards.
7   If the lining on any one disc pad or brake shoe is worn down to the minimum amount given in the Specifications, renew the complete set on the particular axle.

Check the hydraulic brake lines and hoses for damage
8   Thoroughly check all rigid brake lines and flexible hoses for damage, leakage and any signs of chafing, splits or deterioration. Where evident, renew the particular line or hose with reference to Section 23.

2.6 Removing spring clip from the rear disc caliper to view the disc pads

Renew the hydraulic brake fluid
9   Refer to Section 25 for details of this work, however on models with rear drum brakes, first remove the rear drums and check that there is no leakage of fluid from the rear wheel cylinders. Here leakage is evident, renew the wheel cylinder or fit a repair kit of seals (Section 8), then refit the drum.

3   Front disc pads – inspection and renewal

1   The disc pad linings can be checked for wear without removing the front wheels. Apply the handbrake, then jack up the front of the car and support on axle stands. Working beneath the car, insert a mirror between the caliper and wheel and check that the pad linings are not less than the minimum thickness given in the Specifications.
2   To renew the disc pads remove the wheel.
3   Prise the retaining clip from the piston housing and carrier. Hold it with a pair of pliers to avoid its causing personal injury (photo).
4   On early models fitted with wear sensors, pull the wiring connectors apart after releasing them from the spring clip (photo). Note the routing of the wiring for correct reassembly.
5   Using a 7 mm hexagon key unscrew and remove the special guide bolts securing the piston housing to the carrier and withdraw the housing (photos). Support the housing on an axle stand to avoid damage to the hydraulic hose.
6   Pull the inner disc pad from the piston (it is located inside the piston by a spring claw), then remove the outer pad using a

3.3 Removing the retaining clip from the front brake caliper

3.4 Disconnect the wear sensor wiring connector

3.5A Unscrew the guide bolts ...

3.5B ... and withdraw the caliper housing

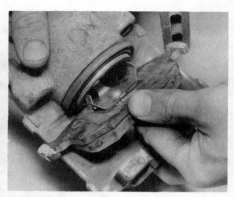

3.6A Inner disc pad removal

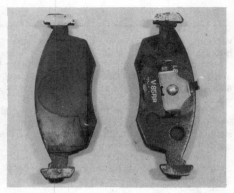

3.6B Outer (left) and inner (right) front disc pads

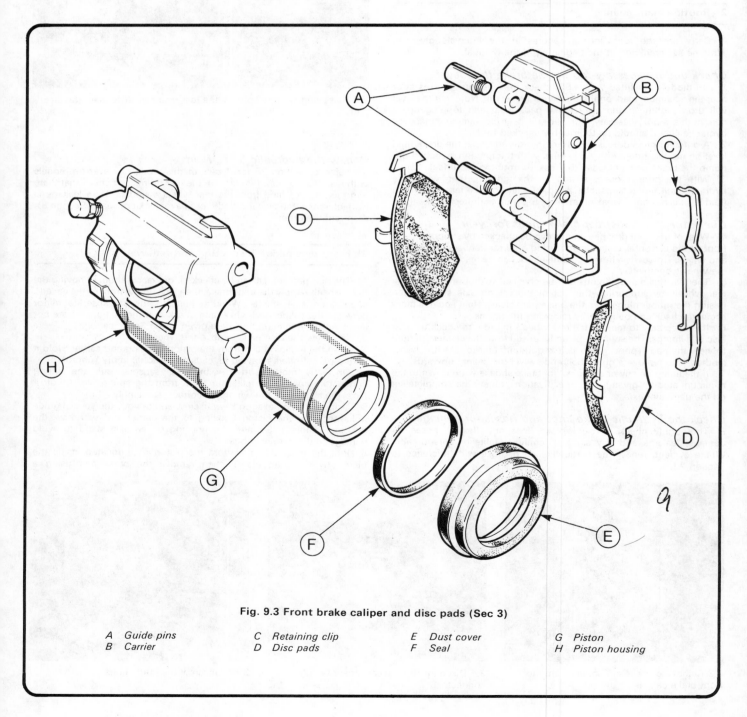

Fig. 9.3 Front brake caliper and disc pads (Sec 3)

A Guide pins	C Retaining clip	E Dust cover	G Piston
B Carrier	D Disc pads	F Seal	H Piston housing

screwdriver if necessary to release it from the anti-rattle compound (photos).

7   Brush the dust and dirt from the housing, piston, carrier, pads and disc, *but do not inhale it as it is injurious to health.* Scrape any scale or rust from the disc.

8   Push the piston back into the housing using a block of wood in order to accommodate the extra thickness of the new disc pads.

9   Locate the new inner disc pad in the piston, then peel the backing paper from the outer pad and press it into position against the outer jaw of the housing.

10   Refit the piston housing and tighten the guide bolts (coated with brake grease) to the specified torque. Reconnect the wear sensor wiring where fitted. Refit the retaining clip and wheel, and lower the car to the ground. Depress the footbrake pedal several times in order to set the disc pads in their normal positions. Avoid heavy braking as far as possible for the first hundred miles or so to allow the new pads to 'bed in'.

4   Rear brake shoes – inspection and renewal

1   The rear brake shoe linings can be checked for wear without removing the rear wheels. First jack up the rear of the car and support on axle stands. Chock the front wheels and release the handbrake.

2   Prise the plug from the brake backplate and using an inspection lamp or torch check that the brake shoe lining thickness is not less than the amount given in the Specifications (photo). If necessary scrape the paint from the edge of the lining and shoe. refit the plug.

3   To renew the brake shoes remove the wheel, then remove the clip and pull off the brake drum where fitted (photo).

4   Remove the hold-down spring from the leading shoe by depressing the cup with pliers and turning it through 90° (photo).

5   Note the fitted position of the return springs, then release the leading shoe from the wheel cylinder and anchor using a screwdriver or adjustable spanner (photos). Note the forward rotation arrows on the brake shoes.

6   Unhook the return springs and remove the leading shoe.

7   Remove the hold-down spring from the trailing shoe by depressing the cup with pliers and turning it through 90°.

8   Withdraw the trailing shoe and disengage the handbrake lever from the cable.

9   Unhook the springs from the trailing shoe and remove the self-adjusting strut.

10   Brush the dust from the backplate, wheel cylinder, shoes, strut and brake drum *but do not inhale it as it is injurious to health.* Scrape any scale or rust from the drum.

11   Apply a little brake grease to the six shoe contact points on the backplate.

12   Lubricate the handbrake lever retaining/pivot rivet with one or two drops of oil, then wipe away any excess oil.

13   Check the wheel cylinder for signs of hydraulic fluid leakage and, if evident, repair or renew the wheel cylinder.

14   Fit the springs to the trailing shoe and attach the self-adjusting strut.

15   Attach the handbrake cable to the lever and position the trailing shoe on the wheel cylinder and anchor. Make sure that the upper return spring is located on the strut.

16   Refit the hold-down spring to the trailing shoe.

17   Connect the return springs to the leading shoe, then locate the lower end in the anchor and lever the upper end onto the toothed quadrant lever and wheel cylinder. Take care to avoid damage to the wheel cylinder dust seal.

18   Refit the hold-down spring to the leading shoe.

19   Using a screwdriver push the self-adjusting toothed quadrant fully towards the backplate to its initial setting.

20   Refit the brake drum and clip where fitted, followed by the wheel. Lower the car to the ground.

21   Depress the footbrake pedal several times in order to set the brake shoes in their normal positions.

4.2 Rear brake shoe lining inspection plug location (arrowed)

4.3 Rear brake drum retaining clip removal

4.4 Rear brake shoe hold-down spring and cup

4.5A Rear brake components

4.5B Rear brake self-adjusting strut and springs

4.5C Rear brake shoe lower anchor and return spring

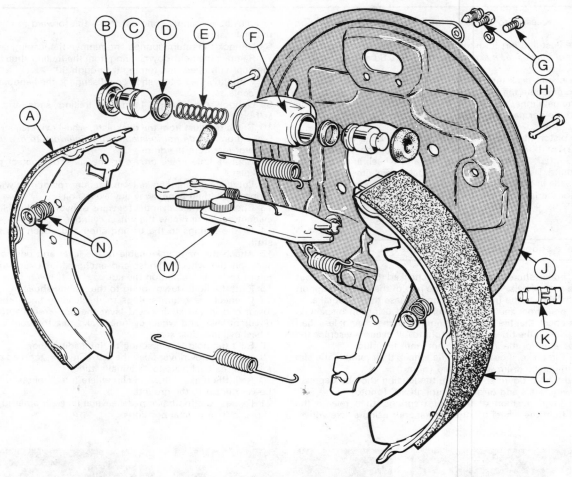

Fig. 9.4 Exploded view of a rear drum brake (Sec 4)

A	Leading shoe	E	Spring
B	Dust cover	F	Wheel cylinder housing
C	Piston	G	Bolts
D	Piston seal		

H	Hold down pin	L	Trailing shoe
J	Backplate	M	Self-adjusting strut
K	Adjustment plunger	N	Hold down spring and cup

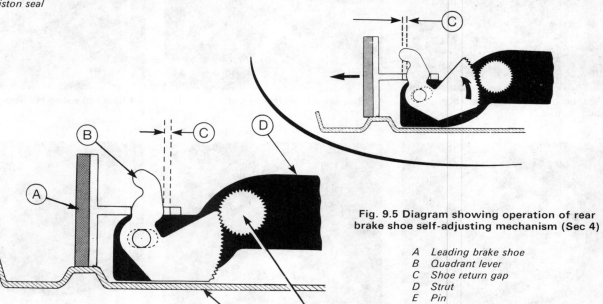

Fig. 9.5 Diagram showing operation of rear brake shoe self-adjusting mechanism (Sec 4)

A   Leading brake shoe
B   Quadrant lever
C   Shoe return gap
D   Strut
E   Pin
F   Backplate
Inset shows brake applied

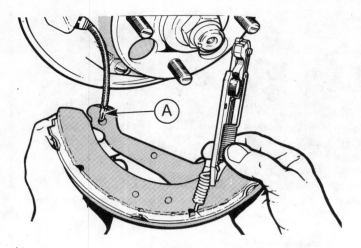

Fig. 9.6 Removing the rear brake trailing shoe (Sec 4)

A   Handbrake cable and slot

Fig. 9.7 Brake grease application points on the backplate (Sec 4)

5 Rear disc pads – inspection and renewal

1   It is necessary to remove the rear wheels in order to inspect the rear pads. The pads can be viewed through the top of the caliper after removing the spring clip (see Section 2). If any one pad is worn down to the minimum specified, all four pads (on both rear wheels) must be renewed.
2   Free the handbrake cable from its clip on the suspension lower arm. Release the handbrake.
3   Remove the caliper guide bolt nearest the front, counterholding the guide with another spanner (photo).
4   Disconnect the pad wear warning wires, when fitted.
5   Swing the caliper rearwards and remove the pads (photo). *Do not press the brake pedal with the caliper removed.*
6   Brush the dust and dirt from the caliper, piston, carrier, pads and disc, but *do not inhale it as it is injurious to health.* Scrape any scale or rust from the disc.
7   Retract the caliper piston, by turning it clockwise, to accommodate the extra thickness of the new pads. There is a Ford tool (No. 12-006) for this purpose, but a pair of circlip pliers or any similar tool can be used instead (photo).
8   Remove any backing paper from the new pads, then fit them to the caliper carrier. Be careful not to contaminate the friction surfaces with oil or grease.
9   Swing the caliper over the pads. Refit and tighten the guide bolt (coated with brake grease).

10   Reconnect the pad wear warning wires, when fitted.
11   Secure the handbrake cable, refit the wheels and lower the car to the ground. Depress the footbrake pedal several times in order to set the disc pads in their normal positions (remember to switch on the ignition first on models with ABS). Avoid heavy braking as far as possible for the first hundred miles or so to allow the new pads to 'bed in'.

6 Front disc caliper – removal, overhaul and refitting

1   On models fitted with ABS, check that the ignition is switched off, then pump the brake pedal at least 20 times (or until it feels hard) to depressurise the hydraulic system.
2   Apply the handbrake, then jack up the front of the car and support on axle stands. Remove the relevant wheel.
3   Fit a brake hose clamp to the flexible brake hose leading to the caliper. Alternatively, remove the filler cap from the brake fluid reservoir, then tighten it down onto a suitable piece of polythene sheeting.
4   Loosen the flexible hose union on the caliper a quarter-turn.
5   Remove the disc pads as described in Section 3.
6   Unscrew the caliper from the flexible hose while holding the hose stationary (photo). Cover the caliper aperture and end of the hose with masking tape to prevent the ingress of dust and dirt.
7   If necessary unbolt the caliper carrier from the spindle carrier (photo).
8   Position a piece of wood inside the caliper, then use low air

5.3 Removing rear caliper guide bolt

5.5 Rear brake pad removal

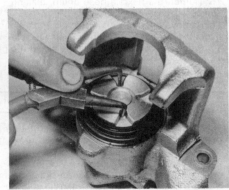

5.7 Rotating the caliper piston to retract it

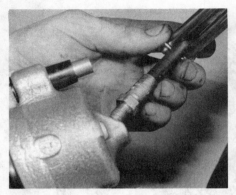

6.6 Removing front caliper – note brake hose clamp

6.7 Removing front caliper carrier

6.9 Removing the dust cover from a front caliper

6.10 Front caliper components

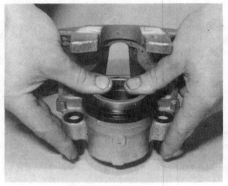

6.11 Pressing the piston into the bore

pressure (ie from a foot pump) to force the piston from the housing.

9   Using a non-metallic instrument, remove the piston seal and dust cover (photo).

10 Clean the piston and housing with methylated spirit and allow to dry (photo). Examine the surfaces of the piston and housing for wear, damage and corrosion. If the piston surface alone is unserviceable, obtain a repair kit which includes a new piston, but if the piston housing is unserviceable, renew the complete caliper. If both surfaces are serviceable, obtain a repair kit of seals.

11 Coat the piston and seals with hydraulic fluid then refit them to the housing (photo).

12 Refit the caliper carrier if removed and tighten the bolts to the specified torque.

13 Screw the caliper onto the flexible hose until the union is finger tight.

14 Refit the disc pads with reference to Section 3.

15 Tighten the flexible hose union, making sure that the hose is not kinked or twisted.

16 Remove the brake hose clamp or polythene sheeting and bleed the hydraulic system as described in Section 24.

17 Refit the wheel and lower the car to the ground.

7   Rear disc caliper – removal, overhaul and refitting

1   On models fitted with ABS, check that the ignition is switched off, then pump the brake pedal at least 20 times (or until it feels hard) to depressurise the hydraulic system.

2   Chock the front wheels, then jack up the rear of the car and support on axle stands. Release the handbrake and remove the relevant wheel.

3   Fit a brake hose clamp to the flexible hose leading from the rear suspension lower arm to the underbody. Alternatively, remove the filler cap from the brake fluid reservoir, then tighten it down onto a suitable piece of polythene sheeting.

4   Disconnect the rigid brake pipe from the flexible hose leading from the caliper by unscrewing the nuts, and detach the flexible hose from the suspension lower arm. Seal the open ends with masking tape.

5   Disconnect the handbrake equaliser yoke from the handbrake lever rod by removing the clevis pin.

6   Disconnect the inner cable from the caliper lever and remove the outer cable (photo). On the right-hand side it will be necessary to extract the circlip first.

7   Unscrew the two guide bolts and lift the caliper off the carrier. Alternatively, unscrew the two carrier bolts and separate the caliper on the bench (photos).

8   Unscrew the flexible hose from the caliper.

9   Clean the caliper externally and mount it in a soft-jawed vice.

10 Rotate the piston anti-clockwise until it is protruding from the bore by about 20 mm (0.8 in). Free the dust boot from the groove in the piston, then carry on unscrewing the piston and remove it. Remove and discard the dust boot.

11 The piston and bore may now be cleaned and examined, and the piston seal and dust boot renewed, as described for the front caliper (Section 6).

12 The piston adjuster nut seal should also be renewed. Remove the circlip from the piston, then extract the thrust washers, wave washer and thrust bearing. Note the fitted sequence of these components. Finally remove the nut (photos).

13 Remove the seal from the nut, noting which way round it is fitted. Clean the nut with methylated spirit. Lubricate the new seal with clean hydraulic fluid and fit it to the nut.

14 To dismantle the caliper further it is necessary to have a tool capable of compressing the return spring. The Ford tool for this job (tool number 12-007) appears to be an adjuster nut reduced in diameter and fitted with a handle. However, it is possible to utilise the actual adjuster nut on the caliper (photo) or a suitable piece of tubing positioned over the threaded pushrod.

15 Using the tool, slightly compress the spring cover, then use a long thin pair of circlip pliers to extract the circlip. Remove the tool followed by the spring cover, spring and washer (photos).

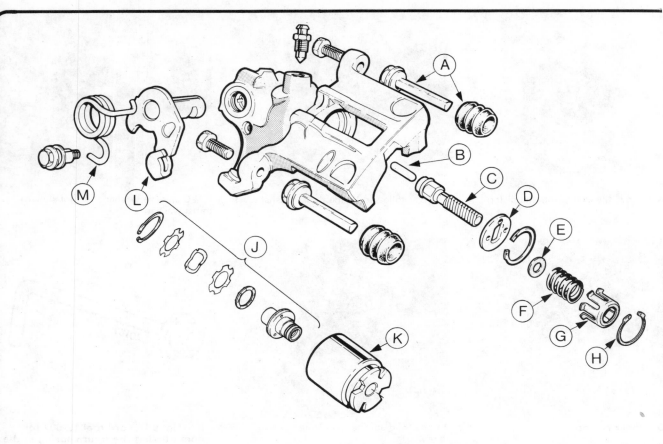

Fig. 9.8 Exploded view of the rear disc caliper (Sec 7)

A	Guide pin and dust cover	G	Spring cover
B	Strut	H	Circlip
C	Threaded pushrod	J	Adjuster nut assembly
D	Keyplate	K	Piston
E	Washer	L	Lever
F	Spring	M	Return spring

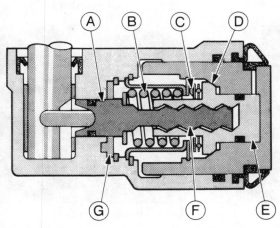

Fig. 9.9 Diagram showing rear caliper self-adjusting mechanism (Sec 7)

A	Handbrake pushrod	E	Adjuster nut
B	Return spring	F	Quick thread
C	Washer	G	Keyplate
D	Clutch face		

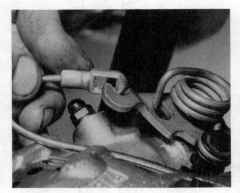

7.6 Disconnecting the handbrake inner cable

7.7A Removing the rear caliper

7.7B Rear caliper carrier mounting bolt (arrowed)

7.12A Remove the circlip from the piston ...

7.12B ... followed by the thrust washer ...

7.12C ... wave washer and (not shown) thrust washer ...

7.12D ... thrust bearing ...

7.12E ... and adjuster nut. Note the seal (arrowed)

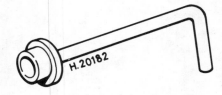

Fig. 9.10 Ford tool 12-007 for compressing the return spring in the rear caliper (Sec 7)

7.14 Using the adjuster nut to compress the caliper spring

7.15A Extract the circlip ...

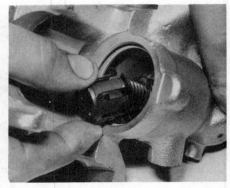

7.15B ... the spring cover ...

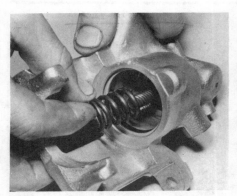

7.15C ... the spring ...

7.15D ... and the washer

7.16 Remove the circlip (ends arrowed) to release the pushrod and keyplate

16 Extract the circlip followed by the pushrod, keyplate and handbrake strut (photo). Remove the O-ring.

17 Remove the handbrake lever return spring and stop bolt. Pull the lever and shaft out of the caliper. Prise out the shaft seal.

18 Clean up the handbrake shaft using wire wool; renew the shaft if it is badly corroded. The shaft bush in the caliper can also be renewed if necessary. Pull out the old bush with an internal puller or slide hammer; press in the new bush to 7.5 mm (0.30 in) below the shaft seal lip. The slot in the side of the bush must line up with the pushrod bore in the caliper.

19 Having renewed components as necessary, commence reassembly by smearing a little brake grease or anti-seize compound on the handbrake shaft and bush.

20 Fit a new handbrake shaft seal to the caliper. Pass the shaft through the seal and into the caliper, being careful not to damage the seal lips.

21 Refit the handbrake lever stop bolt and return spring.

22 Refit the handbrake strut, lubricating it with brake grease.

23 Fit a new O-ring to the base of the pushrod. Refit the pushrod and the key plate, engaging the pip on the key plate with the recess in the caliper. Secure the key plate with the circlip.

24 Refit the washer, spring and spring cover. Compress the spring and refit the circlip, then release the spring compressor.

25 Lubricate the caliper bore with clean hydraulic fluid and fit a new piston seal.

26 Reassemble the piston components. Lubricate the contact face of the adjuster nut with a little brake grease, then fit the adjuster nut (with new seal), thrust bearing, thrust washer, wave washer and the second thrust washer. Secure with the circlip.

27 Fit a new dust boot. The manufacturers recommend that it be fitted to the caliper groove and piston fitted afterwards; it is also possible to fit the boot to the piston first and engage it in the caliper groove afterwards. Either way it is a fiddly business.

28 Refit the piston and screw it into the caliper, then fit whichever lip of the dust boot was left free (photo).

29 Renew the guide pin gaiters and apply a little anti-seize compound to the guide pins when reassembling the caliper to the bracket.

30 Refitting is a reversal of the removal procedure, but before refitting the wheel, bleed the hydraulic system as described in Section 24.

8 Rear wheel cylinder – removal, overhaul and refitting

1 Jack up the rear of the car and support on axle stands. Chock the front wheels and release the handbrake.

2 Remove the wheel then remove the clip (where fitted) and pull off the brake drum.

3 Fit a brake hose clamp to the rear flexible brake hose. Alternatively, remove the brake fluid reservoir filler cap and tighten it down onto a piece of polythene sheeting. This will reduce the loss of hydraulic fluid in the following procedure.

4 Unscrew the union nut and disconnect the hydraulic pipe from the wheel cylinder (photo). Plug the pipe to prevent the ingress of foreign matter.

5 Pull the tops of the brake shoes apart so that the self-adjusting strut holds them clear of the wheel cylinder.

6 Unscrew the bolts and withdraw the wheel cylinder and sealing ring.

7 Prise off the rubber dust covers and withdraw the pistons and central spring, keeping the pistons identified for position.

8 Prise the seals from the pistons.

9 Clean all the components in methylated spirit and allow to dry. Examine the surfaces of the pistons and cylinder bore for wear, scoring and corrosion. If evident, renew the complete wheel cylinder, but if they are in good condition, discard the seals and obtain a repair kit.

10 Dip the inner seals in clean brake fluid and fit them to the piston grooves, using the fingers only to manipulate them. Make sure that the seal lips face into the cylinder as shown in Fig. 9.4.

11 Carefully insert the pistons and central spring then fit the dust covers.

12 Wipe clean the backplate, then fit the wheel cylinder together with a new sealing ring and tighten the bolts.

13 Reconnect the hydraulic pipe and tighten the union nut.

14 Using a screwdriver push the self-adjusting toothed quadrant fully towards the backplate to its initial setting.

15 Refit the brake drum, clip and wheel.

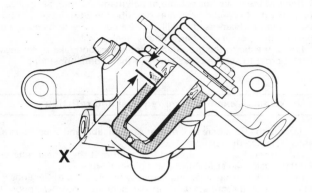

Fig. 9.11 Correct fitted position of handbrake shaft bush (Sec 7)

X = 7.5 mm (0.30 in)

7.28 Dust boot fitted to caliper and piston

8.4 Rear wheel cylinder and hydraulic pipe

16 Remove the brake hose clamp or polythene sheeting as applicable, then bleed the hydraulic system as described in Section 24. If a brake hose clamp has been used it will only be necessary to bleed the one wheel cylinder, otherwise bleed both wheel cylinders.

17 Lower the car to the ground and apply the footbrake pedal several times in order to set the brake shoes in their normal positions.

9 Brake disc – examination, removal and refitting

1 Jack up the front or rear of the car as applicable and support on axle stands. Remove the relevant wheel.

2 Fit washers over the wheel studs, then refit the wheel nuts with their flat sides against the disc and tighten them evenly.

3 Remove the disc caliper and carrier with reference to Sections 6 or 7, but do not disconnect the flexible hydraulic hose. Support the caliper on an axle stand.

4 Rotate the disc and examine it for deep scoring or grooving. Light scoring is normal, but if excessive, the disc should be removed and either renewed or ground by a suitable engineering works.

5 Using a dial gauge or metal block and feeler gauges check that the disc run-out does not exceed the amount given in Specifications.

6 Using a micrometer, measure the thickness of the disc in eight equally-spaced positions 15.0 mm (0.59 in) in from the outer edge (photo). If the results are outside the minimum thickness or maximum variation limits given in the Specifications, renew the disc.

7 To remove the disc, first mark it in relation to the hub, and remove the wheel nuts and washers.

8 Remove the cross-head screw or retaining clip and withdraw the disc from the hub (photos).

9 Refitting is a reversal of removal, but make sure that the mating faces of the disc and hub are clean, and refer to Sections 6 or 7 when refitting the caliper. Note that where the disc run-out is outside the specified limit, and the disc is secured by a cross-head screw, it is permissible to discard the screw and reposition the disc on the hub. However, in this instance, the later type clip must be fitted to one of the wheel studs.

10 Brake drums – examination and renovation

Whenever the brake drums are removed they should be checked for wear and damage. Light scoring of the friction surface is normal, but if excessive or if the surface has worn oval it may be possible to grind it true. This work should be carried out by a qualified engineer, although it is preferable to renew both rear drums.

11 Rear brake backplate – removal and refitting

Drum brakes

1 Remove the rear brake shoes as described in Section 4.

2 Disconnect the handbrake cable from the backplate by extracting the U-clip.

3 Remove the wheel cylinder as described in Section 8.

4 Unclip the driveshaft outer joint plastic cover from the upper brake backplate bolts.

5 Using a socket through the holes in the hub flange unscrew the bolts securing the hub and backplate to the lower suspension arm.

6 Place a container beneath the final drive unit to catch any spilled oil, then withdraw the hub and driveshaft from the final drive unit and remove it from the lower suspension arm.

7 Remove the rear brake backplate.

8 If necessary prise out the handbrake stop button.

9 Refitting is a reversal of removal, but make sure that the mating faces of the hub, backplate and lower suspension arm are clean. Tighten the bolts to the specified torque and refer to Sections 8 and 4 when refitting the wheel cylinder and rear brake shoes. If necessary top up the final drive unit oil level with reference to Chapter 8.

Disc brakes

10 Remove the rear hub as described in Chapter 10.

11 Unbolt the brake caliper carrier plate and remove the backplate from the lower suspension arm.

12 Refitting is a reversal of removal, but make sure that the mating faces of the carrier plate, backplate and lower suspension arm are clean. Tighten the bolts evenly to the specified torque, and refit the rear hub, with reference to Chapter 10.

12 Master cylinder – removal and refitting

1 Depress the footbrake pedal several times to dissipate the vacuum in the servo unit.

2 Disconnect the wiring from the low level switch on the hydraulic fluid reservoir filler cap (photo).

3 Place a suitable container beneath the master cylinder then unscrew the union nuts and disconnect the hydraulic pipes. Plug the pipes or cover them with masking tape to prevent the ingress of foreign matter.

4 Unscrew the mounting nuts and withdraw the master cylinder from the servo unit. Cover the master cylinder with rag to prevent spilling hydraulic fluid on the paintwork. If accidentally spilt, swill off immediately with copious amounts of cold water.

5 Drain the remaining fluid from the master cylinder, and clean the exterior surfaces with methylated spirit.

6 Pull out the reservoir and prise out the sealing rubbers.

7 Mount the master cylinder in a vice, then depress the primary piston slightly and extract the circlip and washer. Withdraw the primary piston assembly.

8 Depress the secondary piston and remove the stop pin from the fluid aperture.

9 Remove the master cylinder from the vice and tap it on the bench to remove the secondary piston assembly.

10 Prise the seals from the secondary piston. Do not attempt to dismantle the primary piston.

11 Clean all the components in methylated spirit and examine them for wear and damage. In particular check the surfaces of the pistons

9.6 Checking brake disc thickness with a micrometer

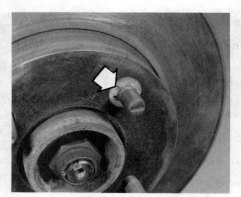
9.8A Brake disc retaining clip (arrowed)

9.8B Removing the brake disc

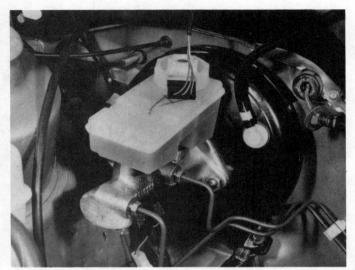

12.2 Brake master cylinder and servo unit. Note the low level switch wiring plug

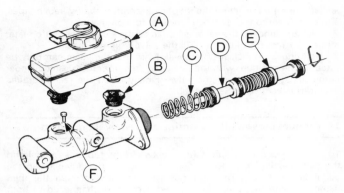

Fig. 9.12 Exploded view of the master cylinder (Sec 12)

A   Reservoir
B   Seal
C   Spring
D   Secondary piston
E   Primary piston
F   Stop pin

and cylinder bore for scoring and corrosion. If the cylinder bore is worn renew the complete master cylinder, otherwise obtain a repair kit including pistons and seals.

12 Check that the inlet and outlet ports are free and unobstructed. Dip the pistons and seals in clean brake fluid.

13 Fit the seals to the secondary piston using the fingers only to manipulate them into the grooves. Note that the sealing lips must face away from each other.

14 Insert the secondary piston and spring into the cylinder. Turn the piston slowly as the first seal enters to avoid trapping the sealing lip. Similarly insert the primary piston and spring then fit the washer and circlip.

15 Depress the primary and secondary pistons and refit the secondary piston stop pin.

16 Fit the sealing rubbers and press the reservoir into them.

17 Refitting is a reversal of removal, but tighten the mounting nuts and pipe union nuts to the specified torque, and finally bleed the hydraulic system as described in Section 24.

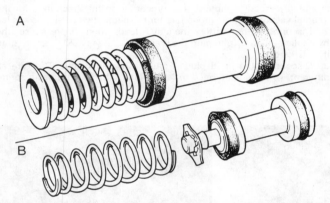

Fig. 9.13 Master cylinder primary piston (A) and secondary piston (B) (Sec 12)

13 Deceleration control valve – removal and refitting

1 The deceleration control valve is fitted to models with rear drum brakes and is located on the left-hand side of the engine compartment (photo). Place a suitable container or rags beneath the valve to catch

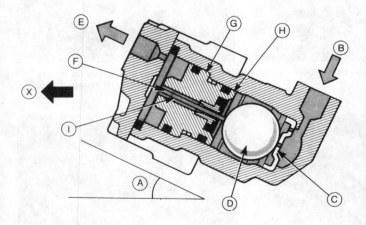

Fig. 9.14 Cross-section of the deceleration valve in the rear drum brake hydraulic circuit (Sec 13)

A   Installation angle
B   Inlet port
C   Diffuser
D   Inertia ball
E   Outlet port
F   Piston bore
G   Large piston
H   Small piston
I   Hollow pin
Arrow X indicates front of car

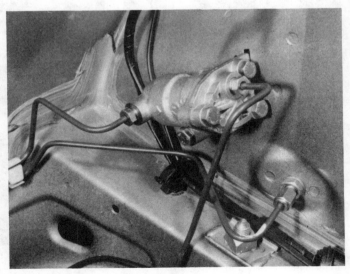

13.1 Brake deceleration control valve

spilled fluid then unscrew the unions, disconnect the hydraulic pipes, and plug them to prevent the ingress of foreign matter.

2   On early models, the valve is bolted to the side panel, but on later models, extract the clip and slide the valve from the bracket.

3   Refitting is a reversal of removal. Note that the valve can only be fitted in one position, with the hydraulic pipe from the master cylinder connected to the rear of the valve. Finally bleed the rear hydraulic circuit as described in Section 24.

14 Vacuum servo unit – description, removal and refitting

1   The vacuum servo unit is fitted between the footbrake pedal and the master cylinder, and provides assistance to the driver when the pedal is depressed. The unit operates by vacuum from the inlet manifold. With the footpedal released vacuum is channelled to both sides of the internal diaphragm, however when the pedal is depressed one side is opened to the atmosphere resulting in assistance to the pedal effort. Should the vacuum servo develop a fault the hydraulic system is not affected, however greater effort will be required at the pedal.

2   To remove the servo unit first remove the master cylinder as described in Section 12.

3   Prise the vacuum hose connection from the servo unit.

4   Working inside the car remove the lower facia panel and disconnect the servo pushrod from the pedal.

5   Unscrew the mounting nuts and withdraw the servo unit from the bulkhead.

6   If necessary remove the hose incorporating the check valve and check that it is only possible to blow through it in one direction.

7   Refitting is a reversal of removal, but when fitting the unit to the bulkhead make sure that the pushrod is correctly located in the pedal. Refit the master cylinder with reference to Section 12.

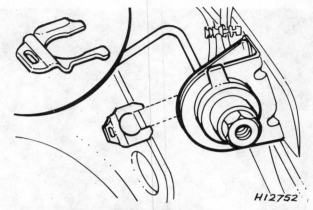

Fig. 9.15 Removal of the later type deceleration valve (Sec 13)

15 ABS hydraulic unit – removal and refitting

1   Note that the valve block may be integral with the hydraulic unit or mounted remotely (photos). The procedure in this Section is for the integral version, but the procedure for the alternative version is similar.

2   Disconnect the battery negative lead, then depressurise the hydraulic system by pumping the brake pedal at least 20 times, or until it feels hard.

3   Disconnect the multi-plugs from the hydraulic unit. They are all different, so there is no need to label them. When a plug has a spring

15.1A ABS hydraulic unit with integral valve block

15.1B ABS hydraulic unit as used with a remote valve block

15.1C Remote valve block located on the left-hand side of the engine compartment

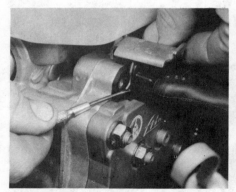

15.3A Disconnecting the valve block multi-plug. Lift the spring clip ...

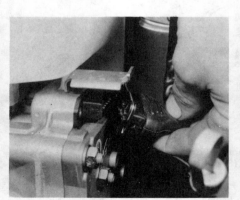

15.3B ... and pull off the plug

15.3C Disconnecting fluid level sensor plug

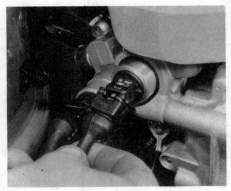

15.3D Disconnecting the main valve plug

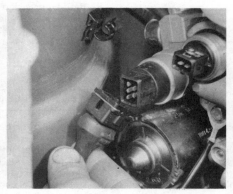

15.3E Disconnecting the pressure switch multi-plug

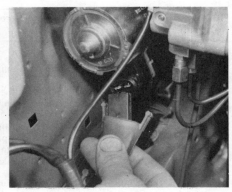

15.3F Disconnecting the pump motor plug

15.4 Earth strap (arrowed) bolted to the hydraulic unit

15.5A Hydraulic pipe connections to the valve block

15.5B One method of capping the hydraulic unions

15.6 Pushrod connection to brake pedal

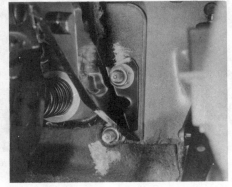

15.7 ABS hydraulic unit mounting nuts (two shown)

clip retainer, lift the clip before pulling out the plug. To release the pump plug, pull back the rubber boot and the plug sleeve (photos).
4   Unbolt the earth strap from the unit (photo).
5   Make arrangements to catch spilt hydraulic fluid. Identify the hydraulic pipes and disconnect them from the base of the unit. Plug or cap the open unions to keep fluid in and dirt out (photos).
6   Remove the lower facia panel on the driver's side. Disconnect the spring clip which secures the hydraulic unit pushrod to the brake pedal (photo).
7   Have an assistant support the hydraulic unit. Remove the four nuts which hold the unit to the bulkhead (photo). Withdraw the unit from the bulkhead.
8   Recover the gasket or sealing compound from the unit and the bulkhead.
9   Drain the hydraulic fluid from the reservoir. *Do not actuate the*

pushrod with the unit removed.
10 Dismantling of the hydraulic unit should be limited to the operations described in the following Sections. These operations can all be carried out without removing the unit from the vehicle if wished.
11 Refit by reversing the removal operations, noting the following points.

(a) *When inserting the unit, take care not to force the pushrod from its rested position*
(b) *Do not refill the reservoir until the end of refitting*
(c) *Use new sealing compound or a new gasket between the unit and the bulkhead*
(d) *Make sure that the hydraulic pipes are reconnected to the correct unions*
(e) *Bleed the complete hydraulic system on completion – see Section 24*

16 ABS hydraulic unit fluid reservoir – removal and refitting

1 Disconnect the battery negative lead.
2 Depressurise the hydraulic system by pumping the brake pedal at least 20 times, or until it feels hard.
3 Disconnect the multi-plugs and remove the reservoir cap (photo).
4 Remove the reservoir securing screw, which is located just above the valve block multi-plug (photo).
5 Make arrangements to catch spilt fluid, then disconnect the low pressure hose from its connections to the pump; the hose is secured by a spring clip (photos). Allow the brake fluid to drain out of the hose.
6 Pull the reservoir out of the seals on the hydraulic unit and remove it (photo).
7 Note the spigot locating bush on the rear inlet union, which may stay in the hydraulic unit or may come out with the reservoir (photo).

8 Refit by reversing the removal operations. Use new seals between the hydraulic unit and the reservoir.
9 Bleed the complete hydraulic system on completion (Section 24). Check for leaks around the disturbed components.

17 ABS hydraulic unit accumulator – removal and refitting

1 Disconnect the battery negative lead.
2 Depressurise the hydraulic system by pumping the brake pedal at least 20 times, or until it feels hard.
3 Wrap a clean rag round the base of the accumulator to catch any spilt fluid.
4 Unscrew the accumulator using a hexagon key. Remove the accumulator, being prepared for fluid spillage (photos).

16.3 ABS hydraulic unit fluid reservoir. Note low fluid sensor wiring multi-plugs

16.4 Undoing the reservoir securing screw

16.5A Extract the spring clip ...

16.5B ... and disconnect the hose

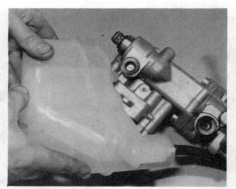

16.6 Hydraulic fluid reservoir removal

16.7 The spigot locating bush fits into this union

17.4A Unscrewing the accumulator

17.4B Accumulator removal. Note O-ring (arrowed)

5 When refitting, fit a new O-ring to the base of the accumulator. Fit the accumulator and tighten it.
6 Reconnect the battery. Switch on the ignition and check that the hydraulic unit pump stops within 60 seconds. If not, there may be a leakage.
7 Bleed the complete hydraulic system (Section 24).

18 ABS hydraulic unit pump and motor – removal and refitting

1 Remove the accumulator as described in the previous Section.
2 Unscrew the union nut and disconnect the high pressure pipe from the pump (some early models may have a flexible hose and banjo union instead). Be prepared for fluid spillage.
3 Disconnect the low pressure hose from the pump. Allow the fluid to drain out of the reservoir through the hose.
4 Disconnect the multi-plugs from the pressure switch and the pump motor.
5 Remove the pump mounting bolt (photo).
6 Pull the pump and motor assembly off the mounting spigot and remove it.
7 Recover the mounting bushes and renew them if necessary.
8 If a new pump is to be fitted, transfer the pressure switch to it, using a new O-ring.
9 Commence refitting by offering the pump to the spigot, then reconnecting the low pressure hose.
10 Refit and tighten the pump mounting bolt.
11 Reconnect the high pressure pipe or hose, using new sealing washers on the banjo union where applicable.
12 Refit the accumulator, using a new O-ring.
13 Reconnect the multi-plugs and the battery.
14 Refill the reservoir, then switch on the ignition and allow the pump to prime itself. Do not let the pump run for more than two minutes – see Section 24. Check for leaks around the disturbed components
15 Bleed the complete hydraulic system (Section 24).

19 ABS hydraulic unit pressure switch – removal and refitting

Note: *To remove the pressure switch from the hydraulic unit in situ, Ford tool No. 12-008, or equivalent, will be required. The switch may be removed without special tools after removing the hydraulic unit complete (Section 15) or the pump (Section 18).*
1 Disconnect the battery negative lead.
2 Depressurise the hydraulic system by pumping the brake pedal at least 20 times, or until it feels hard.

18.5 Hydraulic unit pump mounting bolt

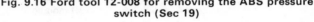
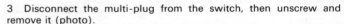

H.20181

Fig. 9.16 Ford tool 12-008 for removing the ABS pressure switch (Sec 19)

3 Disconnect the multi-plug from the switch, then unscrew and remove it (photo).
4 When refitting, use a new O-ring on the switch. Position the plastic sleeve so that the hole in the sleeve is facing the pump motor (photo). Tighten the switch.
5 Reconnect the multi-plug and the battery.
6 Bleed the complete hydraulic system (Section 24).

19.3 Unscrewing the pressure switch

19.4 Refitting the pressure switch. Hole (arrowed) in plastic sleeve must face pump motor

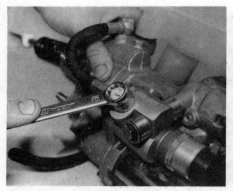

20.4A Undoing a high pressure hose union

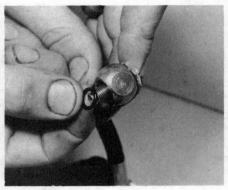

20.4B Fitting new sealing washers to a banjo union

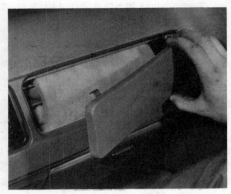

21.3 Remove the small facia panel and packing ...

21.4A ... withdraw the ABS module ...

21.4B ... and disconnect the multi-plug

20 ABS hydraulic unit hose/pipe – removal and refitting

1   The high pressure connection between the booster and pump may be either a hose with banjo unions at each end, or alternatively a rigid pipe with union nuts at each end. A low pressure hose connects the reservoir to the pump inlet.
2   First disconnect the battery and depressurise the hydraulic system by pumping the brake pedal at least 20 times, or until it feels hard.
3   Place a suitable container or absorbent material beneath the hose or pipe to catch the spilt fluid.
4   To remove the high pressure connection, unscrew the banjo bolts or union nuts and recover the sealing washers where applicable (photos). Use new sealing washers on the banjo unions when refitting.
5   To remove the low pressure hose, remove the spring clip and pull the hose off the pump intake. Allow the contents of the reservoir to drain out of the hose into the container, then pull the hose from the reservoir. After refitting the hose, refill the reservoir with fluid.
6   Reconnect the battery and bleed the complete hydraulic system (Section 24). Check for leaks.

21 ABS module – removal and refitting

1   Disconnect the battery negative lead.
2   On pre-February 1987 models, remove the lower facia panel on the driver's side.
3   On February 1987-on models, remove the small panel and packing from the passenger side of the facia panel (photo).
4   The module can now be removed by releasing the catch and disconnecting the multi-plug (photos), but on early models, it will first be necessary to remove the relays and wiring.
5   Refit by reversing the removal operations. Make sure that the multi-plug is fully engaged with the module.

H.12752

Fig. 9.17 Method of disconnecting the multi-plug from the ABS module (Sec 21)

22 ABS wheel sensors – removal and refitting

Front
1   Ensure that the handbrake is applied. Raise and support the front of the vehicle.
2   From under the bonnet disconnect the wheel sensor wiring multi-plug. Unclip the wiring, working towards the sensor.
3   Remove the securing bolt and withdraw the sensor from the spindle carrier (photos).
4   Unclip the wire from the bracket on the strut. Remove the sensor and its wiring.

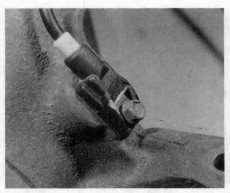

22.3A Remove the bolt ...

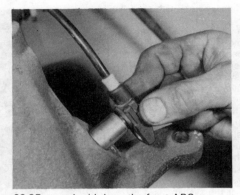

22.3B ... and withdraw the front ABS wheel sensor

22.13 Rear ABS wheel sensor removal

5   Clean any rust or debris from the sensor bore in the spindle carrier. Pack the bore with clean wheel bearing grease.
6   Renew the O-ring on the sensor and smear it with grease.
7   Refit by reversing the removal operations.

Rear

8   Chock the front wheels and release the handbrake. Slacken the rear wheel nuts, raise and support the rear of the vehicle and remove the rear wheel.
9   Fold the rear seat cushion forwards, remove the side kick panel and roll back the carpet to gain access to the sensor multi-plug.
10 Disconnect the multi-plug, release the floor grommet and pass the cable through the floor.
11 Unclip the handbrake cable from the suspension lower arm.
12 Remove the caliper front guide bolt and pivot the caliper rearwards to gain access to the sensor.
13 Remove the sensor securing bolt and withdraw the sensor (photo).
14 Clean up the sensor bore, pack it with grease and renew the sensor O-ring.
15 Refit by reversing the removal operations.

23 Hydraulic brake lines and hoses – removal and refitting

1   On models fitted with ABS, depressurise the hydraulic system by switching off the ignition and pumping the brake pedal 20 times or until it feels hard.
2   To remove a rigid brake line unscrew the union nuts at each end and where necessary release it from the clips (photo).
3   To remove a flexible brake hose first unscrew the union nut(s) and disconnect the rigid brake line(s) from each end. Unscrew the locknut(s) and remove the flexible hose from the bracket(s) (photos). Where applicable, unscrew the hose from the brake caliper.

4   Refitting is a reversal of removal, but bleed the hydraulic system as described in Section 24. New pipes can be bought ready-made, with the unions attached. Some garages and motor factors will make up pipes to order, using the old pipe as a pattern. If purchasing proprietary pipes made of copper alloy or similar material, follow the manufacturer's instructions carefully concerning bending, provision of extra clips etc. Fit and secure the new pipe and tighten the union nuts, then bleed the appropriate part of the hydraulic system.

24 Hydraulic system – bleeding

General

1   If any of the hydraulic components in the braking system have been removed or disconnected, or if the fluid level in the reservoir has been allowed to fall appreciably, it is inevitable that air will have been introduced into the system. The removal of all this air from the hydraulic system is essential if the brakes are to function correctly, and the process of removing it is known as bleeding.
2   There is a number of one-man, do-it-yourself, brake bleeding kits currently available from motor accessory shops. It is recommended that one of these kits should be used wherever possible as they greatly simplify the bleeding operation and also reduce the risk of expelled air and fluid being drawn back into the system. On models fitted with ABS an assistant is required, so it will not be possible to use a one-man bleeding kit as such, although the tube and container may be used separately.
3   If a one-man kit is not available, then it will be necessary to gather together a clean jar and a suitable length of clear plastic tubing which is a tight fit over the bleed screw, and also to engage the help of an assistant.
4   Before commencing the bleeding operation, check that all rigid pipes and flexible hoses are in good condition and that all hydraulic unions are tight. Take great care not to allow hydraulic fluid to come into contact with the vehicle paintwork, otherwise the finish will be

23.2 Union connection between two rigid brake lines

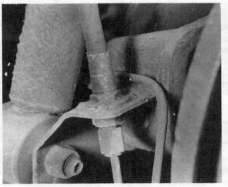

23.3A Flexible hose to rigid brake pipe connection

23.3B Rear flexible brake hose (arrowed)

seriously damaged. Wash off any spilled fluid immediately with cold water.

5   On models fitted with ABS, do not allow the hydraulic unit pump motor to run for more than two minutes at a time. The motor must be allowed to cool (with the ignition off) for at least ten minutes after each two minute spell of running. Remember that brake fluid is poisonous and that the rear brake hydraulic system may be under considerable pressure. *Take care not to allow hydraulic fluid to spray into the face or eyes.*

6   To bleed the system, clean the area around the bleed screw at the caliper or wheel cylinder to be bled and remove the dust cover (photo). If the hydraulic system has only been partially disconnected and suitable precautions were taken to prevent further loss of fluid, it should only be necessary to bleed that part of the system. However, if the entire system is to be bled start at the front left-hand side wheel. Keep the fluid reservoir topped up to the 'MAX' mark during the bleeding operation, and discard fluid bled out of the system, as it is unfit for re-use.

Non-ABS models

7   If a one-man brake bleeding kit is being used, connect the outlet tube to the bleed screw and then open the screw half a turn. If possible position the unit so that it can be viewed from the car, then depress the brake pedal to the floor and slowly release it. The one-way valve in the kit will prevent dispelled air from returning to the system at the end of each stroke. Repeat this operation until clean hydraulic fluid, free from air bubbles, can be seen coming through the tube. Now tighten the bleed screw and remove the outlet tube.

8   If a one-man brake bleeding kit is not available, connect one end of the plastic tubing to the bleed screw and immerse the other end in the jar containing sufficient clean hydraulic fluid to keep the end of the tube submerged (photo). Open the bleed screw one full turn and have your assistant depress the brake pedal to the floor and then slowly release it. Tighten the bleed screw at the end of each downstroke to prevent expelled air and fluid from being drawn back into the system. Repeat this operation until clean hydraulic fluid, free from air bubbles, can be seen coming through the tube. Now tighten the bleed screw and remove the plastic tube.

9   If the entire system is being bled, the procedures described above should now be repeated at the front right-hand side wheel, followed by the rear right-hand side and rear left-hand side wheels. Do not forget to recheck the fluid level in the master cylinder at regular intervals and top up as necessary.

10 When completed, recheck the fluid level in the master cylinder, top up if necessary and refit the cap. Check the 'feel' of the brake pedal, which should be firm and free from any 'sponginess' which would indicate air still present in the system.

ABS models

11 With the ignition switched off, depressurise the hydraulic system by pumping the brake pedal 20 times or until it feels hard.

12 Bleed the front brakes using the procedure described in paragraph 8, the left-hand side first, followed by the right-hand side.

13 Connect the tubing to the bleed screw on the rear left-hand caliper and immerse the end of the tube in the jar as previously described. Open the bleed screw one full turn.

14 Have the assistant depress the brake pedal as far as it will go and hold it down. Switch on the ignition: the hydraulic unit pump will start and fluid will flow from the bleed screw.

15 When clean fluid, free of air bubbles, emerges from the bleed screw, tighten the bleed screw and have the assistant release the pedal.

16 Wait for the hydraulic unit pump to stop, then top up the reservoir and repeat the procedure on the right-hand caliper. This time the brake pedal should only be depressed half-way.

17 Switch off the ignition, top up the reservoir again and refit the reservoir cap. Refit the bleed screw dust caps (if applicable).

25 Hydraulic system – fluid renewal

1   Periodic renewal of the brake fluid is necessary because the fluid absorbs water from the atmosphere. This water lowers the boiling points of the fluid, so increasing the risk of vapour locks, and causes rust and corrosion in braking system components.

2   Simple bleeding of the hydraulic system as described in the previous Section is not adequate for fluid renewal because of the large

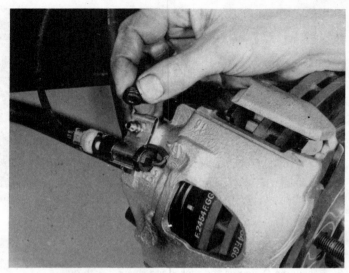

24.6 Removing the dust cover from the bleed screw

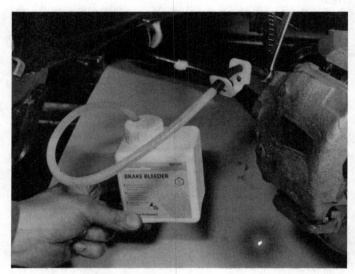

24.8 Bleeding a front brake caliper

quantity of fluid which is normally present in the front calipers.

3   An assistant and the rest of the bleeding equipment will be needed, together with an extra bleed tube and jar. A considerable quantity of hydraulic fluid will be required – probably about 2 litres (nearly half a gallon).

4   Slacken the front wheel nuts. Raise and support the front of the vehicle and remove the front wheels.

5   Remove the hydraulic fluid reservoir cap.

6   Open both front bleed screws one full turn. Attach one bleed tube to each screw, placing the other ends of the tubes in the jars.

7   Pump the brake pedal to expel fluid from the bleed screws. Pause after each upstroke to allow the master cylinder to refill.

8   When air emerges from both bleed screws, stop pumping. Detach the left-hand caliper without disconnecting it and remove the inboard disc pad (see Section 3).

9   Depress the caliper piston, using a purpose-made tool or a blunt item such as a tyre lever, to force more fluid out of the caliper. Hold the piston depressed and have the assistant pump the pedal until air emerges from the bleed screw again.

10 Tighten the bleed screw on the left-hand caliper. Loosely refit the caliper and pad so that the piston is not accidentally ejected.

11 Repeat the purging operation on the right-hand caliper, but do not refit it or tighten the bleed screw yet.

12 Fill the reservoir with fresh hydraulic fluid. Position the bleed jar for the right-hand caliper at least 300 mm (1 foot) above the level of the bleed screw.

13 Have the assistant pump the brake pedal until fluid free of bubbles emerges from the bleed screw. Tighten the bleed screw at the end of a downstroke.

14 Place a piece of wood in the caliper jaws to limit piston travel. Keep your fingers clear of the piston. Have the assistant depress the brake pedal **gently** in order to move the caliper piston out.

15 With the pedal held depressed, slacken the bleed screw on the right-hand caliper and again depress the piston. Tighten the bleed screw when the piston is retracted. The pedal can now be released.

16 Disconnect the bleed tube. Refit the right-hand brake pad and caliper.

17 Remove the left-hand caliper and inboard pad again. Carry out the operations in paragraphs 12 to 16 on the left-hand caliper.

18 Bleed the rear brakes as described in Section 24, paragraphs 13 to 17.

19 Refit the front wheels, lower the vehicle and tighten the wheel nuts.

20 Pump the brake pedal to bring the pads up to the discs, then make a final check of the hydraulic fluid level. Top up and refit the reservoir cap.

26 Handbrake lever – removal and refitting

1 Jack up the rear of the car and support on axle stands. Chock the front wheels and release the handbrake.

2 Extract the clip and clevis pin from the equaliser and disconnect the equaliser from the actuating rod.

3 Working inside the car remove the centre console or rubber gaiter with reference to Chapter 11.

4 Disconnect the wiring from the warning switch then unscrew the mounting bolts and withdraw the handbrake lever (photo). If necessary unbolt the warning switch.

5 Refitting is a reversal of removal, but finally adjust the handbrake cable as described in Sections 27 or 28.

27 Handbrake cable (rear drum brakes) – removal, refitting and adjustment

Removal and refitting

1 Jack up the rear of the car and support on axle stands. Chock the front wheels and release the handbrake.

2 Extract the clip and clevis pin from the equaliser and disconnect the equaliser from the actuating rod.

3 Remove the rear brake shoes as described in Section 4.

4 Extract the U-clips securing the handbrake cables to the rear brake backplates, then release the clips from the suspension arms (photo).

5 Pull both outer cables through the crossmember and withdraw the complete cable from the car.

6 Refitting is a reversal of removal. With reference to Section 4, however, before lowering the car to the ground adjust the cable as follows.

Adjustment

7 Make sure that the handbrake lever is fully released then depress the footbrake pedal several times to set the automatic rear brake adjusters.

8 Using pliers, pull out the nylon lockpin where fitted, then unscrew the locknut from the adjuster located on the left-hand side outer cable and turn the adjuster until the plastic plungers located in the backplates can just be rotated, and the plunger total movement is 0.5 to 1.0 mm (0.02 to 0.04 in) (photo).

9 Tighten the cable adjuster locknut onto the adjuster sleeve, using a suitable spanner or pliers, by between two and four 'clicks', then press in a new lockpin where applicable.

10 Lower the car to the ground.

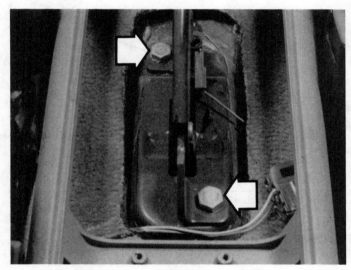

26.4 Handbrake lever mounting bolts (arrowed)

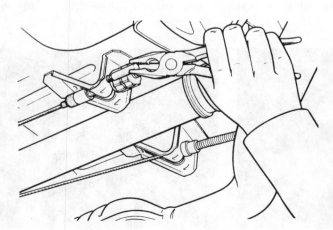

Fig. 9.18 Removing the nylon lockpin from the handbrake cable adjuster (Sec 27)

27.8 Plastic plunger (arrowed) for checking handbrake cable adjustment

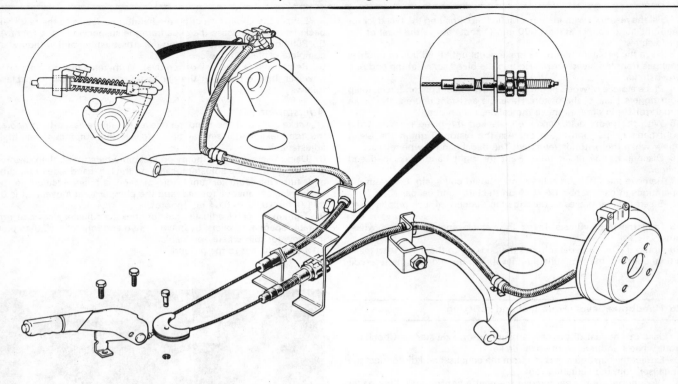

Fig. 9.19 Handbrake cable as fitted to rear disc brake models (Sec 28)

28 Handbrake cable (rear disc brakes) – removal, refitting and adjustment

Removal and refitting

1   Jack up the rear of the car and support on axle stands. Chock the front wheels and release the handbrake. Remove both rear wheels.
2   Remove the lockpin if fitted then slacken off the handbrake cable adjuster locknut and adjuster nut (photo).
3   Free the cable from the equaliser yoke by removing the circlip and clevis pin. Beware of self-tapping screws protruding through the floor in this are.
4   Unhook the inner cable from the handbrake levers on the calipers.
5   Extract the circlip from the right-hand caliper (photo) then release the outer cable from the caliper brackets.

6   Free the cable from the rear suspension lower arm and underbody brackets, and remove it.
7   Refitting is a reversal of removal, but before refitting the rear wheels adjust the cable as follows.

Adjustment

8   Check that both handbrake levers on the calipers are resting against their stops. If not, back off the adjuster nut until they are.
9   Paint alignment marks between each handbrake lever and the caliper body (photo).
10 Tighten the adjuster nut until either handbrake lever just starts to move – as shown by the alignment marks.
11 Apply the handbrake and release it a few times to equalise the cable runs. Check that the handbrake control travel is correct.
12 Tighten the locknut onto the adjuster nut finger tight, then tighten

28.2 Handbrake cable adjuster

28.5 Removing the handbrake cable retaining circlip (arrowed) from the right-hand caliper

28.9 Alignment marks painted on lever and body

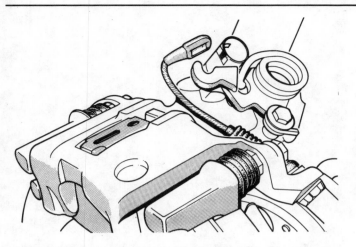

Fig. 9.20 Unhook the inner cable from the handbrake lever (Sec 28)

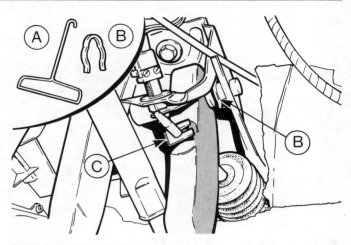

Fig. 9.21 Footbrake pedal removal (Sec 29)

A   Hooked instrument
B   Spring clip and location
C   Pushrod clip

a further two to four 'clicks' using self-locking pliers or a peg spanner.
13 Refit the rear wheels and lower the car to the ground.

29 Footbrake pedal – removal and refitting

1   Disconnect the battery negative lead.
2   Remove the facia lower panel on the driver's side.
3   Using a suitable hooked instrument extract the pivot shaft retaining spring clip located next to the pedal.

4   Extract the clip securing the pushrod to the pedal.
5   Slide the pivot shaft to the clutch pedal sufficiently to withdraw the footbrake pedal. Note the location of the washers and spacers.
6   If necessary prise the rubber from the pedal, and renew the bushes.
7   Refitting is a reversal of removal, but if necessary adjust the stop-lamp switch as described in Chapter 12.

30 Fault diagnosis – braking system

Symptom	Reason(s)
Excessive pedal travel	Air in hydraulic system
Uneven braking and pulling to one side	Contaminated linings Seized wheel cylinder or caliper Incorrect tyre pressures
Brake judder	Worn drums and/or discs Excessively worn brake linings Worn front suspension lower balljoint
Brake pedal feels 'spongy'	Air in hydraulic system Worn master cylinder seals
Excessive effort to stop car	Servo unit faulty Excessively worn brake linings Seized wheel cylinder or caliper Contaminated brake linings Failure of front or rear hydraulic circuit ABS hydraulic pump not working

Chapter 10 Suspension and steering

Contents

Specifications

Front suspension

Type .... Independent MacPherson struts, coil springs and anti-roll bar, double-acting telescopic shock absorbers incorporated in struts

Rear suspension

Type .... Independent, semi-trailing arms and coil springs, double-acting shock absorbers mounted behind the coil springs on Saloon models, but concentric with the coil springs on Estate models, self-levelling shock absorbers on some Estate models

Steering

Type .... Rack-and-pinion steering gear linked to collapsible type steering column by flexible coupling and universal joint. Power-assisted steering standard on some models

Number of turns lock-to-lock:
    Manual steering 4.15
    Power-assisted steering:
        Except 4x4 models .... 2.71 or 2.56
        4x4 models 2.84
Power-steering pump drivebelt tension .... 10.0 mm (0.4 in) deflection midway between water pump and power-steering pump under firm thumb pressure

Power-steering fluid type/specification .... ATF to Ford spec SQM-2C 9010-A (Duckhams D-Matic)

Front wheel alignment
Toe-checking:
    Except 4x4 models .... 0.5 mm (0.02 in) toe-out to 4.5 mm (0.18 in) toe-in
    4x4 models .... 2.5 mm (0.10 in) toe-out to 4.5 mm (0.18 in) toe-in
Toe-setting:
    Except 4x4 models .... 2.0 ± 1.0 mm (0.08 ± 0.04 in) toe-in
    4x4 models .... 1.0 ± 1.0 mm (0.04 ± 0.04 in) toe-in

Nominal castor angle (non-adjustable):
    Saloon (Domestic, excluding 4x4) .... 1° 52'
    Saloon (Heavy Duty, including 4x4) .... 1° 53'
    Estate (Domestic, excluding 4x4) .... 1° 44'
    Estate (Heavy Duty, including 4x4) .... 2° 07'
    Estate (Domestic, Nivomat) .... 1° 42'
    Estate (Heavy Duty, Nivomat) .... 1° 52'
    Estate (Business) .... 1° 50'
Maximum castor variation side-to-side .... 1° 0'
Nominal camber angle (non-adjustable):
    Saloon (Domestic, excluding 4x4) .... −0° 21'
    Saloon (Heavy Duty, including 4x4) .... +0° 04'
    Estate (Domestic, excluding 4x4) .... −0° 25'
    Estate (Heavy Duty, including 4x4) .... +0° 05'
    Estate (Domestic, Nivomat) .... −0° 25'
    Estate (Heavy Duty, Nivomat) .... +0° 05'
    Estate (Business) .... −0° 19'
Maximum camber variation side-to-side .... 1° 15'

Wheels
Type .... Pressed-steel or alloy
Size .... 13 x 5^1/$_2$J or 14 x 5^1/$_2$J

Tyres
Sizes – Saloon .... 165 SR/TR 13, 165 HR 13, 185/70 SR/TR 13, 185/70 HR 13, 195/60
    HR or 195/60 VR 14
Sizes – Estate .... 175 SR/TR 13, 175 HR 13, 195/70 HR 13 or 195/60 HR 14

Pressures (cold) in lbf/in² (bar):

	Front	Rear
All models, normal load*	26 (1.8)	26 (1.8)
Saloon, full load	29 (2.0)	36 (2.5)
Estate, full load:		
175 SR/TR 13 and 175 HR 13	29 (2.0)	40 (2.8)
195/70 HR 13	29 (2.0)	48 (3.3)
195/60 HR 14	29 (2.0)	36 (2.5)

Normal load is defined as up to three passengers (or equivalent). For sustained high speeds add 1.5 lbf/in² (0.1 bar) for every 6 mph (10 km/h) over 100 mph (160 km/h).

Torque wrench settings

	Nm	lbf ft
Front suspension		
Hub retaining nut (except 4x4)	310 to 350	229 to 258
Front driveshaft nut (4x4)	205 to 235	151 to 173
Lower arm balljoint	65 to 85	48 to 63
Strut upper mounting nut	40 to 52	30 to 38
Strut to spindle carrier	77 to 92	57 to 68
Anti-roll bar clamp	57 to 70	42 to 52
Anti-roll bar to lower arm	70 to 110	52 to 81
Crossmember	70 to 90	52 to 66
Lower arm pivot nut:		
Stage 1	45	33
Stage 2	Slacken completely	Slacken completely
Stage 3	15	11
Stage 4	Tighten through further 90°	Tighten through further 90°
Rear suspension		
Rear driveshaft nut	250 to 290	185 to 214
Guide plate to floor	41 to 51	30 to 38
Guide plate to crossmember	69 to 88	51 to 65
Lower arm to crossmember	80 to 95	59 to 70
Anti-roll bar to floor	20 to 25	15 to 18
Hub-to-lower arm bolt – type 'A'	52 to 64	38 to 47
Hub-to-lower arm bolt – type 'B'	80 to 100	59 to 74
Steering (manual)		
Track rod end to steering arm	25 to 30	18 to 22
Track rod end locknut	57 to 68	42 to 50
Track rod inner balljoint	72 to 88	53 to 65
Pinion cover nut	70 to 100	52 to 74
Slipper plug:		
Stage 1	4 to 5	3 to 4
Stage 2	Back off 60° to 70°	Back off 60° to 70°
Coupling shaft to steering shaft	20 to 25	15 to 18
Coupling to pinion	20 to 30	15 to 22
Steering wheel nut	45 to 55	33 to 41
Column mounting pinch-bolt	45 to 55	33 to 41

Torque wrench settings (continued)

	Nm	lbf ft
Steering gear to crossmember:		
Stage 1	45	33
Stage 2	Slacken completely	Slacken completely
Stage 3	15	11
Stage 4	Tighten through further 90°	Tighten through further 90°
Steering (power-assisted)		
Coupling clamp bolts	16 to 20	12 to 25
Coupling pinch-bolts	16 to 20	12 to 15
Slipper cover plate	22 to 24	16 to 18
Coupling nuts	20 to 27	15 to 20
Lower pinion nut	37 to 47	27 to 35
Track rod end to steering arm	25 to 30	18 to 22
Track rod end locknut	57 to 68	42 to 50
Track rod inner balljoint	70 to 77	52 to 57
Pressure hose to sump	26 to 31	19 to 23
Return hose to pump	16 to 21	12 to 15
Pump pulley bolt	10 to 12	7 to 9
Column clamp and nuts	17 to 24	13 to 18
Pump bracket to block	52 to 64	38 to 47
Steering gear to crossmember:		
Except 4x4:		
Stage 1	15	11
Stage 2	Tighten through further 90°	Tighten through further 90°
4x4	35 to 45	26 to 33
Wheels		
Wheel nuts	70 to 100	52 to 74

1 General description

The front suspension is of independent MacPherson strut type incorporating coil springs and double-action telescopic shock absorbers. An anti-roll bar is mounted to the rear of the suspension arms, and controls the fore-and-aft movement of the struts as well as stabilising any roll tendency of the front suspension. All suspension mounting points are of rubber. The lower end of the strut is attached to the suspension arm by a sealed balljoint. The front wheel bearings are of matched self-setting taper roller design and no adjustment is required or possible.

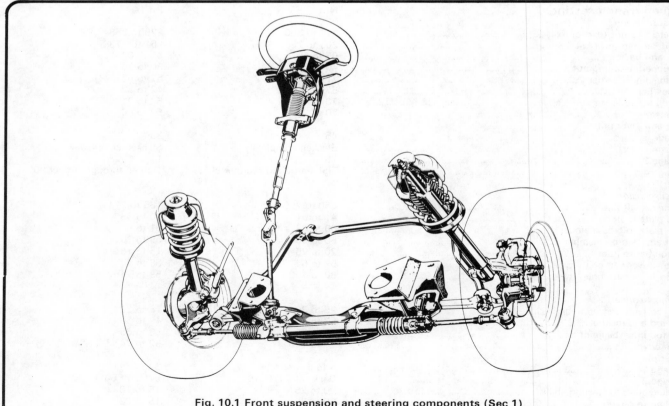

Fig. 10.1 Front suspension and steering components (Sec 1)

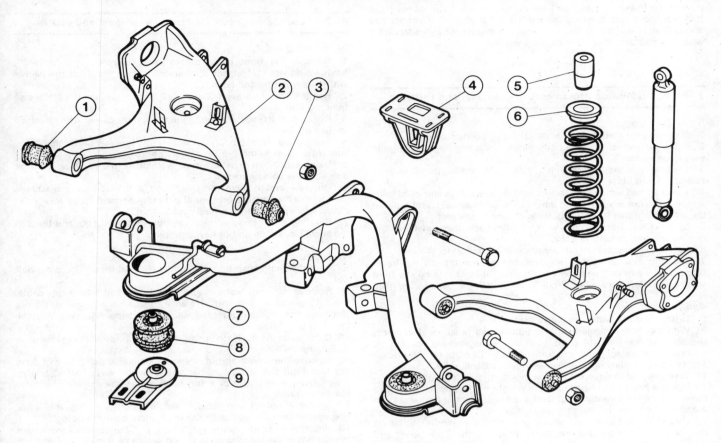

Fig. 10.2 Rear suspension components (Sec 1)

1 Outer rubber bush
2 Lower suspension arm
3 Inner rubber bush
4 Final drive unit rear
   mounting
5 Bump rubber
6 Spring seat pad
7 Rear axle crossmember
8 Mounting rubber
9 Guide plate

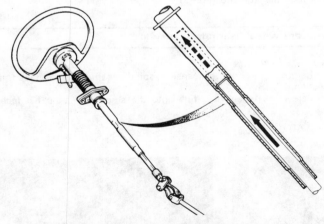

Fig. 10.3 Cross-section of the collapsible safety steering column (Sec 1)

The rear suspension is of independent type incorporating semi-trailing arms, coil springs and double-acting shock absorbers. On Saloon models the shock absorbers are mounted behind the coil springs, but on Estate models they are concentric with the coil springs. Additionally on some Estate models the shock absorbers are of self-levelling type. All suspension mounting points are of rubber. The rear wheel bearings are of double taper-roller design and similar to the front wheel bearings. An anti-roll bar is mounted between the suspension arms.

The steering is of rack-and-pinion type incorporating a safety steering column. Power-assisted steering is fitted to most models covered in this Manual.

2 Routine maintenance

Carry out the following procedures at the intervals given in 'Routine Maintenance' at the beginning of the Manual.

Check tyre for wear and damage
1 Examine the tyre walls and tread for wear and damage, in particular splits and bulges which if evident will require renewal of the tyre. If abnormal tyre wear is evident a thorough check of the suspension should be made. Check and adjust the tyre pressures at the same time (tyres cold).

Check steering components for damage
2 Visually check all steering components, including rubber bellows and dust covers for damage.

Check power steering pump drivebelt(s)
3 Examine the full length of the power steering pump drivebelt(s) for wear, damage and deterioration.
4 Check the drivebelt tension with reference to Chapter 2 and adjust if necessary.

Check steering and suspension components for wear and damage
5 Examine all steering and suspension linkages for wear and damage. Make sure that all dust covers are intact and secure. Check the front

suspension lower balljoints by levering up the suspension arms – the total free movement must not exceed 0.5 mm (0.020 in). The track rod end balljoints can be checked in a similar manner or by observation while an assistant 'rocks' the steering wheel.

3 Front suspension crossmember – removal and refitting

Non-4x4 models

1 Remove the steering gear as described in Section 20 or 22.
2 Unscrew and remove the bolts securing the engine mountings to the crossmember.
3 Slightly raise the engine with a trolley jack and support it with an axle stand and block of wood.
4 Unscrew and remove the self-locking nuts, washers and pivot bolts securing the lower suspension arms to the crossmember, and pull out the arms. Note that the pivot bolt heads face to the rear.
5 Support the crossmember with a trolley jack, then unscrew and remove the four mounting bolts.
6 Lower the crossmember and withdraw it from under the car.
7 Refitting is a reversal of removal, but do not tighten the lower suspension pivot bolt nuts until the weight of the car is on the front suspension. Refer to Section 20 or 22 when refitting the steering gear.

4x4 models

8 Disconnect the battery negative lead.
9 With the front wheels in the straight-ahead position, disconnect the steering intermediate shaft from the inner steering column by unscrewing the single bolt and turning the metal plate to one side.
10 Remove the steering gear as described in Section 22.
11 Unscrew and remove the engine mounting nuts on both sides.
12 Using a hoist and chain, take the weight of the engine just off of the mountings. Alternatively support the engine with a bar resting on wooden blocks on the front suspension struts.
13 Disconnect the lower suspension arms from the spindle carriers on both sides by unscrewing the nuts, removing the Torx bolts, and tapping the arms downwards with a mallet.
14 Unscrew and remove the pivot bolts from the inner ends of the suspension arms.
15 Working on each side separately, pull out the struts and withdraw the inner ends of the driveshafts from the final drive unit and intermediate shaft. Tie the driveshafts to one side.
16 Support the crossmember with a trolley jack, then unscrew and remove the four mounting bolts (photo).
17 Lower the crossmember and withdraw it from under the car.
18 Unbolt the engine mountings from the top of the crossmember.
19 Refitting is a reversal of removal, but do not tighten the lower suspension arm inner pivot bolts until the weight of the car is on the front suspension. Refer to Section 22 when refitting the steering gear. Finally check and if necessary top up the oil level in the front final drive unit (Chapter 8).

4 Front suspension spindle carrier – removal and refitting

Non-4x4 models

1 Remove the front brake caliper with reference to Chapter 9, however do not disconnect the hydraulic hose. Suspend the caliper with wire from the coil spring.
2 Remove the cross-head screw or clip and withdraw the brake disc from the hub.
3 Disconnect the track rod end from the spindle carrier with reference to Section 26.
4 Extract the split pin and unscrew the nut securing the lower suspension arm to the spindle carrier (photo).
5 Using a balljoint separator tool, disconnect the lower suspension arm from the spindle carrier.
6 Unscrew and remove the pinch-bolt and withdraw the spindle carrier from the suspension strut. If difficulty is experienced wedge the clamp legs apart using a suitable cold chisel.
7 Refitting is a reversal of removal, but tighten all nuts and bolts to the specified torque and fit new split pins.

4x4 models

8 Prise the central cap from the roadwheel and loosen the driveshaft nut.
9 Remove the front brake caliper, brake disc, and where applicable, the ABS wheel sensors with reference to Chapter 9, however do not disconnect the hydraulic hose. Suspend the caliper with wire from the coil spring.
10 Disconnect the track rod end from the spindle carrier with reference to Section 26.
11 Remove the driveshaft nut, then use a suitable puller to withdraw the hub from the spindle carrier and over the driveshaft stub end. Alternatively careful use of a soft-head mallet will achieve the same objective (photo).
12 Unscrew the nut and remove the Torx bolt, then tap the lower suspension arm and balljoint from the spindle carrier (photos).
13 Unscrew and remove the pinch-bolt, pull the spindle carrier from the bottom of the suspension strut and withdraw it over the driveshaft stub end. If the carrier is difficult to remove from the strut, use a cold chisel to wedge the clamp legs apart.
14 Refitting is a reversal of removal, but tighten all nuts and bolts to the specified torque. Fit a new split pin to the track rod end nut. Fit a new driveshaft nut, and after tightening, stake the collar into the groove in the stub end (photo).

5 Front wheel bearings – renewal

Non-4x4 models

1 Remove the front suspension spindle carrier as described in Section 4.
2 Screw the wheel nuts fully into the studs with their flat faces

3.16 Removing the crossmember mounting bolts (4x4 models)

4.4 Front suspension lower balljoint and nut on non-4x4 models

4.11 Front wheel hub removal from spindle carrier (4x4 models)

4.12A Unscrew the Torx bolt ...

4.12B ... and withdraw the balljoint from the spindle carrier (4x4 models)

4.14 Locking the driveshaft nut (4x4 models)

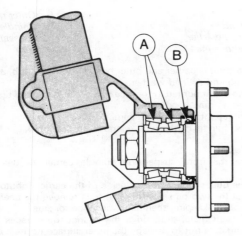

Fig. 10.4 Cross-sectional diagram of front wheel bearings (non-4x4 models) (Sec 5)

A   Matched taper bearings   B   Oil seal

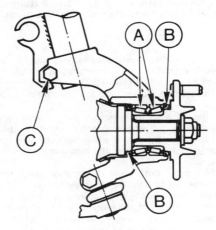

Fig. 10.5 Cross-sectional diagram of front wheel bearings (4x4 models) (Sec 5)

A   Tapered roller bearings
B   Oil seals
C   Spindle carrier-to-strut pinch-bolt

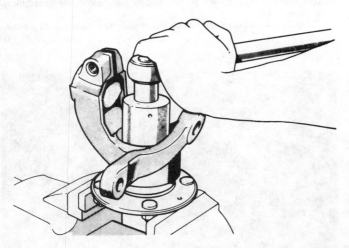

Fig. 10.6 Unscrewing the front hub nut (non-4x4 models) (Sec 5)

5.3 Removing the inner cap from the spindle carrier

towards the flange, then mount the assembly in a vice as shown in Fig. 10.6.

3   Prise the cap from the spindle carrier and unscrew the hub nut with a socket (photo). Note that the nut has a right-hand thread on all models manufactured before late December 1982, but as from this date

Fig. 10.7 Identification of the modified right-hand side front hub with left-hand thread (non-4x4 models) (Sec 5)

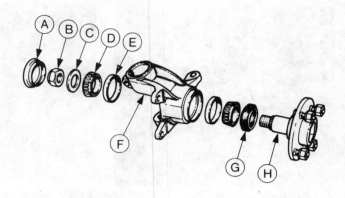

Fig. 10.8 Exploded view of the front hub (non 4x4 models) (Sec 5)

A	Cap	E	Outer race
B	Locknut	F	Spindle carrier
C	Splined washer	G	Oil seal
D	Taper bearing	H	Hub

left-hand thread assemblies were progressively fitted to the right-hand spindle carrier. The modified right-hand hub is identified by the letter 'R' stamped on its outer face (Fig. 10.7).

4   Remove the splined washer and tap the spindle carrier from the hub.

5   Prise out the oil seal, then remove the bearing inner races and rollers from the carrier. If the bearing was tight on the hub, it may have pulled the oil seal from the carrier when the latter was removed. If so, remove the bearing and seal from the hub and clean the hub surface with emery tape.

6   Using a soft metal drift, drive the bearing outer races from the carrier, taking care not to damage the inner surface of the carrier.

7   Clean the carrier and hub with paraffin, wipe dry and examine them for damage and wear. Note that the components are machined to close tolerances. The bearings are supplied in matched pairs, therefore extra care is necessary to ensure that all foreign matter is removed.

8   Using a suitable metal tube drive the bearing outer races fully into the carrier.

9   Pack the inner bearing races and taper rollers with high melting point lithium based grease, and locate the outer bearing in the carrier.

10 Fill the cavities between the sealing lips of the oil seal with grease then drive it fully into the carrier using a block of wood or suitable metal tube.

11 Tap the spindle carrier and outer bearing onto the hub, and fit the inner bearing and splined washer.

12 With the hub mounted in the vice refit the hub nut and tighten it to the specified torque.

13 Tap the cap into the spindle carrier.

14 Refit the spindle carrier with reference to Section 4.

4x4 models

15 Remove the front suspension spindle carrier as described in Section 4.

16 Prise the dust shield from the inside of the carrier (photo).

17 Prise out the two oil seals (photo), then remove the bearing inner races and rollers, keeping them identified side for side.

18 Using a soft metal drift, drive the bearing outer races from the carrier, taking care not to damage the inner surface of the carrier.

19 Clean all the components and examine them for wear and damage.

20 Using a suitable metal tube, drive the new bearing outer races fully into the carrier.

21 Pack the inner bearing races and taper rollers with high melting-point lithium-based grease, and locate them in their matching outer races.

22 Fill the cavities between the sealing lips of the oil seals with grease,

5.16 View of dust shield and bearings from inside the spindle carrier (4x4 models)

5.17 View of oil seal and bearings from outside the spindle carrier (4x4 models)

then drive them fully into the carrier using a block of wood or a suitable metal tube.
23 Press a new dust shield on the inside of the carrier.
24 Refit the carrier with reference to Section 4.

6 Front suspension lower arm – removal, overhaul and refitting

1 Apply the handbrake, then jack up the front of the car and support on axle stands. Remove the relevant wheel.
2 Unscrew and remove the self-locking nut, washer and pivot bolt securing the lower suspension arm to the crossmember, and pull the arm out. Note that the pivot bolt head faces to the rear.
3 On non-4x4 models extract the split pin and unscrew the nut securing the lower suspension arm to the spindle carrier. Using a balljoint separator tool, disconnect the arm from the carrier.
4 On 4x4 models unscrew the nut and remove the Torx bolt, then tap the outer end of the lower suspension arm together with the balljoint from the bottom of the spindle carrier.
5 Unscrew the nut from the end of the anti-roll bar and withdraw the lower arm. Note the location of the dished washers and rubber bushes or plastic cover (photo). Several modifications have been made to the bush; on early models two cupped rubber bush halves were fitted, then in November 1983 plastic covers were fitted between the washers and bushes, and in January 1985 the two rubber bush halves were pressed into the lower arm. Note that the front and rear dished washers are not interchangeable, and that the bush arrangement must be the same on both sides of the car.
6 The inner bush may be removed from the lower arm by using a long bolt with nut, washers and a suitable metal tube. Dip the new bush in soapy water before fitting it using a single continuous action to avoid deformation of the bush. If the balljoint is worn, renew the complete arm, however it is possible to renew the dust seal separately.
7 Where the bush halves are pressed into the lower arm, they may be removed by using a cold chisel. Use a suitable metal tube to drive the new bushes squarely into the arm.
8 Refitting is a reversal of removal, noting that the shallow dished washer goes on the anti-roll bar before fitting the lower arm. Do not tighten the inner pivot until the weight of the car is on the front suspension. Tighten all nuts and bolts to the specified torque, and on non-4x4 models, fit a new split pin to the lower balljoint nut.

6.5 Front suspension lower arm (arrowed)

7 Front anti-roll bar – removal and refitting

1 Apply the handbrake, then jack up the front of the car and support on axle stands. Remove both roadwheels.
2 Where fitted, bend back the locktabs then unscrew the four bolts from the rear mounting clamps (photos).
3 Unscrew the nuts from the front ends of the anti-roll bar and remove the front dished washers and rubber bush or plastic cover.
4 Unscrew and remove the self-locking nut, washer and pivot bolt from the inner end of one of the lower suspension arms. Note that the pivot bolt head faces to the rear.
5 While an assistant pulls the bottom of the strut outwards, withdraw the anti-roll bar from the lower arm (photo), then withdraw it from the arm on the other side. On 4x4 models, it is necessary to ease the driveshaft from the final drive unit or intermediate shaft at the same time.

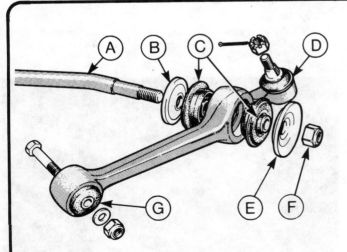

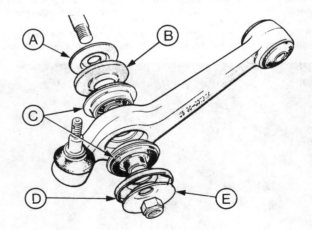

Fig. 10.9 Front anti-roll bar to lower arm mounting on pre-November 1983 models (Sec 6)

A Anti-roll bar	E Front dished washer
B Rear dished washer	F Locknut
C Bush	G Pivot bush
D Balljoint	

Fig. 10.10 Front anti-roll bar to lower arm mounting on January 1985-on models (Sec 6)

A Rear (black) washer	D Plastic cover
B Plastic cover	E Front (yellow) washer
C Bushes	

7.2A Bend back the locktabs ...

7.2B ... unscrew the bolts and remove the anti-roll bar rear mounting clamps

7.5 Removing the front anti-roll bar from the lower arm

6   Remove the bushes, plastic covers, and dished washers from the ends of the anti-roll bar as applicable. Refer to Section 6 for details of the modifications made to the bushes. Also remove the rear clamp rubber bushes.

7   Examine the rubber bushes for damage and deterioration and renew them if necessary. Refer to Section 6 and note that the bushes should be renewed on both sides at the same time.

8   Refitting is a reversal of removal, but do not tighten the rear mounting bolts or the lower suspension arm pivot bolt until the weight of the car is on the front suspension. Where fitted, bend the locktabs onto the rear mounting bolts to lock them.

8   Front suspension strut – removal and refitting

1   Apply the handbrake, then jack up the front of the car and support on axle stands. Remove the relevant wheel.

2   Unscrew and remove the strut pinch-bolt from the spindle carrier and wedge the clamp legs slightly apart using a suitable cold chisel (photo).

3   Where fitted, remove the ABS wheel sensor from the spindle carrier and release the wire from the clip on the strut (photo) (see Chapter 9).

4   Lever the lower suspension arm downwards to separate the spindle carrier from the strut. To prevent any possible damage to the brake caliper flexible hose, locate an axle stand two or three inches below the arm to limit its travel.

5   Working in the engine compartment, prise off the plastic cap (if fitted) then unscrew the strut upper mounting nut, at the same time

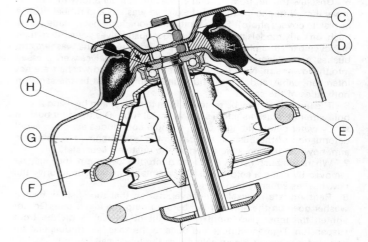

Fig. 10.11 Cross-section of the front suspension strut upper mounting (Sec 8)

A Bearing	E Lower cap
B Nylon spacer	F Spring seat
C Cup	G Bump stop
D Insulator	H Gaiter

8.2 Removing the front suspension strut pinch-bolt

8.3 ABS wheel sensor wire and support clip

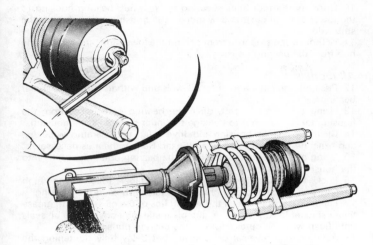

Fig. 10.12 Using spring compressor clamps when dismantling the front suspension strut (Sec 8)

supporting the strut from below (photo). If the strut piston rod rotates hold it stationary with a 6 mm hexagon key.

6 Withdraw the suspension strut from under the wing (photo).

7 Using spring compressor clamps, compress the coil spring. Do not attempt to compress the coil spring without using purpose-made clamps otherwise personal injury may occur.

8 Unscrew the nut from the piston rod and withdraw the cup, bearing, seat, gaiter, coil spring and bump stop (photo).

9 Working in the engine compartment, remove the upper cup and nylon spacer and if necessary prise out the rubber insulator (photos).

10 Clean all the components and examine them for wear and deterioration. Check the action of the strut shock absorber by mounting the strut vertically in a vice and operating the piston rod several times through its full stroke. If any uneven resistance is evident the strut must be renewed.

11 Refitting is a reversal of removal, however the nylon centralizing spacer should be located over the piston rod before fitting the strut to the top mounting. Make sure that the spring ends are correctly located in the shaped seats. Tighten the nuts and bolts to the specified torque.

9 Rear suspension and final drive assembly – removal and refitting

1 Chock the front wheels, then jack up the rear of the car and support with axle stands positioned under the longitudinal underbody members. Release the handbrake.

2 Remove the exhaust system (Chapter 3) and the propeller shaft (Chapter 7).

3 Disconnect the anti-roll bar (where fitted) from the lower arms by prising off the links wih a screwdriver.

4 Disconnect the handbrake cable from the handbrake lever by removing the circlip and pin.

5 Unclip the handbrake outer cables from the underbody.

6 Disconnect the hydraulic brake hoses from the right and left-hand brackets on the underbody with reference to Chapter 9.

7 Place suitable blocks beneath the rear wheels then lower the car so that the rear coil springs are lightly loaded and reposition the axle stands under the underbody members.

8 Support the final drive unit with a trolley jack.

9 Unscrew and remove the bolts securing the guide plates to the underbody and rear suspension crossmember (photo). Remove the guide plates.

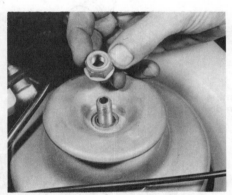

8.5 Front suspension strut upper mounting nut

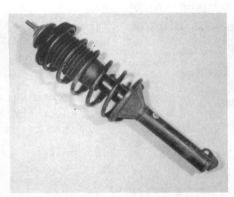

8.6 Front suspension strut

8.8 Front suspension strut upper mounting cap and spring retaining nut

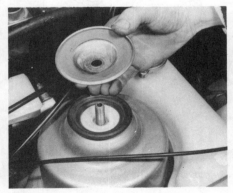

8.9A Front suspension strut upper mounting cap removal

8.9B View of the front suspension strut upper mounting from below

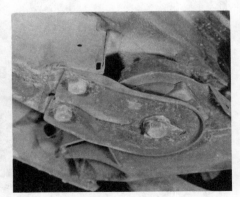

9.9 A rear suspension guide plate

10 Unscrew and remove the bolts securing the final drive rear mounting to the underbody.

11 Working inside the rear of the car unscrew and remove the rear shock absorber upper mounting bolts/nuts. On Saloon models access is gained by removing the trim cover behind the side cushions. On Estate models pull back the floor covering and remove the self-tapping screws from the covers.

12 Using a trolley jack and wooden beam positioned beneath the longitudinal underbody members, raise the rear of the car until the rear suspension and final drive assembly can be withdrawn from under the car.

13 If necessary the individual components may be dismantled from the assembly, with reference to the relevant Sections of this Chapter, and Chapter 8.

14 Refitting is a reversal of removal, but make sure that the rear coil springs are correctly located. Tighten all nuts and bolts to the specified torque. After completion bleed the brakes and adjust the handbrake as described in Chapter 9, and check the final drive unit oil level as described in Chapter 8. Refer to Chapter 7 when refitting the propeller shaft.

10 Rear wheel hub and bearings – removal and refitting

1 Remove the relevant wheel cap as necessary, then apply the handbrake and loosen the driveshaft nut. The nut is tightened to a high torque requiring a long socket extension bar. Note that from September 1983 (build code DJ), the nut on the left-hand side of the car has a **left-hand thread** on rear drum brake models only.

2 Jack up the rear of the car and support on axle stands. Chock the front wheels and release the handbrake. Remove the wheel.

Rear drum brake models

3 Remove the clip and withdraw the brake drum.

4 Unscrew the driveshaft nut and using a suitable puller, withdraw the drive flange from the driveshaft.

5 Prise off the plastic clips and remove the cover from the rear of the backplate.

6 Mark the rear hub bearing housing in relation to the backplate then unscrew the four bolts from the rear suspension lower arm and withdraw the housing. Temporarily refit the brake backplate with two bolts to avoid straining the brake hydraulic pipe.

Rear disc brake models

7 Unscrew the driveshaft nut.

8 Remove the brake disc with reference to Chapter 9.

9 Mark the driveshaft flange and stub axle flange in relation to each other. Using a Torx key unscrew the flange bolts, then tie the driveshaft to one side.

10 Unscrew the four bolts securing the rear hub bearing housing to the lower arm (photo), and withdraw the housing and hub over the stub axle.

11 Withdraw the stub axle from behind the lower arm, and remove the hub from the bearing housing.

All models

12 Prise out the inner and outer oil seals and withdraw the taper roller bearings.

13 Using a soft metal drift, drive the bearing outer races from the housing taking care not to damage the inner surface of the housing.

14 Clean the bearing housing and drive flange with paraffin, wipe dry, and examine them for damage and wear. Renew them as necessary.

15 Using a suitable metal tube drive the bearing outer races fully into the housing.

16 Pack the inner bearing races and taper rollers with high melting-point lithium based grease and locate them in the housing.

17 Fill the cavities between the sealing lips of the oil seals with grease then using a block of wood or suitable metal tube drive in the oil seals until flush with the outer edges of the bearing housing.

18 Refitting is a reversal of removal, but delay fully tightening the

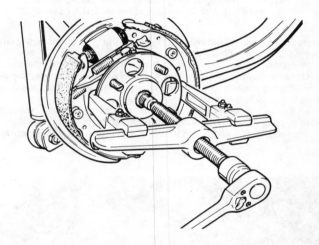

Fig. 10.13 Using a puller to withdraw the rear-wheel-drive flange on drum brake models (Sec 10)

10.10 Rear hub bearing housing bolt removal

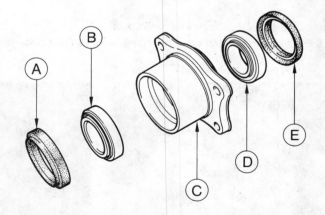

Fig. 10.14 Exploded view of the rear wheel hub (Sec 10)

Note: *Drum brake hub shown, disc brake type similar*

A Outer oil seal	D Inner bearing
B Outer bearing	E Inner oil seal
C Hub	

10.18 Rear driveshaft nut locking method

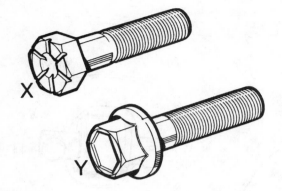

Fig. 10.15 Different types of rear wheel hub-to-suspension lower arm bolts (Sec 10)

X Type 'A'   Y Type 'B'

driveshaft nut (new) until the wheel is on the ground. Where the nut is **not** self-locking, peen the collar into the groove in the driveshaft stub end (photo). Note also that there are two different types of bolt used to secure the hub bearing housing to the lower arm, as shown in Fig. 10.15. The two types of bolt must not be mixed on one vehicle as each has a different tightening torque (see Specifications).

11 Rear shock absorber – removal and refitting

Note: *On Estate models fitted with heavy duty Nivomat shock absorbers follow the procedure given in Section 12 as the coil spring is an integral part of the shock absorber.*

Saloon models
1 With the weight of the car on the rear suspension, work under the car to unscrew and remove the shock absorber lower mounting bolt (photo).
2 Working in the rear compartment, remove the crosshead screws and withdraw the trim cover behind the side cushion (photo).
3 While an assistant supports the shock absorber unscrew and remove the upper mounting bolt (photo).
4 Withdraw the shock absorber from under the car.
5 Refitting is a reversal of removal.

Estate models
6 Chock the front wheels, then jack up the rear of the car and support on axle stands.

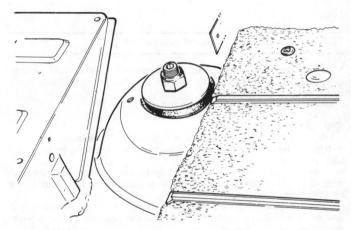

Fig. 10.16 Rear shock absorber upper mounting on Estate models (Sec 11)

7 Support the rear suspension lower arm with a trolley jack.
8 Working in the rear compartment fold the rear seat backrest forwards, remove the screws and lift off the wheel arch trim cover.
9 Unscrew and remove the shock absorber upper mounting nut.
10 Unscrew the lower mounting bolts from the bottom of the rear suspension lower arm and withdraw the shock absorber downwards.
11 Refitting is a reversal of removal.

11.1 Rear shock absorber lower mounting (Saloon models)

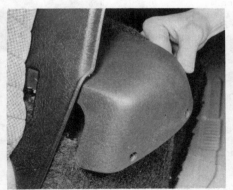

11.2 Remove the trim cover ...

11.3 ... for access to the rear shock absorber upper mounting on Saloon models

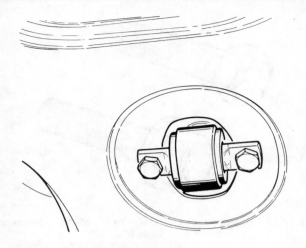

Fig. 10.17 Rear shock absorber lower mounting on Estate models (Sec 11)

12 Rear coil spring – removal and refitting

1   Chock the front wheels, then jack up the rear of the car and support with axle stands positioned under the longitudinal underbody members.
2   Remove the wheel and release the handbrake.

Rear drum brake models
3   Remove the screw or clip and withdraw the brake drum.
4   Unclip the driveshaft outer joint plastic cover from the upper brake backplate bolts.
5   Using a socket through the holes in the drive flange, unscrew and remove the four bolts securing the hub bearing housing and brake backplate to the suspension lower arm.
6   Withdraw the driveshaft complete with hub from the lower arm and final drive unit. Place a container beneath the final drive unit to catch any spilled oil.
7   Temporarily refit the brake backplate with two bolts to avoid straining the brake hydraulic pipe.
8   Unclip the brake hydraulic hose from the underbody mounting bracket. Do not disconnect the hydraulic line.
9   Support the lower suspension arm with a trolley jack.
10 On Saloon models unscrew and remove the shock absorber lower mounting bolt.
11 On Estate models fitted with standard shock absorbers remove the shock absorber as described in Section 11. On Estate models fitted with heavy duty Nivomat shock absorbers disconnect the top and bottom mountings.
12 Unbolt and remove the rear suspension crossmember guide plate from the underbody on the side being worked on.
13 Lower the suspension arm and withdraw the coil spring/heavy duty shock absorber and the rubber spring seat (photo).
14 Refitting is a reversal of removal, but tighten all nuts and bolts to the specified torque. Check and if necessary top up the final drive unit oil level as described in Chapter 8.

Rear disc brake models
15 Mark the driveshaft flange on the side being worked on and the stub axle flange in relation to each other. Using a Torx key unscrew the flange bolts, then tie the driveshaft to one side. This is necessary in order to prevent excessive deflection of the driveshaft when the lower arm is lowered.
16 Disconnect the anti-roll bar (where fitted) from the lower arm by prising off the link with a screwdriver.
17 Unclip the brake hydraulic hose from the underbody mounting bracket without disconnecting the rigid line. Unclip the rigid line from the underbody to allow sufficient movement of the lower arm.
18 Support the lower suspension arm with a trolley jack.
19 Follow the procedure given in paragraphs 10 to 13 inclusive.

20 Refitting is a reversal of removal, but tighten all nuts and bolts to the specified torque.

13 Rear suspension front mounting – renewal

1   Chock the front wheels, then jack up the rear of the car and support on axle stands.
2   Remove the two bolts securing the guide plate to the underbody.
3   Flatten the locktab and unscrew the mounting bolt. Withdraw the guide plate and spacer.
4   Using a length of wood lever the suspension crossmember a few inches from the underbody and insert the wood to retain.
5   Using Ford tool 15-014 (Fig. 10.18) or locally made tool, pull the mounting from the crossmember.
6   Dip the new mounting in soapy water then press it fully into the crossmember. If available use the spindle of Ford tool 15-017 to do this, or alternatively use a long threaded bolt through the floor mounting.
7   Remove the length of wood and insert the guide plate bolts loosely, together with the locktab and spacer.
8   Tighten the mounting bolt then the two remaining bolts to the specified torque and lock the mounting bolt by bending the locktab.
9   Lower the car to the ground.

14 Rear suspension/final drive unit rear mounting – renewal

1   Chock the front wheels, then jack up the rear of the car and support on axle stands.
2   Support the final drive unit with a trolley jack.
3   Unscrew and remove the four mounting bolts.
4   Lower the final drive unit sufficient to unbolt the mounting.
5   Fit the new mounting using a reversal of the removal procedure, but tighten the bolts to the specified torque.

12.13 Rear coil spring and rubber seat (Saloon models)

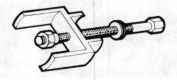

Fig. 10.18 Ford tool 15-014 for removing the rear suspension front mounting (Sec 13)

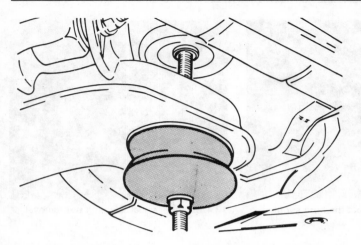

Fig. 10.19 Using Ford tool 15-017 for fitting the rear suspension front mounting (Sec 13)

15 Rear suspension lower arm – removal and refitting

Rear drum brake models

1 Remove the rear coil spring as described in Section 12.
2 Unclip the handbrake cable and brake hydraulic line from the suspension arm. Do not disconnect the hydraulic line.
3 Remove the brake backplate, complete with brake shoes, from the suspension arm and tie it to one side.

Rear disc brake models

4 Remove the relevant wheel cap as necessary, then apply the handbrake and loosen the driveshaft nut. The nut is tightened to a high torque requiring a long socket extension bar. Refer also to paragraph 1 of Section 10.
5 Jack up the rear of the car and support with axle stands positioned under the longitudinal underbody members.
6 Remove the wheel and release the handbrake.
7 Unhook the rear and centre right exhaust mountings, and unbolt the centre left mounting bracket from the underbody. Lower the rear of the exhaust system onto axle stands.
8 Fit a brake hose clamp to the hose leading from the underbody, then remove the rigid brake pipe from the lower arm by unscrewing the union nuts and releasing it from the clip.
9 Unclip the brake hose from the front of the lower arm. Unscrew the locknut and remove the caliper brake hose from the lower arm.
10 Unbolt the brake caliper and carrier from the rear hub bearing

housing, unhook the handbrake outer cable from the lower arm, and tie the assembly to one side.
11 Remove the rear wheel hub with reference to Section 10, paragraphs 7 to 11.
12 Where fitted remove the ABS wheel sensor with reference to Chapter 9.
13 Remove the propeller shaft as described in Chapter 7.
14 Disconnect the anti-roll bar (where fitted) from the lower arm by prising off the link with a screwdriver.
15 Remove the rear coil spring with reference to Section 12, paragraphs 9 to 13.

All models

16 Note the fitted position of the pivot bolts, then unscrew and remove them and withdraw the suspension arm from under the car (photo).
17 If necessary the pivot bushes may be renewed using a long bolt, nut, washers and suitable metal drift. Dip the new bushes in soapy water to facilitate their fitting.
18 Refitting is a reversal of removal, but delay tightening the pivot bolts to the specified torque until the weight of the car is on the rear suspension. Refer to Sections 10 and 12, and Chapters 7 and 9 as applicable and tighten all nuts and bolts to the specified torque. On rear disc brake models, bleed the rear brake hydraulic circuit as described in Chapter 9.

16 Rear anti-roll bar – removal and refitting

1 Slacken the rear wheel nuts, chock the front wheels and raise and securely support the rear of the car. Remove the rear wheels.
2 Prise off the links which connect the anti-roll bar to the lower suspension arms photo).
3 Unbolt the two retaining clamps from the floor and remove the anti-roll bar (photo).
4 Remove the rubber mountings and the connecting straps. Use liquid detergent as a lubricant when fitting new mounting components.
5 Refit in the reverse order of removal. Tighten the retaining clip bolts to the specified torque.

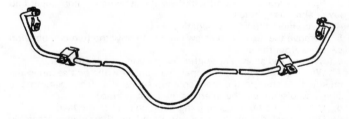

Fig. 10.20 Rear anti-roll bar (Sec 16)

15.16 Rear suspension lower arm pivot bolt

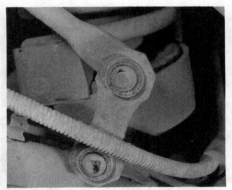

16.2 Rear anti-roll bar link

16.3 Rear anti-roll bar retaining clamp

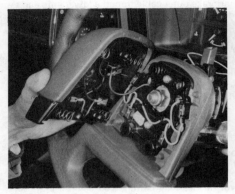
17.2A Prise off the centre insert ...

17.2B ... and disconnect the horn supply wire

17.4 Steering wheel retaining nut removal

17 Steering wheel – removal and refitting

1   Set the front wheels in the straight-ahead position, and disconnect the battery negative lead.
2   Prise the insert from the centre of the steering wheel and disconnect the horn supply wire where applicable (photos).
3   With the ignition key inserted check that the steering lock is disengaged.
4   Unscrew the retaining nut and withdraw the steering wheel from the hexagon shaped inner column (photo).
5   Refitting is a reversal of removal, but first check that the lug on the indicator cam is aligned with the cut-out in the steering wheel. Tighten the retaining nut to the specified torque.

18 Steering column – removal, overhaul and refitting

1   Set the front wheels in the straight-ahead position.
2   Remove the trim panels below the facia (photos).
3   Remove the screws and withdraw the steering column upper and lower shrouds (photos).
4   Disconnect the battery negative lead.
5   Remove the crosshead screws and withdraw the two combination switches from the column.
6   Remove the screw and withdraw the bonnet release lever.
7   Working in the engine compartment unscrew the bolt securing the intermediate shaft to the inner column, swivel the clamp plate to one side, and disconnect the intermediate shaft (photo).
8   Unscrew the nuts securing the outer column to the facia.
9   Disconnect the multi-plugs and withdraw the column assembly upwards.
10 Mount the outer column in a soft jawed vice.
11 Remove the steering wheel as described in Section 17.

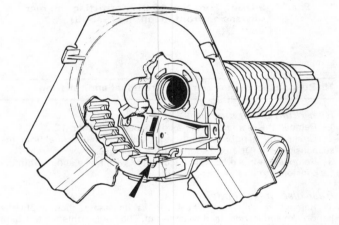
Fig. 10.21 Cut away view of the steering lock (Sec 17)

12 Remove the indicator arm and the bearing thrust washer.
13 Slide the inner column from the outer column, and remove the thrust washer and spring from the inner column.
14 Lever the upper and lower bearings from the outer column.
15 Clamp the bottom of the inner column in a vice and pull of the lower nylon bush. Take care not to collapse the inner column sections otherwise it must be renewed.
16 If necessary insert the ignition key and turn to position '1', depress the spring clip with a suitable instrument and withdraw the steering lock barrel. Remove the two grub screws and withdraw the ignition switch.

18.2A Removing a clip from the lower facia trim

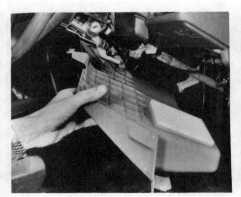
18.2B Removing the lower facia panel

18.2C Side trim removal

18.3A Removing the steering column upper shroud ...

18.3B ... and lower shroud

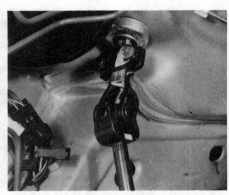

18.7 Intermediate shaft-to-steering column universal joint

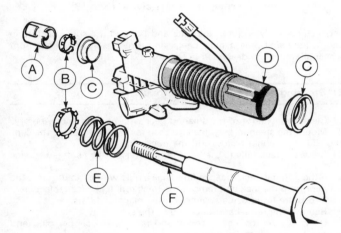

Fig. 10.22 Exploded view of the steering column (Sec 18)

A   Indicator cam   D   Outer column
B   Thrust washers   E   Spring
C   Bearings   F   Inner column

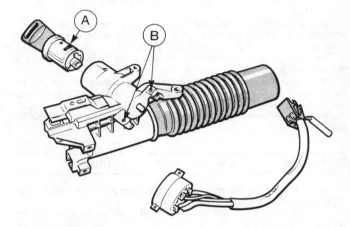

Fig. 10.23 Steering lock barrel securing clip (A) and ignition switch grub screw locations (B) (Sec 18)

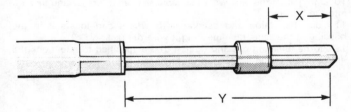

Fig. 10.24 Inner column nylon bush location (Sec 18)

X = 52.0 mm (2.05 in)
Y = 189.0 ± 3.0 mm (7.44 ± 0.12 in)

17 Clean all the components and examine them for wear and damage. Renew them as necessary.
18 Refit the ignition switch and steering lock barrel.
19 With the triangular section of the inner column mounted in a vice, push on the nylon bush to the position shown in Fig. 10.24.
20 Lubricate the upper and lower bearings with grease then push them into the outer column.
21 Locate the spring and thrust washer on the inner column then slide the inner column into the outer column.
22 Fit the upper bearing thrust washer and the indicator cam.
23 Clean the hexagon section of the inner column and refit the steering wheel with reference to Section 17.

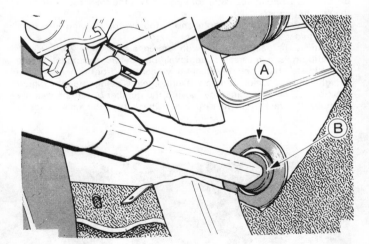

Fig. 10.25 Bulkhead bush (A) and inner column nylon bush (B) (Sec 18)

24 Check the the distance between the lower bearing in the outer column and the welded washer on the inner column is between 11.0 and 13.0 mm (0.43 and 0.51 in). If not, the column has been damaged and should be renewed.
25 Check that the bulkhead bush is serviceable and correctly fitted and renew if necessary. An incorrectly fitted bush can result in the ingress of water.

26 Refit the column assembly in the car and tighten the upper mounting nuts lightly. Loosen the mounting pinch-bolt.
27 Temporarily fit the upper column shroud and adjust the position of the steering column until there is gap of 5.0 mm (0.2 in) between the shroud and the facia.
28 Tighten the pinch-bolt and the mounting nuts and remove the upper column shroud.
29 With the steering wheel in the straight-ahead position reconnect the intermediate shaft and tighten the clamp plate bolt to the specified torque.
30 Refit the bonnet release lever and combination switches and reconnect the multi-plugs.
31 Refit the steering column shrouds and trim panels.
32 Reconnect the battery negative lead.

19 Steering intermediate shaft and coupling – removal and refitting

1 Apply the handbrake, then jack up the front of the car and support on axle stands.
2 Working in the engine compartment unscrew the bolt securing the intermediate shaft to the inner column, swivel the clamp plate to one side, and disconnect the intermediate shaft.
3 Unscrew and remove the clamp bolt securing the lower coupling to the steering gear (photos).
4 Mark the coupling in relation to the pinion then pull off the intermediate shaft and remove it from the car. The pinion has a master spline but marking it will facilitate refitting it.
5 Refitting is a reversal of removal, but tighten the bolts to the specified torque.

20 Steering gear (manual) – removal and refitting

1 Apply the handbrake, then jack up the front of the car and support on axle stands. Remove the front wheels.
2 Set the steering in the straight-ahead position and remove the ignition key to lock it.
3 Unscrew and remove the clamp bolt securing the intermediate shaft to the steering gear (photo).
4 Extract the split pins and unscrew the track rod end nuts.
5 Using a balljoint separator tool disconnect the track rod ends from the steering arms.
6 Unscrew the mounting bolts and withdraw the steering gear from the front suspension crossmember.
7 Remove the track rod ends with reference to Section 26.
8 Refitting is a reversal of removal, but before reconnecting the intermediate shaft, set the steering wheel and front wheels in the straight-ahead position. If a new steering gear is being fitted the pinion position can be ascertained by halving the number of turns necessary to move the rack from lock-to-lock. Check that the master spline

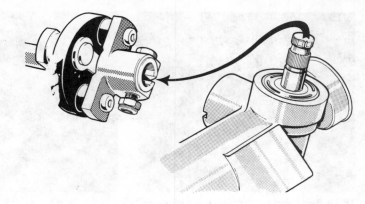

Fig. 10.26 Master spline location on the steering gear pinion and intermediate shaft clamp (Sec 19)

engages correctly. Tighten the nuts and bolts to the specified torque and fit new split pins. Finally check and if necessary adjust the front wheel alignment as described in Section 27.

21 Steering gear (manual) – overhaul

1 Clean the exterior of the steering gear with paraffin and wipe dry.
2 Mount the steering gear in a vice then remove and discard the clips and slide the rubber bellows off the track rods.
3 Move the rack fully to the left and grip the rack in a soft jawed vice (Fig. 10.28).
4 If the original track rods are fitted use a pipe wrench to unscrew the balljoint from the rack and remove the track rod. If service replacement track rods are fitted use a spanner on the machined flats.
5 Remove the right-hand track rod in the same way.
6 Using a hexagon key unscrew and remove the slipper plug and remove the spring and slipper.
7 Prise out the pinion dust cover, then using Ford tool 13-009 or locally made four segment tool, unscrew the pinion retaining nut and withdraw the pinion and bearing using a twisting action.
8 Withdraw the rack from the steering gear housing.
9 Clean all the components in paraffin and wipe dry. Examine them for wear and damage and renew them as necessary. If necessary the rack support bush in the housing can be renewed.
10 Lightly coat the rack with a suitable semi-fluid grease and insert it into the housing.
11 Coat the pinion and bearing with grease and locate it in the housing at the same time meshing it with the rack.
12 Fit the retaining nut and tighten to the specified torque. Lock the nut by peening the housing in four places.

19.3A Intermediate shaft lower coupling on manual steering gear ...

19.3B ... and power-steering gear

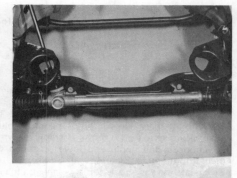

20.3 Manual steering gear location on the front suspension crossmember with engine removed (non-4x4 models)

13 Move the rack to its central position then fit the slipper and spring. Coat the plug threads with locking fluid then immediately fit it, tighten it to a torque of 4 to 5 Nm (3 to 4 lbf ft), and back it off between 60° and 70°.

14 Turn the pinion anti-clockwise 180°. Using a piece of string and a spring balance, check that the turning torque of the pinion while turning it clockwise 360° is between 0.8 and 1.4 Nm (0.6 and 1.0 lbf ft).

15 If adjustment is required, tighten or loosen the slipper plug as necessary, then recheck the setting by repeating the procedure given in paragraph 14. Do this immediately, before the locking fluid begins to set. Once set, lock the plug by peening the housing in three positions around the circumference of the top of the plug.

16 Grip the rack in a soft jawed vice after moving it fully to one side. Coat the threads of the track rod inner balljoint with locking fluid then refit it and tighten to the specified torque.

17 Refit the remaining track rod in the same manner.

18 Refit the rubber bellows to the rack tube using new clips.

19 Refit the pinion dust cover after filling with semi-fluid grease.

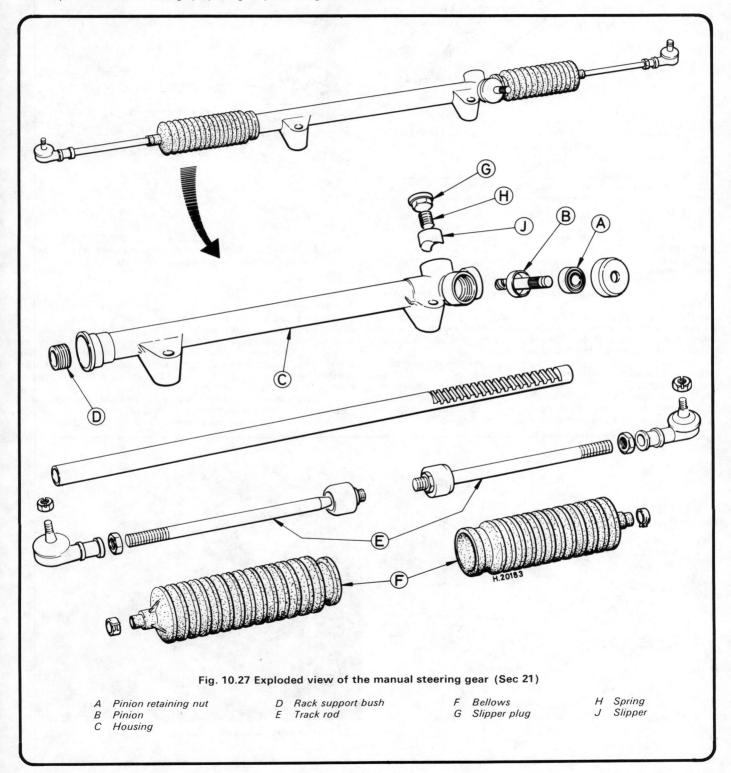

Fig. 10.27 Exploded view of the manual steering gear (Sec 21)

A	Pinion retaining nut	D	Rack support bush	F	Bellows	H	Spring
B	Pinion	E	Track rod	G	Slipper plug	J	Slipper
C	Housing						

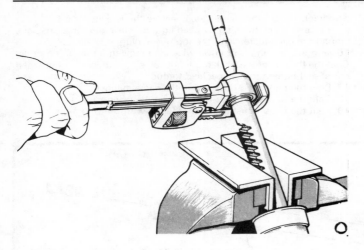

Fig. 10.28 Unscrewing the track rod balljoint from the steering rack (Sec 21)

Fig. 10.29 Ford tool 13-009 for removing the steering gear pinion retaining nut (Sec 21)

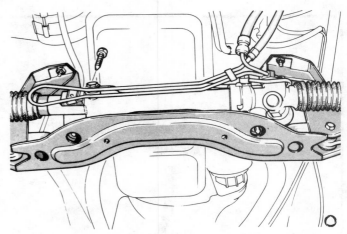

Fig. 10.30 Removing the power-steering gear on non-4x4 models – note the looped cooling pipe (Sec 22)

22 Power-steering gear – removal and refitting

1   Apply the handbrake, then jack up the front of the car and support on axle stands.
2   Set the front wheels in the straight-ahead position, then remove both wheels.
3   Unscrew and remove the clamp bolt securing the intermediate shaft to the steering gear.
4   Extract the split pins and unscrew the track rod end nuts.
5   Using a balljoint separator tool disconnect the track rod ends from the steering arms.
6   Place a suitable container beneath the steering gear then unscrew the pressure and return pipe unions or clamp plate and drain the power steering fluid. Cover the pipe ends and steering gear apertures with masking tape to prevent the ingress of foreign matter.
7   Unscrew the mounting bolts and withdraw the steering gear from the front suspension crossmember. On 4x4 models, refer to Fig. 10.31 for the withdrawal procedure necessary due to the different crossmember (photo). Slide the steering gear in direction (A), swing out the non-pinion end (B), and rotate in direction (C) to remove.
8   Remove the track rod ends with reference to Section 26.

9   Refitting is a reversal of removal, but before reconnecting the intermediate shaft, set the steering wheel and front wheels in the straight-ahead position. If a new steering gear is being fitted the pinion position can be ascertained by halving the number of turns necessary to move the rack from lock-to-lock. Tighten the nuts and bolts to the specified torque and fit new split pins. Where locking tabs are fitted to the steering gear bolts, bend them onto the bolt flats. Take care not to overtighten the unions, and note that with the unions fully tightened it is still possible to rotate and move the pipes. Refill and bleed the power steering as described in Section 23, and finally check and if necessary adjust the front wheel alignment as described in Section 27.

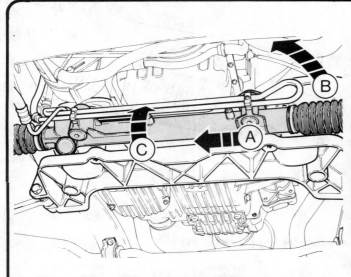

Fig. 10.31 Removal sequence for power-steering gear on 4x4 models (Sec 22)

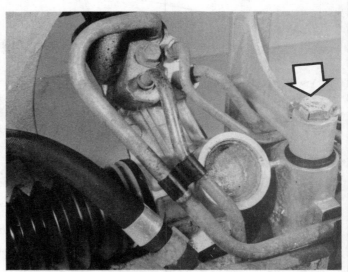

22.7 Power-steering gear and mounting bolt (arrowed)

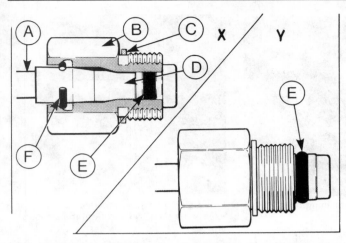

Fig. 10.32 Cutaway view of a pipe union connection for the power-steering gear (Sec 22)

X	*Installed*	C	*PTFE seal*
Y	*O-ring exposed*	D	*Pre-formed end*
A	*Pipe*	E	*O-ring*
B	*Coupling nut*	F	*Snap-ring*

23 Power-steering system – bleeding

Note: *It is important to use only the specified fluid for bleeding, and the fluid must be completely free of air bubbles, otherwise the pump* *will be noisy and the system inefficient. The fluid should be left to stand in the dispensing container for a minimum of 30 minutes before being poured slowly into the fluid reservoir.*

1   Unscrew the filler cap from the power-steering pump and top up the fluid level to the maximum mark (photos).
2   Disconnect the low tension negative lead from the ignition coil and crank the engine several times for two second periods while slowly turning the steering wheel from lock-to-lock. Top up the fluid level if necessary and continue cranking the engine until the fluid is free of air bubbles.
3   Reconnect the coil lead then start the engine and run it for a few seconds. Switch off and top up the level if necessary.
4   Repeat the procedure in paragraph 3 as necessary then refit the filler cap.

24 Power-steering pump – removal and refitting

1   Disconnect the battery negative lead.
2   Place a suitable container under the power-steering pump, disconnect the fluid pipes, and drain the fluid (photos). Considering the position of the alternator, cover it as a precaution where the pump is on the right-hand side of the engine.
3   Loosen the tension bracket bolts or the pump pivot and adjustment bolts as applicable. Slide the bracket or swivel the pump towards the engine and remove the drivebelt(s) from the pulley.
4   Remove the pivot/mounting/adjustment bolts as applicable, and withdraw the pump from the engine (photo).
5   Unbolt the pulley and the mounting plate if necessary.
6   Refitting is a reversal of removal, but tighten the bolts to the specified torque. Tension the drivebelts as described in Chapter 2. Refill the power-steering system with fluid and bleed it as described in Section 23.

23.1A The power-steering pump fluid level dipstick is incorporated in the filler cap

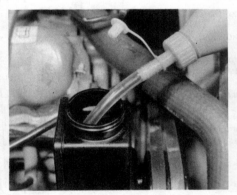

23.1B Topping-up the power-steering fluid level

24.2A Power-steering pump feed ...

24.2B ... and return pipes

24.4 Power-steering pump removed from the engine

25.2 A power-steering gear bellows

26.3 Track rod end and retaining nut

26.4 Using a balljoint separator tool to release the track rod end from the steering arm

25 Steering gear rubber bellows – renewal

1   Remove the track rod end as described in Section 26. Remove the locknut.
2   Remove the clips and slide the bellows from the track rod and steering gear (photo).
3   Slide the new bellows over the track rod and onto the steering gear. Where applicable make sure that the bellows seats in the cut-outs provided in the track rod and housing (support end only).
4   Fit and tighten the clips.
5   Refit the locknut and track rod end as described in Section 2.6

26 Track rod end – removal and refitting

1   Apply the handbrake, then jack up the front of the car and support on axle stands. Remove the relevant wheel.
2   Mark the track rod and track rod end in relation to each other then loosen the locknut a quarter of a turn.
3   Extract the split pin and unscrew the balljoint nut (photo).
4   Using a balljoint separator tool release the track rod end from the steering arm (photo).
5   Unscrew the track rod end from the track rod noting the number of turns necessary to remove it (photo).
6   Refitting is a reversal of removal, but tighten the nuts to the specified torque and fit a new split pin. On completion check and if necessary adjust the front wheel alignment as described in Section 27.

27 Wheel alignment – checking and adjusting

1   Accurate wheel alignment is essential for good steering and slow tyre wear. Before checking it, make sure that the car is only loaded to kerbside weight and that the tyre pressures are correct.
2   Place the car on level ground with the wheels in the straight-ahead position, then roll the car backwards 12 ft (4 metres) and forwards again.

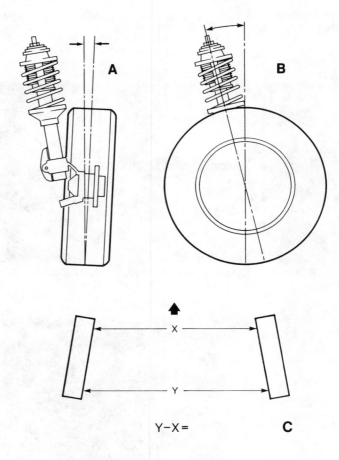

Fig. 10.33 Wheel alignment diagram (Sec 27)

A   Camber
B   Castor
C   Toe setting (toe-in shown)

26.5 Track rod end removed

3 Using a wheel alignment gauge check that the front wheels are aligned as given in the Specifications.

4 If adjustment is necessary loosen the track rod end locknuts and the outer bellows clips, then rotate each track rod by equal amounts until the setting is correct. Hold the track rod ends in their horizontal position with a spanner while making the adjustment. For example, to increase toe-in, both track rods need to be in effect shortened by turning them so that less thread is visible at the track rod ends.

5 Tighten the locknuts and outer bellows clips.

6 Provided the track rods have been adjusted by equal amounts the steering wheel should be central when moving straight-ahead. However if centralising is necessary first ascertain the correction angle in degrees, then rotate both track rods in the same direction approximately 19° for every 1° of correction required. To turn the steering wheel clockwise the track rods must be turned clockwise as viewed from the left-hand side of the car.

7 Camber and castor angles are preset and cannot be adjusted; however, if their accuracy is suspect they can be checked by a suitably equipped garage.

28 Wheels and tyres – general care and maintenance

1 Wheels and tyres should give no real problems in use provided that a close eye is kept on them with regard to excessive wear or damage. To this end, the following points should be noted.

2 Ensure that tyre pressures are checked regularly and maintained correctly. Checking should be carried out with the tyres cold and not immediately after the vehicle has been in use. If the pressures are checked with the tyres hot, an apparently high reading will be obtained owing to heat expansion. Under no circumstances should an attempt be made to reduce the pressures to the quoted cold reading in this instance, or effective underinflation will result.

3 Underinflation will cause overheating of the tyre owing to excessive flexing of the casing, and the tread will not sit correctly on the road surface. This will cause a consequent loss of adhesion and excessive wear, not to mention the danger of sudden tyre failure due to heat build-up.

4 Overinflation will cause rapid wear of the centre part of the tyre tread coupled with reduced adhesion, harsher ride, and the danger of shock damage occurring in the tyre casing.

5 Regularly check the tyres for damage in the form of cuts or bulges, especially in the sidewalls. Remove any nails or stones embedded in the tread before they penetrate the tyre to cause deflation. If removal of a nail *does* reveal that the tyre has been punctured, refit the nail so that its point of penetration is marked. Then immediately change the wheel and have the tyre repaired by a tyre dealer. Do *not* drive on a tyre in such a condition. In many cases a puncture can be simply repaired by the use of an inner tube of the correct size and type. If in any doubt as to the possible consequences of any damage found, consult your local tyre dealer for advice.

6 Periodically remove the wheels and clean any dirt or mud from the inside and outside surfaces. Examine the wheel rims for signs of rusting, corrosion or other damage. Light alloy wheels are easily damaged by 'kerbing' whilst parking, and similarly steel wheels may become dented or buckled. Renewal of the wheel is very often the only course of remedial action possible.

7 The balance of each wheel and tyre assembly should be maintained to avoid excessive wear, not only to the tyres but also to the steering and suspension components. Wheel imbalance is normally signified by vibration through the vehicle's bodyshell, although in many cases it is particularly noticeable through the steering wheel. Conversely, it should be noted that wear or damage in suspension or steering components may cause excessive tyre wear. Out-of-round or out-of-true tyres, damaged wheels and wheel bearing wear/maladjustment also fall into this category. Balancing will not usually cure vibration caused by such wear.

8 Wheel balancing of the front wheels on non-4x4 models may be carried out with the wheel either on or of the car. If balanceing the rear wheels on non-4x4 models on the car, both rear wheels must be clear of the ground and must be driven by the engine; spinning one wheel with the remaining wheel on the grund is not permitted as damage may occur to the viscous defferential unit (where fitted) or differential gears. It is, furthermore, extremely dangerous, particularly so where a viscous unit is fitted.

9 Wheel balancing of all wheels on 4x4 models must be carried out off the car, due to possible damage to the viscous units both in the transfer box and rear final drive unit.

10 Where on-the-car balancing is undertaken, ensure that the wheel-to-hub relationship is marked in some way prior to subsequent wheel removal so that it may be refitted in its original position.

11 General tyre wear is influenced to a large degree by driving style – harsh braking and acceleration or fast cornering will all produce more rapid tyre wear. Interchanging of tyres may result in more even wear, but this should only be carried out where there is no mix of tyre types on the vehicle. However, it is worth bearing in mind that if this is completely effective, the added expense of replacing a complete set of tyres simultaneously is incurred, which may prove financially restrictive for many owners.

12 Front tyres may wear unevenly as a result of wheel misalignment. The front wheels should always be correctly aligned according to the settings specified by the vehicle manufacturer.

13 Legal restrictions apply to the mixing of tyre types on a vehicle. Basically this means that a vehicle must not have tyres of differing construction on the same axle. Although it is not recommended to mix tyre types between front axle and rear axle, the only legally permissible combination is crossply at the front and radial at the rear. When mixing radial ply tyres, textile braced radials must always go on the front axle, with steel braced radials at the rear. An obvious disadvantage of such mixing is the necessity to carry two spare tyres to avoid contravening the law in the event of a puncture.

14 In the UK, the Motor Vehicles Construction and Use Regulations apply to many aspects of tyre fitting and usage. It is suggested that a copy of these regulations is obtained from your local police if in doubt as to the current legal requirements with regard to tyre condition, minimum tread depth, etc.

Fault diagnosis overleaf

29 Fault diagnosis – suspension and steering

Symptom	Reason(s)
Excessive play in steering	Worn rack-and-pinion or steering gear bushes Worn track rod end balljoints Worn lower suspension arm balljoints
Wanders or pulls to one side	Incorrect wheel alignment Worn track road end balljoints Worn lower suspension arm balljoints Uneven tyre pressures Faulty shock absorber
Heavy or stiff steering	Seized track rod end or suspension balljoint Incorrect wheel alignment Low tyre pressures Lack of lubricant in steering gear Faulty power-steering system (where appliable)
Wheel wobble and vibration	Roadwheels out of balance or damaged Faulty shock absorbers Worn wheel bearings Worn track rod ends or suspension arm balljoints
Excessive tyre wear	Incorrect wheel alignment Faulty shock absorbers Incorrect tyre pressures Roadwheels out of balance

Chapter 11 Bodywork and fittings

Contents

Specifications

Torque wrench settings	Nm	lbf ft
Seat belt to front seat frame	25 to 30	18 to 22
Seat belts – all other mountings	30 to 40	22 to 30
Air conditioning:		
Condenser	27 to 33	20 to 24
Fan to condenser	8 to 11	6 to 8
Compressor bracket – M10	85 to 92	63 to 68
Compressor bracket – M12	110 to 120	81 to 89
Compressor	65 to 75	48 to 55
Seats	25 to 32	18 to 24

1 General description

The bodyshell is of all-steel welded construction with front and rear safety cells designed to absorb impact in an accident. Wind tunnel technology has resulted in the contoured styling, giving low drag coefficient. The manufacturing process includes the use of robots and multi-stage corrosion protection with wax injection.

2 Routine maintenance

Carry out the following procedures at the intervals given in *'Routine Maintenance'* at the beginning of the Manual.

Check the seat belts

1   Examine all the seat belt webbing for damage and chafing, particularly where the belt passes through guides.

Lubricate hinges and catches

2   Lubricate the bonnet lock, safety catch, door check straps, fuel filler flap and door private lock barrels with a little oil. Check the operation of each item.
3   Do not attempt to lubricate the steering lock.

Check air conditioning system

4   Examine the compressor drivebelt for damage, fraying or glazing. If in good condition, check and if necessary adjust its tension with reference to Section 44.
5   Remove the radiator grille where applicable and clean any leaves, insects etc from the condenser coil and fins. Be very careful not to damage the condenser fins: use a soft brush, or a compressed air jet, along (not across) the fins.
6   Before refitting the grille, check the refrigerant charge as follows. The engine should be cold and the ambient temperature should be between 64° and 77°F (18° and 25°C).
7   Start the engine and allow it to idle, then switch on the air conditioner and turn the blower control switch to position 3. Observe the refrigerant sight glass. A few bubbles may be seen in the sight glass as the system starts up, but all bubbles should disappear within 10 seconds. Persistent bubbles mean that the refrigerant charge is low. Switch off the system immediately if the charge is low and do not use it again until it has been recharged.
8   Examine the system pipes and hoses for damage and deterioration.

Check underbody protection

9   Raise the front and rear of the car and check the underbody for damage and corrosion. Check the condition of the underseal.

3 Maintenance – bodywork and underframe

The general condition of a vehicle's bodywork is the one thing that significantly affects its value. Maintenance is easy but needs to be regular. Neglect, particularly after minor damage, can lead quickly to further deterioration and costly repair bills. It is important also to keep watch on those parts of the vehicle not immediately visible, for instance the underside, inside all the wheel arches and the lower part of the engine compartment.

The basic maintenance routine for the bodywork is washing – preferably with a lot of water, from a hose. This will remove all the loose solids which may have stuck to the vehicle. It is important to flush these off in such a way as to prevent grit from scratching the finish. The wheel arches and underframe need washing in the same way to remove any accumulated mud which will retain moisture and tend to encourage rust. Paradoxically enough, the best time to clean the underframe and wheel arches is in wet weather when the mud is thoroughly wet and soft. In very wet weather the underframe is usually cleaned of large accumulations automatically and this is a good time for inspection.

Periodically, except on vehicles with a wax-based underbody protective coating, it is a good idea to have the whole of the underframe of the vehicle steam cleaned, engine compartment included, so that a thorough inspection can be carried out to see what minor repairs and renovations are necessary. Steam cleaning is available at many garages and is necessary for removal of the accumulation of oily grime which sometimes is allowed to become thick in certain areas. If steam cleaning facilities are not available, there are one or two excellent grease solvents available which can be brush applied. The dirt can then be simply hosed off. Note that these methods should not be used on vehicles with wax-based underbody protective coating or the coating will be removed. Such vehicles should be inspected annually, preferably just prior to winter, when the underbody should be washed down and any damage to the wax coating repaired. Ideally, a completely fresh coat should be applied. It would also be worth considering the use of such wax-based protection for injection into door panels, sills, box sections, etc, as an additional safeguard against rust damage where such protection is not provided by the vehicle manufacturer.

After washing paintwork, wipe off with a chamois leather to give an unspotted clear finish. A coat of clear protective wax polish will give added protection against chemical pollutants in the air. If the paintwork sheen has dulled or oxidised, use a cleaner/polisher combination to restore the brilliance of the shine. This requires a little effort, but such dulling is usually caused because regular washing has been neglected. Care needs to be taken with metallic paintwork, as special non-abrasive cleaner/polisher is required to avoid damage to the finish. Always check that the door and ventilator opening drain holes and pipes are completely clear so that water can be drained out (photos). Bright work should be treated in the same way as paint work. Windscreens and windows can be kept clear of the smeary film which often appears by the use of a proprietary glass cleaner. Never use any form of wax or other body or chromium polish on glass.

4 Maintenance – upholstery and carpets

Mats and carpets should be brushed or vacuum cleaned regularly to keep them free of grit. If they are badly stained remove them from the vehicle for scrubbing or sponging and make quite sure they are dry before refitting. Seats and interior trim panels can be kept clean by wiping with a damp cloth. If they do become stained (which can be more apparent on light coloured upholstery) use a little liquid detergent and a soft nail brush to scour the grime out of the grain of the material. Do not forget to keep the headlining clean in the same way as the upholstery. When using liquid cleaners inside the vehicle do not over-wet the surfaces being cleaned. Excessive damp could get into the seams and padded interior causing stains, offensive odours or even rot. If the inside of the vehicle gets wet accidentally it is worthwhile taking some trouble to dry it out properly, particularly where carpets are involved. *Do not leave oil or electric heaters inside the vehicle for this purpose.*

3.4A Clearing a door drain hole

3.4B Clearing a sill drain hole

5 Minor body damage – repair

The photographic sequences on pages 190 and 191 illustrate the operations detailed in the following sub-sections.
Note: *For more detailed information about bodywork repair, the Haynes Publishing Group publish a book by Lindsay Porter called The Car Bodywork Repair Manual. This incorporates information on such aspects as rust treatment, painting and glass fibre repairs, as well as details on more ambitious repairs involving welding and panel beating.*

Repair of minor scratches in bodywork

If the scratch is very superficial, and does not penetrate to the metal of the bodywork, repair is very simple. Lightly rub the area of the scratch with a paintwork renovator, or a very fine cutting paste, to remove loose paint from the scratch and to clear the surrounding bodywork of wax polish. Rinse the area with clean water.

Apply touch-up paint to the scratch using a fine paint brush; continue to apply fine layers of paint until the surface of the paint in the scratch is level with the surrounding paintwork. Allow the new paint at least two weeks to harden: then blend it into the surrounding paintwork by rubbing the scratch area with a paintwork renovator or a very fine cutting paste. Finally, apply wax polish.

Where the scratch has penetrated right through to the metal of the bodywork, causing the metal to rust, a different repair technique is required. Remove any loose rust from the bottom of the scratch with a penknife, then apply rust inhibiting paint to prevent the formation of rust in the future. Using a rubber or nylon applicator fill the scratch with bodystopper paste. If required, this paste can be mixed with cellulose thinners to provide a very thin paste which is ideal for filling narrow scratches. Before the stopper-paste in the scratch hardens, wrap a piece of smooth cotton rag around the top of a finger. Dip the finger in cellulose thinners and then quickly sweep it across the surface of the stopper-paste in the scratch; this will ensure that the surface of the stopper-paste is slightly hollowed. The scratch can now be painted over as described earlier in this Section.

Repair of dents in bodywork

When deep denting of the vehicle's bodywork has taken place, the first task is to pull the dent out, until the affected bodywork almost attains its original shape. There is little point in trying to restore the original shape completely, as the metal in the damaged area will have stretched on impact and cannot be reshaped fully to its original contour. It is better to bring the level of the dent up to a point which is about ⅛ in (3 mm) below the level of the surrounding bodywork. In cases where the dent is very shallow anyway, it is not worth trying to pull it out at all. If the underside of the dent is accessible, it can be hammered out gently from behind, using a mallet with a wooden or plastic head. Whilst doing this, hold a suitable block of wood firmly against the outside of the panel to absorb the impact from the hammer blows and thus prevent a large area of the bodywork from being 'belled-out'.

Should the dent be in a section of the bodywork which has a double skin or some other factor making it inaccessible from behind, a different technique is called for. Drill several small holes through the metal inside the area – particularly in the deeper section. Then screw long self-tapping screws into the holes just sufficiently for them to gain a good purchase in the metal. Now the dent can be pulled out by pulling on the protruding heads of the screws with a pair of pliers.

The next stage of the repair is the removal of the paint from the damaged area, and from an inch or so of the surrounding 'sound' bodywork. This is accomplished most easily by using a wire brush or abrasive pad on a power drill, although it can be done just as effectively by hand using sheets of abrasive paper. To complete the preparation for filling, score the surface of the bare metal with a screwdriver or the tang of a file, or alternatively, drill small holes in the affected area. This will provide a really good 'key' for the filler paste.

To complete the repair see the Section on filling and re-spraying.

Repair of rust holes or gashes in bodywork

Remove all paint from the affected area and from an inch or so of the surrounding 'sound' bodywork, using an abrasive pad or a wire brush on a power drill. If these are not available a few sheets of abrasive paper will do the job just as effectively. With the paint removed you will be able to gauge the severity of the corrosion and therefore decide whether to renew the whole panel (if this is possible) or to repair the affected area. New body panels are not as expensive as most people think and it is often quicker and more satisfactory to fit a new panel than to attempt to repair large areas of corrosion.

Remove all fittings from the affected area except those which will act as a guide to the original shape of the damaged bodywork (eg headlamp shells etc). Then, using tin snips or a hacksaw blade, remove all loose metal and any other metal badly affected by corrosion. Hammer the edges of the hole inwards in order to create a slight depression for the filler paste.

Wire brush the affected area to remove the powdery rust from the surface of the remaining metal. Paint the affected area with rust inhibiting paint; if the back of the rusted area is accessible treat this also.

Before filling can take place it will be necessary to block the hole in some way. This can be achieved by the use of aluminium or plastic mesh, or aluminium tape.

Aluminium or plastic mesh is probably the best material to use for a large hole. Cut a piece to the approximate size and shape of the hole to be filled, then position it in the hole so that its edges are below the level of the surrounding bodywork. It can be retained in position by several blobs of filler paste around its periphery.

Aluminium tape should be used for small or very narrow holes. Pull a piece off the roll and trim it to the approximate size and shape required, then pull off the backing paper (if used) and stick the tape over the hole; it can be overlapped if the thickness of one piece is insufficient. Burnish down the edges of the tape with the handle of a screwdriver or similar, to ensure that the tape is securely attached to the metal underneath.

Bodywork repairs – filling and re-spraying

Before using this Section, see the Sections on dent, deep scratch, rust holes and gash repairs.

Many types of bodyfiller are available, but generally speaking those proprietary kits which contain a tin of filler paste and a tube of resin hardener are best for this type of repair. A wide, flexible plastic or nylon applicator will be found invaluable for imparting a smooth and well contoured finish to the surface of the filler.

Mix up a little filler on a clean piece of card or board – measure the hardener carefully (follow the maker's instructions on the pack) otherwise the filler will set too rapidly or too slowly. Using the applicator apply the filler paste to the prepared area; draw the applicator across the surface of the filler to achieve the correct contour and to level the filler surface. As soon as a contour that approximates to the correct one is achieved, stop working the paste – if you carry on too long the paste will become sticky and begin to 'pick up' on the applicator. Continue to add thin layers of filler paste at twenty-minute intervals until the level of the filler is just proud of the surrounding bodywork.

This sequence of photographs deals with the repair of the dent and paintwork damage shown in this photo. The procedure will be similar for the repair of a hole. It should be noted that the procedures given here are simplified — more explicit instructions will be found in the text

In the case of a dent the first job — after removing surrounding trim — is to hammer out the dent where access is possible. This will minimise filling. Here, the large dent having been hammered out, the damaged area is being made slightly concave

Now all paint must be removed from the damaged area, by rubbing with coarse abrasive paper. Alternatively, a wire brush or abrasive pad can be used in a power drill. Where the repair area meets good paintwork, the edge of the paintwork should be 'feathered', using a finer grade of abrasive paper

In the case of a hole caused by rusting, all damaged sheet-metal should be cut away before proceeding to this stage. Here, the damaged area is being treated with rust remover and inhibitor before being filled

Mix the body filler according to its manufacturer's instructions. In the case of corrosion damage, it will be necessary to block off any large holes before filling — this can be done with aluminium or plastic mesh, or aluminium tape. Make sure the area is absolutely clean before ...

... applying the filler. Filler should be applied with a flexible applicator, as shown, for best results; the wooden spatula being used for confined areas. Apply thin layers of filler at 20-minute intervals, until the surface of the filler is slightly proud of the surrounding bodywork

Initial shaping can be done with a Surform plane or Dreadnought file. Then, using progressively finer grades of wet-and-dry paper, wrapped around a sanding block, and copious amounts of clean water, rub down the filler until really smooth and flat. Again, feather the edges of adjoining paintwork

The whole repair area can now be sprayed or brush-painted with primer. If spraying, ensure adjoining areas are protected from over-spray. Note that at least one inch of the surrounding sound paintwork should be coated with primer. Primer has a 'thick' consistency, so will find small imperfections

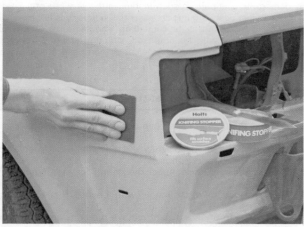

Again, using plenty of water, rub down the primer with a fine grade wet-and-dry paper (400 grade is probably best) until it is really smooth and well blended into the surrounding paintwork. Any remaining imperfections can now be filled by carefully applied knifing stopper paste

When the stopper has hardened, rub down the repair area again before applying the final coat of primer. Before rubbing down this last coat of primer, ensure the repair area is blemish-free — use more stopper if necessary. To ensure that the surface of the primer is really smooth use some finishing compound

The top coat can now be applied. When working out of doors, pick a dry, warm and wind-free day. Ensure surrounding areas are protected from over-spray. Agitate the aerosol thoroughly, then spray the centre of the repair area, working outwards with a circular motion. Apply the paint as several thin coats

After a period of about two weeks, which the paint needs to harden fully, the surface of the repaired area can be 'cut' with a mild cutting compound prior to wax polishing. When carrying out bodywork repairs, remember that the quality of the finished job is proportional to the time and effort expended

Once the filler has hardened, excess can be removed using a metal plane or file. From then on, progressively finer grades of abrasive paper should be used, starting with a 40 grade production paper and finishing with 400 grade wet-and-dry paper. Always wrap the abrasive paper around a flat rubber, cork, or wooden block – otherwise the surface of the filler will not be completely flat. During the smoothing of the filler surface the wet-and-dry paper should be periodically rinsed in water. This will ensure that a very smooth finish is imparted to the filler at the final stage.

At this stage the 'dent' should be surrounded by a ring of bare metal, which in turn should be encircled by the finely 'feathered' edge of the good paintwork. Rinse the repair area with clean water, until all of the dust produced by the rubbing-down operation has gone.

Spray the whole repair area with a light coat of primer – this will show up any imperfections in the surface of the filler. Repair these imperfections with fresh filler paste or bodystopper, and once more smooth the surface with abrasive paper. If bodystopper is used, it can be mixed with cellulose thinners to form a really thin paste which is ideal for filling small holes. Repeat this spray and repair procedure until you are satisfied that the surface of the filler, and the feathered edge of the paintwork are perfect. Clean the repair area with clean water and allow to dry fully.

The repair area is now ready for final spraying. Paint spraying must be carried out in a warm, dry, windless and dust free atmosphere. This condition can be created artificially if you have access to a large indoor working area, but if you are forced to work in the open, you will have to pick your day very carefully. If you are working indoors, dousing the floor in the work area with water will help to settle the dust which would otherwise be in the atmosphere. If the repair area is confined to one body panel, mask off the surrounding panels; this will help to minimise the effects of a slight mis-match in paint colours. Bodywork fittings (eg chrome strips, door handles etc) will also need to be masked off. Use genuine masking tape and several thicknesses of newspaper for the masking operations.

Before commencing to spray, agitate the aerosol can thoroughly, then spray a test area (an old tin, or .similar) until the technique is mastered. Cover the repair area with a thick coat of primer; the thickness should be built up using several thin layers of paint rather than one thick one. Using 400 grade wet-and-dry paper, rub down the surface of the primer until it is really smooth. While doing this, the work area should be thoroughly doused with water, and the wet-and-dry paper periodically rinsed in water. Allow to dry before spraying on more paint.

Spray on the top coat, again building up the thickness by using several thin layers of paint. Start spraying in the centre of the repair area and then, using a circular motion, work outwards until the whole repair area and about 2 inches of the surrounding original paintwork is covered. Remove all masking material 10 to 15 minutes after spraying on the final coat of paint.

Allow the new paint at least two weeks to harden, then, using a paintwork renovator or a very fine cutting paste, blend the edges of the paint into the existing paintwork. Finally, apply wax polish.

Plastic components

With the use of more and more plastic body components by the vehicle manufacturers (eg bumpers, spoilers, and in some cases major body panels), rectification of more serious damage to such items has become a matter of either entrusting repair work to a specialist in this field, or renewing complete components. Repair of such damage by the DIY owner is not really feasible owing to the cost of the equipment and materials required for effecting such repairs. The basic technique involves making a groove along the line of the crack in the plastic using a rotary burr in a power drill. The damaged part is then welded back together by using a hot air gun to heat up and fuse a plastic filler rod into the groove. Any excess plastic is then removed and the area rubbed down to a smooth finish. It is important that a filler rod of the correct plastic is used, as body components can be made of a variety of different types (eg polycarbonate, ABS, polypropylene).

Damage of a less serious nature (abrasions, minor cracks etc) can be repaired by the DIY owner using a two-part epoxy filler repair material. Once mixed in equal proportions, this is used in similar fashion to the bodywork filler used on metal panels. The filler is usually cured in twenty to thirty minutes, ready for sanding and painting.

If the owner is renewing a complete component himself, or he has repaired it with epoxy filler, he will be left with the problem of finding a suitable paint for finishing which is compatible with the type of plastic used. At one time the use of a universal paint was not possible owing to the complex range of plastics encountered in body component applications. Standard paints, generally speaking, will not bond to plastic or rubber satisfactorily. However, it is now possible to obtain a plastic body parts finishing kit which consists of a pre-primer treatment, a primer and coloured top coat. Full instructions are normally supplied with a kit, but basically the method of use is to first apply the pre-primer to the component concerned and allow it to dry for up to 30 minutes. Then the primer is applied and left to dry for about an hour before finally applying the special coloured top coat. The result is a correctly coloured component where the paint will flex with the plastic or rubber, a property that standard paint does not normally possess.

6 Major body damage – repair

Where serious damage has occurred or large areas need renewal due to neglect, it means certainly that completely new sections or panels will need welding in and this is best left to professionals. If the damage is due to impact, it will also be necessary to completely check the alignment of the bodyshell structure. Due to the principle of construction, the strength and shape of the whole car can be affected by damage to one part. In such instances the services of a Ford agent with specialist checking jigs are essential. If a body is left misaligned, it is first of all dangerous as the car will not handle properly, and secondly uneven stresses will be imposed on the steering, engine and transmission, causing abnormal wear or complete failure. Tyre wear may also be excessive.

7 Bonnet – removal and refitting

1 Support the bonnet in its open position and place some cardboard or rags beneath the corners.
2 Unscrew the cross-head screw and remove the earth cable from the rear edge of the bonnet (photo).
3 Where applicable disconnect the wiring for the engine compartment light.
4 Mark the location of the hinges with a pencil, then loosen the four bolts (photo).
5 With the help of an assistant remove the bolts and lift the bonnet from the car (photo).
6 Refitting is a reversal of removal, but adjust the hinges to their original positions before tightening the bolts. Check that the bonnet is central within its aperture and aligned with the surrounding bodywork. If necessary adjust the front bump stops so that the front edge of the bonnet is slightly below the level of the front panel (Fig. 11.1). Adjust the striker or lock to ensure correct engagement as the bonnet is closed (photos).

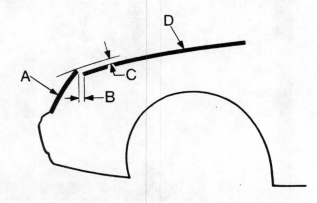

Fig. 11.1 Bonnet alignment diagram (Sec 7)

A Front panel
B = 5 ± 1 mm (0.2 ± 0.04 in)
C = 1 to 2 mm (0.04 to 0.08 in)
D Bonnet

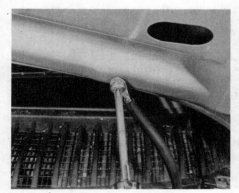

7.2 Removing the bonnet earth cable

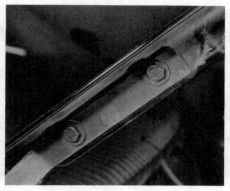

7.4 Bonnet hinge bolts

7.5 Lifting the bonnet from the car

7.6A Bonnet adjustable bump stop

7.6B Bonnet striker and safety catch
(pre-February 1987 models)

8.3 Bonnet lock and cable (pre-February
1987 models)

8 Bonnet lock cable – removal and refitting

Note: *If the cable breaks, the bonnet may be opened by inserting a screwdriver through the special hole under the lock.*
1 Remove the screws and withdraw the lower steering column shroud.
2 Remove the single screw and withdraw the lock cable bracket from the steering column.
3 Working in the engine compartment, pull the outer cable end fitting from the bracket and release the inner cable end fitting from the lock lever (photo).
4 Release the cable from the clips in the engine compartment.
5 Pull the cable through the bulkhead into the passenger compartment.
6 Refitting is a reversal of removal, but make sure that the rubber grommet is correctly located in the bulkhead.

9 Bonnet lock – removal and refitting

1 Working in the engine compartment, pull the outer cable end fitting from the bracket and release the inner cable end fitting from the lock lever.
2 Remove the three cross-head screws (pre-February 1987) or two bolts (February 1987-on) and withdraw the lock from the front panel (photo).
3 Refitting is a reversal of removal, but on February 1987-on models adjust the position of the lock within the elongated bolt holes so that the striker enters the lock centrally.

10 Tailgate – removal and refitting

1 Disconnect the battery negative lead.
2 Open the tailgate and prise out the trim panel using a wide blade screwdriver

9.2 Bonnet lock and cable (February 1987-on models)

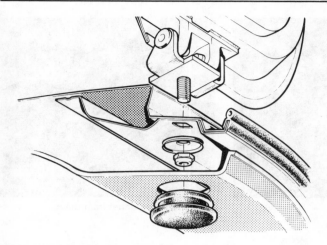

Fig. 11.2 Tailgate hinge (Sec 10)

3   Disconnect the wiring as applicable from the heated rear window, lock solenoid and remote release, interior light switch, rear wash/wipe and door ajar sensor. Before pulling the wiring from the tailgate, tie string to each wire so that the wire can be positioned correctly.
4   While an assistant supports the tailgate, disconnect the struts by prising out the retaining clips (photo). Do not remove the clips completely, just raise them by 4 mm (0.16 in) maximum and then pull the strut off its mounting.
5   Remove the plugs from the headlining, unscrew the hinge nuts, and withdraw the tailgate from the car (photo).
6   Refitting is a reversal of removal, but renew the sealing pads on the

hings studs and do not fully tighten the hinge nuts until the tailgate is positioned centrally in its aperture. If necessary adjust the striker so that the tailgate shuts correctly (photo).

11 Tailgate lock – removal and refitting

1   Open the tailgate and prise out the trim panel using a wide blade screwdriver. Recover the plastic clips where applicable (photo).
2   Prise out the clip and withdraw the lock barrel (photos).
3   Unbolt the support bracket (photos).
4   Remove the special screws (if necessary using a suitable key) and withdraw the lock assembly (photos). Disconnect the central locking wiring if applicable.
5   Refitting is a reversal of removal.

12 Tailgate strut – removal and refitting

1   Support the tailgate in its open position with a suitable prop.
2   Using a small screwdriver, prise out the two end clips approximately 4 mm (0.16 in) and disconnect the strut from the ball-studs (photo).
3   Refitting is a reversal of removal, but make sure that the piston rod end of the strut is fitted to the main body.

13 Radiator front panel (pre-February 1987 models) – removal and refitting

1   Remove the cross-head screws from the top of the panel (photo).
2   Lift the panel from the rubber inserts and withdraw from the car (photo).
3   Refitting is a reversal of removal.

10.4 Releasing a tailgate strut spring clip

10.5 Tailgate hinge

10.6 Tailgate striker

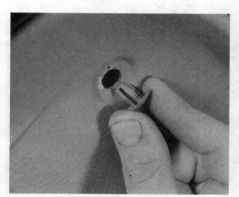

11.1 Tailgate trim panel plastic clip

11.2A Prise out the clip (arrowed) ...

11.2B ... and withdraw the lock barrel

11.3A Unscrew the bolts ...

11.3B ... and remove the support bracket

11.4A Removing the tailgate lock securing screws

11.4B Tailgate lock – note solenoid not fitted to all models

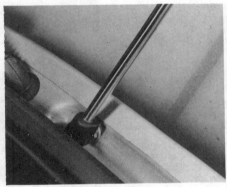

12.2 The piston rod end of the strut must be fitted to the main body

13.1 Removing the radiator front panel upper screws (pre-February 1987 models)

13.2 Radiator front panel removal from rubber inserts

14.2 Door check arm location

14.7 Door hinge

14 Doors – removal and refitting

1 On models equipped with an electric mirror, electric windows, door-mounted speakers, or door ajar sensors, remove the trim panel as described in Section 15 and disconnect the wiring inside the door.
2 Unscrew and remove the bolt securing the check arm to the pillar (photo).
3 On front doors, remove the side trim panel, and on rear doors remove pillar trim.
4 On the front driver's door remove the lower facia panels and disconnect the face level vent hose.

5 On the front passenger door remove the face level vent cover.
6 Support the door on blocks of wood.
7 Unscrew the hinge nuts and remove the support plates from the door pillar (photo).
8 Withdraw the door from the car.
9 Refitting is a reversal of removal, but do not tighten the hinge nuts until the door is positioned centrally in the body aperture and aligned with the surrounding bodywork. If necessary adjust the lock striker so that it enters the lock centrally – on early models the striker has a hexagon head, but on later models the striker is loop-shaped and secured by two Torx screws (photos). The loop and pin of the later type must be positioned horizontally.

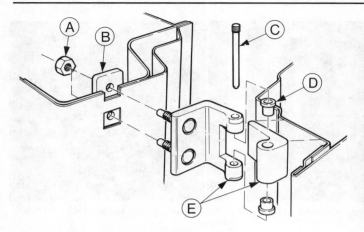

Fig. 11.3 Front door hinge components (Sec 14)

A   Nut
B   Plate
C   Hinge pin
D   Bush
E   Hinge assembly

14.9A Door lock striker on early models

14.9B Door lock striker on later models

15 Door inner trim panel – removal and refitting

1   Where applicable, note the position of the window regulator handle with the window shut. Prise out the plastic cover, remove the cross-head screw and withdraw the handle and bezel (photos).
2   On pre-February 1987 models, remove the screw and withdraw the small trim panel from behind the door grip (if fitted). Remove the additional screws, lift the interior door handle, and withdraw the surround and grip. Remove the screws and release the door pocket from the trim panel. On models with electric mirrors, prise out the switch and disconnect the multi-plug on the driver's side. Where applicable, remove the screws securing the edge of the trim panel to the door (photos).
3   On February 1987-on models, remove the screws and withdraw the interior handle finger plate, armrest and door pocket (photos). Remove the mirror control panel trim with reference to Section 25, then remove the exposed screw.
4   On all models prise the trim panel away from the door and remove it (photo), taking care not to tear the plastic clips from the panel. To do this, use a wide blade screwdriver directly under the clip, or better still, make a removal tool to the dimensions shown in Fig. 11.4. If a clip will not release even with the aid of the tool, sever it with a chisel or knife and fit a new clip on reassembly. Where applicable disconnect the wiring from the door-mounted speaker.
5   If necessary peel the polythene sheet from the door. Note the location of the air release flap and window regulator spacer.

6   Refitting is a reversal of removal, but make sure that all the retaining clips are correctly aligned before pressing them into the door, and make sure that the upper lip of the panel locates under the exterior mirror control panel.

15.1A Prise out the cover ...

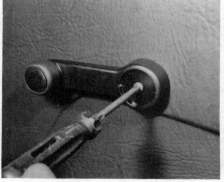

15.1B ... remove the screw ...

15.1C ... and withdraw the window regulator handle ...

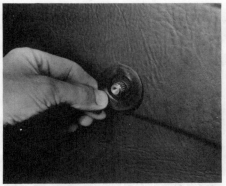

15.1D ... and bezel

15.2A Door grip inner trim panel removal (early models)

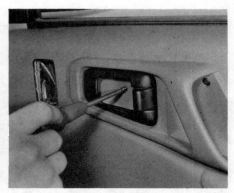

15.2B Remove the screws ...

15.2C ... and withdraw the surround and grip

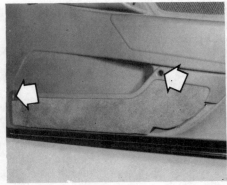

15.2D Door pocket retaining screw locations (arrowed)

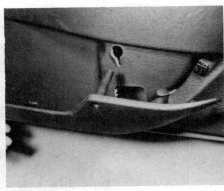

15.2E The door pocket

15.2F Screw securing edge of door inner trim panel

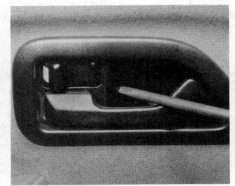

15.3A Remove the screw ...

15.3B ... and the finger plate (February 1987-on models)

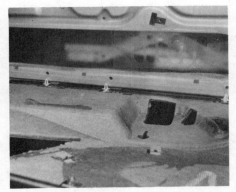

15.4 Door inner trim panel removal, showing plastic clips and polythene sheet air release flap

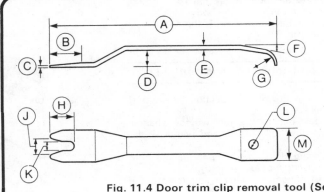

A	178 mm (7 in)
B	25 mm (1 in)
C	1 mm (0.04 in)
D	13 mm (0.5 in)
E	3 mm (0.12 in)
F	5 mm (0.2 in)
G	10 mm (0.4 in)
H	19 mm (0.75 in)
J	13 mm (0.5 in)
K	8 mm (0.3 in)
L	8 mm (0.3 in)
M	25 mm (1 in)

Fig. 11.4 Door trim clip removal tool (Sec 15)

16.2A Remove the screws ...

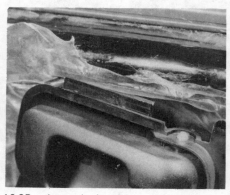
16.2B ... lower the interior handle from the upper tab ...

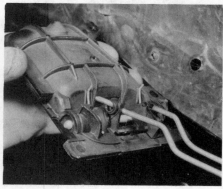
16.3 ... and disconnect the control rods

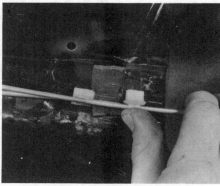
16.4 The remote control rod guides are pressed into the door panel

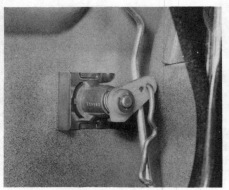
18.3 Inner view of the door private lock

16 Door interior handle remote control – removal and refitting

1   Remove the inner trim panel as described in Section 15.
2   Remove the cross-head screws and slide the control downwards from the door aperture (photos).
3   Disconnect the two rods and withdraw the control (photo).
4   Refitting is a reversal of removal, but check that the two rods are correctly located in the guides (photo).

17 Door check arm – removal and refitting

1   Remove the inner trim panel as described in Section 15.
2   Remove the single bolt securing the arm to the body.
3   Unbolt the check arm and withdraw it from inside the door.
4   Refitting is a reversal of removal.

18 Door private lock – removal, inspection and refitting

1   Remove the inner trim panel as described in Section 15 and peel back the polythene sheet as necessary.
2   On February 1987-on models, remove the front window channel lower rear screw with the window fully raised, and withdraw the channel.
3   Pull out the retaining clip using pliers, then unhook the lock from the rod and withdraw it from outside the door (photo).
4   To dismantle the lock first extract the circlip and remove the endplate and nylon lever.
5   Remove the return spring.

Pre-February 1987 models
6   Prise the cap from the key end of the lock and discard it.
7   Insert the key and pull out the lock barrel.
8   Hold the tumblers in position with the finger and thumb then remove the key and shutter plate.
9   Remove the tumblers *keeping them in strict order.* Remove the springs.
10 Clean all the components in paraffin and wipe dry, then examine them for wear and damage. Renew any components as necessary.

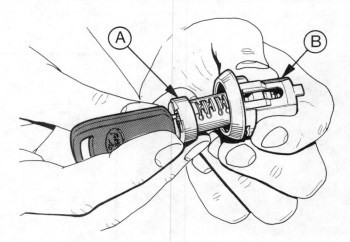
Fig. 11.5 Door private lock barrel (A) removal from the housing (B) on pre-February 1987 models (Sec 18)

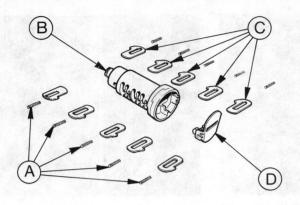

Fig. 11.6 Exploded view of private lock on pre-February 1987 models (Sec 18)

A Springs
B Lock barrel

C Tumblers
D Shutter plate

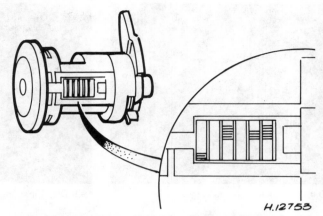

Fig. 11.7 Private lock coding for February 1987-on models (Sec 18)

Example code reads 143423

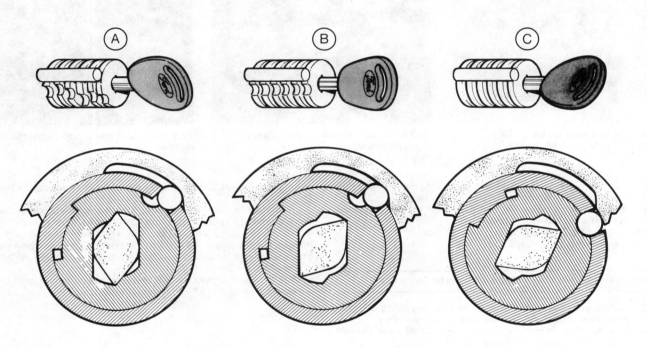

Fig. 11.8 Private lock operation for February 1987-on models (Sec 18)

A Key inserted   B Initial rotation to align tumblers   C Further rotation to allow roller to drop

11 Reassembly and refitting is a reversal of dismantling and removal, but lightly lubricate the lock barrel with a little oil and apply a little grease inside the shutter plate. Fit a new cap over the shutter plate and bend it back over the lock housing. Fit a new gasket between the lock and the door panel.

February 1987-on models

12 Before removing the magazine, position the drain slot upwards and read the code by counting the notches on each tumbler. Where there are no notches, the code is '4'.

13 Remove the magazine, roller and tumblers.

14 Clean all the components in paraffin and wipe dry, then examine them for wear and damage. Renew any components as necessary.

15 Reassembly and refitting is a reversal of dismantling and removal,

but apply a little grease to the magazine before inserting it. Use a socket to press the castellated retainer into the lock housing.

19 Door lock – removal and refitting

1 Remove the inner trim panel as described in Section 15 with the window shut. Peel back the polythene sheeting as necessary.

2 On February 1987-on models, remove the front window channel lower rear screw and withdraw the channel. Where applicable, remove the three screws securing the door lock motor, disconnect the operating rod and wiring multi-plug, and withdraw the motor.

3 Remove the interior handle remote control as described in Section 16 and prise out the two guides.

19.4 Door lock retaining screws

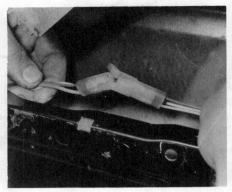

19.5 Disconnecting the central locking wiring

19.6A Removing the door lock

19.6B Door lock with central locking solenoid – not fitted to all models

20.3 Inner view of door exterior handle retaining screws

22.3 Front door rear window channel screw removal

4   Remove the cross-head screws, then reach inside the door and turn the lock to disconnect it from the control rods (photo).
5   Where applicable, disconnect the door ajar switch or central locking solenoid switch wiring (photo).
6   Withdraw the lock from inside the door (photos).
7   Refitting is a reversal of removal.

20 Door exterior handle – removal and refitting

1   Remove the inner trim panel as described in Section 15 with the window shut. Peel back the polythene sheeting as necessary.
2   On February 1987-on models, remove the front window channel lower rear screw and withdraw the channel.
3   Remove the screws (photo), disconnect the operating rod and remove the handle.
4   Refitting is a reversal of removal.

21 Windscreen, tailgate and fixed rear quarter windows – removal and refitting

The windscreen, tailgate and fixed quarter windows are direct-glazed to the body using special adhesive. Purpose-made tools are required to remove the old glass and fit the new glass, therefore this work is best entrusted to a specialist.

22 Front door window – removal and refitting

1   With the window shut remove the inner trim panel as described in Section 15. Peel off the polythene sheeting as necessary.
2   Remove the exterior mirror complete (February 1987-on models) or the mirror inner quadrant (earlier models) with reference to Section 25.
3   From the rear of the door remove the single screw securing the rear window channel (photo), then unclip and remove the rear channel.
4   Lower the window until the lower support channel is visible through the aperture at the bottom of the door. Prise the regulator arms from the sockets in the channel, then lower the window to the bottom of the door.
5   Pull the channel from the rear of the window aperture, then tilt the window forwards and lift it out through the aperture.

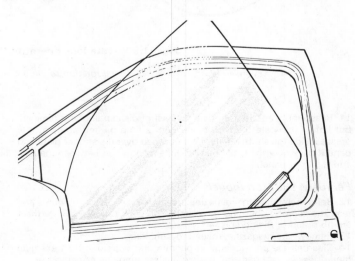

Fig. 11.9 Removing the front door window (Sec 22)

6 Refitting is a reversal of removal, but position the rear window channel screw to give the window approximately 5.0 mm (0.2 in) fore-and-aft clearance.

23 Rear door window – removal and refitting

1 With the window shut remove the inner trim panel as described in Section 15. Peel off the polythene sheeting as necessary.
2 Prise off the quarter trim panel from inside the door, then remove the screw and withdraw the outer trim panel.
3 Remove the three screws and withdraw the rear window channel.
4 Lower the window until the lower support channel is visible through the aperture at the bottom of the door. Prise the regulator arm from the socket in the channel, then lower the window to the bottom of the door.
5 Pull the channel from the front of the window aperture, then tilt the window rearwards and lift it out through the aperture.
6 Refitting is a reversal of removal, but position the rear window channel screws to give the window approximately 5.0 mm (0.2 in) fore-and-aft clearance.

24 Window regulator – removal and refitting

1 With the window shut remove the inner trim panel as described in Section 15. Peel off the polythene sheeting as necessary.
2 Lower the window until the lower support channel is visible through the aperture at the bottom of the door (photo). Prise the regulator arm(s) from the socket(s) in the channel, then lower the window to the bottom of the door.
3 Drill out the rivets retaining the window regulator. On front doors also drill out the rivets retaining the guide channel.

4 Withdraw the regulator and where applicable the guide channel through the door aperture. Where applicable disconnect the wiring from the electric motor; the motor may be unbolted from the regulator if necessary (photos).
5 Refitting is a reversal of removal, but fit new rivets using a hand riveter (photo).

25 Door mirror – removal and refitting

1 On pre-February 1987 model electric mirrors, first remove the door inner trim panel as described in Section 15 and disconnect the wiring multi-plug. Prise off the inner trim front edge and release from the clips (photos).
2 On February 1987-on model electric mirrors, prise out the plastic cover and remove the screw. Prise off the inner trim front edge and release from the clips, then disconnect the wiring plug from the switch (photos).
3 On all cable-operated mirrors, unscrew the bezel from the control knob, then prise off the inner trim front edge and release from the clips (photos). On all standard mirrors, prise off the trim as previously described.
4 Remove the screws and withdraw the mirror from the door (photo); disconnect the additional wiring multi-plug where applicable.
5 Refitting is a reversal of removal.

26 Door mirror glass – removal and refitting

1 On standard mirrors, carefully lever out the glass from the internal balljoint. To refit, press on until the balljoint is engaged.
2 On cable-operated and electric mirrors, insert a screwdriver through the small hole in the bottom of the mirror case and turn the

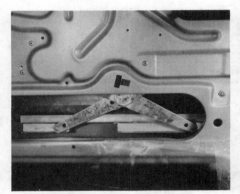

24.2 Front door window lower support channel and regulator arms

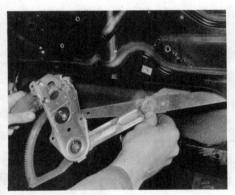

24.4A Removing the front door window regulator (electric)

24.4B Front door window regulator (electric)

24.4C Window regulator electric motor mounting bolts (arrowed)

24.5 Using a hand riveter to secure the window regulator

25.1A Disconnecting the electric door mirror wiring (pre-February 1987 models)

25.1B Removing the door mirror inner trim
(pre-February 1987 models)

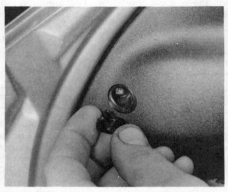

25.2A Electric door mirror inner trim securing
screw (February 1987-on models)

25.2B Removing the electric door mirror
inner trim (February 1987-on models)

25.3A Unscrew the bezel ...

25.3B ... and remove the cable-operated door
mirror inner trim

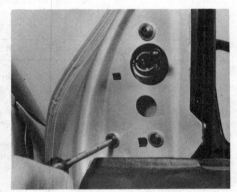

25.4 Removing the door mirror

locking ring as shown in Fig. 11.10. Disconnect the wires from the heating element where applicable (photo).
3   Refitting is a reversal of removal.

27 Rear quarter window (opening) – removal and refitting

1   Remove the trim from around the window. It is secured by five screws.
2   Remove the two screws which secure the locking catch (photo) to the body.
3   Remove the screw covers from the hinges. Support the glass and remove the hinge screws, lift out the glass.
4   If a new window is being fitted, transfer the locking catch to it.
5   Refit in the reverse order of removal.

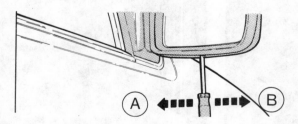

Fig. 11.10 Door mirror glass removal for cable-operated and
electric mirrors (Sec 26)

A   Lock   B   Unlock

28 Bumpers – removal and refitting

Pre-February 1987 models

1   On the front bumper remove the radiator front panel as described in Section 13, and also disconnect the direction indicator and fog lamps as necessary with reference to Chapter 12.

26.2 Removing a door mirror glass – note wires for heating element
and electric motor

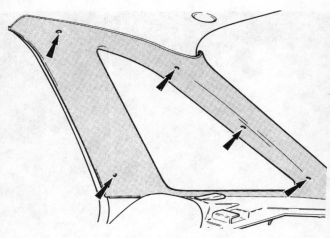

Fig. 11.11 Rear quarter window trim screw locations (Sec 27)

27.2 Rear quarter window locking catch

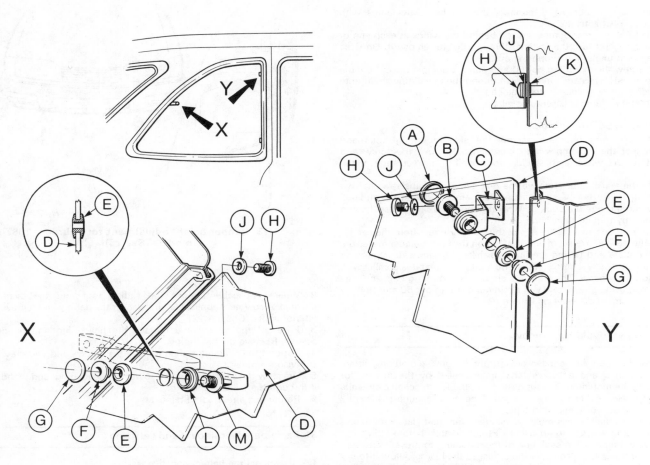

Fig. 11.12 Rear quarter window catch (X) and hinge (Y) components (Sec 27)

A Cap	D Glass	G Cap	K Nut
B Screw	E Grommet	H Screw	L Spacer
C Hinge	F Nut	J Washer	M Catch

28.4A Front bumper mounting bolt

28.4B Rear bumper mounting bolts

2   On the rear bumper disconnect the number plate lamps with reference to Chapter 12.
3   On front and rear bumpers reach behind the wings at each end of the bumper and turn the fastener through 90° to remove it. On Ghia models also unclip the support straps.
4   Unscrew the mounting bolt(s) and pull the bumper direct from the car (photos). Resistance may be felt during the initial movement until the side pegs are released from the clips.
5   Refitting is a reversal of removal.

February 1987-on models
6   On the front bumper unscrew the side mounting bolts and disconnect the foglamp wiring multiplugs. Remove the screw and withdraw the wheel arch shields from behind the rear edge of the bumper.
7   On the rear bumper remove the rear carpet and unscrew the two mounting bolts. Remove the number plate lamps (Chapter 12) and pull the wiring through the bumper. Working under the car, release the two fasteners by turning them through 90°.
8   On front and rear bumpers pull the bumper direct from the car.
9   Refitting is a reversal of removal, but on the front bumper make sure that the plate and O-ring are fitted to the right-hand side. Where an adjustment facility is fitted, adjust the bumper so that it is parallel with the side body panel. The adjusters are on the mounting bars and may be turned using a Torx key with a minimum length of 150 mm (5.9 in) and a maximum diameter of 12 mm (0.47 in).

29 Bumper moulding – renewal

1   New bumpers are supplied without the decorative moulding fitted. Special primer and adhesive tape are specified by the makers for retaining the moulding: it is suggested that the DIY mechanic consults a Ford dealer, either to have the job done or to acquire sufficiently small quantities of primer and tape.
2   The moulding recess must be cleaned with methylated spirit, and the moulding warmed to 45°C (113°F) immediately before fitting.
3   Apply the primer to each end of the moulding to prevent moisture discolouring it, and also apply the primer to the recess. Allow it to dry for three minutes before pressing the moulding firmly into position. A small plastic roller is ideal for removing the air pockets and wrinkles.

30 Headlining – removal and refitting

1   The headlining is of moulded type and can be removed in one piece through the tailgate aperture. First loosen the upper screws of the trim panels touching the headlining.

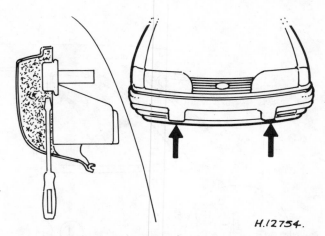

H.12754.

Fig. 11.13 Bumper height adjustment for February 1987-on models (Sec 28)

2   Where applicable remove the sliding roof and the overhead console. Also where applicable, disconnect the battery and remove the interior lights (Chapter 12).
3   Prise off the covers and remove the headlining and handgrip screws. Remove the handgrips.
4   Support the headlining then remove the screws and withdraw the sun visors and clips.
5   Unscrew the special fasteners, lower the headlining, and withdraw it through the tailgate aperture.
6   Refitting is a reversal of removal.

31 Facia panel – removal and refitting

1   Disconnect the battery negative lead.
2   Remove the screws and withdraw the upper and lower shrouds from the steering column.
3   Remove the screws and withdraw the driver's side lower facia panel. Where applicable disconnect the radio speaker wiring.
4   Pull out the ashtray, remove the screws and withdraw the pocket or cassette compartment as applicable (photos).
5   Unscrew the knob from the gearstick then remove the screws and withdraw the rubber gaiter and surround.
6   Remove the screws and push the console rearwards.

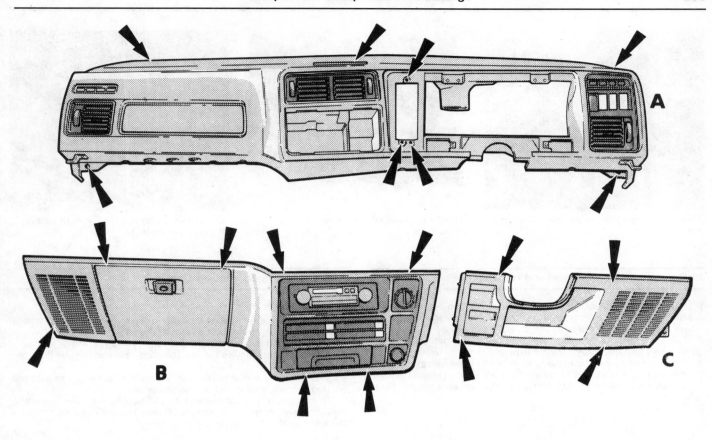

Fig. 11.14 Facia panel screw locations (Sec 31)

A   Upper facia panel   B   Lower facia panel (passenger side)   C   Lower facia panel (driver's side)

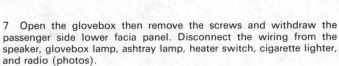

31.4A Removing the ashtray ...

31.4B ... and facia pocket

7   Open the glovebox then remove the screws and withdraw the passenger side lower facia panel. Disconnect the wiring from the speaker, glovebox lamp, ashtray lamp, heater switch, cigarette lighter, and radio (photos).
8   Remove the instrument panel as described in Chapter 12.
9   Remove the trip computer and door ajar monitor as applicable, with reference to Chapter 12.

10   Remove the foglamp and heated rear window switches.
11   Remove the heater switch controls with reference to Section 39.
12   Disconnect the auxiliary warning or graphic display multi-plug.
13   Remove the retaining screws and withdraw the main facia panel through the passenger door, at the same time disconnect the heater vent hoses.
14   Refitting is a reversal of removal.

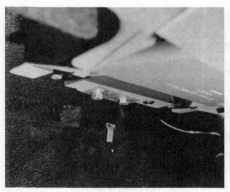

31.7A Passenger side lower facia mounting bolts

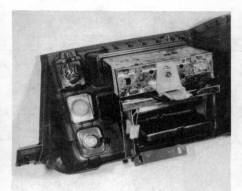

31.7B Rear view of the passenger side lower facia

32.1 Retaining screws for the front section of the centre console

32 Centre console – removal and refitting

1   Remove the screws from the front console and lift it over the gearstick, at the same time releasing the rubber gaiter (photo) and where applicable disconnecting the switch multi-plugs.
2   Open the cassette case lid, then prise out the tailgate lock switch where fitted and disconnect the multi-plug.
3   Remove the screws from the bottom of the cassette case and the front mounting screws and lift away the rear console (photos).
4   Remove the screws and withdraw the lower console panel (photos).
5   Refitting is a reversal of removal.

33 Seats – removal and refitting

Front seats
1   Adjust the seat fully forwards, and on seats with height adjustment unhook the spring from the rear cross tube.
2   Unscrew and remove the rear mounting bolts (photo).
3   Adjust the seat fully to the rear then unscrew and remove the front mounting bolts.
4   Withdraw the seat from the car. Where applicable disconnect the heating element wiring and air cushion pipe.
5   Refitting is a reversal of removal, but tighten the inner mounting bolts first. On seats with height adjustment locate the spring between the weld 'pips' on the cross tube.

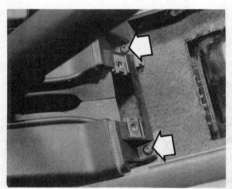

32.3A Front screws (arrowed) ...

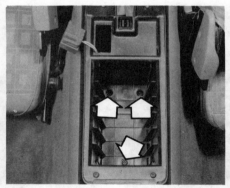

32.3B ... and rear screws for the rear section of the centre console

32.4A Lower console panel front screws ...

32.4B ... centre screws ...

32.4C ... and rear screws

33.2 Front seat rear mounting bolts

Rear seat cushion

6   Remove the mounting screws below the front of the cushion. On split seat versions the centre screws secure the hinge.
7   Lift out the cushion.
8   Refitting is a reversal of removal.

Rear seat backrest

9   Fold the rear seat backrest forwards.
10 Remove the screws securing the hinges to the backrest, and withdraw the backrest.
11 If necessary the hinge and pivot assemblies can be removed after removing the screws.
12 Refitting is a reversal of removal.

34 Rear seat armrest – removal and refitting

1   Fold the rear seat backrest forwards and remove the three armrest securing screws.
2   Lift the backrest, pull out the armrest, and prise apart the clips retaining the material.
3   Refitting is a reversal of removal.

35 Rear seat catch – removal and refitting

1   Fold the rear seat backrest forwards.

Knob type catch

2   Unscrew the catch knob from the top of the seat.
3   Pull the cushion and cover aside, then unbolt and remove the catch from the backrest. If necessary remove the screws and withdraw the strikers.
4   Refitting is a reversal of removal, but make sure that the catch operating rod is located correctly in the guide.

Lever type catch

5   With the parcel shelf removed, remove the screws and withdraw the cover for access to the catch.

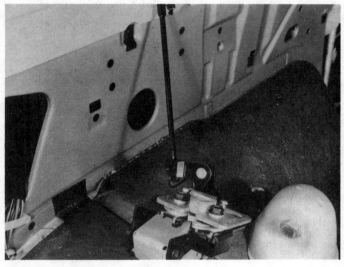

35.6 Lever type rear seat catch

6   Unbolt the catch from the mounting bracket (photo).
7   Using a small screwdriver push out the pin securing the catch to the link.
8   Withdraw the catch from under the parcel shelf side-member.
9   If necessary lift the catch lever, push out the pin, and remove the link. The lever can be removed by drilling out the rivets.
10 Refitting is a reversal of removal.

36 Seat belts – removal and refitting

Front seat belt

1   Remove the front seat as described in Section 33.
2   Unscrew the Torx bolts and remove the stalk from the seat.

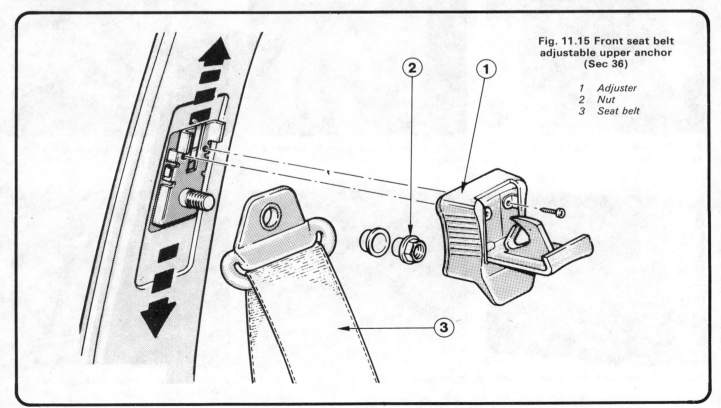

Fig. 11.15 Front seat belt adjustable upper anchor (Sec 36)

1   Adjuster
2   Nut
3   Seat belt

3 Prise the cover from the upper anchor and where the anchor is adjustable remove the two screws and adjuster.
4 Unscrew the anchor bolt/nut and remove the buckle noting the location of the washers.
5 Remove the pillar trim and unbolt the inertia reel unit. On three-door models, remove the rear quarter trim, belt guide and lower anchor rail.
6 Refitting is a reversal of removal, but tighten the nut/bolts to the specfied torque.

Rear seat belt

7 Remove the rear seat cushion with reference to Section 33.
8 Unbolt the anchor bolts from the floor.
9 Where the buckle is held in the backrest by an elastic strap, push out the retaining dowel but insert a rod or suitable tool through the strap to prevent it retracting into the backrest.
10 On Estate models remove the rear quarter trim panel.
11 Prise up the plastic cap then unbolt the inertia reel unit (photo).
12 On Hatchback models prise the guide from the side parcel shelf and feed the anchor through the aperture.
13 Refitting is a reversal of removal, but make sure that the cut-outs in the floor mounting plates locate over the dimple (Fig. 11.16).

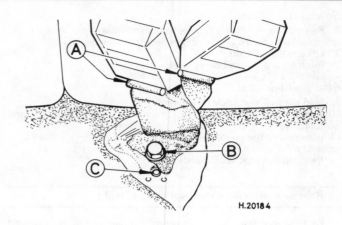

H.20184

Fig. 11.16 Rear seat belt floor mounting (Sec 36)

A   *Retaining dowel*   C   *Location dimple*
B   *Bolt*

37 Rear parcel shelf side-member – removal and refitting

1 Remove the centre parcel shelf.
2 Unhook and remove the rear seat side cushion (photo).
3 With the rear seat backrest folded forwards, lift the catch lever and push out the pin to disconnect it from the link (photo).
4 Remove the screws and withdraw the rear parcel shelf sidemember. If necessary for access to the aerial, prise the trim from the inner panel (photos).
5 Refitting is a reversal of removal.

38 Sliding roof – removal, refitting and adjustment

Removal and refitting

1 Fully open the sliding roof then remove the control screw and remove the handle.
2 Working from above, remove the screws from the perimeter (photo).
3 Lift the front rail and withdraw the assembly forward from the aperture. Do not damage the paintwork.

36.11 Rear seat belt inertia reel unit and mounting bolt

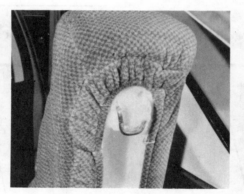

37.2 Rear seat side cushion and mounting hook

37.3 Disconnecting the rear seat catch link from the lever

37.4A Rear panel shelf side-member screw removal

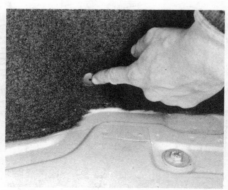

37.4B Rear side trim clip

37.4C Aerial location with rear side trim removed

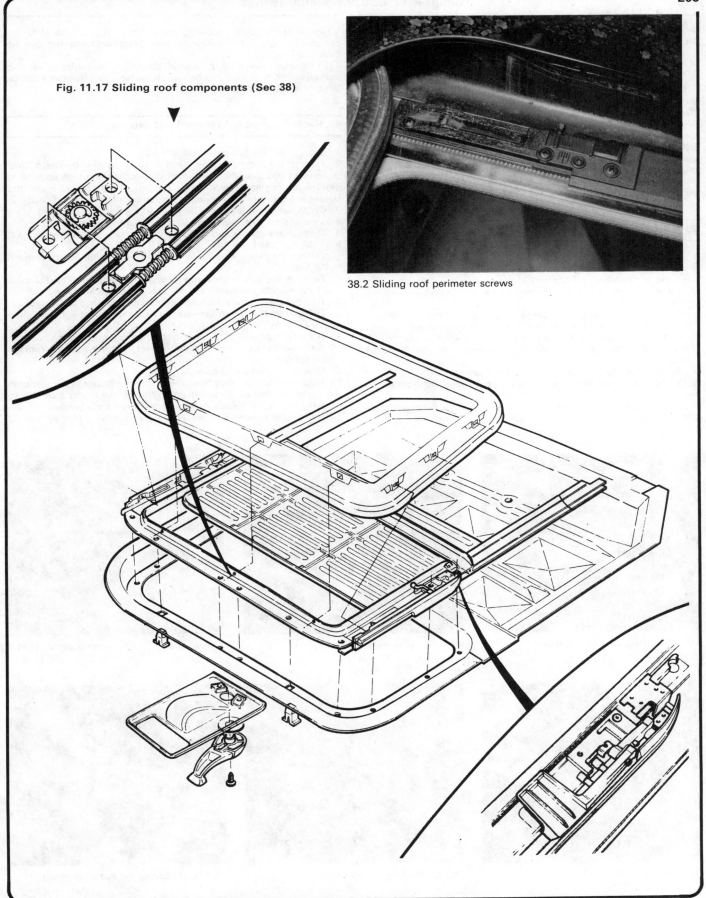

Fig. 11.17 Sliding roof components (Sec 38)

38.2 Sliding roof perimeter screws

4 Refitting is a reversal of removal, but make sure that the guide rails are correctly located. Finally adjust the sliding roof as follows.

Adjustment

5 Fully open and close the sliding roof then check that the front edge is flush with or a maximum of 2.0 mm (0.079 in) *below* thje adjacent roof panel. The rear edge should be flush with or a maximum of 2.0 mm (0.079 in) *above* the adjacent roof panel.
6 If adjustment is necessary, remove the three screws securing the lower frame to the glass and slide the lower frame back into the roof. Loosen the centre screws and either the front or rear screws located on the sides of the glass. Reposition the glass as necessary then tighten thé screws.
7 After making the adjustment slide the lower frame forward and fit the three screws.

39 Heater controls – removal and refitting

1 Disconnect the battery negative lead.
2 Remove the steering column shrouds and instrument panel surround as described in Chapter 10.
3 Detach the centre console as described in Section 32 and move it to the rear.
4 Remove the passenger footwell side trim panel and, on February 1987-on models, unclip the driver's footwell side trim panel.
5 Remove the heater switch and bezel with reference to Chapter 12.
6 Disconnect the wiring from the glove compartment light and cigar lighter.
7 Remove the lower facia panel from the passenger side.
8 Remove the two screws and disconnect the control cables from the heater.
9 Where applicable, pull the two vent hoses from the right-hand side of the heater.

10 Remove the screws securing the controls to the facia, slide the controls through and withdraw the assembly downwards. Remove the bulb and holder.
11 Refitting is a reversal of removal, but adjust the cables by moving the levers fully to the top and bottom stops. Note that resistance will be felt as the cables are repositioned.

40 Heater assembly – removal and refitting

1 Disconnect the battery negative lead.
2 Note the location of the heater hoses on the bulkhead then disconnect and plug them. Alternatively secure them high enough to prevent the coolant from draining (photo). If the coolant is still hot release the pressure in the cooling system with reference to Chapter 2.
3 To prevent unnecessary spillage when the heater is removed, blow into the upper heater pipe until all the coolant is removed.
4 Remove the screws and withdraw the heater pipe cover and gasket from the bulkhead (photo).
5 Detach the centre console as described in Section 32 and move it to the rear.
6 Remove the passenger footwell side trim panel and, on February 1987-on models, unclip the driver's footwell side trim panel.
7 Remove the heater switch and bezel with reference to Chapter 12.
8 Disconnect the wiring from the glove compartment light and cigar lighter (photo).
9 Remove the lower facia panel from the passenger side.
10 Remove the two screws and disconnect the control cables from the heater (photo).
11 Disconnect the vent hoses.
12 Unscrew the mounting bolts then move the heater to the rear until the pipes are clear of the bulkhead. Withdraw the heater assembly to the left (photos). If necessary remove the lower facia bracket.
13 Refitting is a reversal of removal, but adjust the cables by moving

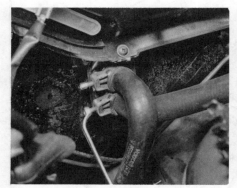
40.2 Removing the heater hoses

40.4 Heater pipes and cover

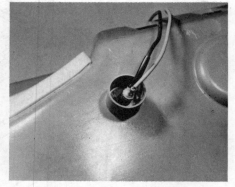
40.8 Rear view of glove compartment light and wiring

40.10 Heater control cable

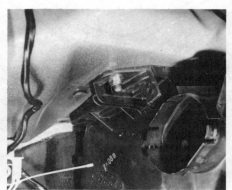
40.12A Heater mounting bolt

40.12B Removing the heater assembly

40.12C Side view of the heater assembly

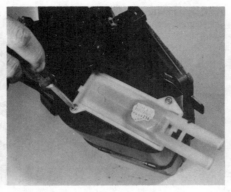
41.1A Remove the screws ...

41.1B ... and withdraw the heater matrix

41.3 Heater air valve

42.4A Remove the bolts ...

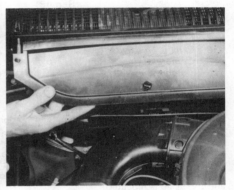
42.4B ... and withdraw the heater motor cover

the levers fully to the top and bottom stops. Note that resistance will be felt as the cables are repositioned. Finally fill the cooling system as described in Chapter 2.

41 Heater assembly – overhaul

1   With the heater assembly removed, remove the screws and slide the matrix from the casing (photos).
2   Cut the gasket in line with the casing joint, then use screwdrivers to prise off the clips and separate the casing halves.
3   Remove the air valves, then align the levers as necessary and press them from the casing (photo).
4   Clean all the components and hose the matrix to ensure that any debris is removed. If necessary use a chemical cleaner to clear the inner tubes of the matrix. Renew the components as necessary.
5   Reassembly is a reversal of the dismantling procedure.

42 Heater motor – removal and refitting

1   Disconnect the battery negative lead.
2   Pull the rubber moulding from the front of the plenum chamber.
3   Remove the windscreen washer hoses and where applicable the wiring from the heater motor cover.
4   Unbolt the heater motor cover (photos).
5   Disconnect the multi-plug from the resistor assembly and detach the earth lead from the bracket (photo).
6   Unscrew the mounting nuts and withdraw the motor from the bulkhead.
7   Unclip and remove the casing halves.
8   Disconnect the wiring, then prise open the clamp and withdraw the heater motor and fans.
9   Refitting is a reversal of removal.

43 Air conditioning system – description and precautions

An air conditioning system is available as an optional extra on certain larger-engined models. In conjunction with the heater the system enables any reasonable air temperaure to be achieved inside the car; it also reduces the humidity of the incoming air, aiding demisting even when cooling is not required.

The refrigeration side of the air conditioning system functions in a

42.5 Heater motor and wiring

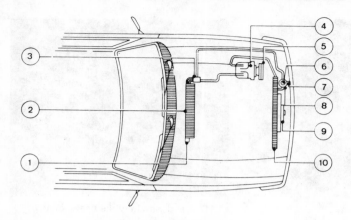

Fig. 11.18 Layout of air conditioning system components (Sec 43)

1	De-ice thermostat	6	Pressure switch
2	Evaporator	7	Sight glass
3	Expansion valve	8	Dehydrator/collector
4	Compressor	9	Cooling fan
5	Compressor clutch	10	Condenser

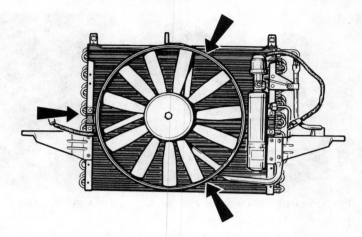

Fig. 11.19 Condenser fan securing bolt locations (arrowed) (Sec 44)

similar way to a domestic refrigerant. A compressor, belt-driven from the crankshaft pulley, draws refrigerant in its gaseous phase from an evaporator. The compressed refrigerant passes through a condenser where it loses heat and enters its liquid phase. After dehydration the refrigerant returns to the evaporator where it absorbs heat from air passing over the evaporator fins. The refrigerant becomes a gas again and the cycle is repeated.

Various subsidiary controls and sensors protect the system against excessive temperature and pressures. Addtionally, engine idle speed is increased when the system is in use to compensate for the additional load imposed by the compressor.

Although the refrigerant is not itself toxic, in the presence of a naked flame (or a lighted cigarette) it forms a highly toxic gas. Liquid refrigerant spilled on the skin will cause frostbite. If refrigerant enters the eyes, rinse them with a dilute solution of boric acid and seek medical advice immediately.

In view of the above points, and of the need for specialised equipment for evacuating and recharging the system, any work which requires the disconnection of a refrigerant line must be left to a specialist.

Do not allow refrigerant lines to be exposed to temperature above 230°F (110°C) – eg during welding or paint drying operations.

Do not operate the air conditioning system if it is known to be short of refrigerant, or further damage may result.

44 Air conditioning system components – removal and refitting

Note: *Only those items which can be removed without discharging the system are described here. Other items must be dealt with by a Ford dealer or air conditioning specialist.*

Compressor drivebelt

1   Disconnect the battery negative lead.
2   Loosen the compressor adjustment and pivot bolts, swivel the compressor towards the engine and remove the drivebelt.

3   Fit the new drivebelt and lever out the compressor until its deflection midway along the longest run is approximately 10 mm (0.4 in) under firm thumb pressure. Tighten the adjustment and pivot bolts.
4   Recheck the belt tension after it has run for at least 10 minutes under load.

Condenser fan and motor

5   Disconnect the battery negative lead.
6   On pre-February 1987 models remove the radiator front panel, and on Ghia models, the complete front bumper. Disconnect the fan wiring connector at the right-hand side of the condenser.
7   On February 1987-on models, remove the bonnet lock and unbolt the support from beneath it. Unclip the fan cowl and separate the fan motor ccnnector.
8   Apply the handbrake then jack up the front of the car and support on axle stands.
9   Unbolt the fan from the condenser. On pre-February 1987 models, turn the frame to position the fan wiring on the dehydrator side to avoid damaging the wiring. Take care also not to damage the condenser fins or tube. On February 1987-on models, detach the condenser from the radiator (2 bolts and 3 clips) before removing the fan.
10   To remove the fan blades from the motor, remove the retaining nut and circlip. The nut has a **left-hand thread,** ie it is undone clockwise.
11   With the blades removed, the motor can be unscrewed from the frame.
12   Reassemble and refit in the reverse order of dismantling and removal.

De-ice thermostat

13   Disconnect the battery and remove it.
14   Remove the plenum chamber cover plate, disconnecting vacuum hoses and washer hoses as necessary.
15   Disconnect the thermostat from the evaporator casing and remove it. Also remove the thermostat probe.
16   Refit in the reverse order of removal.

Heater/air conditioning controls

17   The procedure is similar to that described in Section 39 but additionally the vacuum hoses must be disconnected from the control unit vacuum valve during removal, and reconnected when refitting.

Chapter 12 Electrical system

Contents

Specifications

System type .... 12 volt, negative earth

Battery

Rating:
8 plates per cell type	270A/50RC
10 plates per cell type	360A/60RC
13 plates per cell type	500A/75RC
15 plates per cell type	610A/110RC
17 plates per cell type	700A/150RC

Charge condition:
Poor	12.4 volt
Normal	12.6 volt
Good	12.7 volt

Alternator

Make .... Bosch, Lucas, Motorola or Mitsubishi
Output .... 35, 45, 55, 70 or 90 amp
Stator winding resistance (ohm):

	Bosch	Lucas	Motorola	Mitsubishi
35 amp	0.130 to 0.143	0.128 to 0.138	0.333 to 0.368	–
45 amp	0.090 to 0.099	Delta type 0.285 to 0.305 Star type 0.088 to 0.108	0.266 to 0.294	–

Stator winding resistance (ohm) (contd.):

	Bosch	Lucas	Motorola	Mitsubishi
55 amp	0.070 to 0.077	0.193 to 0.213	0.228 to 0.252	0.760 to 0.840
70 amp	0.050 to 0.055	0.134	0.138 to 0.152	–
90 amp	0.090 to 0.099	–	–	–
Rotor winding resistance (ohm):				
35, 45 and 55 amp	3.40 to 3.74	3.04 to 3.36	3.80 to 4.20	2.70 to 3.10
70 and 90 amp	2.80 to 3.08	3.04 to 3.36	3.80 to 4.20	–
Minimum brush length	5.0 mm (0.197 in)	5.0 mm (0.197 in)	4.0 mm (0.157 in)	5.0 mm (0.197 in)
Regulated voltage at 4000 rpm and 3 to 7 amp load (volt)	13.7 to 14.6	13.7 to 14.6	13.7 to 14.6	13.7 to 14.6

Starter motor

Type .... Pre-engaged
Make .... Bosch or Lucas
Minimum brush length:
    Bosch .... 10.0 mm (0.394 in) [1.1 kW] or 8.0 mm (0.315 in)
    Lucas .... 8.0 mm (0.315 in)
Minimum commutator diameter:
    Bosch .... 32.8 mm (1.29 in)
    Lucas .... No value given
Minimum commutator thickness:
    Bosch .... No value given
    Lucas .... 2.05 mm (0.081 in)
Armature endfloat:
    Bosch .... 0.30 mm (0.012 in)
    Lucas .... 0.25 mm (0.010 in)

Fuses and relays (early models – typical)

Fuse	Rating (amps)	Circuit
1	20	Electric windows
2	30	Heated rear screen, heated door mirror
3	10	Clock, intermittent wiper control, econo-warning lights, door locks, defective exterior light bulb warning light
4	30	Heater motor, rear screen wiper, windscreen washer pump
5	30	Headlamp wash/wipe, reversing light
6	15	Horn
7	15	Auxiliary driving lamps
8	15	Wiper motor
9	15	Indicators, brake lights
10	15	Foglamps
11	30	Tailgate, central locking
12	20	Floor area lights, heated seats, delayed action courtesy light, load floor light, digital clock, cigar lighter, trip computer, vanity mirror
13	10	Hazard flasher warning light
14	10	Main beam left
15	10	Main beam right
16	10	Dipped beam left
17	10	Dipped beam right
18	10	Side and tail lights right, glove compartment light, switch illumination, instrument panel illumination
19	10	Switch illumination for front/rear foglamps, side and tail lights left, number plate light, engine compartment light
20	–	–

Relays	Circuit
1	Automatic transmission inhibitor switch
2	Horn
3	
4	Auxiliary driving lamps
5	Front foglamps
6	Electrically operated tailgate lock
7	Intermittent wiper motor – front
8	Headlamp wash/wipe
9	Seat belt warning light
10	Ignition switch lock
11	Intermittent wiper motor – rear
12	Delayed action courtesy light
13	Heated rear screen and heated door mirror with automatic 'cut-off'

Fuses and relays (later models – typical)

Fuse	Rating (amps)	Circuit
1	30	Power windows
2	30	Heated rear screen, heated door mirror
3	15	Wiper motor
4	30	Heater blower motor, rear screen wipers, windscreen washer pump
5	30	Headlamp wash, reversing light
6	15	Horn (steering wheel mounted)
7	15	Auxiliary driving lamps
8	10	Clock, intermittent wiper control, econo-warning lights, warning lights for door ajar and defective exterior light bulbs
9	15	Indicators, brake lights
10	15	Foglamps
11	30	Remote tailgate release, central locking
12	25	Floor area lights, heated seats, delayed action courtesy light, load floor light, digital clock, cigar lighter, trip computer, vanity mirror
13	10	Hazard flasher warning light, horn (on multi-function switch)
14	10	Main beam left
15	10	Main beam right
16	10	Dipped beam left
17	10	Dipped beam right
18	10	Switch illumination for front/rear foglamps, side and tail lights left, number plate light, engine compartment light
19	10	Side and tail lights right, glove compartment light, switch illumination, instrument panel illumination
20	25	Fuel system cooling fan

Relays	Circuit
I	Driving lamps
II	Foglamps
III	Remote Control Tailgate Release
IV	Start Inhibitor – Automatic Transmission
V	Horn
VI	Daytime Running Lights (Sweden)
VII	Ignition Switch
VIII	Headlamp Washers
IX	Warning Lamp – Seat Belts
X	Intermittent wipe – front wiper
Grey	Heated rear screen/mirrors
Orange	Rear Wiper – Intermittent Operation
Yellow	Courtesy Light Delay

Fuses and relays (1987-on models)

Fuse	Rating (amps)	Circuit
1	20	Main beam left, auxiliary driving lamp left
2	20	Main beam right, auxiliary driving lamp right
3	10	Dipped beam left
4	10	Dipped beam right
5	10	Sidelights left
6	10	Sidelights right
7	15	Instrument panel illumination, number plate lights
8	–	–
9	30	Headlamp wash/wipe, automatic transmission kickdown
10	20	Central locking, interior lights, clock, electric mirrors
11	20	Fuel pump – air conditioner (carburettor version)
12	10	Hazard warning lights
13	30	Cigar lighter
14	30	Horn
15	30	Wiper motor(s), washer pump(s)
16	30	Heated rear window, heated exterior mirrors
17	20	Front foglamps, dim-dip lighting
18	30	Heater motor
19	–	–
20	15	Direction indicators, reversing lights
21	15	Stop-lights
22	10	Instruments and controls
23	20	Fuel pump (2.8 models)
24	C30	Power windows (C = circuit breaker)
30	20	Anti-lock braking (ABS)
31	30	ABS pump
33	15	Fuel pump
35	1	Engine management

Relays	Circuit
I	Ignition switch
II	Dim-dip lighting
III	Headlamp wash/wipe
IV	–
V	Intermittent wiper control – front
VI	Time delay – interior lights
VII	Anti-lock braking (ABS)
VIII	Automatic transmission kickdown
IX	Fuel pump – air conditioning (carburettor version)
X	Main beam
XI	Engine management
XII	Automatic transmission inhibitor
A	–
B	Rear foglamp
C	Horn
D	Engine management
E	Electric exterior mirror
F	Dipped beam
G	–
H	Front foglamps
LI	Direction indicators, hazard flashers
NI	Bulb outage
M3	Air conditioner
M4	Fan (air conditioner)
M6	ABS pump
M9	Hot start relay
PI	ABS System
P2	Fuel injection system
P3	Auxiliary warning system
L2	Heated front screen (time relay)
L3	Heated front windscreen

Torque wrench settings

	Nm	lbf ft
Wiper motor bracket	6 to 7	4 to 5
Wiper arm nut	17 to 18	12 to 13
Alternator bolts:		
Coloured threads	41 to 51	30 to 38
Non-coloured threads	20 to 25	15 to 18

1 General description

The electrical system is of the 12 volt, negative earth type. Electricity is generated by an alternator, belt-driven from the crankshaft pulley. A lead-acid storage battery provides a reserve of power for use when the demands of the system temporarily exceed the alternator output, and for starting.

The battery negative terminal is connected to 'earth' – vehicle metal – and most electrical system components are wired so that they only receive a positive feed, the current returning via vehicle metal. This means that the component mounting forms part of the circuit. Loose or corroded mountings can therefore cause apparent electrical faults.

Many semiconductor devices are used in the electrical system, both in the 'black boxes' which control vehicle functions and in other components. Semiconductors are very sensitive to excessive (or wrong polarity) voltage, and to extremes of heat. Observe the appropriate precautions to avoid damage.

Although some repair procedures are given in this Chapter, sometimes renewal of a well-used item will prove more satisfactory. The reader whose interests extend beyond component renewal should obtain a copy of the 'Automobile Electrical Manual,' available from the publishers of this book.

Before starting work on the electrical system, read the precautions listed in 'Safety first!' at the beginning of the manual.

2 Routine maintenance

Carry out the following procedures at the intervals given in 'Routine Maintenance' at the beginning of the Manual.

Check operation of exterior lights

1 With the help of an assistant, check the operation of headlamps, sidelamps, tail lamps, direction indicator lamps and reversing lamps. Also check the direction indicator warning lights.
2 Where fitted, check that the graphic information module functions correctly.

Top up washer reservoirs

3 Check the level of washer fluid in the front and rear reservoirs and if necessary top up.

Check operation of all electrical equipment

4 Check the operation of all switches, interior lights, horn, instruments and any optional equipment.

Check battery electrolyte level

5 Except where a 'maintenance-free' battery is fitted, check the battery electrolyte level and top up if necessary with reference to Section 3.

3 Battery – maintenance

1 The battery fitted as original equipment is either of 'low maintenance' or 'maintenance-free' type. The 'low maintenance' battery requires checking at 4 year intervals.

2 To clean the battery terminals, disconnect them, negative (earth) first. Use a wire brush or abrasive paper to clean the terminals. Bad corrosion or 'fungus' should be treated with a solution of bicarbonate of soda, applied with an old toothbrush. Do not let this solution get inside the battery.

3 Coat the battery terminals with petroleum jelly or a proprietary anti-corrosive compound before reconnecting them. Reconnect and tighten the positive (live) lead first, followed by the negative (earth) lead. Do not overtighten.

4 Keep the top of the battery clean and dry. Periodically inspect the battery tray for corrosion, and make good as necessary.

5 If a 'traditional' type battery is fitted as a replacement, remove the cell covers at major service intervals and check that the plate separators in each cell are covered by approximately 6 mm (0.25 in) of electrolyte. If the battery case is translucent, the cell covers need not be removed to check the level. Top up if necessary with distilled or de-ionized water; do not overfill, and mop up any spillage at once.

6 Persistent need for topping-up the battery electrolyte suggests that the alternator output is excessive.

7 If the car covers a small annual mileage it is worthwhile checking the specific gravity of the electrolyte every three months to determine the state of charge of the battery. Use a hydrometer to make the check and compare the results with the following table:

	Ambient temperature above 25°C (77°F)	Ambient temperature below 25°C (77°F)
Fully charged	1.210 to 1.230	1.270 to 1.290
70% charged	1.170 to 1.190	1.230 to 1.250
Fully discharged	1.050 to 1.070	1.110 to 1.130

Note that the specific gravity readings assume an electrolyte temperature of 15°C (60°F); for every 10°C (18°F) below 15°C (60°F) subtract 0.007. For every 10°C (18°F) above 15°C (60°F) add 0.007.

8 If the battery condition is suspect, first check the specific gravity of electrolyte in each cell. A variation of 0.040 or more between any cells indicates loss of electrolyte or deterioration of the internal plates.

9 A further test can be made using a voltmeter. Connect the voltmeter across the battery and compare the result with those given in the Specifications under 'charge condition'. The test is only accurate if the battery has not been subject to any kind of charge for the previous six hours. If this is not the case switch on the headlights for 30 seconds then wait four to five minutes before testing the battery.

4 Battery – charging

1 In normal use the battery should not require charging from an external source, unless the vehicle is laid up for long periods, when it should be recharged every six weeks or so. If vehicle use consists entirely of short runs in darkness it is also possible for the battery to become discharged. Otherwise, a regular need for recharging points to a fault in the battery or elsewhere in the charging system.

2 As a precaution against possible damage to transistorized modules (eg ignition, fuel injection, ABS) **both** battery terminals should be disconnected before charging. Remove the battery cell caps.

3 Domestic battery chargers (up to about 6 amps output) may safely be used overnight without special precautions. Make sure that the charger is set to deliver 12 volts before connecting it. Connect the leads (red or positive terminal, black or negative to the negative terminal) **before** switching the charger on at the mains.

4 When charging is complete, switch off at the mains **before** disconnecting the charger from the battery. Remember that the battery will be giving off hydrogen gas, which is potentially explosive.

5 Charging at a higher rate should only be carried out under carefully controlled conditions. Very rapid or 'boost' charging should be avoided if possible, as it is liable to cause permanent damage to the battery through overheating.

6 During any sort of charging, battery electrolyte temperature should never exceed 38°C (100°F). If the battery becomes hot, or the electrolyte is 'gassing' vigorously, charging should be stopped.

5 Battery – removal and refitting

1 The battery is located in the engine compartment on the left-hand side of the bulkhead (photo).

2 Note the location of the leads then unscrew the bolt and disconnect the negative lead.

3 Lift the plastic cover then unscrew the bolt and disconnect the positive lead.

4 Unscrew the clamp bolt and lift the battery from the platform, taking care not to spill any electrolyte on the bodywork (photo).

5 Refitting is a reversal of removal, however do not over-tighten the clamp and terminal bolts.

6 Alternator – precautions

1 To avoid damage to the alternator semiconductors, and indeed to any other components, the following precautions should be observed:

   (a) *Do not disconnect the battery or the alternator whilst the engine is running*

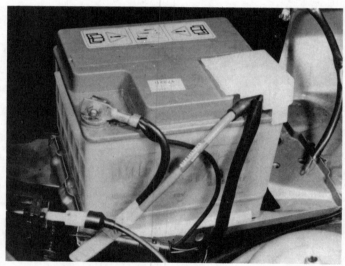

5.1 Battery and leads

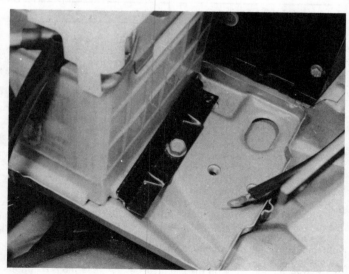

5.4 Battery clamp

(b) *Do not allow the engine to turn the alternator when the latter is not connected*

(c) *Do not test for output from the alternator by 'flashing' the output lead to earth*

(d) *Do not use a battery charger of more than 12 volts output, even as a starting aid*

(e) *Disconnect the battery and the alternator before carrying out electric arc welding on the vehicle*

(f) *Always observe correct battery polarity*

7 Alternator – fault finding and testing

Note: *To carry out the complete test procedure use only the following test equipment – a 0 to 20 volt moving coil voltmeter, a 0 to 100 amp moving coil ammeter, and a 0 to 30 amp rheostat.*

1 Check that the battery is at least 70% charged by using a hydrometer as described in Section 3.

2 Check the drivebelt tension with reference to Chapter 2.

3 Check the security of the battery leads, alternator multi-plug, and interconnecting wire.

4 *To check the cable continuity,* pull the multi-plug from the alternator and switch on the ignition being careful not to crank the engine. Connect the voltmeter between a good earth and each of the terminals in the multi-plug in turn. If battery voltage is not indicated, there is an open circuit in the wiring which may be due to a blown ignition warning light bulb if on the small terminal.

5 *To check the alternator output,* connect the voltmeter, ammeter and rheostat as shown in Fig. 12.1. Run the engine at 3000 rpm and switch on the headlamps, heater blower and the heated rear window. Vary the resistance to increase the current and check that the alternator rated output is reached without the voltage dropping below 13 volts.

6 *To check the positive side of the charging circuit,* connect the voltmeter as shown in Fig. 12.2. Start the engine and switch on the headlamps. Run the engine at 3000 rpm and check that the indicated voltage drop does not exceed 0.5 volt. A higher reading indicates a high resistance such as a dirty connection on the positive side of the charging circuit.

7 *To check the negative side of the charging circuit,* connect the voltmeter as shown in Fig. 12.3. Start the engine and switch on the headlamps. Run the engine at 3000 rpm and check that the indicated voltage drop does not exceed 0.25 volt. A higher reading indicates a high resistance such as a dirty connection on the negative side of the charging circuit.

8 *To check the alternator voltage regulator,* connect the voltmeter and ammeter as shown in Fig. 12.4. Run the engine at 3000 rpm and, when the ammeter records a current of 3 to 5 amp, check that the voltmeter records 13.7 to 14.5 volt. If the result is outside the limits the regulator is faulty.

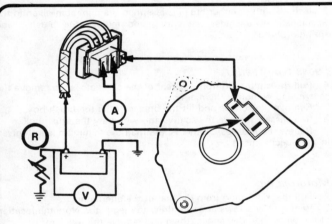

Fig. 12.1 Alternator output test circuit (Sec 7)

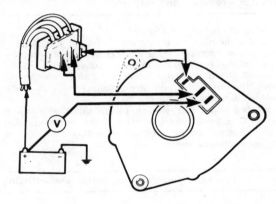

Fig. 12.2 Alternator positive check circuit (Sec 7)

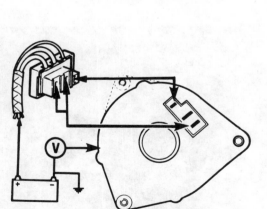

Fig. 12.3 Alternator negative check circuit (Sec 7)

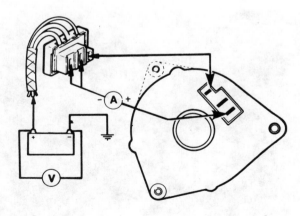

Fig. 12.4 Alternator voltage regulator test circuit (Sec 7)

8.2 Alternator and adjustment link

8.4 Wiring to the rear of the alternator

8   Alternator – removal and refitting

1   Disconnect the battery negative lead.
2   Loosen the alternator mounting and adjustment nuts and bolts, then swivel the alternator in towards the cylinder block (photo).
3   Slip the drivebelt(s) from the alternator pulley(s).
4   Disconnect the wiring from the rear of the alternator (photo).
5   Remove the mounting and adjustment nuts and bolts, and withdraw the alternator from the engine.
6   Refitting is a reversal of removal, but tension the drivebelt(s) as described in Chapter 2. Where applicable the front mounting bolt should be tightened before the rear mounting bolt, as the rear mounting incorporates a sliding bush.

9   Alternator brushes – removal, inspection and refitting

1   Disconnect the battery negative lead.

Bosch type (also later Lucas type)

2   Remove the screws and withdraw the regulator and brush box from the rear of the alternator (photos).

3   If the length of either brush is less than the minimum given in the Specifications, unsolder the wiring and remove the brushes and springs (photo).

Lucas type (early)

4   Pull the multi-plug from the rear of the alternator then remove the screws and withdraw the rear cover.
5   Remove the screws and lift the brushes from the brush box.
6   If necessary remove the screws and withdraw the brush box.
7   Renew the brushes if either is less than the minimum length given in the Specifications.

Motorola type

8   Pull the multi-plug from the rear of the alternator.
9   Remove the screws and withdraw the regulator. Note the location of the wires then disconnect them and remove the regulator.
10 Remove the single screw (35 and 45 amp types) or two screws (55 and 70 amp types) and carefully withdraw the brush box.
11 If the length of either brush is less than the minimum given in the Specifications, obtain a new brush box.

9.2A Removing the alternator regulator and brush box (Bosch)

9.2B Alternator regulator and brush box (Bosch)

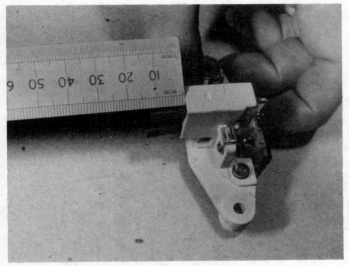

9.3 Checking the length of the alternator brushes (Bosch)

Fig. 12.5 Exploded view of the Bosch alternator (Sec 9)

A Fan
B Spacer
C Drive end housing
D Drive end bearing retaining
   plate
E Slip ring end bearing
F Slip ring end housing
G Brush box and regulator
H Rectifier (diode) pack
   (Inset shows N1-70A diode
   pack)
J Stator
K Slip rings
L Rotor
M Drive end bearing
N Spacer
O Pulley

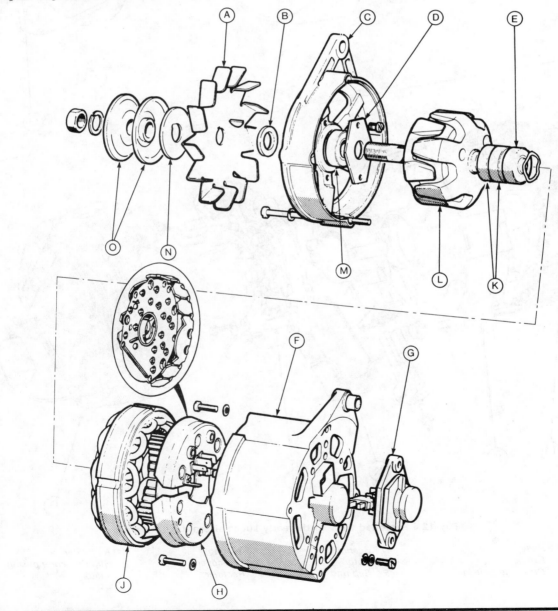

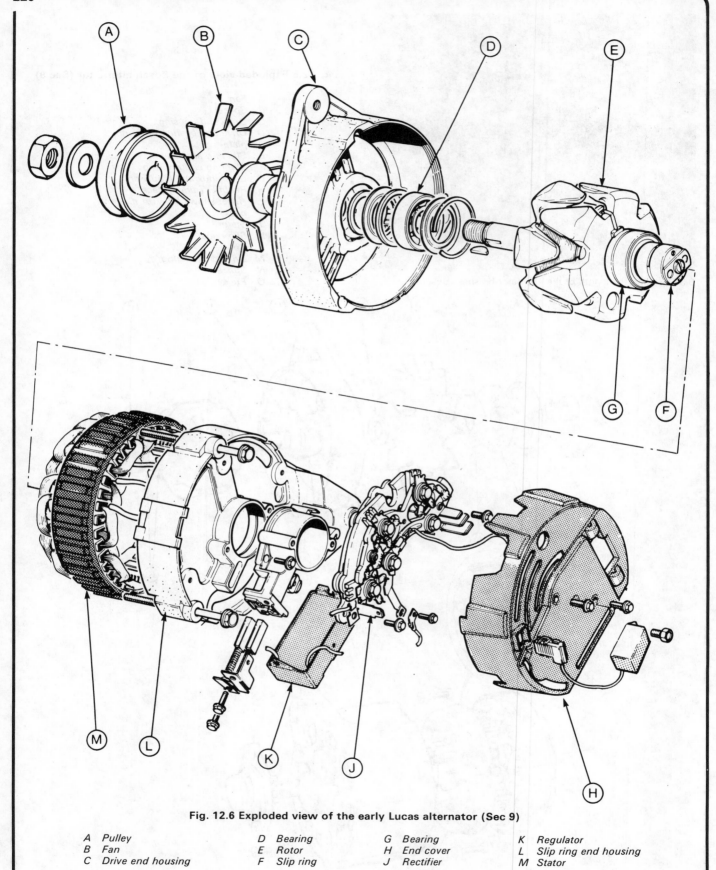

Fig. 12.6 Exploded view of the early Lucas alternator (Sec 9)

A	Pulley	D	Bearing	G	Bearing	K	Regulator
B	Fan	E	Rotor	H	End cover	L	Slip ring end housing
C	Drive end housing	F	Slip ring	J	Rectifier	M	Stator

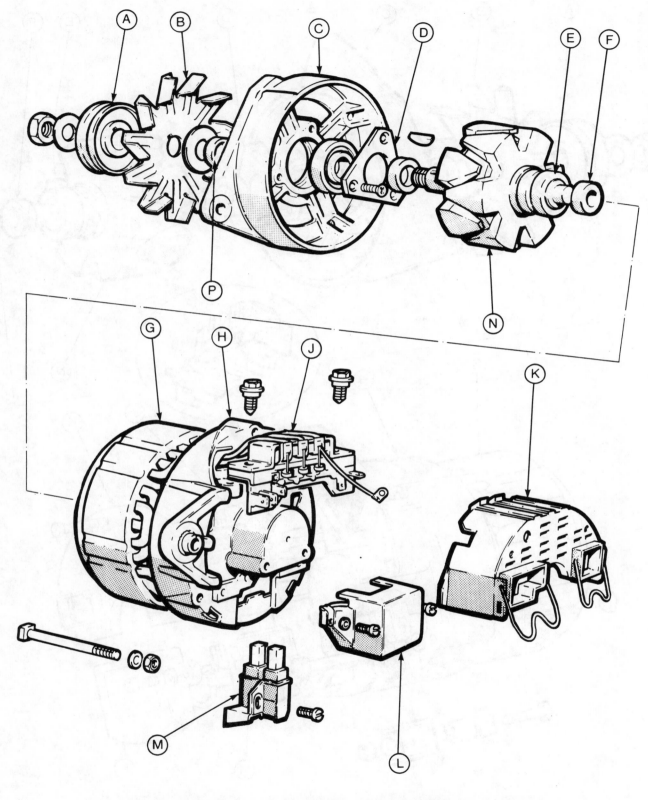

Fig. 12.7 Exploded view of the Motorola 35 and 45 amp alternator (Sec 9)

A Pulley	D Drive end bearing retaining	F Slip ring end bearing	J Diode bridge	M Brush box
B Fan	plate	G Stator	K End cover	N Rotor
C Drive end housing	E Slip ring	H Slip ring end housing	L Regulator	P Spacer

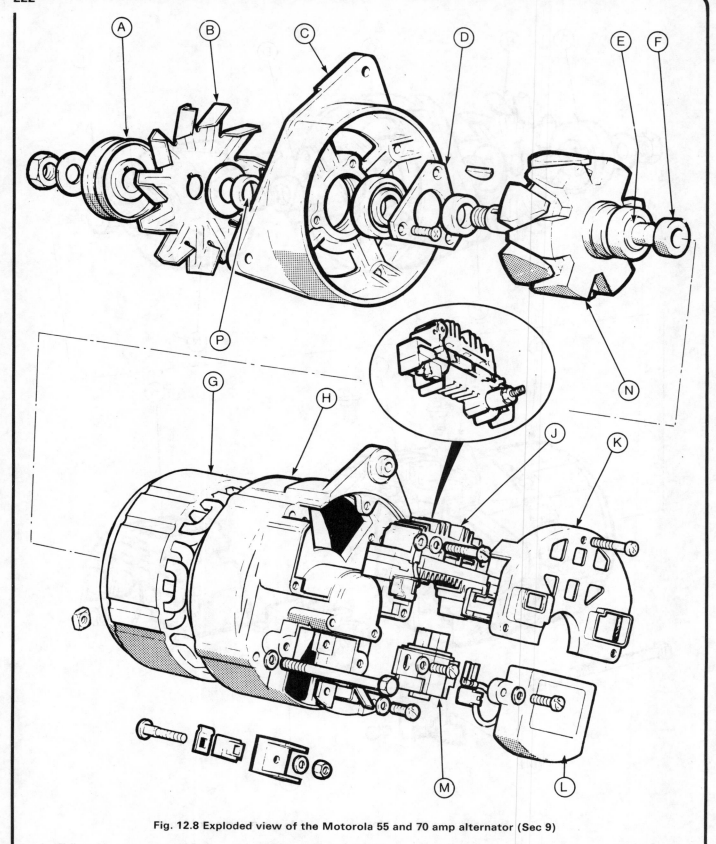

Fig. 12.8 Exploded view of the Motorola 55 and 70 amp alternator (Sec 9)

A	Pulley
B	Fan
C	Drive end housing
D	Drive end bearing retaining plate
E	Slip ring
F	Slip ring end bearing
G	Stator
H	Slip ring end housing
J	Diode bridge
K	End cover
L	Regulator
M	Brush box
N	Rotor
P	Spacer

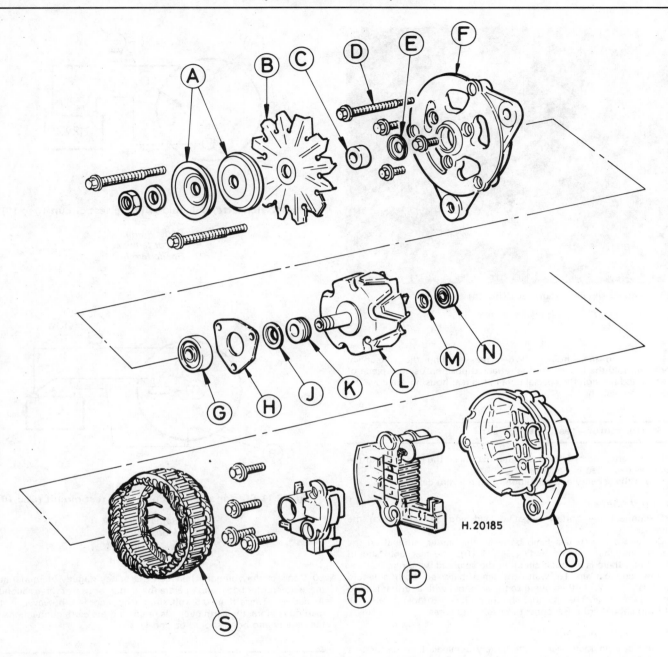

Fig. 12.9 Exploded view of the Mitsubishi alternator (Sec 9)

A Pulley	E Dust shield	J Dust cap	M Seal	P Diode pack
B Fan	F Drive end housing	K Spacer (thin)	N Bearing	R Brush box
C Spacer (thick)	G Bearing	L Rotor	O Commutator end housing	S Stator
D Through-bolt	H Retainer			

Mitsubishi type

12 Remove the alternator as described in Section 8.

13 Unscrew the pulley nut and remove the washer. Hold the rotor shaft stationary using an 8 mm hexagon key in the end of the shaft. Alternatively use an oil filter removal strap on the pulley.

14 Remove the pulley, cooling fan, spacer and dust shield from the rotor shaft.

15 Mark the front and rear housings and stator in relation to each other.

16 Unscrew the through-bolts then remove the front housing from the rotor shaft followed by the dust seal and spacer.

17 Remove the rotor from the rear housing and stator. If difficulty is experienced, heat the rear housing with a 200 watt soldering iron for 3 or 4 minutes.

18 Unbolt the rectifier and stator from the rear housing.

19 Unsolder the stator and brush box from the rectifier, but use only the minimum heat necessary. Use a pair of pliers to reduce the spread of heat to the diodes.

All types

20 Wipe clean the slip rings with a fuel-moistened cloth – if they are very dirty use fine glasspaper to clean them then wipe with the cloth (photo).

21 Refitting is a reversal of removal, but make sure that the brushes

9.20 Alternator slip rings (arrowed) (Bosch)

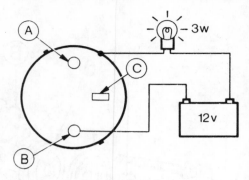

Fig. 12.10 Starter solenoid winding test circuit (Sec 10)

    A   Battery terminal
    B   Motor terminal
    C   Spade terminal

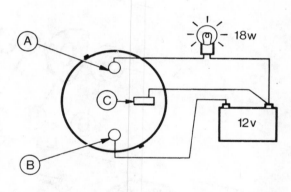

Fig. 12.11 Starter solenoid continuity test circuit (Sec 10)

    A   Battery terminal
    B   Motor terminal
    C   Spade terminal

move freely in their holders. When reassembling the Mitsubishi alternator, hold the brushes in the retracted position using a piece of wire inserted through the special hole in the rear housing. Remove the wire on completion.

10 Starter motor – testing in the car

1   If the starter motor fails to operate first check the condition of the battery as described in Section 3.
2   Check the security and condition of all relevant cables.

Solenoid check

3   Disconnect the battery negative lead and all leads from the solenoid.
4   Connect a 3 watt test lamp between the starter terminal on the solenoid and the solenoid body (Fig. 12.10). The test lamp should light. If not, there is an open circuit in the solenoid windings.
5   Now connect an 18 watt test lamp between both solenoid terminals (Fig. 12.11) then energise the solenoid with a further lead to the spade terminal. The solenoid should be heard to operate and the test lamp should light. Reconnect the solenoid wires.

On load voltage check

6   Connect a voltmeter across the battery terminals then disconnect the low tension lead from the coil positive terminal and operate the starter by turning the ignition switch. Note the reading on the voltmeter which should not be less than 10.5 volts.
7   Now connect the voltmeter between the starter motor terminal on the solenoid and the starter motor body. With the coil low tension lead still disconnected operate the starter and check that the recorded voltage is not more than 1 volt lower than that noted in paragraph 6. If the voltage drop is more than 1 volt a fault exists in the wiring from the battery to the starter.
8   Connect the voltmeter between the battery positive terminal and the terminal on the starter motor. With the coil low tension lead disconnected operate the starter for two or three seconds. Battery voltage should be indicated initially, then dropping to less than 1 volt. If the reading is more than 1 volt there is a high resistance in the wiring from the battery to the starter and the check in paragraph 9 should be made. If the reading is less than 1 volt proceed to paragraph 10.
9   Connect the voltmeter between the two main solenoid terminals and operate the starter for two or three seconds. Battery voltage should be indicated initially then dropping to less than 0.5 volt. If the reading is more than 0.5 volt the ignition switch and connections may be faulty.

10   Connect the voltmeter between the battey negative terminal and the starter motor body, and operate the starter for two or three seconds. A reading of less than 0.5 volt should be recorded, however, if the reading is more, the earth circuit is faulty and the earth connections to the battery and body should be checked.

11 Starter motor – removal and refitting

1   Jack up the front of the car and support on axle stands. Apply the handbrake.
2   Disconnect the battery negative lead.
3   Working beneath the car unscrew the nut and disconnect the main cable from the solenoid (photo).
4   Disconnect the ignition switch wire from the solenoid.
5   Unscrew the mounting bolts and withdraw the starter motor from the gearbox (photo).
6   Refitting is a reversal of removal.

12 Starter motor – overhaul

Note: *This Section covers the overhaul of the early Bosch starter motor. However, overhaul of the later Bosch and Lucas starter motors is similar with reference to Figs. 12.13 and 12.14.*
1   Unscrew the nut securing the field winding cable to the lower solenoid terminal (photo). Remove the washer and unhook the cable.

11.3 Main cable on the starter solenoid (arrowed)

11.5 Starter motor mounting bolts (arrowed) (4x4)

12.1 Disconnecting the field winding cable

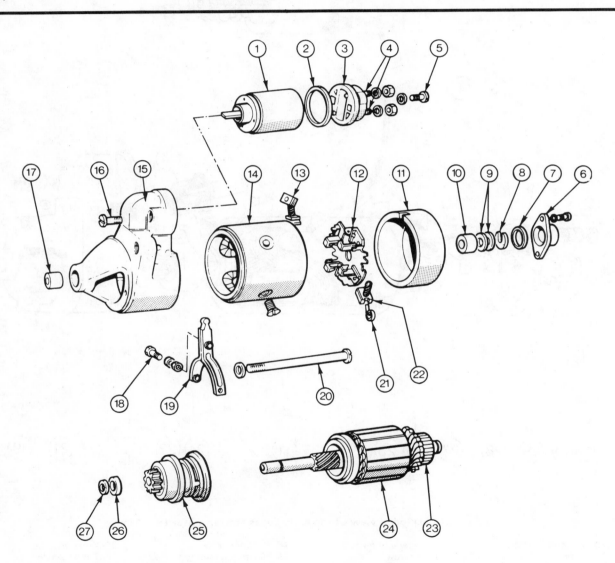

Fig. 12.12 Exploded view of the early Bosch starter motor (Sec 12)

1	Solenoid body	8	C-clip	15	Drive end housing	22	Brush
2	Gasket	9	Shim washer	16	Solenoid retaining screw	23	Commutator
3	Switch contacts and cover	10	Bearing bush	17	Bearing bush	24	Armature
4	Terminals (main)	11	Commutator end housing	18	Pivot screw	25	Drive pinion and roller
5	Retaining screw	12	Brushbox assembly	19	Actuating lever		clutch assembly
6	End cover	13	Connector link	20	Through-bolt	26	Thrust collar
7	Seal	14	Main casing (yoke)	21	Brush spring	27	C-clip

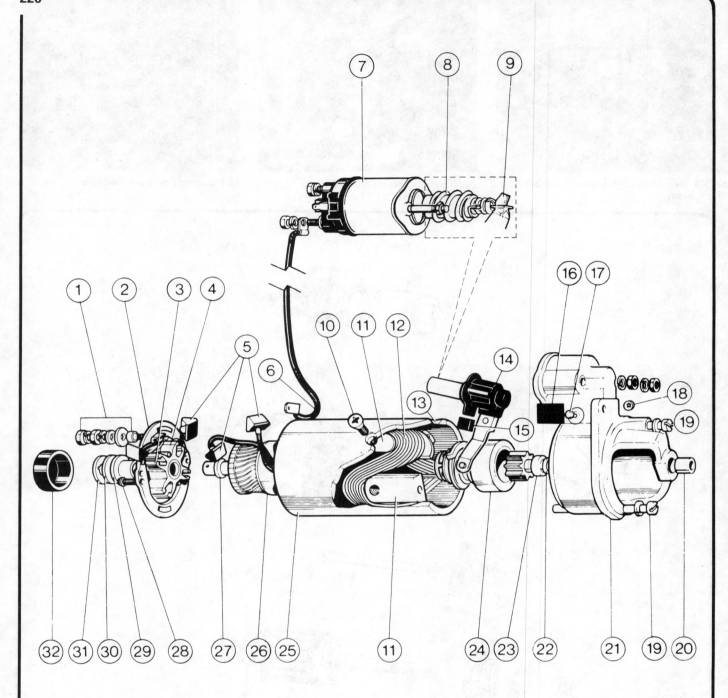

Fig. 12.13 Exploded view of the early Lucas starter motor (Sec 12)

1	Terminal nuts and washers	9	Engagement lever
2	Commutator end plate	10	Pole screw
3	Brush housing	11	Pole shoe
4	Brush springs	12	Field coils
5	Brushes	13	Field to earth connection
6	Connector link, solenoid to starter	14	Rubber seal
7	Solenoid unit	15	Rubber dust pad
8	Return spring	16	Rubber dust cover
		17	Pivot pin

18	Retaining clip	26	Armature
19	Housing retaining screws (2)	27	Thrust washer
20	Bearing bush	28	Commutator end plate retaining screws (2)
21	Drive end housing	29	Bearing bush
22	C-clip	30	Thrust plate
23	Thrust collar	31	Star clip
24	Drive assembly	32	Dust cover
25	Main casing (yoke)		

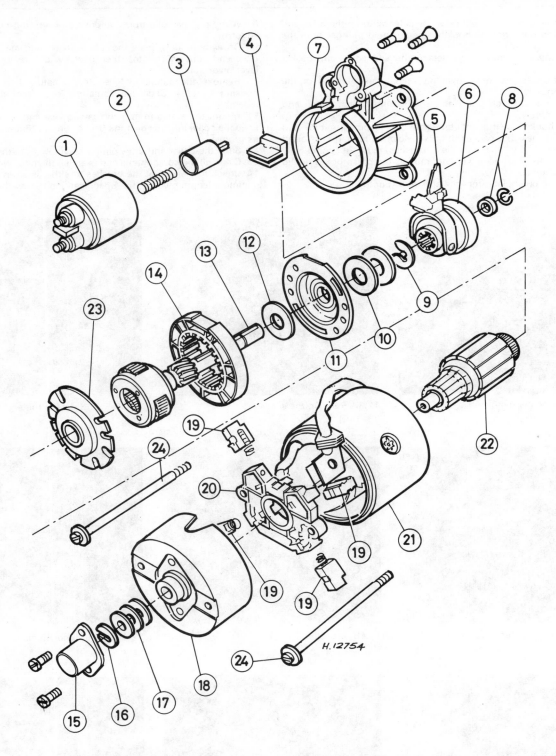

Fig. 12.14 Exploded view of the Bosch reduction gear starter motor (Sec 12)

H.12754

1	Solenoid	7	Drive end housing	13	Output shaft and planet gear assembly	19	Brushes
2	Return spring	8	C-clip and collar	14	Ring gear	20	Brushplate
3	Armature (solenoid)	9	Circlip	15	End cap	21	Yoke
4	Rubber block	10	Spacers	16	C-clip	22	Armature
5	Actuating fork	11	Cover	17	Spacers	23	Retaining plate
6	Drive assembly	12	Spacer	18	Commutator end housing	24	Through-bolt

2   Remove the screws and withdraw the solenoid from the drive end housing, at the same time unhooking the solenoid plunger from the actuating lever (photo).

3   Remove the two screws and detach the end cover and gasket (photos).

4   Extract the C-clip and remove the shims from the end of the armature (photos).

5   Unscrew the through-bolts and remove the commutator end housing (photos).

6   Using a hooked instrument, lift each brush spring in turn and remove the brushes. The two earth brushes can be lodged in a raised position (photo), but the two field brushes must be completely removed from the brushplate. On later models the brush boxes unclip from the brushplate.

7   Remove the brushplate from the armature (photo).

8   Withdraw the yoke from the drive end housing over the armature (photo).

9   On early models, prise the rubber insert and metal disc from the drive end housing (photo), then unscrew and remove the actuating lever pivot bolt.

10 Remove the actuating lever and armature from the drive end housing (photo). Slide the actuating lever from the drive pinion assembly.

11 Mount the armature in a soft-jawed vice and use a metal tube to drive the collar inwards over the C-clip (photo). Extract the C-clip from its groove.

12 Slide the collar and drive pinion assembly from the armature.

13 Clean all the components and examine them for wear and damage.

14 Check the length of the brushes. If either is worn to less than the minimum length given in the Specifications, renew them by soldering

12.2 Solenoid screw removal

12.3A Remove the screws ...

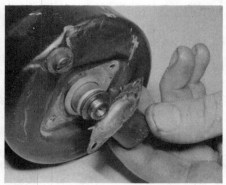

12.3B ... and detach the end cover

12.4A Remove the outer shim ...

12.4B ... C-clip ...

12.4C ... and inner shims

12.5A Remove the through-bolts ...

12.5B ... and the commutator end housing

12.6 Brushplate on the armature

12.7 Brushplate with earth brushes in raised position

12.8 Yoke removal

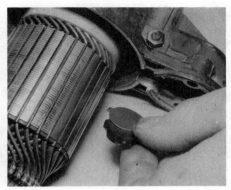

12.9 Removing the rubber insert and metal disc

12.10 Removing the actuating lever and armature from the drive end housing

12.11 Collar and C-clip

12.15 Armature commutator (arrowed)

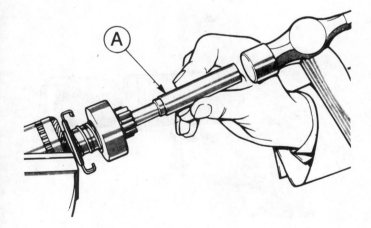

Fig. 12.15 Using a tube (A) to release the collar on the starter armature shaft (Sec 12)

on the new ones or by securing the brush leads with the screws.

15 Clean the commutator (photo) with fine glasspaper then wipe clean with a fuel-moistened cloth. If it is excessively worn it may be skimmed in a lathe and then polished, provided that it is not reduced to under the minimum diameter given in the Specifications. Clean any burrs from the insulation slots, but do not increase the width of the slots.

16 Check the armature windings for good insulation by connecting a test lamp and leads between each commutator segment in turn and the armature shaft; if the bulb glows the insulation is faulty.

17 Check the field windings in the yoke for security and for the condition of soldered joints. Check the continuity and insulation of the windings using a testlamp and leads.

18 Check the bearing bushes for wear and if necessary renew them using a soft metal drift. The bushes should be immersed in clean SAE 30/40 grade oil for a minimum of 20 minutes before being fitted. The bushes are made of self-lubricating porous bronze and must not be reamed otherwise the self-lubricating quality will be impaired.

19 Refitting is a reversal of dismantling, but lubricate the bearings and actuating lever with lithium based grease. Check that the armature endfloat is as given in the Specifications, and if necessary fit shims to correct.

13 Fuses and relays – general

1 The fuses and relays are located in the engine compartment on the right-hand side of the bulkhead and, on certain models, some additional relays are located beneath the facia panel, on the steering column bracket, and on the right-hand side of the driver's footwell (photo).

2 Always renew a fuse with one of identical rating and never renew it more than once without finding the source of the trouble (usually a short circuit). Always switch off the ignition before renewing a fuse or relay, and when renewing the wiper motor fuse keep the hands clear of the wiper linkage as it may return to the parked position.

3 Access to the fuses and relays in the fusebox is gained by removing the loose cover and spring clip (if fitted), pulling the plastic clip and removing the cover. All fuses and relays are a push fit (photos).

4 Fuse and relay locations are shown on the fusebox cover and are listed in Specifications.

5 On later models the battery positive lead is protected by a fusible link.

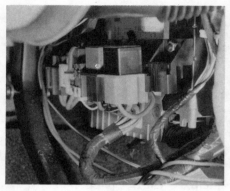

13.1 Relays on the right-hand side of the driver's footwell

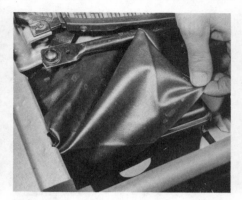

13.3A Remove the fusebox loose cover ...

13.3B ... spring clip ...

13.3C ... and cover

13.3D Fuses and relays

6   The fuses are colour coded as follows:

Red .... 10 amp
Blue .... 15 amp
Yellow .... 20 amp
Clear .... 25 amp
Green .... 30 amp

14 Direction indicator switch – removal and refitting

1   Disconnect the battery negative lead.
2   Remove the screws and withdraw the upper and lower shrouds from the steering column.
3   Remove the two cross-head screws and withdraw the switch from the steering column, also disconnect the two multi-plugs.
4   Refitting is a reversal of removal.

15 Ignition switch and lock barrel – removal and refitting

1   Disconnect the battery negative lead.
2   Remove the screws and withdraw the upper and lower shrouds from the steering column.
3   Insert the ignition key and turn to position 'I' then depress the spring clip with a suitable instrument and withdraw the steering lock barrel. Slight movement of the key will be necessary in order to align the cam.
4   With the key fully inserted, extract the spring clip taking care not to damage its location, then withdraw the key approximately 5 mm (0.2 in) and remove the barrel from the cylinder.
5   Disconnect the wiring multi-plug then remove the two grub screws and withdraw the ignition switch.

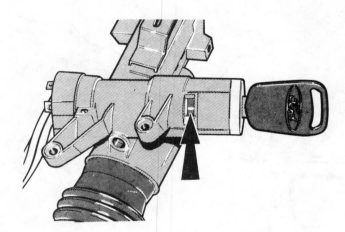

Fig. 12.16 Ignition key lock barrel spring clip location (arrowed) (Sec 15)

6   Refitting is a reversal of removal, but check the operation of the steering lock in all switch positions.

16 Lighting switch – removal and refitting

The procedure is identical to that for the direction indicator switch in Section 14 except for the additional removal and refitting of an earth lead.

17 Reversing light switch – removal and refitting

1   Jack up the front of the car and support on axle stands. Apply the handbrake.
2   Working beneath the car, disconnect the wiring and unscrew the switch from the gearbox extension.
3   Refitting is a reversal of removal, but make sure that the wiring is secured clear of the exhaust system.

18 Instrument panel illumination switch – removal and refitting

1   Disconnect the battery negative lead.
2   Using a thin screwdriver prise the switch from the facia.
3   Disconnect the wiring multi-plug and remove the switch (photo).
4   Refitting is a reversal of removal.

19 Courtesy light switch – removal and refitting

1   Open the door and unscrew the cross-head screw.
2   Remove the switch from the door pillar and pull the wire out sufficiently to prevent it from springing back into the pillar (photo).
3   Disconnect the wire and remove the switch.
4   Refitting is a reversal of removal.

20 Luggage compartment light switch – removal and refitting

1   A level-sensitive switch is incorporated into the luggage compartment light circuit and is located in the tailgate.

2   Prise the trim panel from inside the tailgate.
3   Disconnect the wiring then remove the screw and withdraw the switch. Note the fitted position of the switch to ensure correct refitting (photos).
4   Refitting is a reversal of removal.

21 Electric window switch – removal and refitting

1   Disconnect the battery negative lead.
2   Using a thin screwdriver and pad prise the front or rear switch assembly (as applicable) from the console or rear door armrests (photo).
3   Disconnect the wiring and remove the switch.
4   Refitting is a reversal of removal.

22 Heater motor switch – removal and refitting

1   Pull off the switch knob using pliers with padded jaws if necessary.
2   Prise out the switch front plate.
3   Squeeze the tabs and withdraw the switch sufficiently to disconnect the multi-plug (photo).
4   Refitting is a reversal of removal.

23 Door mirror switch – removal and refitting

1   Disconnect the battery negative lead.
2   On pre February 1987 models, prise out the switch using a thin screwdriver and disconnect the multi-plug (photo).
3   On February 1987-on models, prise out the plastic cover, remove the screw and release the door mirror inner trim from the clips.

18.3 Removing the instrument panel illumination switch

19.2 Courtesy light switch removal

20.3A Luggage compartment light switch and mounting screw

20.3B Luggage compartment light switch removed

21.2 Removing the electric window switch from the centre console

22.3 Rear view of heater motor switch

23.2 Door mirror switch removal
(pre-February 1987 models)

24.2 Handbrake warning switch

25.2 Brake stop-light switch

Disconnect the multi-plug then depress the clips and withdraw the switch.
4   Refitting is a reversal of removal.

24 Handbrake warning switch – removal and refitting

1   Remove the centre console as described in Chapter 11.
2   Disconnect the wiring then remove the screws and withdraw the switch from the handbrake assembly (photo).
3   Refitting is a reversal of removal.

25 Brake stop-light switch – removal and refitting

1   Remove the lower facia panel.
2   Disconnect the wiring then twist the switch anti-clockwise and withdraw it from the pedal bracket (photo).
3   To refit the switch, check that the brake pedal is resting on its stop. Insert the switch into the lock ring so that the switch barrel is just touching the pedal, then twist it clockwise to lock.
4   Reconnect the wiring and refit the lower facia panel.

26 Windscreen wiper switch – removal and refitting

The procedure is identical to that for the direction indicator switch in Section 14.

27 Tailgate lock switch – removal and refitting

1   Disconnect the battery negative lead.
2   Lift the cassette case lid, and prise out the switch using a thin screwdriver.
3   Disconnect the wiring multi-plug (photo).
4   Refitting is a reversal of removal.

28 Door ajar switch – removal and refitting

1   Remove the door inner trim panel (Chapter 11).
2   Pull the switch out of its location in the lock, disconnect its wiring plug and remove it.
3   Refit in the reverse order of removal. Check the switch for correct operation before refitting the trim panel.

29 Low washer fluid level switch – removal and refitting

1   Empty the washer reservoir to below the level of the switch.

2   Disconnect the switch wiring plug and prise the switch out of its grommet.
3   Refit in the reverse order of removal, using a new grommet if necessary. Check for leaks, and for correct operation of the switch, when refilling the reservoir.

30 Low coolant warning switch – removal and refitting

1   Drain the cooling system as described in Chapter 2.
2   Disconnect the wiring multi-plug then unscrew the collar and pull the switch from the rubber grommet (photo).
3   Refitting is a reversal of removal. Refer to Chapter 2 when refilling the cooling system.

31 Warning light control – removal and refitting

1   Remove the lower facia cover from behind the glove compartment.
2   Pull off the cylindrical clips and lower the control bracket (photo).
3   Disconnect the multi-plug then remove the screws and withdraw the control unit. Where two units are fitted note the multi-plugs are colour-coded – the warning light control multi-plug is brown. The green multi-plug is fitted to the bulb failure monitor.
4   Refitting is a reversal of removal.

32 Instrument panel – removal and refitting

1   Disconnect the battery negative lead.
2   Remove the screws and withdraw the steering column upper and lower shrouds.
3   Where fitted, remove the rheostat and intermittent wiper control.
4   Remove the screws and withdraw the panel surround. Note that the right-hand side screw is covered with a plastic cap. Disconnect the plug from the illumination switch (photos).
5   Remove the screws and withdraw the instrument panel sufficiently to disconnect the speedometer cable and multi-plugs (photos).
6   Refitting is a reversal of removal.

33 Speedometer cable – removal and refitting

1   On models fitted with a trip computer remove the speed sender as described in Section 41.
2   Remove the instrument panel as described in Section 32.
3   Jack up the front of the car and support on axle stands. Apply the handbrake.
4   On manual gearbox non-4x4 models extract the circlip and remove the speedometer cable from the extension housing (photos). On 4x4 models, unscrew the nut and remove the speedometer cable from the intermediate shaft bearing cover on the left-hand side of the engine sump (photo).

27.3 Disconnecting the tailgate lock switch multi-plug

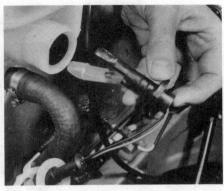

30.2 Removing the low coolant warning switch

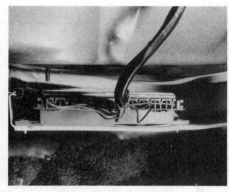

31.2 Warning light control location

32.4A Remove the plastic cap ...

32.4B ... unscrew the instrument panel surround lower screws ...

32.4C ... and upper screws ...

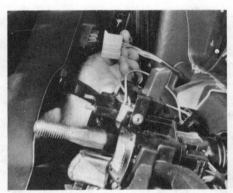

32.4D ... and disconnect the plug from the illumination switch

32.5A Remove the screws ...

32.5B ... withdraw the instrument panel ...

32.5C ... and disconnect the multi-plugs and speedometer cable

33.4A On manual gearbox models extract the circlip (arrowed) ...

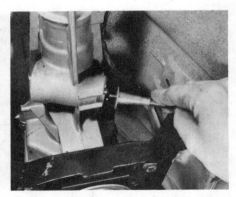

33.4B ... and remove the speedometer cable

33.4C On 4x4 models remove the speedometer cable from the intermediate shaft bearing cover

35.2 Auxiliary warning light panel removal

35.3 Graphic information module retaining screw removal

5   On automatic transmission models unscrew the bolt and remove the clamp and speedometer cable from the transmission housing.
6   Pull the cable through the bulkhead into the engine compartment then bend open the retaining clips and remove the cable.
7   Refitting is a reversal of removal, but make sure that the bulkhead grommet is correctly located. Position the cable according to the colour band locations. The first band must coincide with the grommet, the second band with the first side member clip, and the third band with the side-member bracket.

34 Instrument panel gauges – removal and refitting

1   Remove the instrument panel, as described in Section 32.

Speedometer head
2   Remove the cross-head screws and withdraw the lens or front assembly.
3   Remove the two screws and spacers and withdraw the speedometer head from the panel.
4   Refitting is a reversal of removal.

Tachometer
5   Remove the cross-head screws amd withdraw the lens or front assembly.
6   Remove the nuts and washers and withdraw the tachometer.
7   Refitting is a reversal of removal.

Fuel and temperature gauges
8   Remove the cross-head screws and withdraw the lens or front assembly.
9   Remove the nuts and washers or screws and withdraw the gauge assembly. On later models it is necessary to remove the warning light bulbs and printed circuit from the area behind the gauges.
10 Refitting is a reversal of removal.

35 Graphic information module – removal and refitting

1   Disconnect the battery negative lead.
2   Remove the upper screw and pull the auxiliary warning light panel from the facia (photo). Note that the multi-plug is disconnected as the panel is withdrawn.
3   Remove the retaining screw and the retainer (photo).
4   Pull out the module and release the multi-plug using a small screwdriver (photo).
5   Refitting is a reversal of removal.

36 Clock – removal and refitting

1   Disconnect the battery negative lead.

Standard model
2   Prise the clock from the facia using a thin screwdriver then disconnect the multi-plug. On models with an auxiliary warning light panel, remove the panel first (1 screw).
3   Refitting is a reversal of removal.

Multi-function digital analogue model
4   Remove the upper screw and pull the auxiliary warning light panel from the facia.
5   Remove the screws and withdraw the clock sufficiently to disconnect the multi-plug (photo).
6   Refitting is a reversal of removal.

37 Ice warning sender unit – removal and refitting

1   Remove the horn as described in Section 43.
2   Depress the two tangs, disconnect the multi-plug and withdraw the sender unit from the slot on the front panel.
3   Refitting is a reversal of removal.

35.4 Disconnecting the multi-plug from the graphic information module

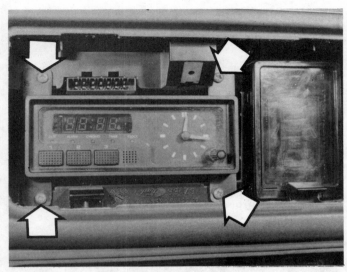

36.5 Digital clock and retaining screws (arrowed)

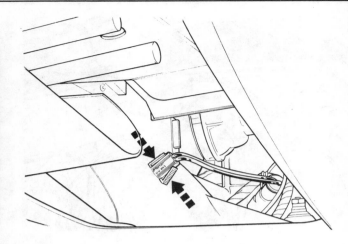

Fig. 12.17 Ice warning sender unit removal (Sec 37)

Depress the tangs (arrowed)

38 Cigarette lighter – removal and refitting

1   Disconnect the battery negative lead.
2   Reach up behind the lower centre console and push out the lighter after disconnecting the wiring (photo).
3   Remove the bulbholder and ring assembly.
4   Refitting is a reversal of removal.

39 Auxiliary warning system – general

1   Fitted to 2.3 models and also the XR4i, the auxiliary warning system (AWS) monitors the levels of fuel, coolant, washer fluid and (at start-up only) engine oil, it also gives warning of brake pad wear. The five warning lights should all illuminate for a few seconds when the ignition is first switched on, then all go out. If a light remains on, the appropriate fluid level or system should be checked as soon as possible. If a light flashes, a circuit fault is indicated and the appropriate circuit should be checked.
2   On some models the AWS also includes a graphic display unit, consisting of an outline of the car and symbols representing its doors and lights. Warning is given to the driver of doors ajar and of running light bulb failure (except main beam). The stop-light circuit is also checked; after switch-on the stop-light symbols will remain lit until the brake pedal is first depressed. If all is well they will then extinguish.
3   The graphic display unit carries a central snowflake symbol, which will show yellow when the outside temperature falls to 4°C (39°F), and red at or below 0°C (32°F).
4   The coolant and washer fluid sensors are reed switches, operated by floating magnets. The fuel level sensor is incorporated in the gauge sender unit. The oil level sensor is built into a special dipstick.
5   Brake pad wear warning is achieved by incorporating a wire loop in the friction material of one pad on each caliper. When the loop is broken, the warning light illuminates.
6   All AWS sensors, including the 'door ajar' switches, incorporate resistors in such an arrangement that the control assembly can read the difference between open sensor contacts and an open-circuit in the wiring.
7   The AWS control unit, and (when fitted) the bulb failure monitor, are located behind the glovebox.
8   Thorough testing and fault finding should be left to a Ford dealer, or other competent electrical specialist, having the necessary test equipment. Unskilled or uninformed testing may cause damage.
9   Investigation of malfunctions should begin by checking that all wiring is intact and securely connected. If checking wires or sensors

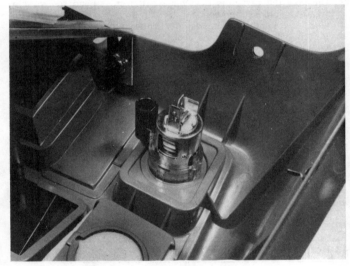

38.2 Rear view of the cigarette lighter

for continuity, always disconnect the control unit and/or bulb failure monitor before so doing, otherwise damage may be caused.

40 Trip computer models – removal and refitting

1   Disconnect the battery negative lead.
2   Remove the upper screw and pull the auxiliary warning light panel from the facia. Note that the multi-plug is disconnected as the panel is withdrawn.
3   Remove the screws and withdraw the module sufficiently to disconnect the multi-plug.
4   Where applicable unscrew the nuts and separate the bracket from the module.
5   Refitting is a reversal of removal.

41 Trip computer speed sender unit – removal and refitting

1   The speed sender unit is located in the engine compartment on the right-hand side of the bulkhead.
2   Disconnect the multi-plug from the sender unit.

Fig. 12.18 Trip computer speed sender unit location in the bulkhead (Sec 41)

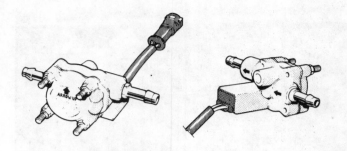

Fig. 12.19 Trip computer fuel-flow sensor flow and mounting arrows – carburettor version (Sec 42)

3   Unscrew the two nuts then remove the cross-head screws and withdraw the bracket and sender.
4   Unscrew the nut and separate the sender from the bracket.
5   Refitting is a reversal of removal.

42   Trip computer fuel-flow sensor – removal and refitting

1   The fuel flow sensor is located on the left-hand side of the engine compartment.
2   Note the location of the fuel pipes then disconnect them from the sensor.
3   Disconnect the multi-plug.
4   Remove the screws and withdraw the sensor and bracket.
5   Unscrew the nuts or bolts and separate the sensor from the bracket.
6   Refitting is a reversal of removal, however note the markings which indicate the direction of fuel flow and the top of the unit.

43   Horn – removal and refitting

1   The horns are located just in front of the radiator on each side beneath the front panel.
2   Disconnect the battery negative lead.
3   Disconnect the wiring then unscrew the bolt and detach the horn and bracket from the front panel (photo).
4   Refitting is a reversal of removal.

44   Headlamps – alignment

1   It is recommended that the headlamp alignment is carried out by a Ford garage using modern beam setting equipment. However in an emergency the following procedure will provide an acceptable light pattern.
2   Position the car on a level surface with tyres correctly inflated approximately 10 metres (33 feet) in front of, and at right-angles to, a wall or garage door.
3   Draw a vertical line on the wall corresponding to the centre line of the car. The position of the line can be ascertained by marking the centre of the front and rear screens with crayon then viewing the wall from the rear of the car.
4   Complete the lines shown in Fig. 12.20.
5   Switch the headlamps on dipped beam and adjust them as necessary using the knobs located behind the headlamps (photo). Cover the headlamp not being checked with cloth.

43.3 Horn location

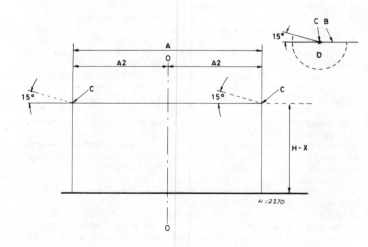

Fig. 12.20 Headlamp alignment chart (Sec 44)

A   Distance between headlamp centres
B   Light-dark boundary
C   Beam centre dipped
D   Dipped beam pattern

H   Height from ground to centre of headlamps
O   Centre line
x   All variants – 16.0 cm (6.3 in or 1.0°)

44.5 Main headlamp (A) and auxiliary driving light (B) beam alignment knobs

2   Full information will be given in the driver's handbook, but basically the dim-dip lamps are in operation whenever the light switch is in the first 'ON' position and the ignition is switched on.
3   All Sierras built after October 1st 1986 (build code GR) are equipped with additional relays to enable the dim-dip system to be fitted.

46 Headlamps and headlamp bulbs – removal and refitting

1   To remove a headlamp bulb, open the bonnet then remove the cover by turning it anti-clockwise.
2   Pull off the connector then, according to type, release the spring clip or turn the bulbholder anti-clockwise (photo).
3   Withdraw the bulb but do not touch the bulb glass (photo). If it is accidentally touched, clean it with methylated spirit.

Pre-February 1987 models
4   To remove the headlamp unit first remove the front grille panel by unscrewing the upper screws.
5   Disconnect the multi-plug from the rear of the unit (photo). When applicable disconnect the headlamp washers.
6   Unscrew the mounting bolts and the lower sliding clamp bracket bolt on the rear of the unit, then withdraw the unit from the car (photos).
7   If required, the headlamp lens can now be removed by releasing the spring clips around its edge (photos).
8   Refitting is a reversal of removal, but do not tighten the headlamp mounting bolts until it is aligned with the front grille panel. When refitting the bulb make sure that the lugs locate in the slots in the holder. Finally check the headlamp alignment as described in Section 44.

February 1987-on models
9   To remove the headlamp unit first, where applicable, remove the headlamp wiper arm as described in Section 53 and the direction indicator lamp as described in Section 47.

45 Dim-dip lighting system – general

1   Recent legislation requires that all vehicles registered after the 1st April 1987 should be equipped with a dim-dip lighting system. The system provides the headlamps with a brightness between that of the sidelamps and the headlamps on normal dipped beam. The purpose of the system is to prevent vehicles being driven on sidelamps only.

46.2A Headlamp bulb connector

46.2B Headlamp bulb and retaining spring clips

46.3 Removing the headlamp bulb

46.5 Disconnecting headlamp multi-plug (pre-February 1987 models)

46.6A Headlamp upper bolts ...

46.6B ... rear bolt ...

46.6C ... and slide bolt (pre-February 1987 models)

46.6D Headlamp removal (pre-February 1987 models)

46.6E Rear view of removed headlamp (pre-February 1987 models)

46.7A Release the clips ...

46.7B ... and remove the headlamp lens

46.10A Remove the screws ...

46.10B ... and withdraw the plastic trim (February 1987-on models)

46.10C Plastic trim locating guides beneath the headlamp (February 1987-on models)

46.10D Plastic trim side location (February 1987-on models)

46.11 Wiper motor-to-headlamp securing bolts (February 1987-on models)

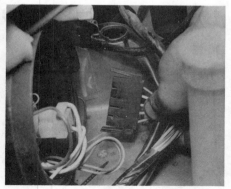

46.12A Disconnect the multi-plug ...

46.12B ... and unscrew the rear mounting bolt ...

46.12C ... and upper mounting nut ...

46.12D ... and side mounting nut (February 1987-on models)

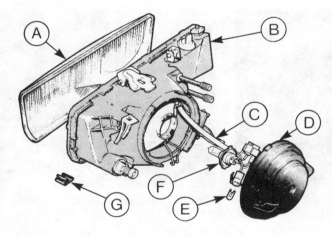

Fig. 12.21 Exploded view of the High Series headlamp (Sec 46)

A Lens
B Body
C Loom
D Cover
E Sidelamp bulb
F Headlamp bulb
G Retaining clip

10 Remove the screws and carefully ease the plastic trim away from its location over the front bumper (photos).
11 Where applicable unscrew the bolts securing the wiper motor to the headlamp and slide the motor rearwards (photo).
12 Disconnect the wiring multi-plug then unscrew the headlamp mounting nut and bolts (photos).

13 Withdraw the headlamp unit; tilting it as necessary to release the outer peg from the bracket (photos).
14 If required, the headlamp lens can now be removed by releasing the spring clips around its edge.
15 Refitting is a reversal of removal, but before tightening the mounting nut and bolts, temporarily close the bonnet and align the headlamp with it.

47 Lamp bulbs – renewal

Sidelamps
1 Open the bonnet and remove the headlamp rear cover by turning it anti-clockwise.
2 Pull and turn the sidelamp bulbholder from the reflector leaving the rubber sleeve in position (photo). On most models it is necessary to depress a tab to remove the bulbholder.
3 Pull the wedge type bulb from the bulbholder.

Auxiliary driving lamps (pre-February 1987 models)
4 Twist the cover on top of the headlamp anti-clockwise and remove it (photo).
5 Remove the clip and withdraw the bulb (photo).
6 Disconnect the wiring and remove the bulb.
7 Reconnect the wiring last when refitting the bulb (photo).

Auxiliary driving lamps (February 1987-on models)
8 Release the spring clip and remove the rear cover (photo).
9 Release the spring clips and withdraw the bulb (photo).
10 Disconnect the wiring.

Front direction indicator lamps (pre-February 1987 models)
11 On some 2.3 models push the lamp rearward into its aperture until the plastic tang is locked then extract the lamp.

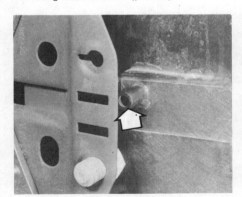

46.13A Headlamp outer peg (arrowed) ...

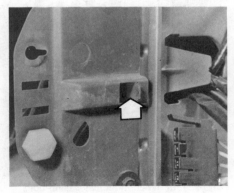

46.13B ... and bracket location hole (arrowed) (February 1987-on models)

47.2 Sidelamp bulb removal

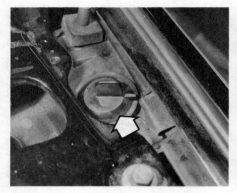

47.4 Auxiliary driving lamp bulb cover (arrowed) (pre-February 1987 models)

47.5 Auxiliary driving lamp bulb removal (pre-February 1987 models)

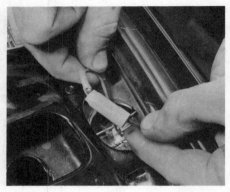

47.7 Reconnecting the auxiliary driving lamp bulb wiring (pre-February 1987 models)

47.8 Auxiliary driving lamp rear cover and spring clip (February 1987-on models)

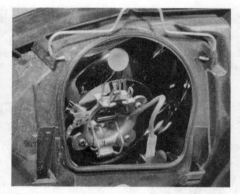

47.9 Auxiliary driving lamp bulb and wiring (February 1987-on models)

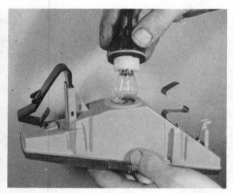

47.13 Front direction indicator lamp bulb removal (pre-February 1987 models)

12 On 2.8 and Ghia models push the release lever up into the bumper recess and extract the lamp.

13 Twist the bulbholer anti-clockwise and remove it from the lamp then push and twist the bulb to remove it (photo).

14 On Low Series models release the plastic tang before refitting the lamp.

Front direction indicator lamps (February 1987-on models)

15 Unhook the spring from behind the lamp and release the location pegs as the lamp is withdrawn (photo).

16 Turn the bulbholder anti-clockwise and remove it from the lamp body (photo).

17 Depress and twist the bulb to remove it.

Front foglamps (pre-February 1987 models)

18 Remove the front direction indicator lamp as described in paragraphs 11 to 14.

19 Unhook the clip, withdraw the lamp so that the plug can be disconnected, then remove the lamp.

20 Turn the bulb cover anti-clockwise then release the spring clips and remove the bulb.

47.15 Removing the front direction indicator lamp (February 1987-on models)

47.16 Front direction indicator lamp bulb removal (February 1987-on models)

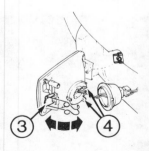

Fig. 12.22 Front foglamp removal on pre-February 1987 models (Sec 47)

3   Tab
4   Bulb retaining spring

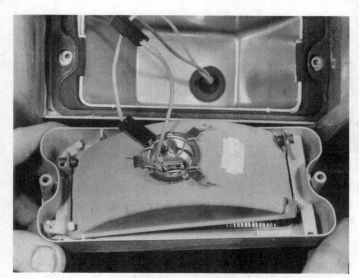

47.21 Removing the front foglamp lens and reflector (February 1987-on models)

Front foglamps (February 1987-on models)

21 Remove the two screws and withdraw the lens and reflector (photo).
22 Disconnect the wiring then release the spring clip and remove the bulb.
23 Take care not to trap the wiring when refitting, and align the beam if necessary by turning the adjustment screw in the upper corner.

Side repeater lamps (early models)

24 Turn the steering full lock to the side being worked on.
25 Remove the screws securing the splash shield to the inner body panel, noting the location of the screw covers in the engine compartment (photo).
26 Squeeze the retainers and withdraw the lamp.
27 Twist the bulbholder anti-clockwise and remove it from the lamp then pull out the wedge type bulb (photo).

Side repeater lamps (later models)

28 Twist the lamp clockwise and withdraw it from the front wing.
29 Turn the bulbholder anti-clockwise and separate it from the lamp.
30 Pull the bulb from the socket.

Rear lamp cluster (Saloon)

31 Working in the luggage compartment press the plastic tab inwards and withdraw the bulbholder (photos).
32 Press and twist the bulbs to remove them (photo).

Rear lamp cluster (Estate)

33 Working in the luggage compartment turn the tabs a quarter-turn and remove the cover.
34 Push out the retaining tabs and withdraw the bulbholder.
35 Press and twist the bulbs to remove them.

Rear number plate lamp

36 Prise the lamp from the rear bumper using a small screwdriver to depress the two spring clips (photos).
37 Twist the bulbholder anti-clockwise and remove it from the lamp then pull out the wedge type bulb (photo).

Interior lamp and luggage compartment lamp

38 With the lamp switched on prise out the lamp with a screwdriver (photo).
39 Press and twist the bulb to remove it (photos).

47.25 Splash shield removal for access to side repeater lamp (early models)

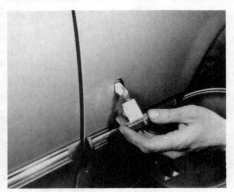

47.27 Removing the side repeater lamp (early models)

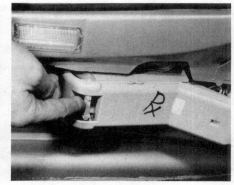

47.31A Press in the plastic tab ...

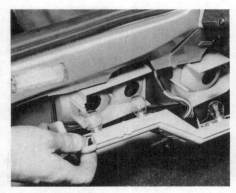

47.31B ... and withdraw the rear lamp cluster (Saloon)

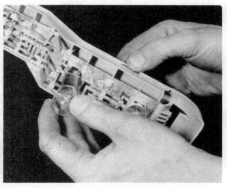

47.32 Rear lamp cluster bulb removal

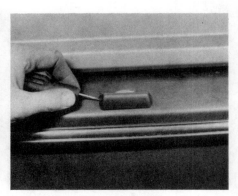

47.36A Depress the spring clips ...

47.36B ... and remove the rear number plate lamp

47.37 Rear number plate bulb removal

47.38 Prise out the interior lamp ...

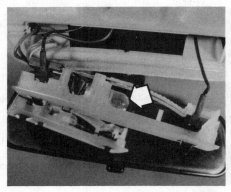

47.39A ... for access to the bulb (arrowed)

47.39B Luggage compartment lamp and bulb

Glove compartment lamp
40 Open the glove compartment lid and pull the wedge type bulb from the bulbholder.

Ashtray lamp
41 Remove the ashtray drawer, pull out the bulbholder, and pull out the wedge type bulb.

Heater motor switch lamp
42 Pull off the switch knob using padded pliers if necessary.
43 Press and twist the bulb to remove it.

Map reading lamp
44 Remove the interior lamp as described in paragraphs 38 and 39 then insert a finger in the interior lamp aperture and push out the map

reading lamp. Alternatively prise out the lamp with a small screwdriver (photo).
45 Pull out the bulbholder then pull out the wedge type bulb (photo).

Heater control lamp
46 Remove the instrument panel as described in Section 32.
47 Prise off the bezel and pull out the wedge type bulb.

Vanity mirror lamp
48 Pull down the sun visor then prise off the mirror and lens.
49 Extract the festoon type bulbs from the spring contacts.
50 To remove the sun visor remove the two screws, lower the unit from the headlining, and disconnect the wire (photo).

47.44 Map reading lamp removal

47.45 Removing the bulbholder from the map reading lamp

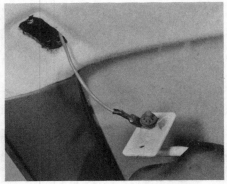

47.50 Vanity mirror lamp wiring when removing the sun visor

47.56A Removing a small bulbholder from the instrument panel

47.56B Removing a large bulbholder from the instrument panel

47.57 The bulb can be separated from the small bulbholder

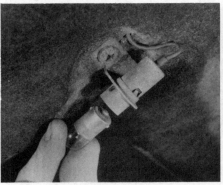

47.58 Engine compartment lamp bulb removal

47.60 Auxiliary warning lamp bulb removal

Facia warning lamp

51 Remove the centre facia screw and withdraw the warning lamp assembly at the same time disconnect the multi-plug.
52 Twist the bulbholder through 90° and remove it. The bulb cannot be removed from the bulbholder.

Hazard warning lamp

53 Remove the upper steering column shroud (1 screw).
54 With the switch off, pull off the cover then pull out the wedge type bulb using small pliers if necessary.

Instrument panel lamp

55 Remove the instrument panel as described in Section 32.
56 Twist the bulbholder through 90° and remove it (photos).
57 On the small black bulbholders the bulb can be removed but on the large white bulbholders this is not possible (photo).

Engine compartment lamp

58 Open the bonnet then depress and twist the bulb to remove it from the bulbholder (photo).

Auxiliary warning lamp

59 Remove the upper screw and pull the auxiliary warning light panel from the facia. Note that the multi-plug is disconnected as the panel is withdrawn.
60 Twist the bulbholder through 90° and remove it (photo). The bulb cannot be removed from the bulbholder.

Automatic transmission quadrant lamp

61 Unscrew the selector lever handle.
62 Remove the centre console tray with reference to Chapter 11.
63 Remove the gate cover and unclip the bulbholder.
64 Pull off the top cover then depress and twist the bulb to remove it.

Clock illumination lamp

65 Remove the clock as described in Section 36.
66 Twist the bulbholder through 90° and remove it.

Trip computer module illumination lamp

67 Remove the trip computer module as described in Section 40.
68 Using long-nosed pliers or tweezers, turn the bulbholder anti-clockwise and remove it.
69 Remove the bulb from the bulbholder.

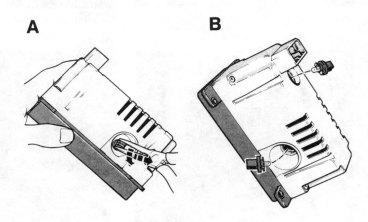

A   B

Fig. 12.23 Trip computer bulb renewal (Sec 47)

48 Windscreen wiper motor and linkage – removal and refitting

1   Remove the wiper arms as described in Section 51.
2   Open the bonnet and disconnect the washer tube.
3   Unscrew the front screws from the ribbed cowl panel, then close the bonnet and unscrew the rear screws having first removed the screw covers. Remove the cowl panel.
4   Disconnect the multi-plug to the wiper motor.
5   Unbolt the mounting bracket and remove it, together with the linkage and motor (photo).
6   Unscrew the spindle nut and the mounting bolts and separate the motor from the linkage and bracket.
7   Refitting is a reversal of removal, but tighten the nuts and bolts to the specified torque.

49 Rear screen wiper motor – removal and refitting

1   Remove the wiper arm as described in Section 51.
2   Open the tailgate and carefully prise off the trim panel using a wide-bladed screwdriver.
3   Unscrew the mounting bolts and the earth lead and disconnect the multi-plug (photo).
4   Withdraw the wiper motor and bracket and disconnect the washer hose. If necessary unbolt the wiper motor from the bracket.
5   Refitting is a reversal of removal, but tighten the bolts to the specified torque.

50 Wiper blades – renewal

1   The wiper blades should be renewed when they no longer clean the windscreen or tailgate window effectively.

2   Lift the wiper arm away from the windscreen or tailgate window.
3   With the blade at 90° to the arm depress the spring clip and slide the blade clear of the hook then slide it up off the arm (photo).
4   If necessary extract the two metal inserts and unhook the wiper rubber.
5   Fit the new rubber and blade in reverse order making sure where necessary that the cut-outs in the metal inserts face each other.

51 Wiper arms – removal and refitting

1   Remove the wiper blades as described in Section 50.
2   Lift the hinged covers and remove the nuts and washers securing the arms to the spindles (photo).
3   Mark the arms and spindles in relation to each other then prise off the arms using a screwdriver. Take care not to damage the paintwork.
4   Refitting is a reversal of removal.

52 Headlamp wiper motor – removal and refitting

1   Disconnect the battery negative lead.
2   Lift the hinged cover and unscrew the nut retaining the wiper arm to the spindle (photo). Remove the washer.
3   Note the parked position of the blade then remove the arm from the spindle (photo). Disconnect the washer hose.
4   Remove the headlamp unit as described in Section 46.
5   Disconnect the wiring and remove the motor (photo).
6   Refitting is a reversal of removal.

53 Washer pump – removal and refitting

1   Remove the washer reservoir by unscrewing the mounting screws. Access to the rear washer pump is gained by removing the rear left-hand side trim.

48.5 Windscreen wiper motor

49.3 Rear screen wiper motor and wiring

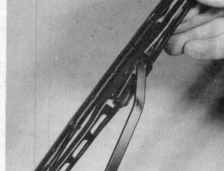

50.3 Removing a wiper blade

51.2 Wiper arm retaining nut location

52.2 Unscrew the nut ...

52.3 ... and remove the headlamp wiper arm

52.5 Headlamp wiper motor (arrowed)

54.2 Flasher unit (arrowed) removal

55.2 Radio retaining clips (arrowed) on early models

2   Pour out the fluid and prise the pump from the grommet.
3   Disconnect the wiring and hose.
4   Refitting is a reversal of removal. Finally refill the reservoir.

54 Flasher unit – removal and refitting

1   The direction indicator/hazard warning flasher unit is clipped to a bracket above the steering column. Gain access by removing the lower facia panel on the driver's side.
2   Unclip the flasher unit and disconnect its multi-plug (photo).
3   Refitting is a reversal of removal.

55 Radio (standard) – removal and refitting

1   Disconnect the battery negative lead.
2   On early models unscrew the two nuts and plain washers and remove the trim panel. Using a hooked instrument, pull the mounting tangs towards the centre of the radio and extract the radio from the aperture (photo).
3   On later models, two special clips are required and should be obtained from an in-car entertainment specialist. Insert the clips fully into the holes in the front of the radio then withdraw the radio from the aperture (photo). Remove the clips.
4   Refitting is a reversal of removal.

56 Radio aerial – removal and refitting

1   Remove the rear parcel shelf side-member on the side concerned.
2   Remove the upper retaining nut, spacer and sealing washer from the top of the aerial. Collapse the aerial mast.

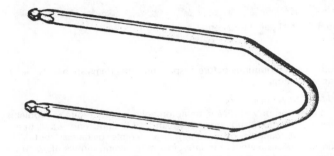

Fig. 12.24 Clip for removing radio on later models (Sec 55)

3   On power-operated aerials, remove the lower mounting support bracket screw and disconnect the power lead (photo).
4   Pull the aerial into the car and disconnect the aerial lead. Note that the lead may have a screw fitting instead of the usual pull-off type (photo).
5   The aerial leads runs through the roof. If it is wished to renew the lead, it may be considered easier to leave the old lead in place and run a new one under the carpet. Follow existing wire runs where possible.
6   Refit in the reverse order of removal. With non-power aerials, make sure that the foot of the aerial enters its mounting (photo).

57 Radio equipment – suppression of interference

1   The radio equipment installed in production is adequately suppressed for interference and should not normally require attention. If a problem occurs, check all wiring including aerials, earth leads and

55.3 Radio removal on later models using special clips (arrowed)

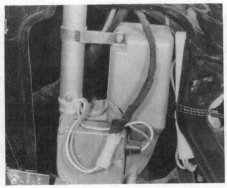

56.3 View of power-operated aerial

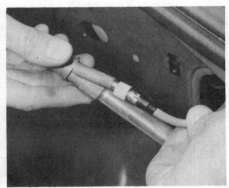

56.4 Disconnecting the radio aerial lead

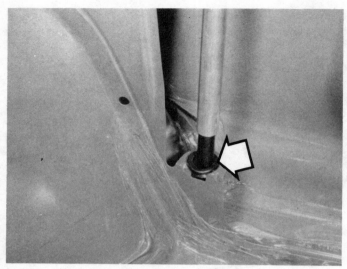

56.6 Foot of aerial must enter mounting (arrowed)

component mountings before suspecting other items such as HT leads and capacitors.

VHF/FM broadcasts

2   Reception of VHF/FM in an automobile is more prone to problems than the medium and long wavebands. Medium/long wave transmitters are capable of covering considerable distances, but VHF transmitters are restricted to line of sight, meaning ranges of 10 to 50 miles, depending upon the terrain, the effects of buildings and the transmitter power.

3   Because of the limited range it is necessary to retune on a long journey, and it may be better for those habitually travelling long distances or living in areas of poor provision of transmitters to use an AM radio working on medium/long wavebands.

4   When conditions are poor interference can arise, and some suppression devices fall off in performance at very high frequencies unless specifically designed for the VHF band. Available suppression devices include reactive HT cable, resistive distributor caps, screened plug caps, screened leads and resistive spark plugs.

Citizens' Band radio (CB)

5   Aerials are the key to effective transmission and reception.

Regulations limit the aerial length to 1.65 metres including the loading coil and any associated circuitry, so tuning the aerial is necessary to obtain optimum results. The choice of a CB aerial is dependent on whether it is to be permanently installed or removable, and the performance will hinge on correct tuning and the location point on the vehicle. Common practice is to clip the aerial to the roof gutter or to employ wing mounting where the aerial can be rapidly unscrewed. An alternative is to use the boot rim to render the aerial theftproof, but a popular solution is to use the 'magamount' – a type of mounting having a strong magnetic base clamping to the vehicle at any point, usually the roof.

6   Aerial location determines the signal distribution for both transmission and reception, but it is wise to choose a point away from the engine compartment to minimise interference from vehicle electrical equipment.

7   The aerial is subject to considerable wind and acceleration forces. Cheaper units will whip backwards and forwards and in so doing will alter the relationship with the metal surface of the vehicle with which it forms a ground plane aerial system. The radiation pattern will change correspondingly, giving rise to break-up of both incoming and outgoing signals.

8   Interference problems on the vehicle carrying CB equipment fall into two categories:

(a)   Interference to nearby TV and radio receivers when transmitting.

(b)   Interference to CB set reception due to electrical equipment on the vehicle.

9   Problems of break-through to TV and radio are not frequent, but can be difficult to solve. Mostly, trouble is not detected or reported because the vehicle is moving and the symptoms rapidly disappear at the TV/radio receiver, but when the CB set is used as a base station any trouble with nearby receivers will soon result in a complaint.

10 It must not be assumed by the CB operator that his equipment is faultless, for much depends upon the design. Harmonics (that is, multiples) of 27 MHz may be transmitted unknowingly and these can fall into other user's bands. Where trouble of this nature occurs, low pass filters in the aerial or supply leads can help, and should be fitted in base station aerials as a matter of course. In stubborn cases it may be necessary to call for assistance from the licensing authority, or, if possible to have the equipment checked by the manufacturers.

11 Interference received on the CB set from the vehicle equipment is, fortunately, not usually a severe problem, but the following is worth noting.

12 It is common practice to use a slide-mount on CB equipment enabling the set to be easily removed for use as a base station, for example. Care must be taken that the slide mount fittings are properly earthed and that first class connection occurs between the set and slide-mount.

58 Fault diagnosis – electrical system

Symptom	Reason(s)
Starter fails to turn engine	Battery discharged or defective Battery terminal and/or earth leads loose Starter motor connections loose Starter solenoid faulty Starter brushes worn or sticking Starter commutator dirty or worn
Starter turns engine very slowly	Battery discharged Starter motor connections loose Starter brushes worn or sticking
Starter noisy	Pinion or flywheel ring gear teeth badly worn Mounting bolts loose
Battery will not hold charge for more than a few days	Battery defective internally Electrolyte level too low Battery terminals loose Alternator drivebelt(s) slipping Alternator or regulator faulty Short circuit
Ignition light stays on	Alternator faulty Alternator drivebelt(s) broken
Ignition light fails to come on	Warning bulb blown or open circuit Alternator faulty
Instrument readings increase with engine speed	Voltage stabilizer faulty
Fuel or temperature gauge gives no reading	Wiring open circuit Sender unit faulty Gauge faulty
Fuel or temperature gauge gives maximum reading all the time	Wiring short circuit Gauge faulty
Lights inoperative	Bulb blown Fuse blown Battery discharged Switch faulty Wiring open circuit Bad connection due to corrosion
Failure of component motor	Commutator dirty or burnt Armature faulty Brushes sticking or worn Armature bearings seized Fuse blown Wiring loose or broken Field coils faulty

Wiring diagrams overleaf

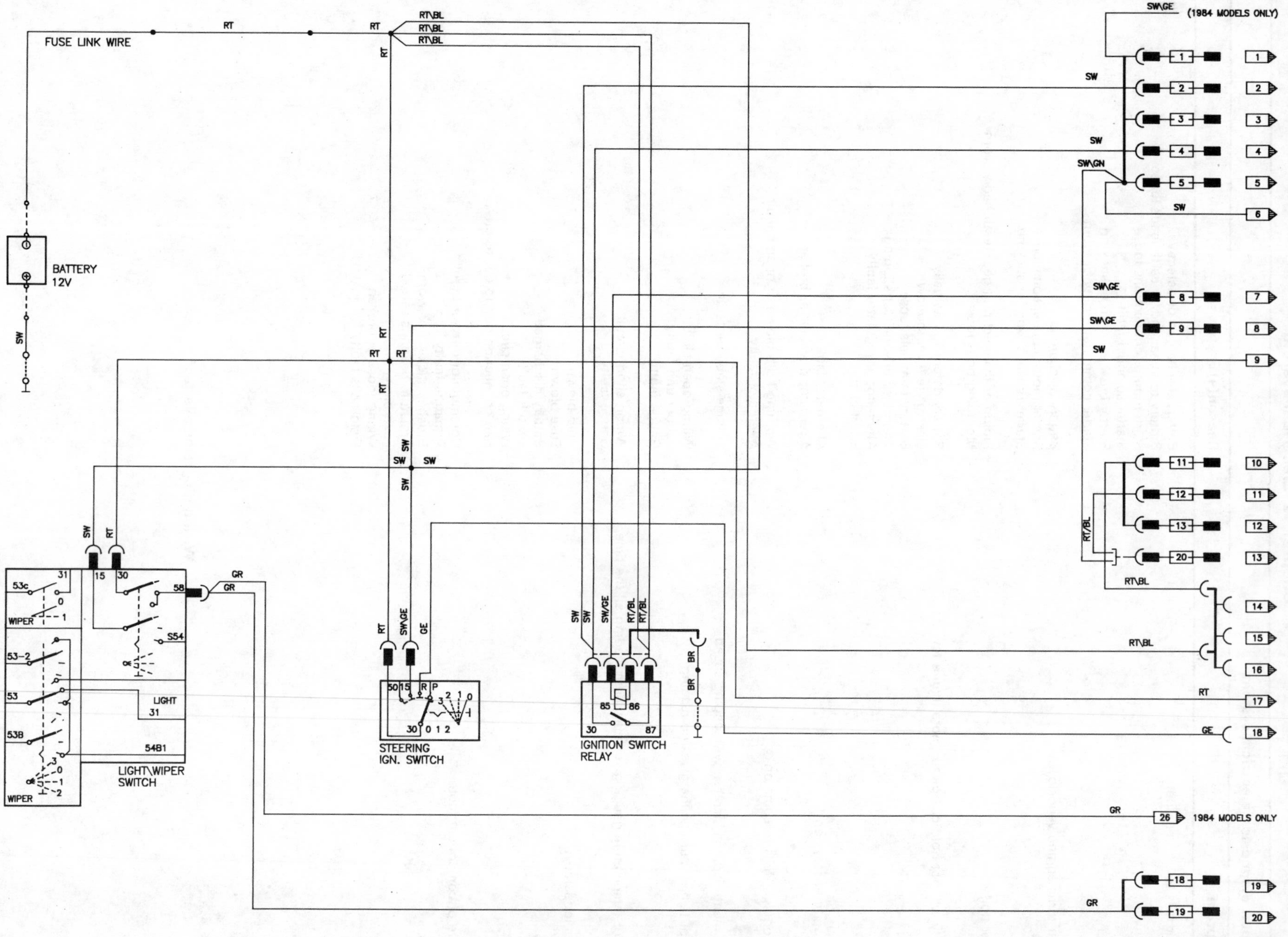

Fig. 12.25 Power distribution – up to 1986

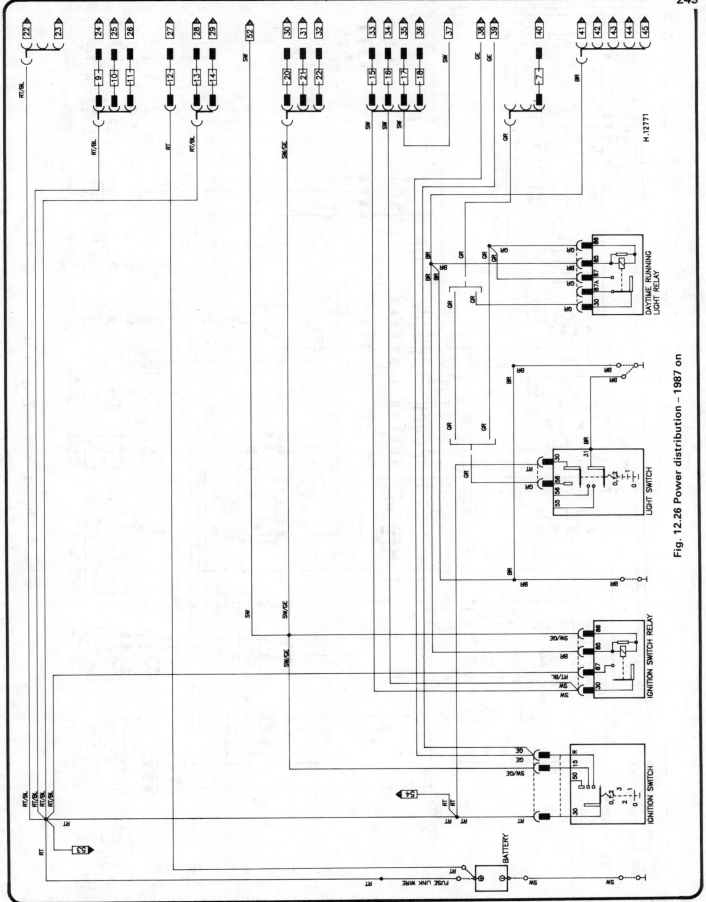

Fig. 12.26 Power distribution – 1987 on

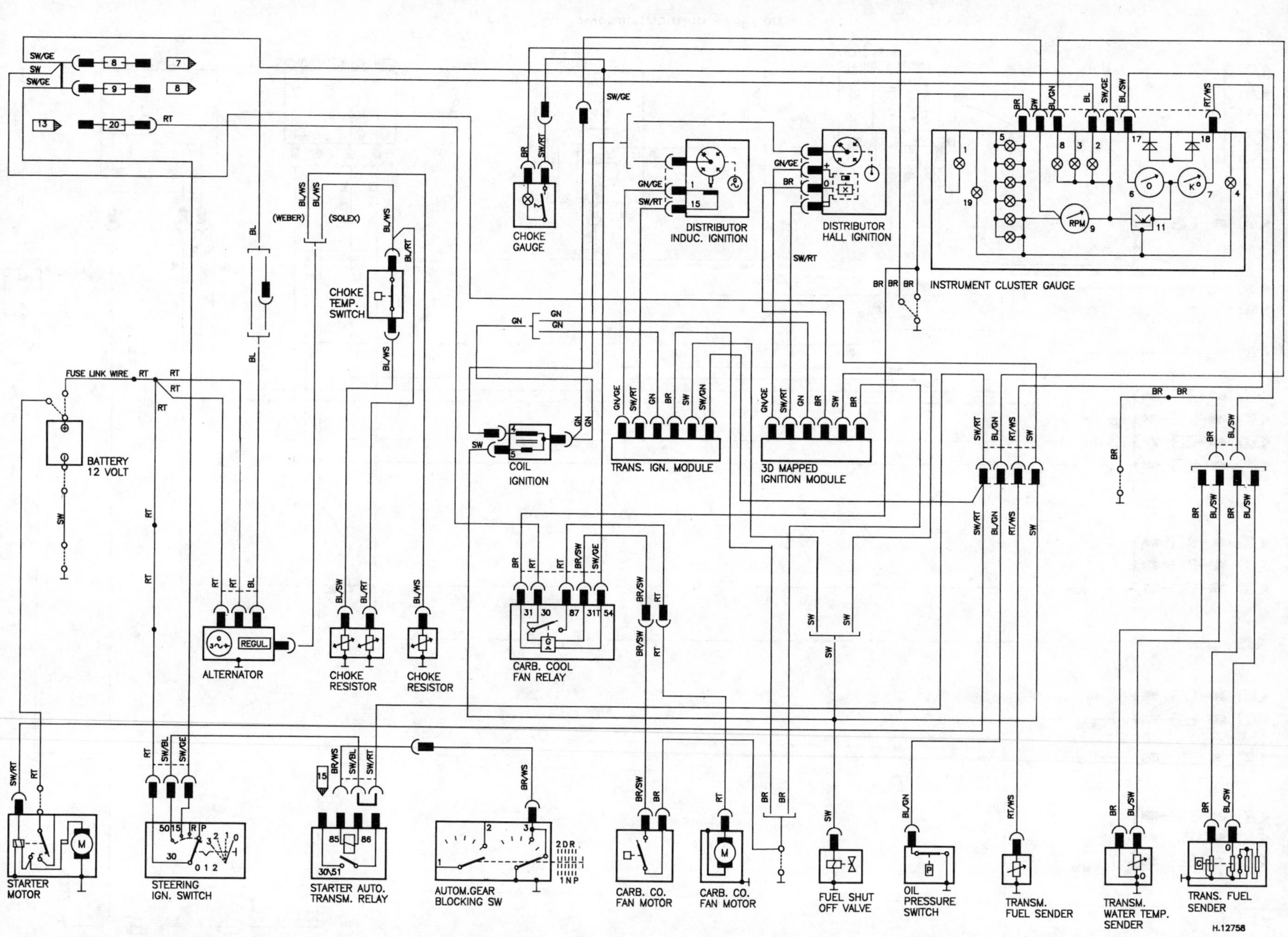

Fig. 12.27 Starting and charging – up to 1984

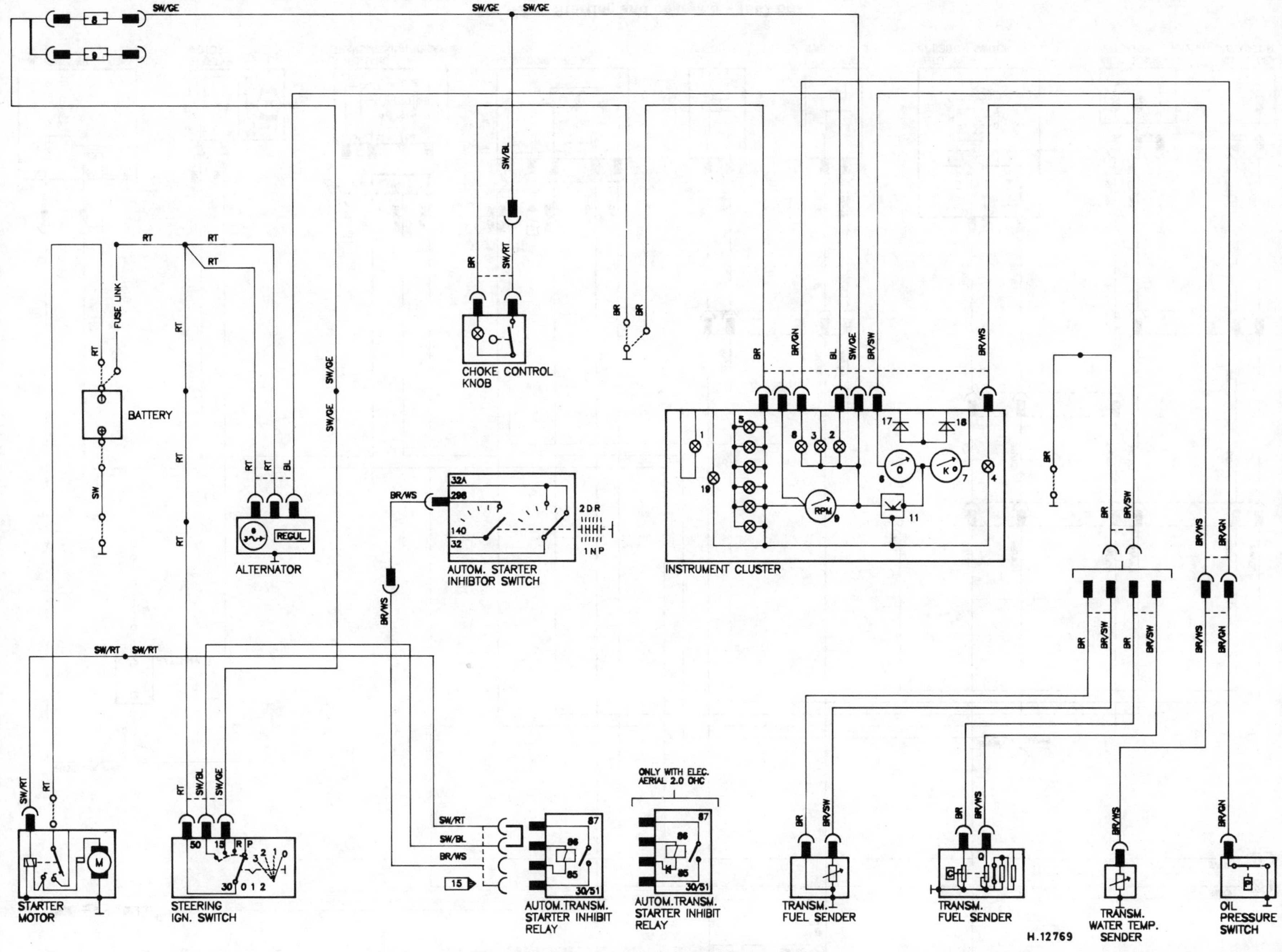

Fig. 12.28 Starting and charging – 1985 to 1986

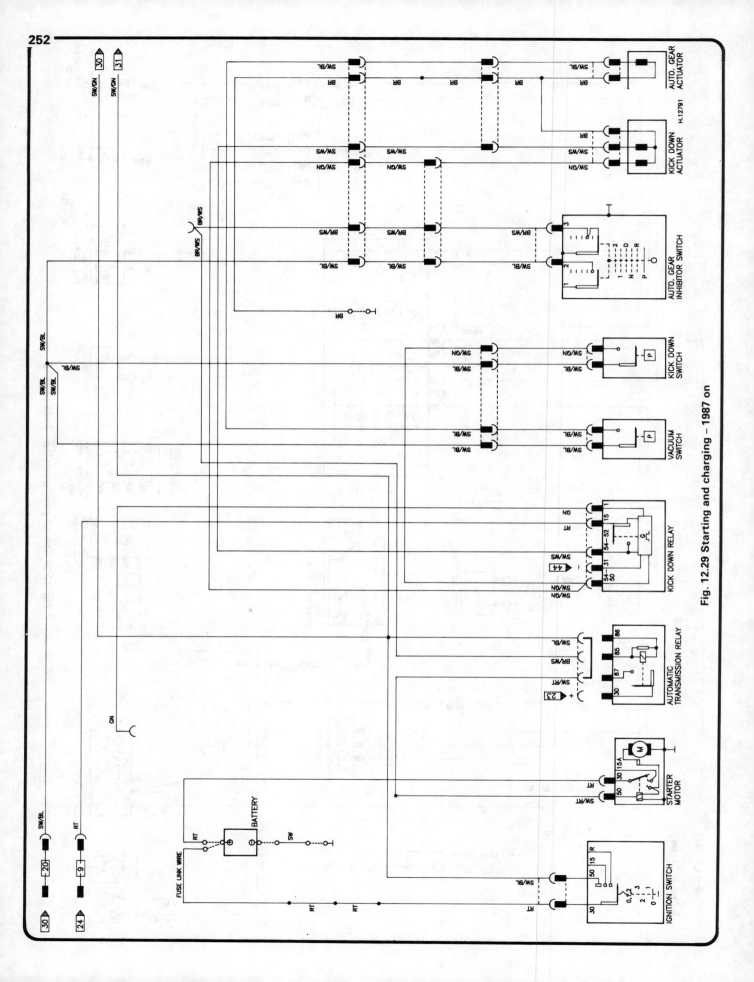

Fig. 12.29 Starting and charging – 1987 on

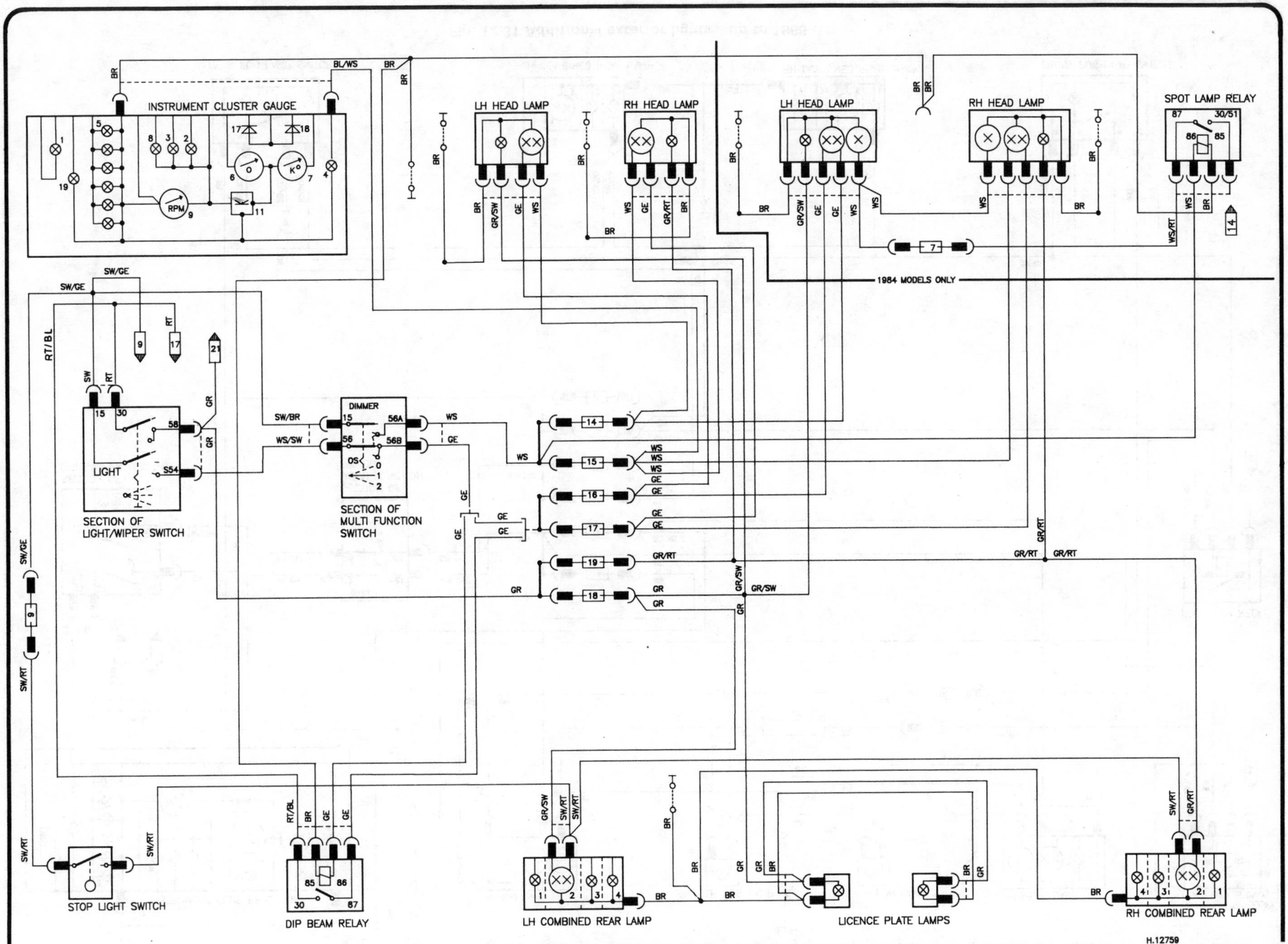

Fig. 12.30 Exterior lights – up to 1986

H.12759

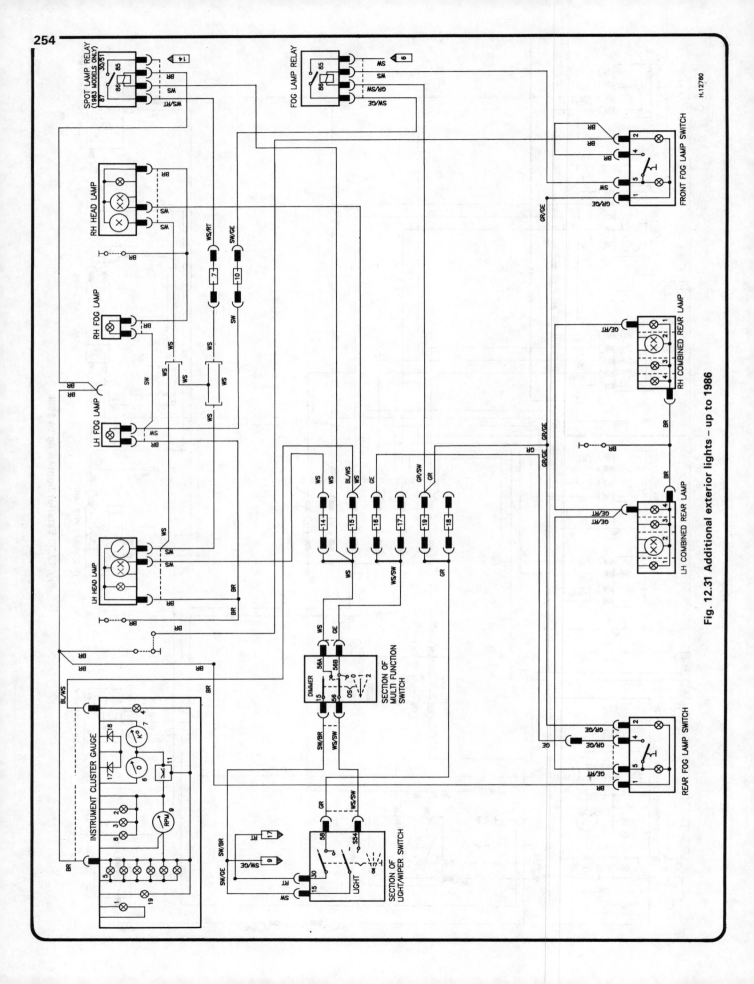

Fig. 12.31 Additional exterior lights – up to 1986

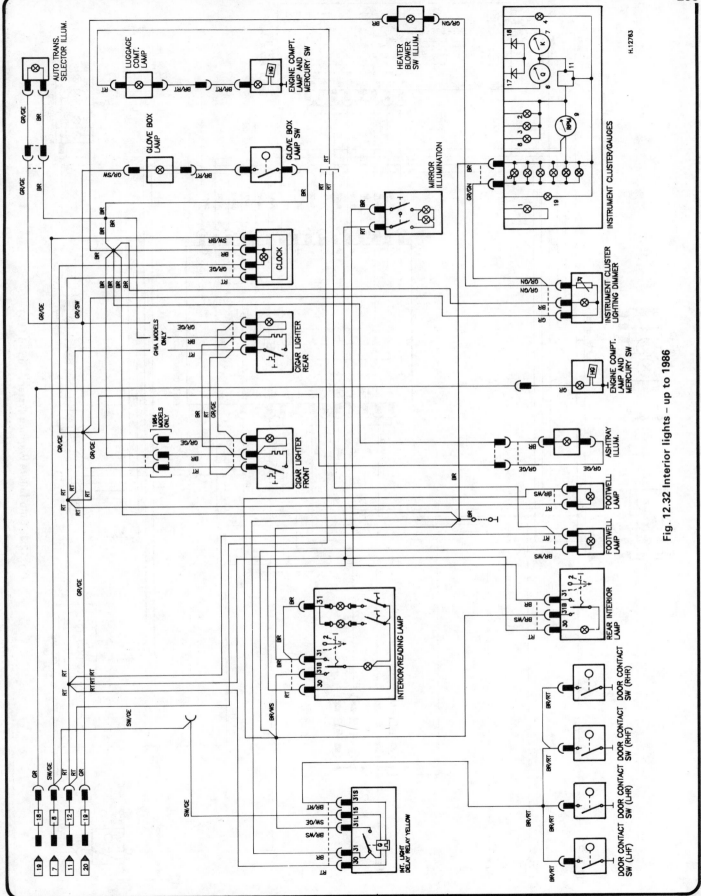

Fig. 12.32 Interior lights – up to 1986

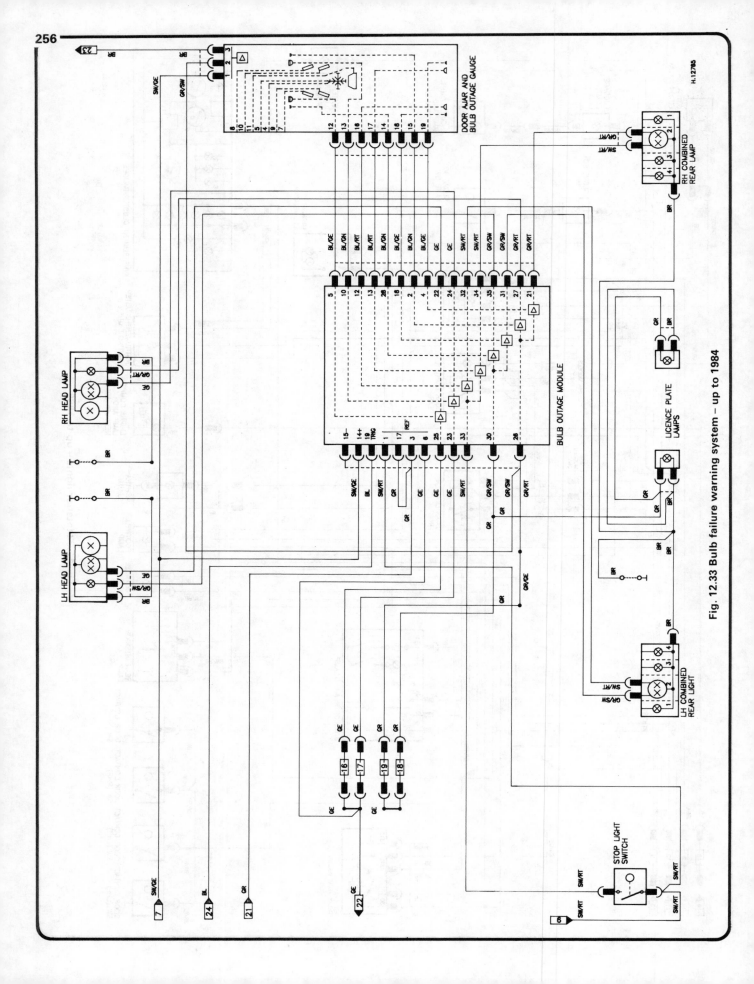

Fig. 12.33 Bulb failure warning system – up to 1984

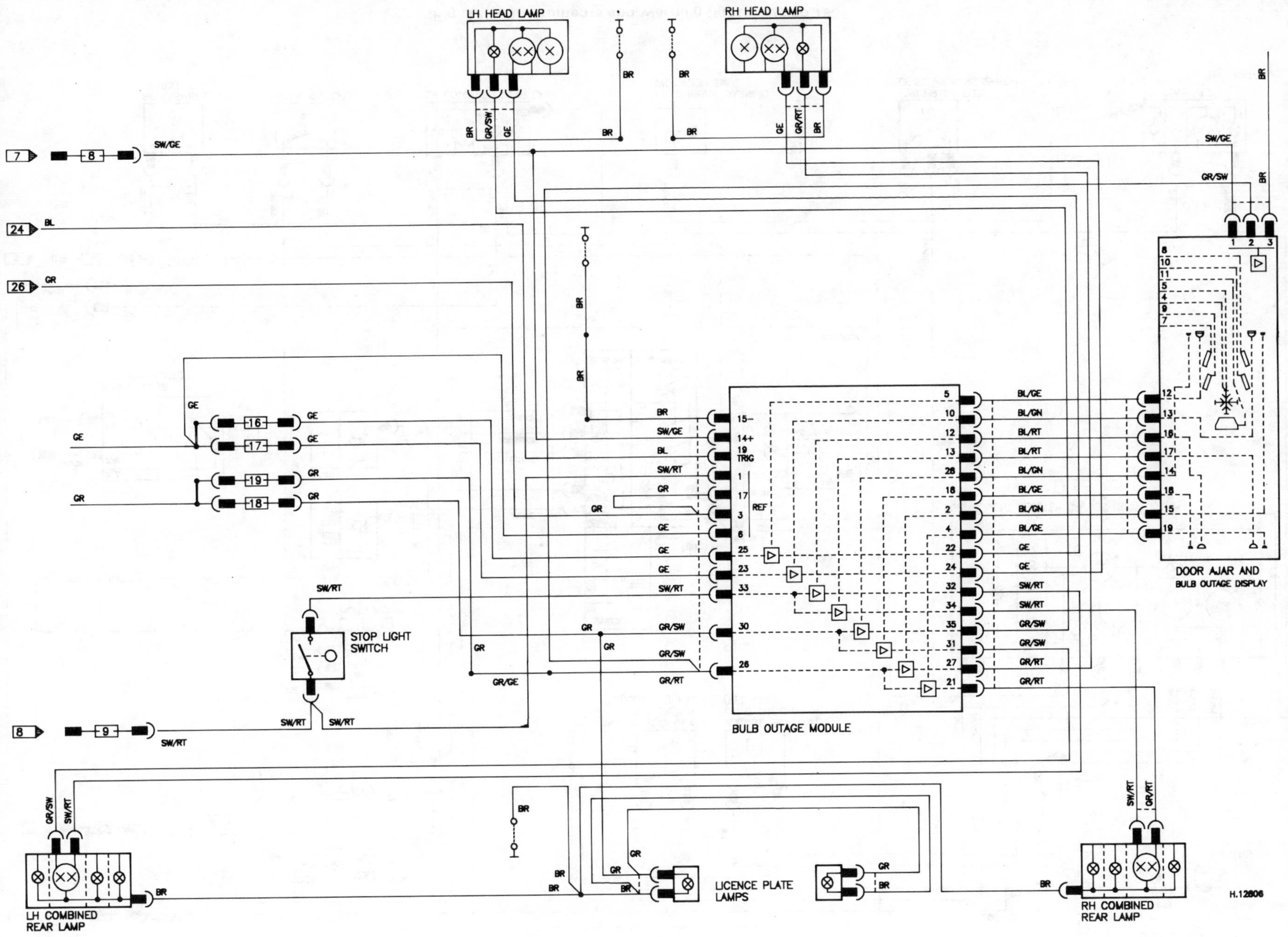

Fig. 12.34 Bulb failure warning system – 1985 to 1986

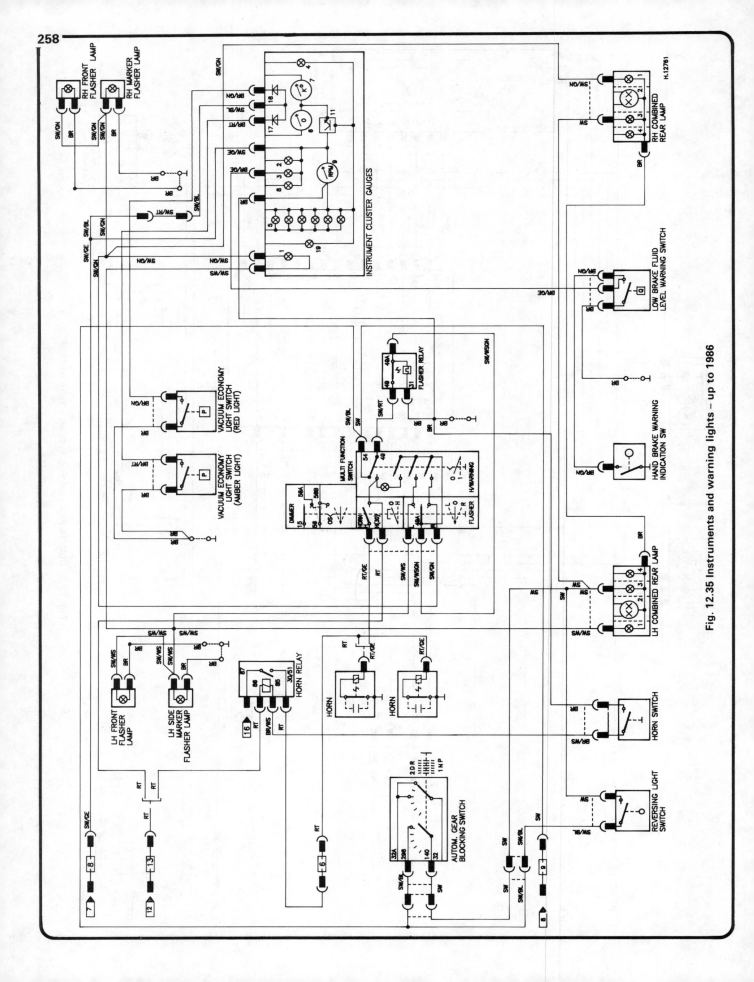

Fig. 12.35 Instruments and warning lights – up to 1986

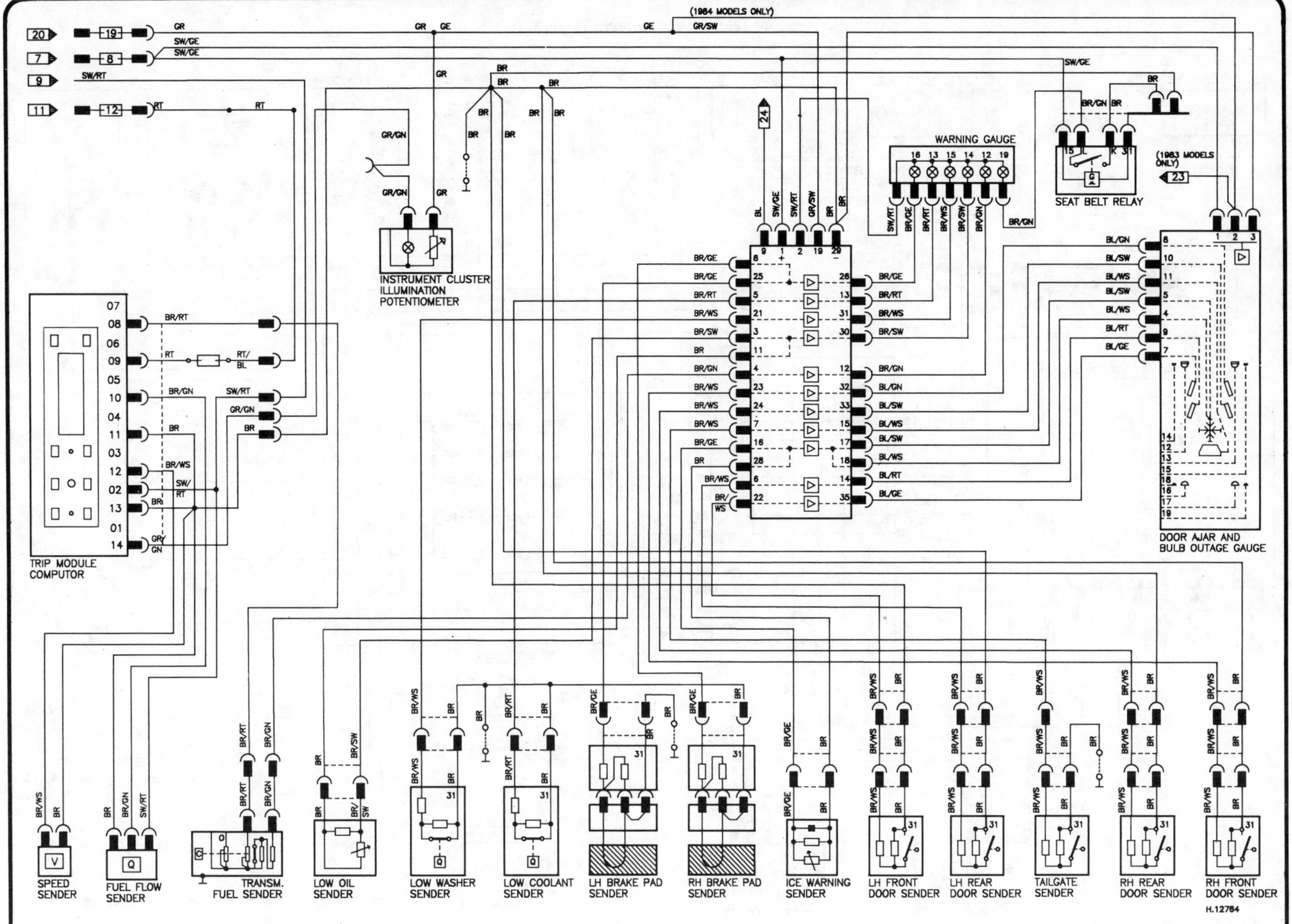

Fig. 12.36 Auxiliary warning system – up to 1986

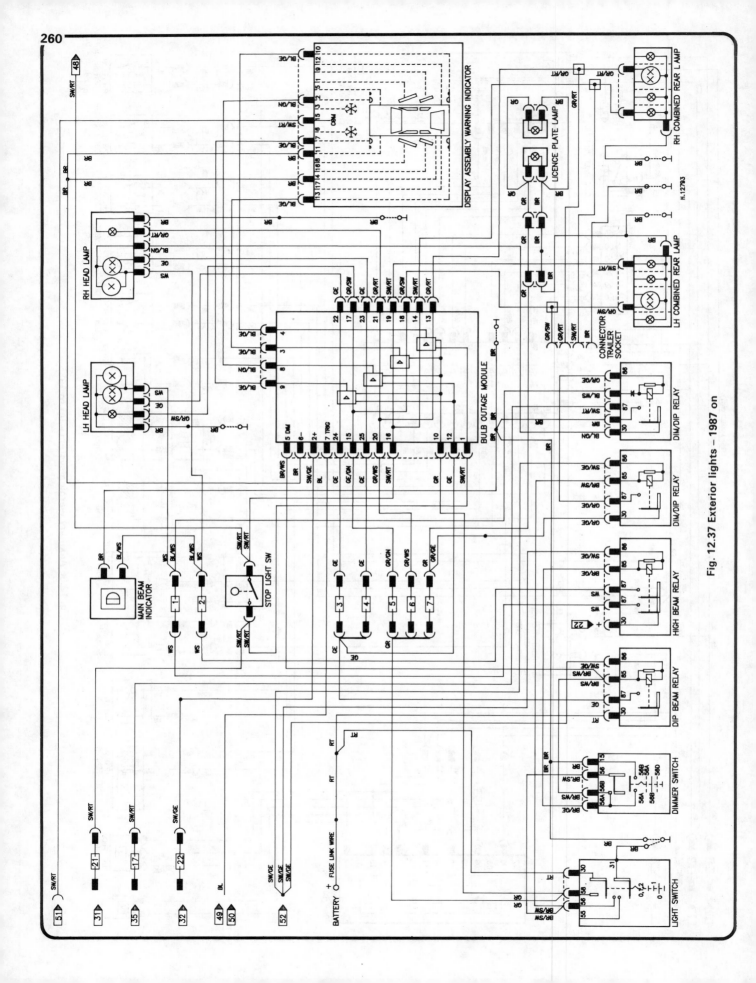

Fig. 12.37 Exterior lights – 1987 on

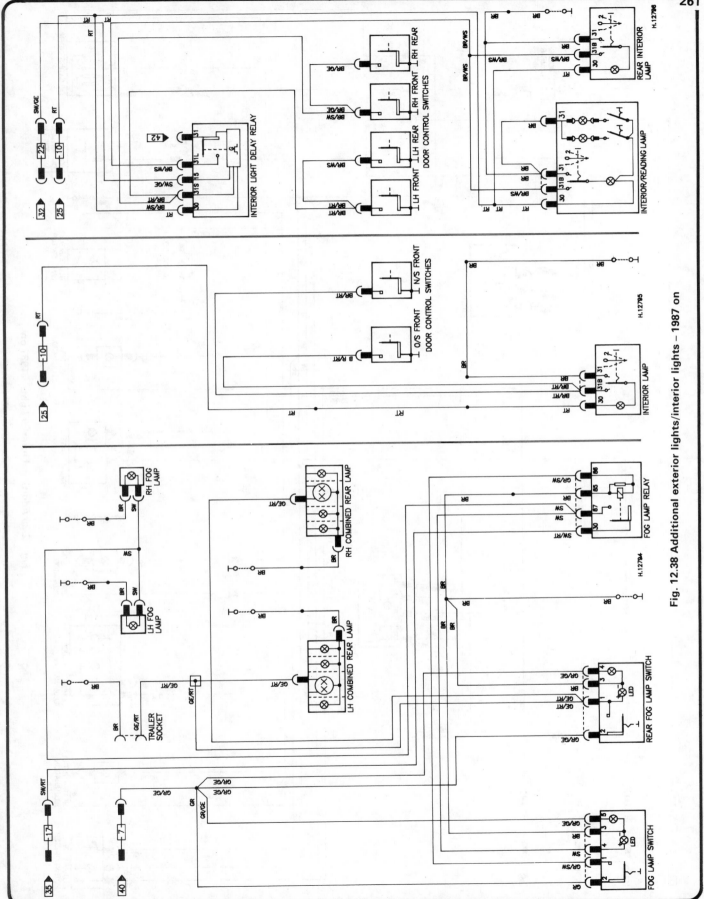

Fig. 12.38 Additional exterior lights/interior lights – 1987 on

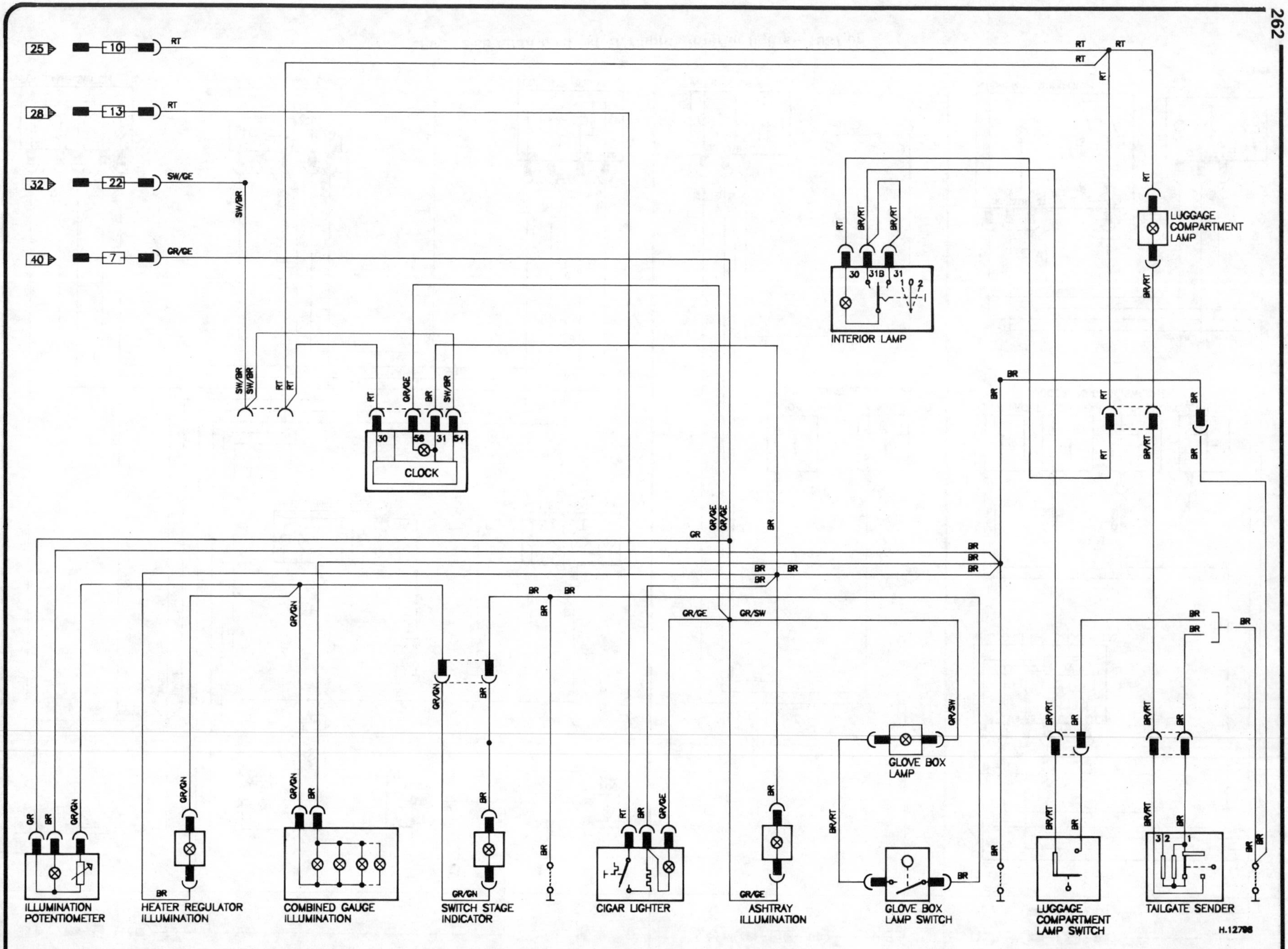

H.12708

LUGGAGE COMPARTMENT LAMP

TAILGATE SENDER

LUGGAGE COMPARTMENT LAMP SWITCH

INTERIOR LAMP

GLOVE BOX LAMP

GLOVE BOX LAMP SWITCH

ASHTRAY ILLUMINATION

CIGAR LIGHTER

SWITCH STAGE INDICATOR

CLOCK

COMBINED GAUGE ILLUMINATION

HEATER REGULATOR ILLUMINATION

ILLUMINATION POTENTIOMETER

25
28
32
40

Fig. 12.39 Additional interior lights – 1987 on

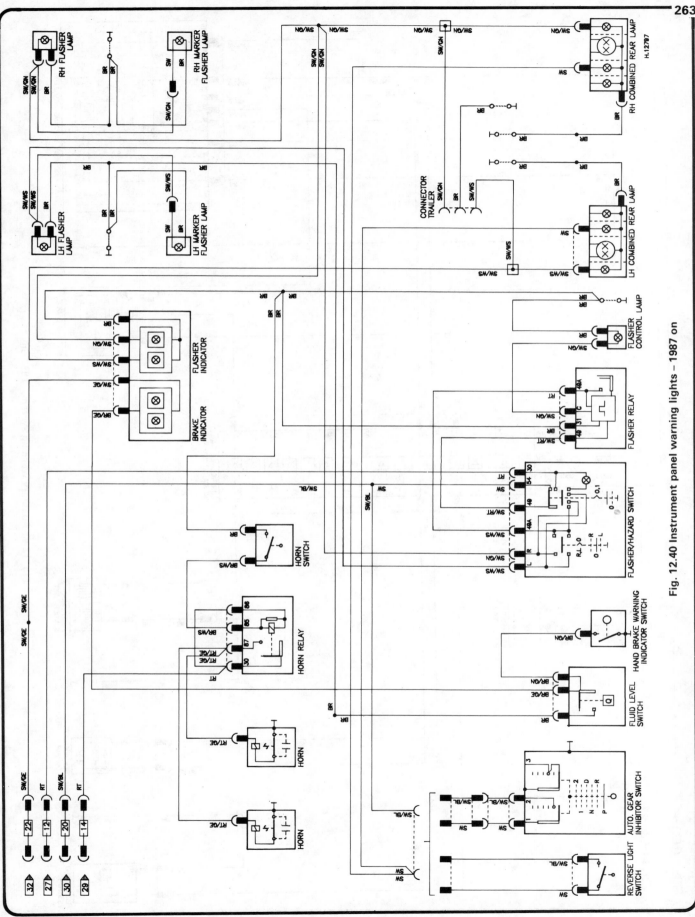

Fig. 12.40 Instrument panel warning lights – 1987 on

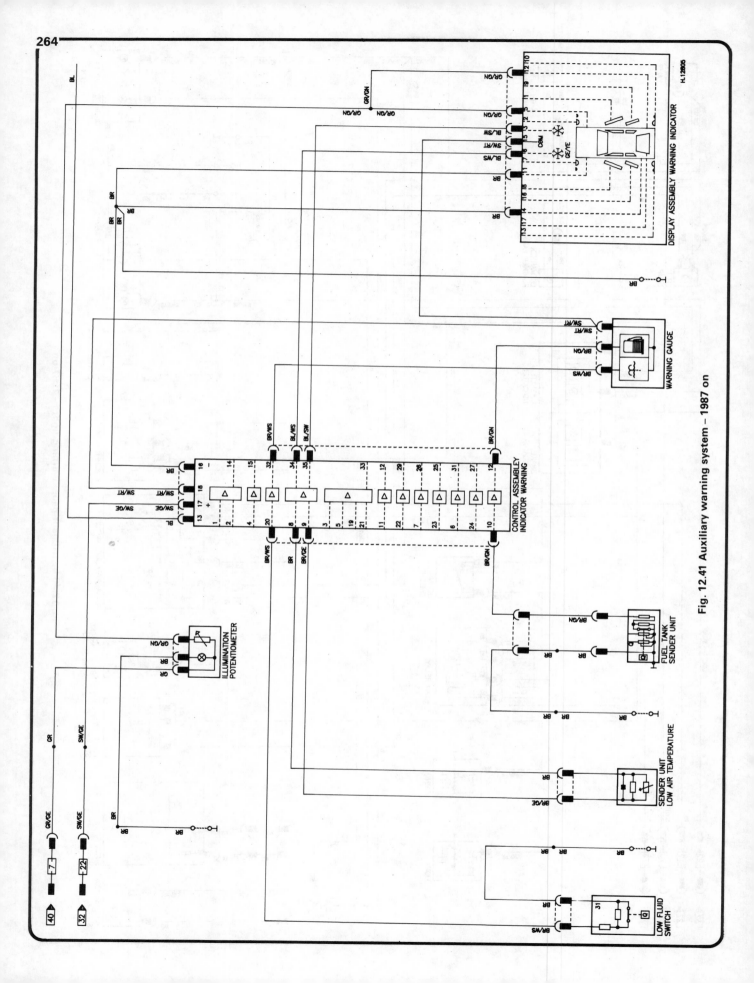

Fig. 12.41 Auxiliary warning system – 1987 on

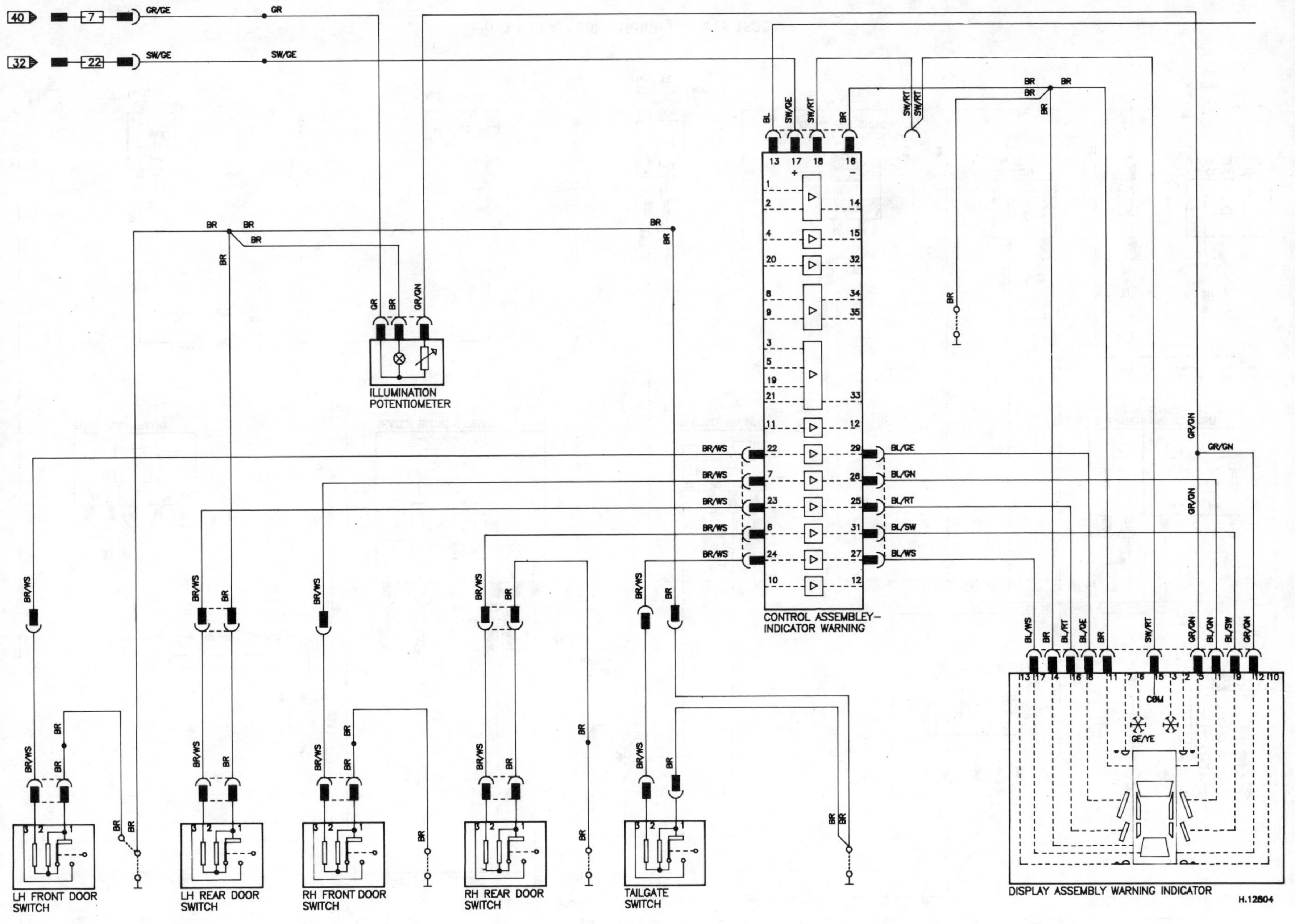

Fig. 12.42 Door ajar warning system – 1987 on

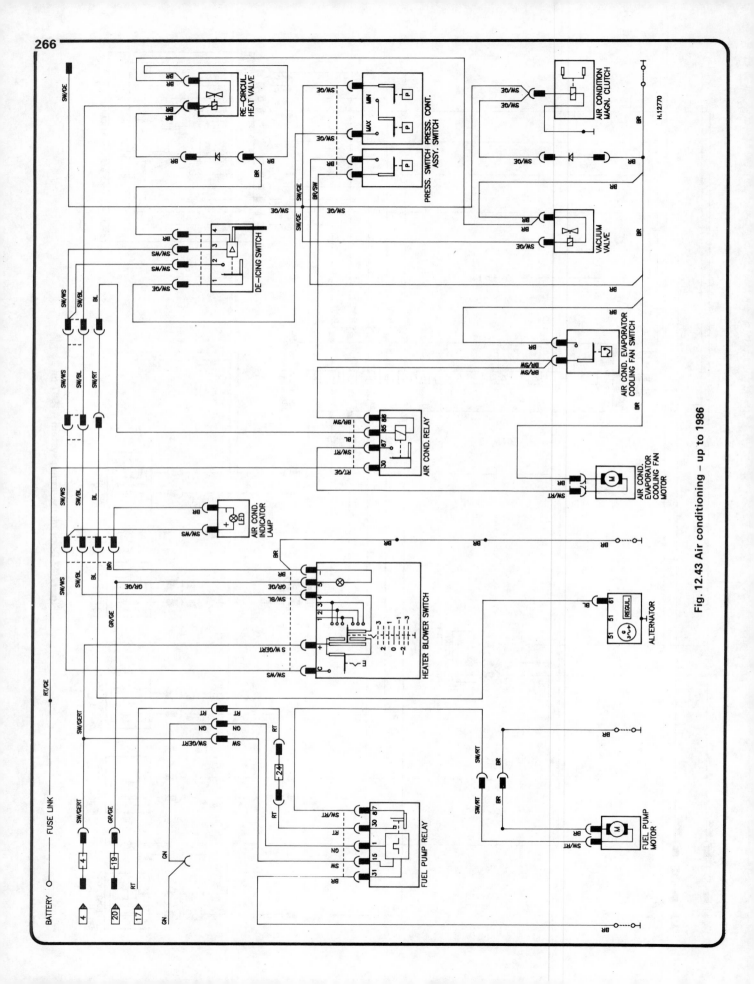

Fig. 12.43 Air conditioning – up to 1986

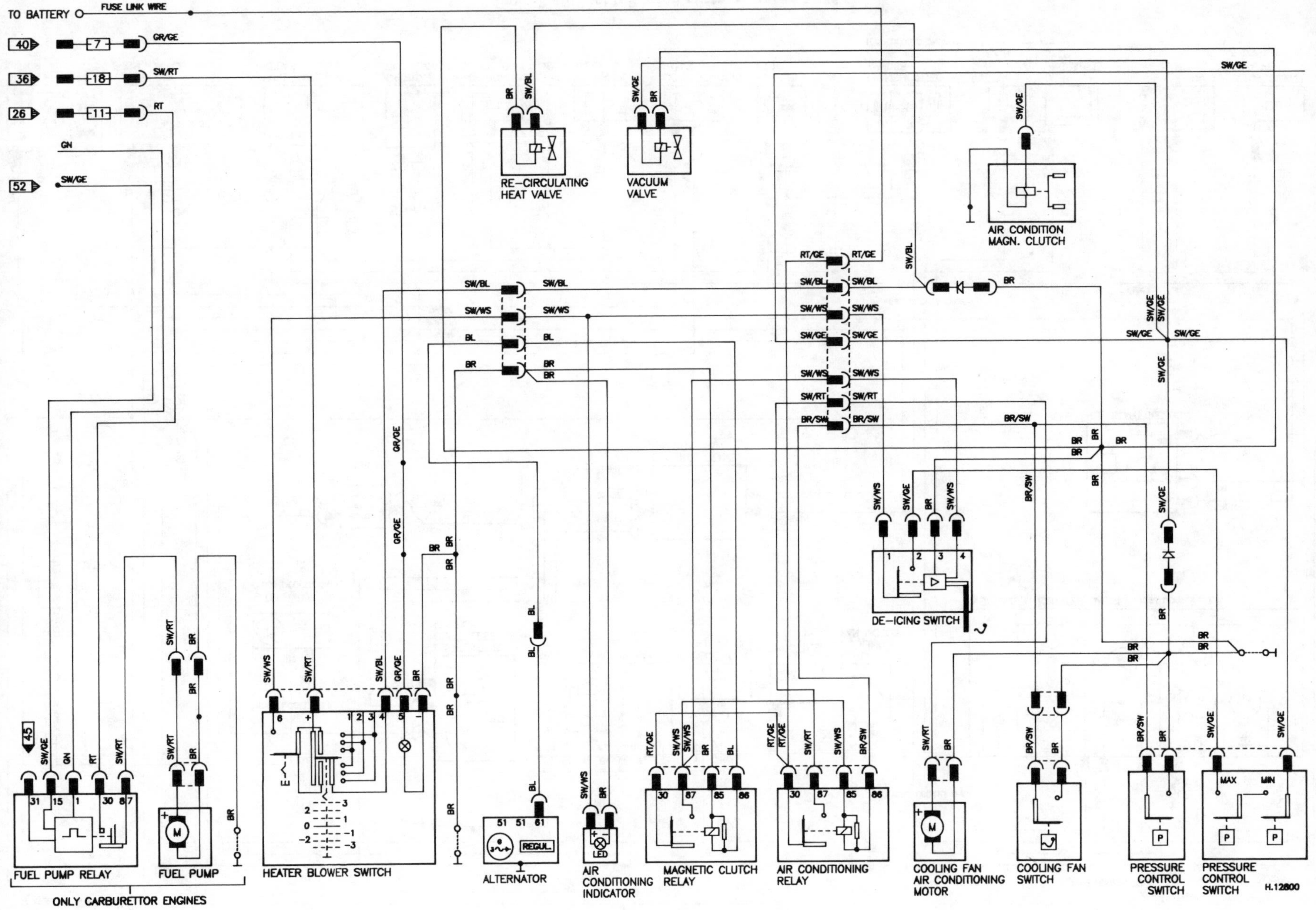

Fig. 12.44 Air conditioning – 1987 on

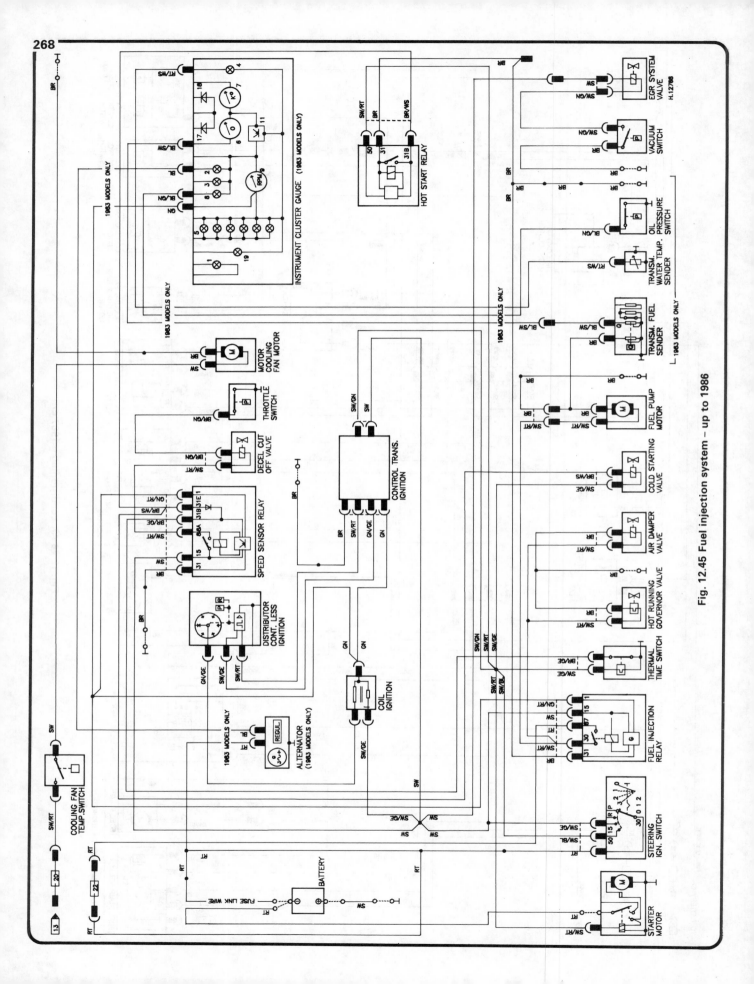

Fig. 12.45 Fuel injection system – up to 1986

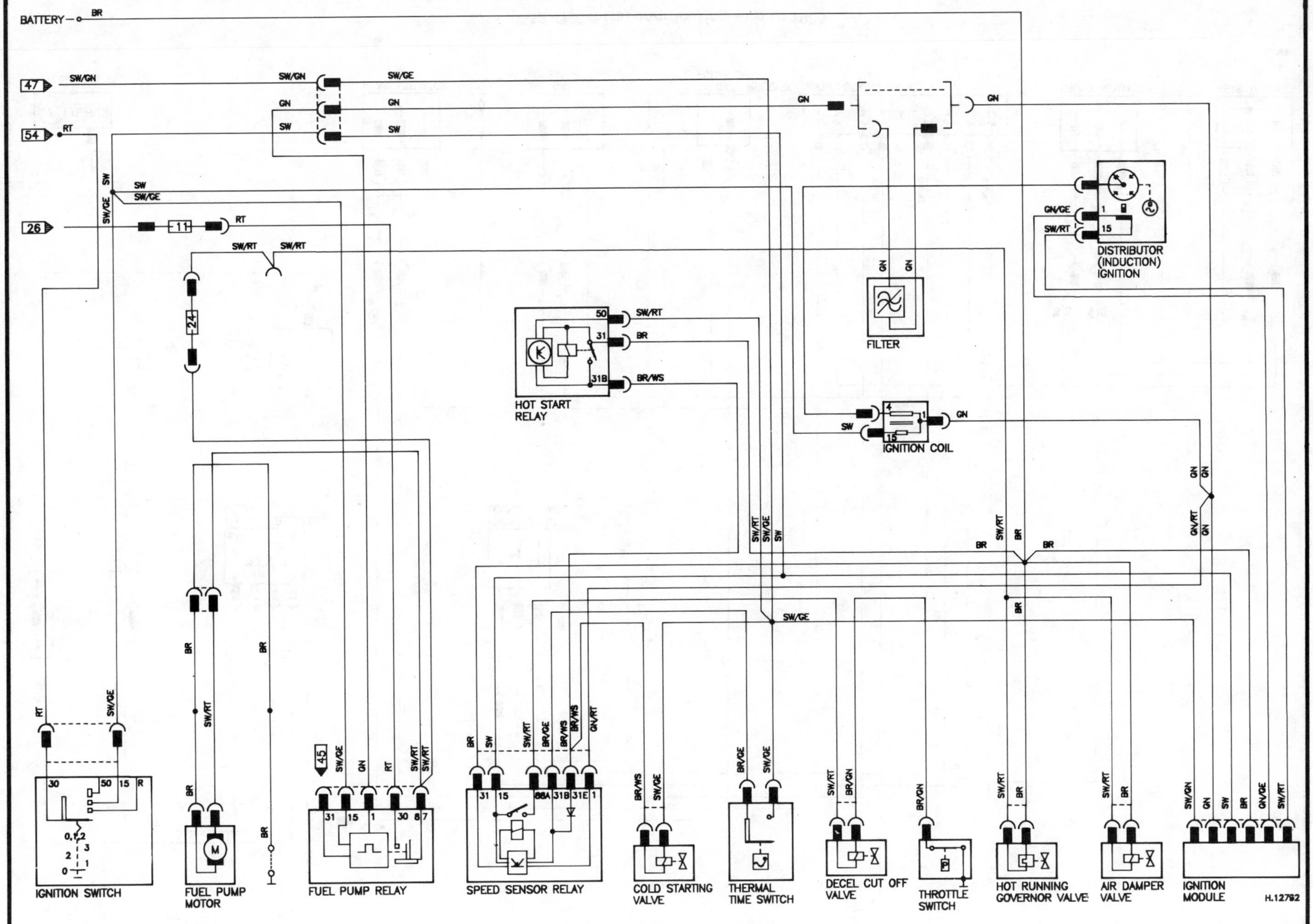

Fig. 12.46 Fuel injection system – 1987 on

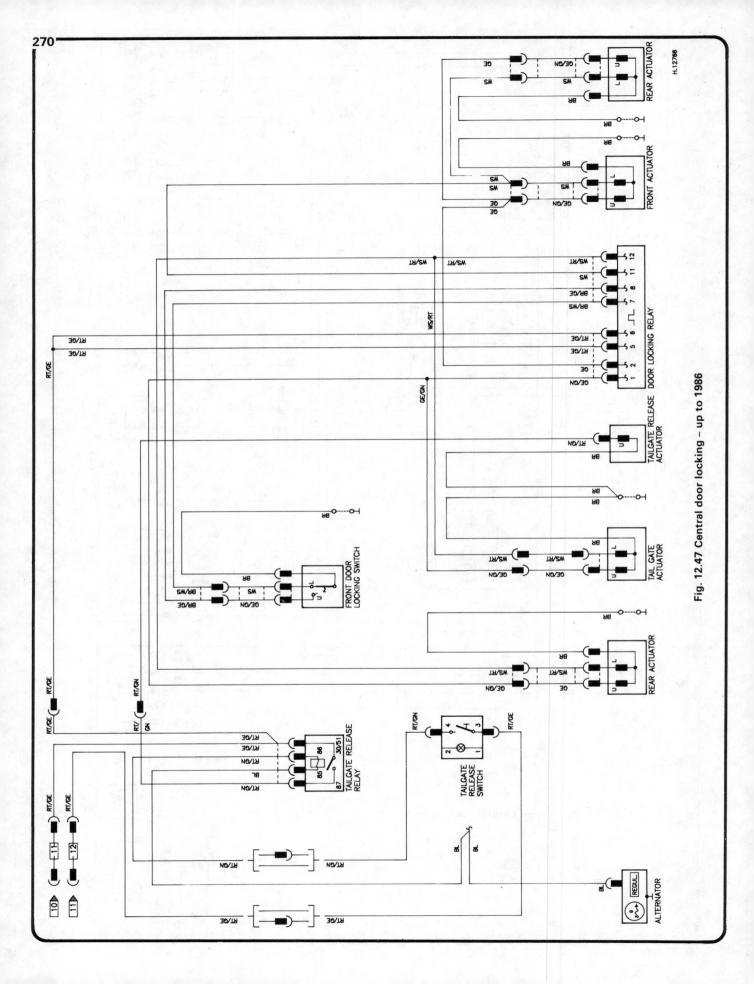

Fig. 12.47 Central door locking – up to 1986

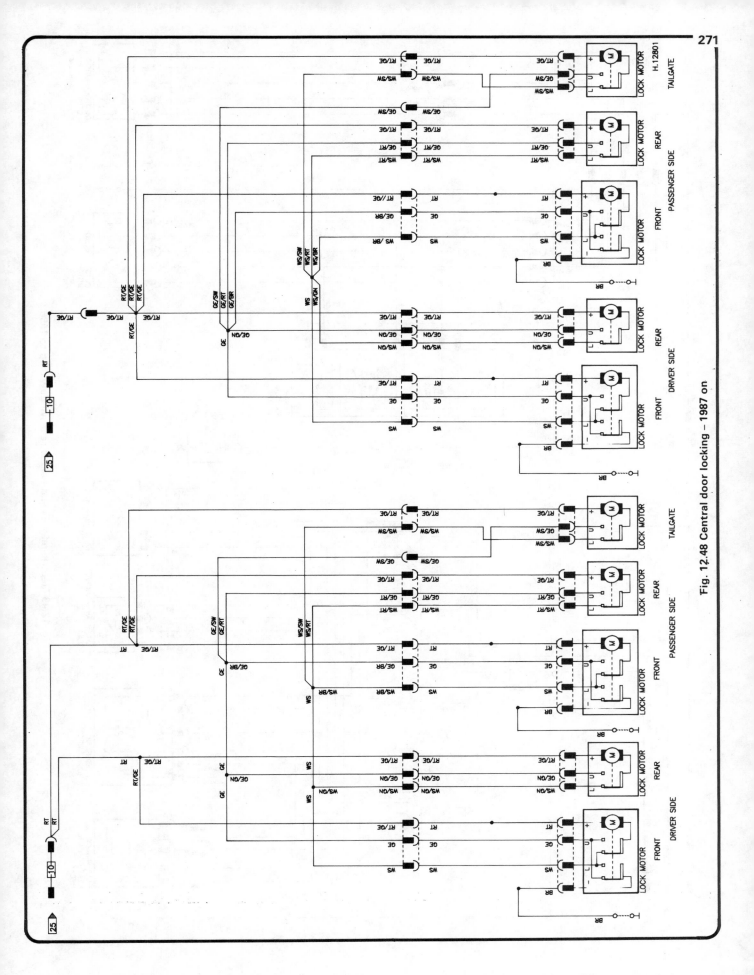

Fig. 12.48 Central door locking – 1987 on

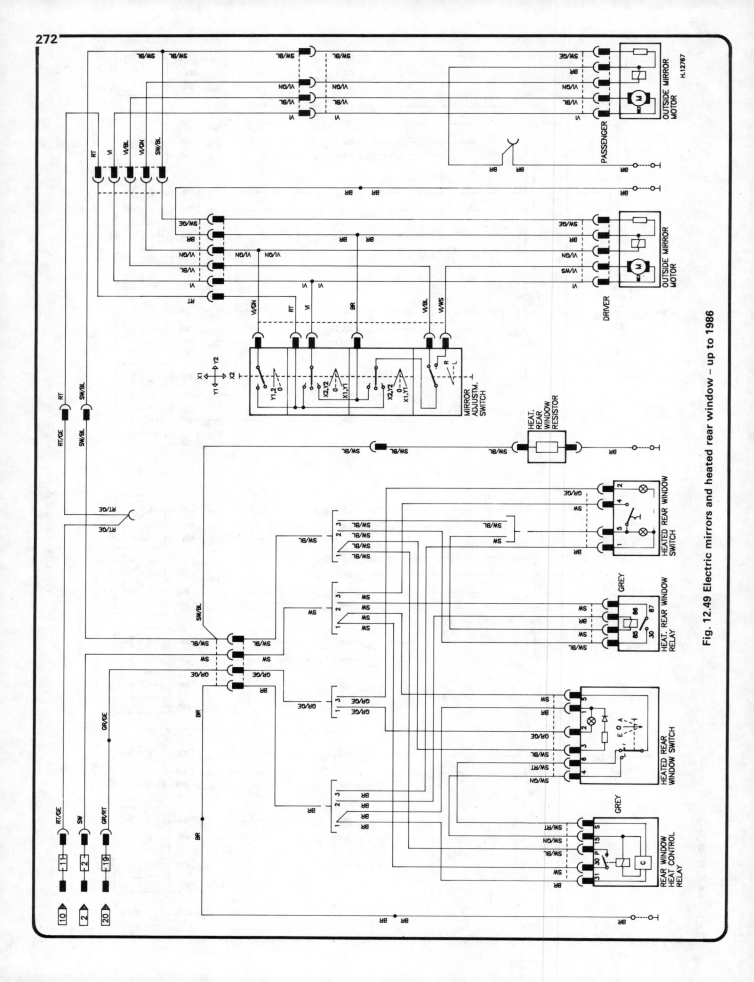

Fig. 12.49 Electric mirrors and heated rear window – up to 1986

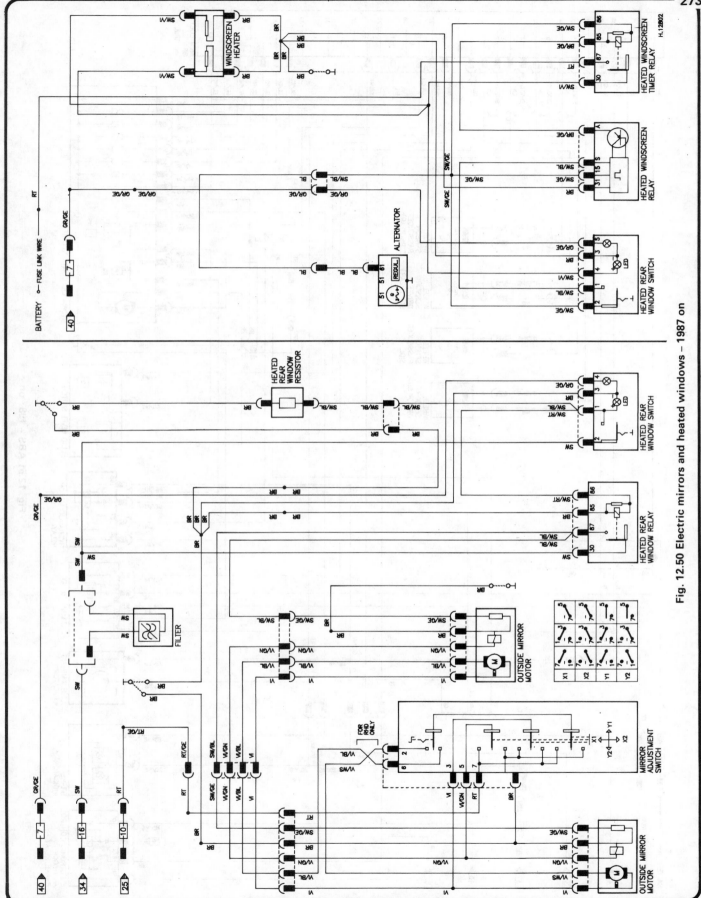

Fig. 12.50 Electric mirrors and heated windows – 1987 on

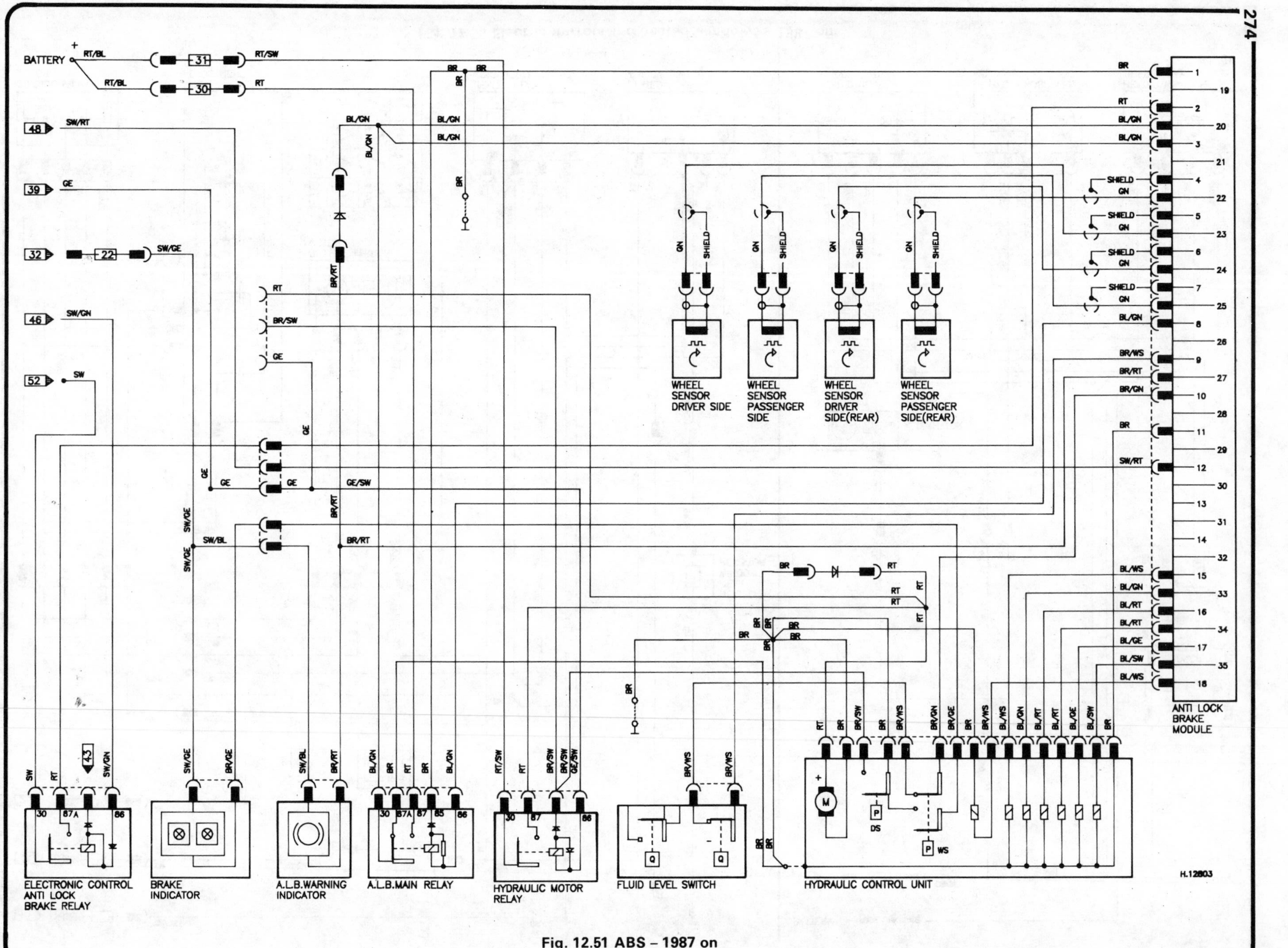

Fig. 12.51 ABS – 1987 on

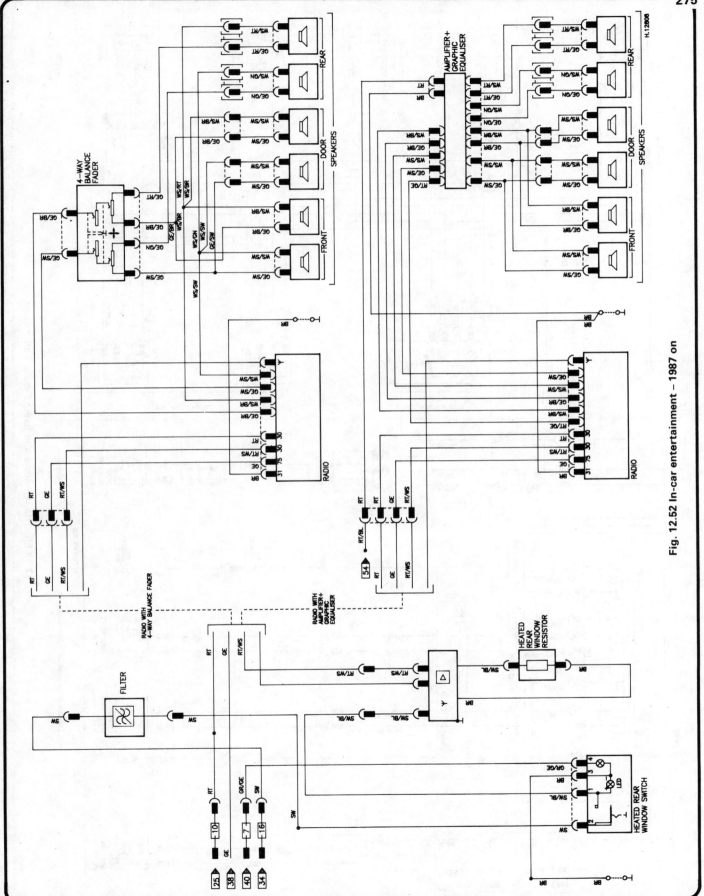

Fig. 12.52 In-car entertainment – 1987 on

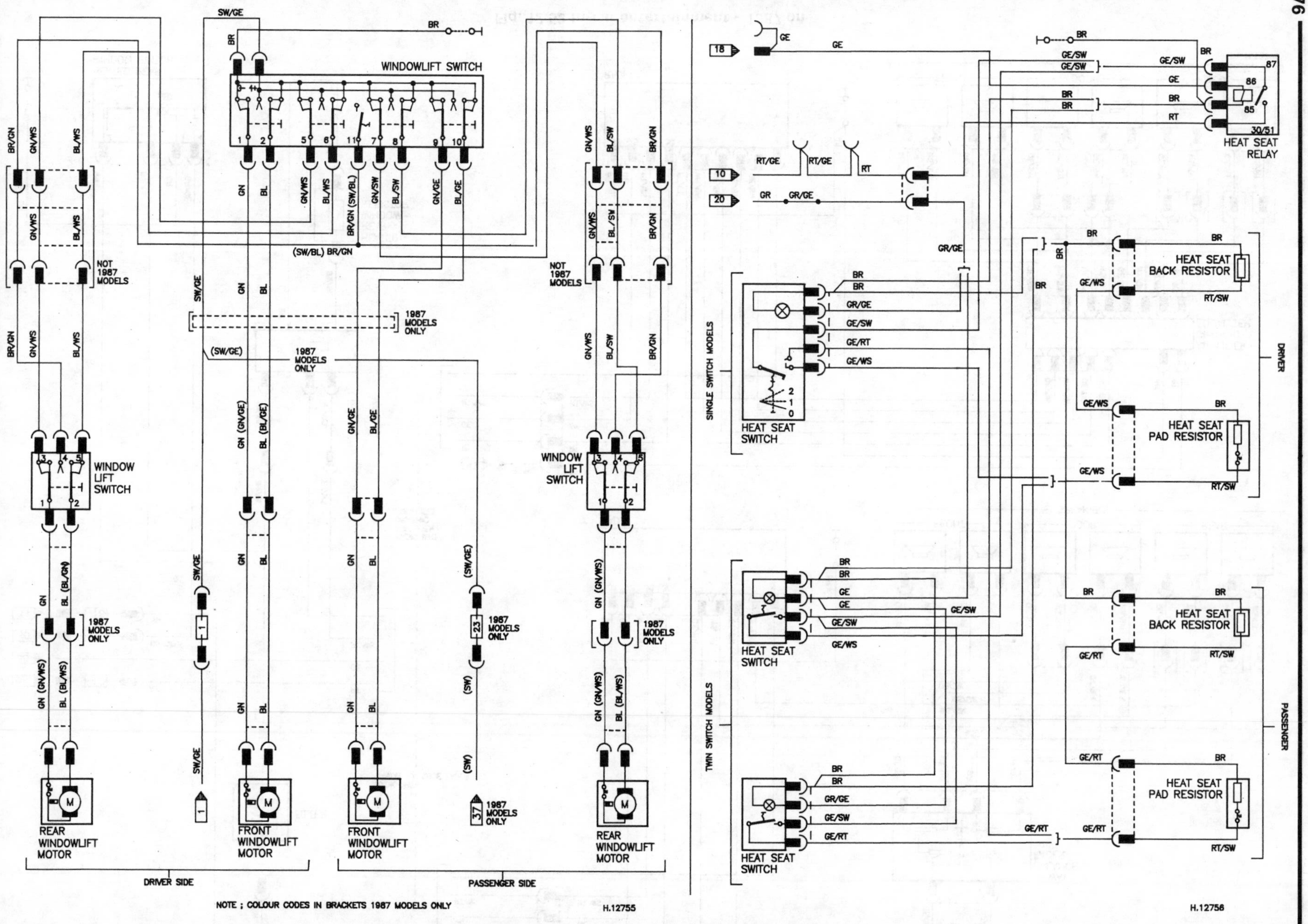

Fig. 12.53 Electric windows and heated seats – all models

NOTE : COLOUR CODES IN BRACKETS 1987 MODELS ONLY

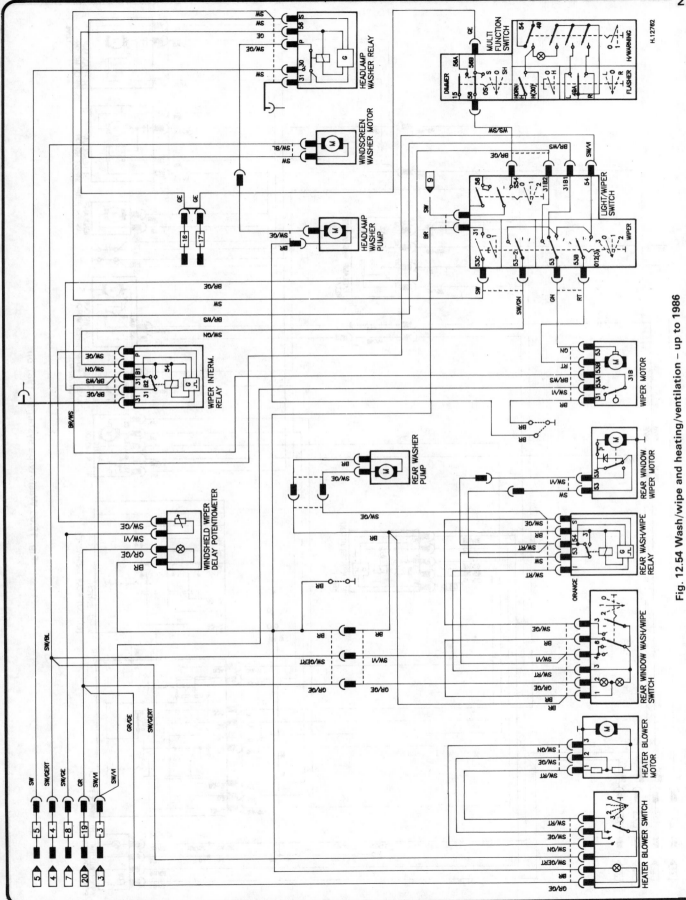

Fig. 12.54 Wash/wipe and heating/ventilation – up to 1986

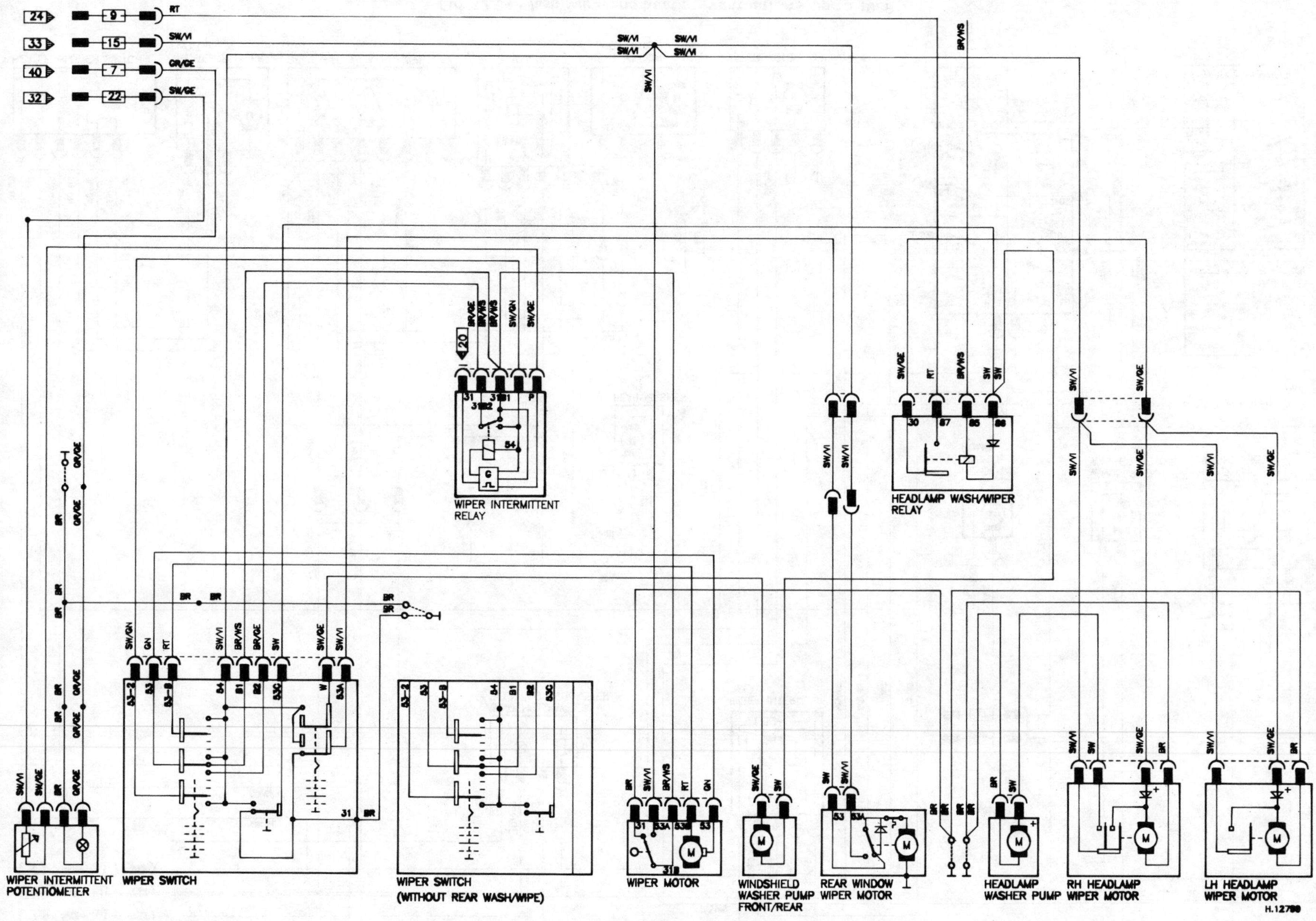

Fig. 12.55 Wash/wipe systems – 1987 on

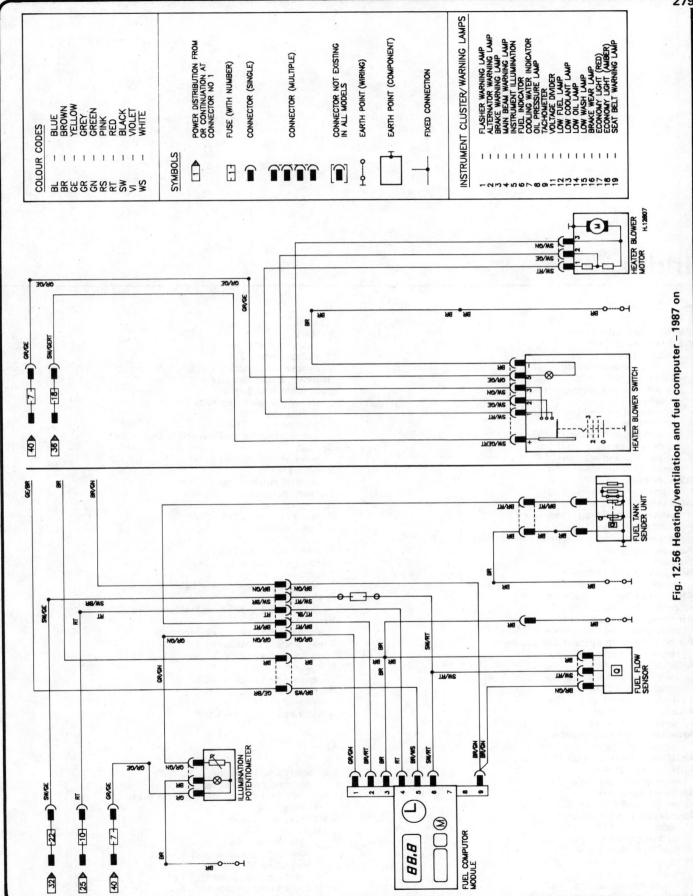

Fig. 12.56 Heating/ventilation and fuel computer – 1987 on

Index

Printed by
J H Haynes & Co Ltd
Sparkford Nr Yeovil
Somerset BA22 7JJ England